DIAL HOUSE abc GUIDE TO FOOTBALL GROUNDS

JON LADD

DIAL HOUSE

D0233647

First published 1995

ISBN 0 7110 2402 2

Published by Dial House

an imprint of Ian Allan Ltd,
Terminal House, Station Approach,
Shepperton, Surrey TW17 8AS.
Printed by Ian Allan Printing Ltd,
Coombelands House, Coombelands Lane,
Addlestone, Surrey KT15 1HY.

Front cover: Huddersfield Town's Alfred McAlpine Stadium. *Empics*

Back cover: Sheffield Wednesday's Hillsborough Stadium. *Aerofilms*

Below: A view of Bristol City's ground. *Aerofilms*

This book is dedicated with my love to Liz, who for 11 years, without complaint, has put up with my obsession for the game and, more recently, my many mood swings as this project moved slowly towards completion/production.

ACKNOWLEDGEMENTS

There are literally hundreds of people without whom this book could not have completed, and to everyone who took the time to complete the questionnaires I sent out, as well as any supporters, stewards, fanzine sellers and members of HM Constabulary whom I accosted trying to find information about pubs, parking, programmes etc. I offer my heartfelt thanks.

A few name checks for people who gave above and beyond the call of duty. Liz Bulbeck, for helping with the typing of the manuscript, as well as obtaining numerous bits of vital information from various clubs for me over the telephone.

Maureen Walton, who gave freely of countless lunch-hours helping me to pore through maps trying to establish the best route to each ground, and who is also the best damned netty checker south of Blyth. Keep ah'ad pet!

Stuart Evans for an inordinate amount of help in getting the initial project off the ground.

Also:
My Mum and Dad, Sheila, Kate, Brian, Anne-Marie, Catherine, Gareth, Charles Richards (a good man), Angela Ryan, Will (The Don), Danny (The Saint), Conor, and all at Ian Allan.

CONTENTS

INTRODUCTION

OK, let's get this straight from the start: this is a guide to football league grounds, not a Bible. It was compiled over 18 months via a series of questionnaires sent to every league club (the last of which went out in April 1995), and at least one visit to every ground over the same period. The total number of matches I've seen over the same period is just over 150 (hmmm, the phrase 'get a life' has sprung into my mind for some reason).

No doubt there will be changes during the late summer months regarding issues such as club colours, kit sponsors etc., but the aim of this book is to give any would-be visitors a feel of each ground and the town it is sited in.

To my knowledge all information is accurate at least until the end of the 1994/5 season, and in many cases will cover the whole of the 1995/6 season and beyond as well. Special efforts wenre made in trying to obtain details of any ground developments and what impact they would have on away supporters between August 1995 and May 1996.

It is a personal irritation that many clubs continue to treat supporters — who are after all their customers and their lifeblood — with suspicion; although policing at grounds has improved over the last few years, there remain certain elements who seem to regard it as their duty to make the visitors' day out as unpleasant as possible. I have tried to put this book together in a fairly light-hearted way, but I have been told by some people that I am overly cynical and in one case I was berated by a club official who, after reading a piece I'd written, stated that it was 'easy' to knock their club (they were right as well, it was very easy). The 1994/5 season was not a great one for the game: at one stage seemingly every other day a new scandal was hitting the back pages of the papers. Ten years on from Bradford and Heysel it is vital that we never forget the lessons that these events along with Hillsborough taught us. However, I still believe that football is a game of beauty, that football is God's game, and more importantly that football is my game and your game. I hope that this book in some small way can make your travels a bit easier.

Remember, like the Murphy's I'm not bitter.
All the best.

Jon Ladd
June 1995

PUBLISHER'S NOTE

The views and comments in this book are made as a result of the author's practical knowledge and a visit to the grounds. Changes may have been made since the author's visit.

The Publisher would like to hear comments and suggestions from all supporters — home and away — concerning the Premiership and Endsleigh League grounds.

Football clubs are selling a commodity and do not like unfair criticism. As with all businesses, most complaints are acted on and the higher up the chain one goes, the greater is the likelihood of this happening, but a football club obviously does have financial restrictions on the extent of its facilities.

Furthermore, football is a mass market business; it reflects wider social and economic developments and frequently football clubs have been forced to make changes in order to accommodate this.

The author of *abc Guide to Football Grounds* is an enthusiast who is writing for the average fan who would like to be treated well but who realises that there have to be restrictions. The author has visited each ground in the book in the last 18 months and has first-hand knowledge of what actually happened during his visit.

Obviously some clubs are disappointed with their entry — it may have been just a case of harassed staff or police on the day or they may be disappointed by general criticism — but of the 93 grounds we have listed we got corrections, which we have been happy to incorporate, from the following clubs:

Arsenal
Barnet
Birmingham City
Bournemouth
Bradford City
Brighton & Hove Albion
Bristol City
Bristol Rovers
Burnley
Bury
Cambridge United
Cardiff City
Carlisle United
Charlton Athletic
Chelsea

Chester City
Colchester United
Coventry City
Crewe Alexandra
Crystal Palace
Darlington
Derby County
Everton
Exeter City
Fulham
Grimsby Town
Hartlepool United
Hereford United / MACCLESFIELD
Huddersfield Town (Leeds road)
Hull City
Ipswich Town
Leeds United
Leicester City
Leyton Orient
Luton Town
Manchester City
Millwall
Northampton Town
Norwich City
Nottingham Forest
Notts County
Oldham Athletic
Oxford United
Peterborough United
Plymouth Argyle
Port Vale
Preston North End
Reading
Rochdale
Scarborough
Sheffield United
Shrewsbury Town
Southampton
Southend United
Stockport County
Stoke City
Sunderland
Swindon Town
Torquay United
Tranmere Rovers
Walsall
Watford
West Bromwich Albion
West Ham United
Wigan Athletic
Wimbledon
Wolverhampton Wanderers
Wycombe Wanderers
York City.

The following clubs did not reply when we sent them a copy of their entry:

Aston Villa
Blackburn Rovers
Blackpool
Bolton Wanderers
Brentford
Carlisle United
Gillingham
Liverpool
Mansfield Town
Middlesbrough
Newcastle United
Portsmouth
Queens Park Rangers
Rotherham United
Sheffield Wednesday
Swansea City
Wrexham.

We hope that the information provided is accurate and we would be happy to incorporate their corrections in the future.

The following clubs did not want to be associated with this book, mainly due to the tone of their entry:

Barnsley
Chesterfield
Lincoln City
Manchester United
Scunthorpe United
Tottenham Hotspur
Wembley PLC.

We would like to reiterate that this book is not intended to knock football clubs. It *is* intended to be a useful but humourous guide for a public which deserves the best possible service (and in order for football to reach the same heights of service of many sports abroad it needs substantial improvements in many instances, as long as these can be afforded). The views and comments therefore are those of a fan committed to football.

A note also has to be made on behalf of the police and stewards at football matches: they do a difficult job and it is not surprising that there are occasional instances when this strain shows.

ARSENAL

ADDRESS: Arsenal Stadium,
Avenell Road, Highbury
London N5 1BU
TELEPHONE No: 0171 226 0304
TICKET OFFICE: 0171 354 5404
FAX: 0171 226 0329
CLUBCALL: 0891 20 20 21
NICKNAME: The Gunners
RECORD ATTENDANCE:
73,295 v Sunderland Div 1 9 March 1935
(Surprisingly a 0-0 draw)

CLUB COLOURS:
HOME: Shirts: Red Red/White Sleeves;
Shorts: White; Socks: Red with White Hoops
AWAY: Shirts: Blue with Teal Lightning Flash;
Shorts: Navy; Socks: Navy with Teal Hoops
There was almost a big fuss about the amount of
white, or lack of it, in the home shirt sleeves. It's easy
to see why the club were taken by surprise by the out-
cry, having seen their fans even take the garish yellow
and green effort to their hearts a couple of years back.

KIT SPONSORS: JVC
MANUFACTURERS: Nike

GROUND INFO
The only concessionary prices available are in the
Family (West) Stand for members only at a cost of £11
adults and £5.50 juniors. There are no cash turnstiles
at the ground, and if you intend paying by Credit Card,
the booking must be taken at least 72 hours before the
match. Note that the Clock End is only covered from
row 18.

If you are either a neutral or can keep a lid on your
enthusiasm, why not sample the pleasures of the new
North Bank? In this 12,400-capacity seated stand all
the upper-tier seats are upholstered and have arms,
there are 12 fast food outlets and a 200-seat restaurant, together with a couple of bars and an amusement
area for children, the toilets positively sparkle and
there is a balcony overlooking the lower mall.

Together with the new stands is a state-of-the-art
scoreboard for pre-match entertainment, which also
displays the names and numbers of all the players during the game — very useful for knowing exactly at
whom to direct your anger after a clumsy challenge.

CAPACITY: Stands: 38,500; Terrace: Nil;
Total: 38,500
AWAY FANS: Clock End South Corner: 1,800;
Total: 1,800
This can be increased to include the Clock End Block

T (an extra 800 spaces) or the whole of the Clock End
(capacity 6,000) if the level of visiting support
demands. Although away fans don't get concessions,
you can't really complain about the prices at the Clock
End (also referred to as the South Stand) as it is rare
to find a club where the cheapest adult seats are given
to the visitors. While this is very nice, you can't help
wondering whether it is financially sensible.

DISABLED FACILITIES: 184 spaces
(including 92 for helpers) are available in front of the
East Stand towards the Clock End, and there is no
charge for either disabled fans or helpers. Most places
are allocated to Arsenal season-ticket holders but
there are usually some available on a match-to-match
basis. However, it is essential to pre-book, as you
should for match commentaries for the blind. The club
do not have any special parking facilities, which is a
real nuisance given the general lack of places in the
immediate ground area.

PROGRAMME: £1.50
FANZINES:
The Gooner	£1
One-Nil Down, Two-One Up	£1
An Imperfect Match	£1.80
Up The Arse	50p
The Highbury Wizard	50p

Of the five, *The Gooner* possibly just shades it as
being the best, with its glossy format of the serious, the
funny, and the fans' opinions — although any of the
top three are worth an investment. Thankfully none of
the above are written by the over-hyped Nick Hornby
(who my spell check suggests should be Nick Horny —
I think not!!!).

TRAVEL
NEAREST RAILWAY STATION:
Finsbury Park (from King's Cross and the north)
(0171 922 9091)
NEAREST TUBE STATION:
Arsenal (Piccadilly Line). The club's famous manager
Herbert Chapman persuaded London Underground to
change the name of the station from Gillespie Road to
Arsenal. This was done to honour the club and not, as
some scurrilous Spurs fans have suggested, because
otherwise the Arsenal fans wouldn't be able to figure
when to get out!

On leaving the tube you will be greeted by big
signs 'Warning; Arsenal FC are playing at home today.
Is your car safe?' I'm not sure what is being suggested
here, but it certainly has the effect of making you
worry, even if your car is locked up in a garage 200
miles away!

Getting back on to the tube after matches can be a
confusing business. The police don't let the fans go

directly into the station, line them up by the side. To prevent people cutting in the queue there are crash barriers which everybody likes to try and climb over, and because the barriers are not fixed they tend to topple over in big crowds. Finsbury Park (Piccadilly Line) and Highbury & Islington (Victoria Line) are also walkable if you want to avoid the crowds.

BY CAR:

NORTH: Leave the M1 at J2 and follow the signs for the City. Keep going for about seven miles until you see Holloway Road tube station. Once you have passed the tube station, take the third left; this will take you into Drayton Park. 0.75 mile later take a right into Aubert Park, where the third left will then take you into Avenell Road.

SOUTH/EAST: Cross the Thames at London Bridge, and then follow signs first for Bank of England, and then Angel (Islington). When you get to a major set of traffic lights, turn right (signposted 'The North') and after about a mile you will come to the Highbury Roundabout. Take a deep breath and go straight across. this takes you into the Holloway Road, where the third right takes you into Drayton Park Road. Then as north.

WEST: Take M4 to J1, then get on to the A315 to Chiswick. One mile down A315 turn left on to the A402 to M41, A40(M), and the A501. At Angel, turn left and continue to Highbury Roundabout. Then as south.

PARKING: There is very restricted parking at Arsenal, with a residents' parking scheme in operation. Do not think that a blind eye will be turned to anyone who parks without a permit, because you will certainly end up being towed away if you break the rules. It can be worth parking a little away from the ground and

travelling in on the tube; otherwise there normally is somewhere to leave the car around Finsbury Park.

FUTURE DEVELOPMENTS
None.

OTHER INFORMATION

Because the stands are so impressive at Arsenal, away fans don't always realise the true (lack of) size of the pitch, which at 7,810sq yd is the smallest in the Premier. However, if you have the misfortune to be at a dull match, the number of times the ball travels from one keeper directly to the other starts to take on a strange fascination.

One of the few people actually to welcome the introduction of all-seater stadia must be the peanut seller at Highbury, a character who, no matter the game, no matter the crowd, would inevitably pop up under your nose on the terraces tempting you with the delights of monkey nuts. After these were purchased he would evaporate into the crowd — leaving you to a futile 10min trying to crack open the nuts and get the booty into your mouth without it being knocked on to the floor by the throngs around you. Much has been made of the state of the toilets which, it has to be said, are probably the best in the League, although it's all very well having nice Arsenal patterned tiles about the place, but if, as on my last visit, there is no toilet paper in the cubicles, you still aren't quite providing the service (and the programme cannot be described as 'soft strong and very very long!').

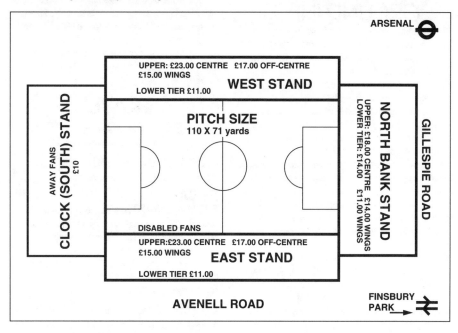

ASTON VILLA

ADDRESS: Villa Park
Trinity Road
Birmingham B6 6HE
TELEPHONE No: 0121 327 2299
TICKET OFFICE: 0121 327 5353
FAX: 0121 322 2107
CLUBCALL: 0891 12 11 48
NICKNAME: The Villains
RECORD ATTENDANCE:
76,588 v Derby FA Cup 6th 2 March 1946 (L 3-4)

CLUB COLOURS:
HOME: Shirts: Claret with Blue stripes;
Shorts: White; Socks: White
AWAY: Shirts: Black with Green stripes;
Shorts: Black; Socks: Black
Villa fans everywhere (certainly the ones with a degree of colour co-ordination) must be breathing a sigh of relief that the latter of these two kits is likely to be no more at some point during the 1995/6 season as it was quite simply horrible (although sadly they are not the worse by far of those that are currently knocking around).

KIT SPONSORS: AST Computers

MANUFACTURERS: Asics

GROUND INFO

The Holte End was living proof of why standing at football grounds was special — it was simply magnificent and was capable of generating a fantastic atmosphere, although some felt its inhabitants' fixation with Birmingham City meant that it didn't always give Villa the 'goal start' it could have done.

The away fans are sited in the lower tier of what is now called the Doug Ellis Stand (and who suggested that little re-christening? Presumably not Big Ron) and North Stand. The latter of which has what you might describe as a holographic roof — when the rain comes down, supporters find themselves getting soaked when they might have believed they were under cover. If you don't know where the away fans' entrance is, just look for the only turnstiles with the home colours of Claret and Blue above them. Yep, they are the ones.

You may find a bit of a problem getting into the ground, if you have not got a ticket. I got the run-around from the stewards and ticket office, all of whom appeared to think it a bit of a wheeze to send one round and round the ground in search of the elusive selling point. For the vast majority of matches you will probably find that (despite what you may be told initially) you can actually pay on the turnstile. Having entered the ground, stop and ponder a moment as to whose bright idea it was to put the programme hut and the food serving hatches right at the top entrance of the corridor by the entrance to the actual seats. There again, you may feel that your time will be better spent fighting through the masses and heading for your seat. (A little tip, go to the toilet, before you start this epic voyage, as if you get to your allocated position only to find that you've got to go through it all again to relieve yourself it may just ruin your day!)

CAPACITY: Stands: 40,310; Terrace: Nil;
Total: 40,310

AWAY FANS: North Stand Lower Tier (R Block): 2,567; Doug Ellis Q Block: 2,023;
Total: 4,590

DISABLED FACILITIES: There are 56 spaces available for wheelchair-bound supporters, with disabled fans being admitted for nothing and helpers paying the standard match day price of £12. There are no special parking facilities at the Club. Match commentaries for the blind are available, pre-booking for which, as with the disabled spaces, is essential.

PROGRAMME: £1.20.
Not too bad: The Aston Villa News and Record,

FANZINES:
Heroes and Villains	£1
The Holy Trinity	50p
The Villa Bugle	£1

The first of these is of the up-market type with a glossy cover. It is packed with articles but is let down by its print style, or lack of it, which makes it a bit daunting to the eye. *The Holy Trinity* is cheap and cheerful, a half-time read which, like a half-time burger, is best enjoyed briefly and then forgotten. *The Villa Bugle* is a new one on me, so who knows?

TRAVEL
NEAREST RAILWAY STATION:
Witton (0121 643 2711 — Birmingham New Street)

BUSES: Birmingham Central (Midland Road)
(0121 200 2700 — Centro Hotline)

BY CAR:
FROM ALL PARTS: M6 to J6 (Spaghetti Junction). When you exit the motorway, follow the signs for Birmingham NE. At the roundabout, take the fourth exit on to the A38 (signposted Aston) and half-a-mile later turn right into Aston Hall Road. Turn right at the end of Aston Hall Road for Witton Lane (B4137) and the ground is 200yd on the right.

PARKING: Asda Car Park in Aston Hall Road, or by Aston Villa Leisure Centre. An alternative that some locals recommend is to come off the M6 at J7 and take the A34 Walsall Road (signposted Perry Barr). After

2.5 miles you will see Parry Barr greyhound stadium and the BR station where you can park and take a train the one stop to Witton, or if you feel energetic walk the 1.25 miles to the ground. The advantage of parking here becomes obvious as you walk past the jam-packed streets around the ground at 4.45. There are plenty of 'Mind your car Misters?' around; these tend to be open to negotiation about the value of the service they offer, but they do tend to stick by the cars and often seem happy to risk life and limb slowing down the traffic to allow you to pull out when you want to leave.

FUTURE DEVELOPMENTS

The conversion of the Holte End to seats was completed in the 1994/5 season, and this represents the end of current developments.

OTHER INFORMATION

Villa is the terrain of the West Midlands police force whose strict football watch code tends to be something of a bugbear for visiting fans, who inevitably come away from Villa Park with tales of being pulled out for no apparent reason, as well as being antagonised by excessive body searches etc. As a general rule, if you get told to jump by one of these boys in blue then don't stand there arguing, just do it, unless like one visitor to

Villa Park you want to be ejected for the heinous crime of 'Cheeking me'!

The Aston Tavern outside the ground bills itself as a friendly pub, although if you are wearing away colours you may beg to differ. Either way, it takes an age to get served in there. The Holte Suite is for Aston Villa Supporters Club Members only, and the stewards on the door keep it that way — the old 'I've left my card at home' routine will only provoke the response 'Well you better pop back and get it'. Many away fans will mourn the passing of the Holte pub right by the ground where they could always be assured of a warm welcome and a relaxing pint… Not! With the fast and frequent train service to Witton from New Street, it can be as well to stay around Birmingham city centre if you fancy a pre- or post-match pint. There are plenty of mobile snack bars around the ground, including one which is done up like a mock Tudor cottage, complete with leaded windows! Inside the ground the pies are quite tasty but the tea is dreadful — although with the kind of logic only football clubs can display, a complaint about its lack of taste brought forth the response 'Well at least it comes in a big cup'.

The club is into advertising in a big way with all the stewards decked out in Asics baseball caps, and when any Villa player scores, the scoreboard flashes up not the time of the goal or some such similar fact, but the legend 'So-and-so scores with Rover'. Who says football has sold out?

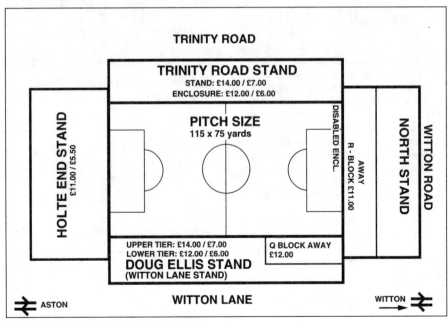

BARNET

ADDRESS: Underhill Stadium
Westcombe Drive
Barnet
Herts EN5 2BE
TELEPHONE No: 0181 441 6932
TICKET OFFICE: 0181 441 1677
FAX: 0181 447 0655
BUZZLINE: 0839 33 30 33
NICKNAME: The Bees
RECORD ATTENDANCE:
11,026 v Wycombe Wanderers Am Cup QF
23 February 1952 (W 2-0)

CLUB COLOURS:
HOME: Shirts: Amber; Shorts: Black; Socks: Black
with Amber top
AWAY: Shirts: Green and White; Shorts: Green;
Socks: Green

KIT SPONSORS: The Printing Company

MANUFACTURERS: Vandanel

GROUND INFO

Away fans are sited in the South End of the East
Terrace, the outside of which, when I last visited, was a
delightful mixture of flaky green paint and rust. Whilst
there is no official away allocation in the Main Stand
you will not find yourself ejected by stewards if you
decide that's where you want to go. Two definites for
away fans are: firstly, a pair of wellingtons, as the mer-
est hint of rain makes the areas around the terrace
reminiscent of a Louisiana swamp, and secondly, some
muscle rub for the stiff neck you'll get from having to
look up from the bottom end of a monumentally sloping
pitch. (Mind you, don't think to complain, as it is a great
improvement from the club's amateur days when there
was a 9ft difference between one goal and the other.)

The prices at Underhill, like the pitch, are a little
steep. However, the club deserves a huge pat on the
back for ensuring that away fans were offered concessions even during the most financially bleak times.
Prices for 1995/6 are:

Main Stand	£12 and £6
East Terrace	£7 (concessions £3.50)
NW Terracre	£6 (concessions £3)
Family Stand	£18 family ticket (three match tickets including one concession)

CAPACITY: Stands: 1,487; Terrace: 2,485;
Total: 3,972

AWAY FANS: Priory Grove (East Terrace —
South Side): 714 max.
Temp seating: 500 approx.

DISABLED FACILITIES: There are 10
spaces for wheelchair-bound fans and helpers, these
being in the southwest corner of the ground. Admission
is via the Barnet Lane gate and is free, though the club
does recommend you pre-book. There are adequate
parking and toilet facilities for disabled supporters at
the ground. However, no matchday commentary facility
is available.

PROGRAMME: £1.20.
A very average affair, although it does throw up the
occasional gem such as the fan file where the
responses to the questions 'Player I'd Like To See
Most At Underhill', and 'Changes I'd Make To The
Ground' were 'Phil Griedelet' (who?) and 'None'
(????!). Presumably as the respondent was in his 70s
it can be put down to age rather than a damning reflection of every Bee's desire (or lack of it).

FANZINES:
There's Villa's Ground	50p
Two Together	£1

Both of these are a decent enough read combining
some good humour and a love of their team's spirit
with a healthy cynicism about the club's administration.

TRAVEL
NEAREST RAILWAY STATION:
New Barnet (Great Northern Line from Moorgate on
weekdays, King's Cross weekends) (0171 922 6061)
NEAREST TUBE STATION: High
Barnet (Northern Line)

BUS: London Transport (0171 222 1234)

BY CAR:
FROM ALL PARTS: M25 or A1 to the intersection of the two (J23 of M25). Take A1081 St Albans
Road (signposted Barnet). As you approach Barnet
town centre the road merges with the A1000. Continue
along this road past High Barnet tube turning right 0.25
miles later into Fairfield Way, and then into
Westcombe Drive for the ground. A possible alternative for those coming from the south is to go up the A1
to Stirling Corner and turn right on to the A411 Barnet
Road. Turn right after 0.25 miles into Barnet Gate
which becomes May's Lane along which after one mile
you can turn right into Barnet Lane for the ground.

PARKING: There is on-street parking around the
ground, or if you prefer you can park at High Barnet
tube. If you opt for the latter be careful as it is a very,
very tight left turn off the A1000. The other hassle with
parking here is that, because you have to turn right to
get out, it can take a bit of time to escape after the
match. Fortunately as there are plenty of sets of traffic
lights along the road you don't have to rely entirely on
the legendary courtesy of London drivers.

FUTURE DEVELOPMENTS

Given the recent financial straits in which the club has found itself, the main policy must be to survive. Some progress has been made with respect to the toilets and also work is being done on improving the access points, although it still remains a mystery how the club has got away with using the word 'stadium' in its address. However, things may be about to change. The club has announced plans to redevelop the South End of the ground with a 2,500-seat stand to be built for opening sometime in 1996. During the initial stages of construction it may be able to use the terrace area, although if this is the case its capacity will be reduced to approximately 600. There appears to be slight confusion as to what will happen to the away fans during the building process, with one view being they will be allocated the South Terrace itself, and another saying they will be in the southeast corner of the ground. Whichever scenario is opted for, eventually this will not result in a major change in capacity or facilities. (Latest information from the club is that, as it is unlikely that the current site will meet League regulations, a new ground will be developed in two to three years.)

OTHER INFORMATION

The Old Red Lion by Fairfield Way is the nearest pub to the ground. Away fans are always welcome, and if the weather isn't too inclement there are tables outside where you can sit and inhale the fumes from the traffic on the Great North Road. Otherwise walk down Barnet Hill for the Queen's Arms, which is big and OK, or the Weaver, which is smaller and nicer. Between the two is a bookies for your fixed odds. The area is sadly lacking a decent chip shop — Fat Sams on the High Street is an above average American Diner, but it is a very long walk from the ground.

The catering facilities for 1995/6 have been revamped with tea bars and burger stalls in every part of the ground. A tea bar has also been constructed in the old offices. Application has also been made for a licence. A new club shop is also available.

The team emerge onto the pitch to the strains of Springsteen's 'Glory Days' with its lyrics of 'Glory days, well they pass you by...' — inspirational stuff, eh? Sadly this season seems to have seen the disappearance of the Barnet Bee, who used to try and gee everyone up during the pre-match warm up but had a lamentable lack of success. Like the Lone Ranger, no one seemed to know who lay behind the mask, but as the bee always looked slightly dodgy and had an extensive waistline, maybe if you ever see him you should ask if he's got a spare cup final ticket on him.

The home supporters seem to be able to take everything that is thrown at them, and there is a definite spirit about the place that means even if you hate the ground — which you may well do — you will retain a sneaking admiration for the club which will leave you hoping it survives.

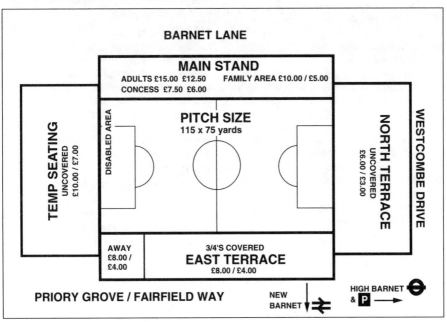

BARNSLEY

ADDRESS: Oakwell Ground
Grove Street
Barnsley
S71 1ET

TELEPHONE No: 01226 295353
TICKET OFFICE: 01226 295353
FAX: 01226 201000
CLUBCALL: 0891 12 11 52
NICKNAME: Colliers, Tykes, Reds
RECORD ATTENDANCE:

40,255 v Stoke FA Cup 5th 15 February 1936 (W 2-1)

CLUB COLOURS:
HOME: Shirts: Red; Shorts: White; Socks: Red
AWAY: Shirts: Green with Red/White pinstripes;
Shorts: Green; Socks: Green

KIT SPONSORS: ORA Electronics
MANUFACTURERS: Pelada

GROUND INFO

If you haven't been to Oakwell for a while then you're in for a pleasant surprise, as the old Brewery Stand has been replaced by a brand-new two-tier construction. NB: On matchdays the police may direct traffic to the ground by alternative routes.

Unfortunately, the visiting supporters get stuck in the West Stand which is archaic, poorly lit and uncomfortable. Why any home fans choose to sit there and pay either the same as or more than they would fork out for a seat in the new construction beggars belief. With the improvements being made to the Pontefract Road End, away fans should have no worries that they will look completely out of place for the 1995/6 season. More bad news concerns the away concessions; there aren't any! So in summary, not only do you get the poorest quality but you get to pay through the nose for it. Thank you and goodnight!

CAPACITY: Stands: 18,643; Terrace: Nil;
Total: 18,643

These figures reflect changes arising from the development of the West Stand Lower Tier and the Pontefract Road End

AWAY FANS: West Stand Block A and B: 841;
West Stand Overspill: 1,323;
Spion Kop: 2,036; Total: 4,200

DISABLED FACILITIES: Barnsley were the first club in the league to construct a purpose-built stand for disabled fans and this holds 55. Admission to this stand if free for disabled fans, with their helpers paying £6. Other than for all-ticket matches, there is no need to book this facility. The club also offers match commentaries for the blind, and once again this is free of charge and you can just turn up on the day. There is no specific parking for disabled fans but there is a large car park adjacent to the ground.

PROGRAMME: £1.30

A real example of a 'bog standard' programme.

FANZINES:

South Riding Fanzine 50p

To make up for one of the dullest names in the fanzine world, the *SRF* now incorporates 'Throw Yer Spare Ribs Behind The Telly'. Wacky, eh! Contents are miles better than the cover or the title suggests (a nice change from the other way round, which is so often the case). Nothing brilliant, but worth a read.

TRAVEL

NEAREST RAILWAY STATION:

Barnsley (0114 272 6411 — Sheffield Enquiries)
The train station at Barnsley is one of the nicest buildings in the town and looks like a new shopping centre. Some may feel it would be better if the trains were more frequent and the carriages were clean, but hey, we can't have everything!

NEAREST BUS:

East bus station (0114 276 8688)
You can take either a 115,116 or 117 from the station to Pontefract Road and walk up to the ground from there, but in truth it's more hassle than it's worth. If you do decide to travel by bus, watch out for the bus stops which have revolving information boards on them. These seem to have been specially designed to pitch anyone who leans on them on to the ground (much to the amusement of the locals).

BY CAR:

NORTH/SOUTH/WEST: M1 to J37, and travel towards Barnsley on the A628 (Dodsworth Road), keeping in the right-hand lane. After 0.25 miles you get to a crossroads and some traffic lights; turn right here (signposted Wakefield A6133, Pontefract and Doncaster). Continue along the A6133 (NB: 30mph restrictions on the dual carriageway) until you get to a crossroads where you see the Coach & Horses opposite you. Turn left, and then right by the next traffic lights into Oakwell Lane. At the bottom of this road turn left and immediately right into Grove Street. The ground is on your right.
EAST: Take the A628, first crossing the River Dearne and then driving past Beevor Hall (anyone of a delicate disposition should refrain from asking some of the locals how they refer to this place). Turn right 200yd past the Hall into Grove Street and the ground is on your right.

PARKING: There are car parks at both ends of the ground. Stick to the main one that you see as you turn into Grove Street rather than the one by the away supporters' terrace entrance (unless you want to see 6,000-odd people hit the road before you). There is also plenty of street parking around, although if you go for this, make sure your handbrake is in good order and that you've been practising your hill-starts!

FUTURE DEVELOPMENTS

The development of the old West Stand Paddock into a 2,500-seat Lower Tier of the West Stand has now been completed. In addition, a 4,500 seater stand is currently under construction at the Pontefract Road End which should be open for the start of the new season.

OTHER INFORMATION

If you want to check out the local hospitality, the nearest pub to the ground — excepting the Barnsley FC Social Club, which I couldn't get into as there was a man with a tie on the door whose only phrase was 'No membership card, no pint' (the man that is rather than the tie) — is the Mount on Pontefract Road. In general

though, it's usually worth avoiding pubs which are mocked-up like a castle on the outside(!) so you could try the Beer Engine in the town, although neither is necessarily to be recommended. As for food, inside the ground it was nothing special, but if on your travels you get a chance to sample a Potters Pie, go for it!

The public address at Oakwell has to be one of the loudest you'll ever come across; you can hear the team changes being announced while you're still in the town centre. What's more, the announcer (Jason) has the dubious claim to fame of having once stood in for one of the front men in Black Lace (altogether now: Aaaaaa Gaaaaa Do Do Do....). One thing you can't fail to miss at the ground is the fact that the players' tunnel is longer than average and has about a one-in-three gradient. So even the most lumbering of centre-halfs can't avoid breaking into a trot as they descend it.

Having moaned (and rightly so) about some of the club's policies and attitudes, it has to be said that they are getting better and I've found that the lower down the hierarchy you go, the friendlier the people are. In addition, the fans are generally good for a chat about football, and they won't even let their natural distrust of all things southern (well actually southern, eastern, western and north of Barnsley) get in the way of having a laugh in the pub with you over a pint.

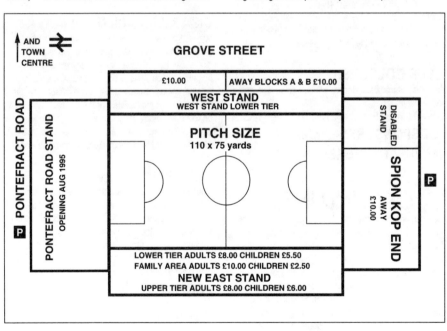

AND TOWN CENTRE

GROVE STREET

£10.00 — AWAY BLOCKS A & B £10.00

WEST STAND
WEST STAND LOWER TIER

PITCH SIZE
110 x 75 yards

PONTEFRACT ROAD

PONTEFRACT ROAD STAND
OPENING AUG 1995

DISABLED STAND

SPION KOP END
AWAY £10.00

LOWER TIER ADULTS £8.00 CHILDREN £5.50
FAMILY AREA ADULTS £10.00 CHILDREN £2.50
NEW EAST STAND
UPPER TIER ADULTS £8.00 CHILDREN £6.00

BIRMINGHAM CITY

ADDRESS: St Andrew's
St Andrew's Street
Birmingham B9 4NH

TELEPHONE No: 0121 772 0101

TICKET OFFICE:

0121 766 5743 — Main

0121 753 3408 — Kop

Ooh! Two ticket office numbers, there's posh for you!

FAX: 0121 766 7866

CLUBCALL: 0891 12 11 88

NICKNAME: The Blues

RECORD ATTENDANCE:

67,341 v Everton FA Cup 5th 11 February 1939 (D 2-2)

Various other record/fact books tend to give the attendance at this match as either 68,844 or 66,844. However, when I asked the club for confirmation as to which of these figures was correct, they quoted yet another figure. Presumably they know what they are talking about, and given that the Director's paper does have a nipple count in it, I guess we can't really question their addition!

CLUB COLOURS:

HOME: Shirts: Blue; Shorts: White; Socks: Blue and White hoops

AWAY: Shirts: Red; Shorts: Red; Socks: Red

KIT SPONSORS: Auto Windscreens

MANUFACTURERS: JWS

GROUND INFO

One can only hope that the club has more luck with its developed stadium than it has had in the past. Perhaps top of the bad luck table is the time when the fire brigade was called to put out a brazier, but when they arrived instead of going for the traditional method of using water, they doused it liberally with petrol instead, and virtually gutted one of the stands in the process. Actually, with the old stadium, gutting one of the stands would have probably done upwards of £13.20 in damage, but that was before the transformation of St Andrew's. Between the summer of 1994 and the middle of the 1994/5 season St Andrew's underwent the kind of face-lift that Joan Collins only dreams about! Gone are the sprawling terraces to be replaced by superb sweeping stands, which are very impressive to behold. You can't fail to admire the speed with which the metamorphosis took place, although the touting of the redeveloped ground as the 'Old Trafford of the Midlands' may be stretching it slightly. I've got to say I do miss the sight of the old Kop which ran the full length of the pitch, but I am just a sad traditionalist, and you won't hear the Blues fans who go to the ground week-in week-out complaining much. They still manage to create a fairly good atmosphere there as well, and their rendition of 'Keep Right On To The End Of The Road' doesn't seem to have suffered too much. The Railway Paddock suffers a bit in comparison to the standards of the Tilton and Kop Stands but it still offers a reasonable view of the action for visiting supporters even if the toilets are a bit on the dodgy side.

It's just a shame that amongst all the redevelopment the club hasn't managed to find it in its heart to offer concessions to away fans; still I don't suppose we can have everything in this old life can we? Home fans do get concessions if they are members of the club's Beau Brummie scheme (and it should give fans money off for inflicting such a dodgy pun on them!) or within the family enclosure.

CAPACITY: Stands: 25,000; Terrace: Nil; Total: 25,000

AWAY FANS: Railway Paddock: 3,600; Total: 3,600

DISABLED FACILITIES: There are 20 spaces for wheelchair-bound fans available at the ground, which means that pre-booking is required. The club states that the cost for disabled fans and their helpers is 'to be decided'. As it was also unable to say whether match commentaries were available you get the feeling that the facilities for the disabled is an area on which Ms Brady has still to work her magic touch. Still, if it turns out as well as the other projects she has turned her hand to at the stadium, it should be worth the wait.

PROGRAMME: £1.50.

Don't worry about not being able to get a programme outside the ground as vendors wander around the stands during the match. You will no doubt think this is a splendid idea the first time they go past you. However, as your view of the game's only goal is obscured by a seller searching for change your opinion may differ slightly.

FANZINES:

The Heathen   50p

Readable, without being particularly outstanding.

TRAVEL

NEAREST RAILWAY STATION:

Bordesley (0121 643 2711 — Birmingham New Street)

BUS: Birmingham Central — Midland Road (0121 200 2700 — Centro Hotline)

BY CAR:
FROM ALL PARTS:

M6 to J6 (Spaghetti Junction) and take the A38 Aston

Expressway. After 1.5 miles you get to the second exit from the Expressway; leave at this point and take the first exit at the roundabout on to the Dartford Middleway A4540 (signposted Bordesley). Go straight over the next three roundabouts and 0.75 miles later turn left into Kingston Road. At the bottom of Kingston Road turn left into Coventry Road and keep to the left for Cattell Road and the ground.

PARKING:
There is a car park at the ground at which the admission price was reduced at one stage to £3; apparently this charitable step was undertaken because of the increased incidence of fans' cars parked on side streets being broken into or stolen (and most definitely not because people were just not using what they considered to be a very overpriced facility). Don't necessarily let this put you off(!) but, as with all grounds, use your common sense; if a street is deserted there is probably a good reason for this. My own favourite parking place is in the side street by The Roost off Cattell Road where I've never encountered any problems (the expression 'tempting fate' seems to have popped into my head for some reason).

FUTURE DEVELOPMENTS
The club has got long-term plans which are likely to involve developing the Railway End and linking it to the roof of the Kop Stand. However, nothing has been formalised at present as to when exactly this will happen, or what will happen to away supporters when it does.

OTHER INFORMATION
It is difficult to know what to make of the dynamic duo at Birmingham of MD Karren Brady and Director David Sullivan. Certainly you may have reservations about how he has earnt his fortune, but let's be honest, it is that fortune that has kept the Blues alive and has paid for the transformation of St Andrew's. The club has become much more responsive to the needs of the fans since Brady's arrival and this has resulted in a more open two-way communication process where the fans' needs and opinions are positively encouraged. The crowds the club attracted last season — including the phenomenal 20,000+ for several Autoglass ties — are testimony not only to the resurgence in fortunes of the club, but to the fact that when treated like human beings and customers, as opposed to a constant source of revenue who will accept anything thrown at them, fans will respond positively. (Of course, winning more matches than you lose doesn't hurt either!) One slightly disturbing thing is the logo which accompanies the club's adopted motto of 'the caring family club'. On it the family in question seem to be about to be attacked by an oversized, poorly drawn and slightly unnerving cartoon dog. This same dog also appears elsewhere on the club literature in a shower, although rather surprisingly, when it does, it is fully dressed! Perhaps the involvement with the club is mellowing Mr Sullivan!

Nearest pub to the ground (open to non-members) is the Royal George on Tilton Road, but it's one of those where on match days it's a case of waiting ages to get served and then losing half your drinks as you fight your way back through the heaving multitude.

A piece on St Andrew's wouldn't be complete without the traditional West Midlands police story, so here goes: on one of my last visits, a sergeant informed away fans that if they 'so much as squeaked' they'd be nicked, and 'don't think you can escape us, we've got you on video and we can be breaking down your door by six tomorrow morning'.

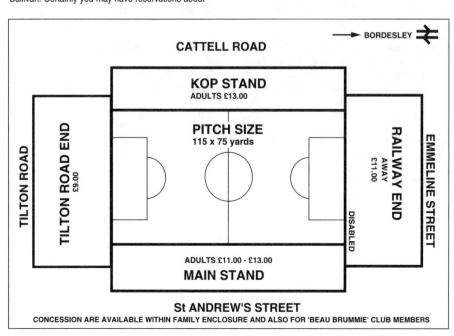

CATTELL ROAD

→ BORDESLEY

KOP STAND
ADULTS £13.00

PITCH SIZE
115 x 75 yards

TILTON ROAD

TILTON ROAD END
£9.00

RAILWAY END
AWAY
£11.00

DISABLED

EMMELINE STREET

ADULTS £11.00 - £13.00
MAIN STAND

St ANDREW'S STREET

CONCESSION ARE AVAILABLE WITHIN FAMILY ENCLOSURE AND ALSO FOR 'BEAU BRUMMIE' CLUB MEMBERS

BLACKBURN ROVERS

ADDRESS: Ewood Park
Bolton Road
Blackburn
BB2 4JF

TELEPHONE No: 01254 698888
TICKET OFFICE: 01254 696767
FAX: 01254 671042
CLUBCALL: 0891 12 11 79
NICKNAME: Rovers or Blue and Whites.

Which just goes to show, it doesn't matter how rich you are, you can't buy originality.

RECORD ATTENDANCE:
61,783 v Bolton FA Cup 6th 2 March 1929 (D 1-1)

CLUB COLOURS:
HOME: Shirts: Blue and White halves;
Shorts: White; Socks: Blue
AWAY: Shirts: Red and Black stripes; Shorts: Black;
Socks: Black

KIT SPONSORS: McEwans
MANUFACTURERS: Asics

GROUND INFO

Prior to your visit to Ewood you could be forgiven for thinking that 'Our Jack' Walker was some kind of megalomaniac, but this couldn't be further from the truth. Jack has simply been busy building a very impressive stadium, the facilities within which are excellent. It is a place where you can enjoy a pre-match pint whilst watching TV or listening to 'Radio Rovers', have a flutter at Ladbrokes, telephone your other half to tell them you'll be late home, and as well as the usual pies and Bovril you can sample scampi and chips or chicken nuggets.

Almost miraculously, the club does offer concessions to visiting supporters. *However*, it will only do this if the visiting team offer Rovers a reciprocal arrangement. Which makes it a bit difficult to complain about if you are charged full price for the kids. (If you are insistent on wanting a moan, then stick to safer grounds and ask them if they think that a two-category pricing system is really fair.)

CAPACITY: Stands: 30,500; Terrace: Nil;
Total: 30,500

AWAY FANS: Darwen End: 8,000; Total: 8,000
The above capacity at the Darwen End is the maximum available and is reduced according to the levels of support. There is a section within the family enclosure for visitors who are members of their own club's family scheme.

DISABLED FACILITIES: Brilliant! The front row of each end of the ground is allocated to disabled fans and their helpers (a grand total of 822 places!), visitors are welcome, and the design means you can actually get to be near your mates which makes a welcome change from the unspoken attitude of 'Goodness gracious me! Do disabled supporters have "normal" friends?'. Although there is plenty of room you should pre-book, admission is free for disabled fans with helpers paying standard matchday prices. There is supervised parking at the ground. Headphones are available for matchday commentaries at the Blackburn End, and again these should be pre-booked. If you can't organise a set of headphones, bring a radio and tune in to Radio Rovers for match commentaries.

PROGRAMME: £1.50.
Available both inside and outside the ground, and very readable.

FANZINES:
Loadsamoney £1
4,000 Holes £1
The latter's title is not a reference to the way Shearer and Sutton may well leave your defence but rather from the track 'Day In The Life' on the Beatles 'Sgt Pepper' album which John Lennon stuck in after reading/hearing that that was the amount of potholes in the roads of 'Blackburn, Lancashire'. Sadly this fact is more interesting than the fanzine itself, which is a bit dull and uncontroversial; still it seems very unlikely that Rovers fans have got anything much to complain about. Perhaps typically for Blackburn contributors to this epistle get *paid* for their efforts.

TRAVEL

NEAREST RAILWAY STATION:
Blackburn Central (01772 259439 — Preston Enquiries)

NEAREST BUS STATION:
Blackburn Central (01254 51112)
The number 346 (Darwen) bus runs from both the station and the town centre to the ground.

BY CAR:
NORTH/WEST: M6 to J31, take the A666 (Oooer! Yon tarmac hath the number of the beast!) towards Samlesbury and Blackburn. As you travel along the road you will see signs for Nova Scotia and Ewood. Go past the Infirmary and 0.5 mile later turn left into Kidder Street; the ground is on your right.
SOUTH: M6 to J29. When you leave the motorway turn left onto the A6 (signposted Chorley), turning left after a mile onto the B5256. Turn right onto the A6061 by the Fielden Arms pub (Livesey Park Road) and continue for approx two miles.

You will climb a hill, and as you descend it you will see the ground loom up in front of you. Continue to the bottom of the hill and turn right at the roundabout onto the Bolton Road for the stadium.

NB: This way takes you on about 5-6 miles of winding narrow roads, and it may be as well, if the traffic is bad, to take the M6 to J31 and go in via the north directions.

EAST: M65 to J6. When you leave the motorway go straight over at the exit roundabout, and take the next left into Whitebirk Road, then right onto the A679 Accrington Road (signposted Audley). After 1.5 miles the road (now called Lower Audley Street) is crossed by two roads — Park Road and Great Bolton Street. Turn left into the second of these, this is the A666 (signposted Bolton Road, Ewood), then as north.

PARKING: The car parks at the ground are for permit holders only. There is a free car park on the first roundabout as you head towards Blackburn town centre from the ground on the Bolton Road, but unless you arrive very early, you've no chance of getting in! Alternatively try the Fernhurst pub 0.25 mile south of the ground on the A666.

If you don't want to pay you can park in the side roads off the A666; but remember, if you want a quick getaway, park as close to the A666 on these side streets as you legally and physically can otherwise you can find yourself blocked in, not least of all by the disgruntled local residents.

FUTURE DEVELOPMENTS

The story circulating about JW being about to purchase a row of terrace houses, which would then be knocked down to form a tree-lined boulevard leading to the ground, was dismissed by the club as 'paper talk', still stranger things…

OTHER INFORMATION

The town is famous for its curry houses, and if you've got the time you should go into Darwen for one particularly fine one. If your tastes are simpler, check out the excellent meat and potato pies sold from the window of a converted house opposite the ground.

If you fancy a pint then it is worth climbing the hill that leads out of the town for about 0.75 to the White Bull, the Brown Cow or the Moorgate; the third of these is a bit small, but all serve a decent pint.

If you have a problem or query about a forthcoming visit to Ewood Park then contact the club by telephone rather than by mail, as if you do write it is likely you will end up with a nice sheet of headed notepaper explaining that the club is very busy and hasn't got time to write you a reply(?). Over the phone it is more helpful, and once you are actually at the ground it seems prepared to do anything it can to assist you.

Whatever your tastes, the new Ewood Park is well worth a visit, if just to see how the other half lives, and it may go some way towards convincing doubters that the arrival of all-seater stadia does not necessarily mean the onset of all things dreadful.

However, another abiding memory may be the nagging question 'why isn't this ground full?'. It seems hard to explain; after all, the club have bought the best players and developed a magnificent football stadium to which admission does not cost the earth. Maybe — and it's just a thought — amongst all the money and changes, the fans have felt slightly alienated from the club and would have preferred to earn success rather than buy it. I reiterate that this comment is not intended as a slight against Rovers but rather as a genuine thought as to a mystifying issue. Bottom line — if football could find another 91 Jack Walkers, things would be a lot easier!

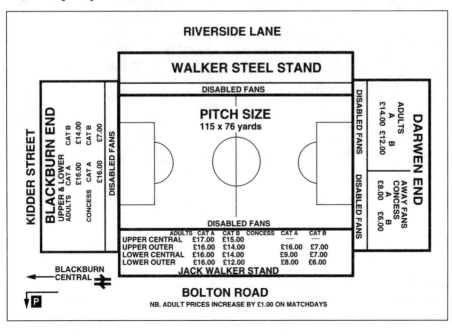

RIVERSIDE LANE

WALKER STEEL STAND

DISABLED FANS

PITCH SIZE
115 x 76 yards

DISABLED FANS

KIDDER STREET

BLACKBURN END

	ADULTS	CAT A	CAT B
UPPER & LOWER	£16.00	£16.00	£14.00
CONCESS	£16.00		£7.00

DISABLED FANS

DISABLED FANS

DISABLED FANS

DARWEN END

ADULTS	A	£14.00
	B	£12.00
AWAY FANS CONCESS	A	£8.00
	B	£6.00

DISABLED FANS

	ADULTS CAT A	CAT B	CONCESS CAT A	CAT B
UPPER CENTRAL	£17.00	£15.00	—	—
UPPER OUTER	£16.00	£14.00	£16.00	£7.00
LOWER CENTRAL	£16.00	£14.00	£9.00	£7.00
LOWER OUTER	£16.00	£12.00	£8.00	£6.00

JACK WALKER STAND

BLACKBURN CENTRAL

P

BOLTON ROAD

NB. ADULT PRICES INCREASE BY £1.00 ON MATCHDAYS

BLACKPOOL

ADDRESS: Bloomfield Road
Blackpool
Lancashire
FY1 6JJ
TELEPHONE No: 01253 404331
TICKET OFFICE: 01253 404331
FAX: 01253 405011
CLUBCALL: 0891 12 16 48
NICKNAME: Seasiders
RECORD ATTENDANCE:
39,118 v Man Utd Div 1 19 April 1952 (D 2-2)

CLUB COLOURS:
HOME: Shirts: Tangerine; Shorts: White;
Socks: Tangerine
AWAY: Shirts: Navy and Sky Blue Stripes;
Shorts: Navy; Socks: Navy

KIT SPONSORS: Rebecca's Jewellers
Southport. Perhaps one of the more parochial and
obscure of sponsors, but at least they are (or should
that be she is) putting money into the club.

MANUFACTURERS: Pelada

GROUND INFO

An old and very tired-looking ground which only serves
to bring home that the club's glory days have long
since passed. No concessions for away supporters
(which is good in a way because if, when at the pleasure beach, little Johnny wants to have a go on something that you think might kill you, explain to him the
fact that the rotten old Seasiders don't give concessions means you've spent too much and can't afford
to!). For home supporters, concessionary rates also
apply to unemployed supporters. Proof of status will be
required on entry to the ground.

The away terrace is basic and uncovered, which
means that when the wind and rain get up (and you
must remember that as one of England's best tourist
resorts, this is virtually compulsory) it can be a bleak
place to spend an afternoon.

CAPACITY: Stands: 2,940; Terrace: 7,397;
Total: 10,337

AWAY FANS: Spion Kop: 1,700; East Paddock
North: 800; East Paddock Centre: 700*; East Paddock
South: 1,300*; West Stand Family Enc: 120*; West
Stand: 237*; Total: 4,857
*These areas only available if the away team have suf-
ficient support; otherwise these sections are for the
use of home supporters.

DISABLED FACILITIES: There are
spaces for 10 wheelchair-bound fans in the South
Stand by the players' tunnel, and there is no admission
charge for either disabled fans or their helpers. The
club state that pre-booking is not required, but given
the limited number of places it is better to be safe than
sorry. Match commentaries for the blind are available;
these must be pre-booked. There is also plenty of
parking at the ground, with some spaces allocated for
the use of disabled supporters.

PROGRAMME: £1.50.
This has a bit of a back-to-front feel about it, with the
match facts — including each game's man of the
match, and virtually as many details on the stiffs as on
the first team — being on page three, and the inside of
the back cover having action from previous matches.
Other than the unusual layout it doesn't really have
much to commend it.

FANZINES:
View From The Tower   £1

TRAVEL

NEAREST RAILWAY STATION:
Blackpool South Shore/Blackpool North (01772
259349)
South Shore is the nearest railway station to the
ground, but only has about a third of the trains serving
it that North does. Both are a walkable distance, but
you can catch a bus or tram — or a very over-priced
pony and trap — to get either to Bloomfield Road itself,
or at least a good bit closer.

NEAREST BUS STATION:
Blackpool Transport (01253 23931)

BY CAR:
FROM ALL PARTS: M6 to J32. At J32 exit on to
the M55; continue to the end of the motorway, and
carry straight on along the spine road (Yeardon Way).
Go straight over the first two roundabouts, then when
you get to a mini-roundabout, turn right and the ground
is 0.5 mile on the right.

NB If you are driving to the ground from the
town/beach area, then head towards the Tower (driving from the Pleasure Beach area) along the sea
front. Turn right off the Promenade then left on to
Lytham Road. Continue until you get to some traffic
lights beyond which is the Old Bridge pub, at which
you should turn right into Bloomfield Road and the
ground is 250yd on the left. If in any doubt head
towards 'Rigby' car parks (signposted in green).

PARKING: There is a large pay-and-display
adjacent to the ground (Rigby Car Park), which is
cheap and easy to get away from. Some on-street
parking is also available in the vicinity.

FUTURE DEVELOPMENTS

Bloomfield Road has really begun to look tatty over the last few years. However, the club is hoping to develop a 20,000 all-seater stadium on the same site, the breakdown of which will be as follows:

Spion Kop: 7,078 seats West Stand 2,876 seats
(four disabled places)
South Stand: 7,289 seats (42 disabled places)
East Stand: 2,534 seats (64 disabled places)

In addition, there will be 712 private box seats, but the most spectacular feature of the new development is the retractable roof which will be drawn across on rainy days to keep the playing surface in peak condition.

Final planning permission has apparently been granted for this vision of the future. Having considered moving out of Bloomfield Road for a couple of years while the ground was constructed (it was mooted that they would ground share at Wigan!!) the club has decided to develop the new ground on extra land it owns around the Bloomfield Road site, thus in effect creating a new stadium yards away from the old one. The club is unsure when the first brick will be laid, but remain confident that New Bloomfield (or the Coliseum as it has been suggested the ground will be called) will be open for 1998.

OTHER INFORMATION

Blackpool is one of those places where football almost seems secondary to the day out (heresy!). Don't go to the place with any ideas other than to simply enjoy the day/night/weekend. You always tend to get one or two people who get sniffy at the fact that there are 3ft by 2ft signs for fart powder, and yes it is tacky, but more importantly, it's fun, and besides, where else in the world would you find a shop that is half dedicated to selling spectacles with the other half selling marital aids? (The window display is wild!!!)

There are rakes of pubs (although not that many very close to the ground), night-clubs, and things to do, and B&B will set you back from a tenner.

Inside the ground the food is passable and if you are going out of the tourist season, is probably better than some of the chip shops where you are never quite sure how old the stock is. The tea is hot but weak, and you might opt for the hot blackcurrant instead, which is fine.

If the match is dull you can always spend your time looking at the Tower which has a hypnotic light going round and round it. Also keep an eye/ear open for the newspaper seller who spends about two hours before a game circling the outside of the ground, and the full 90min of the match walking round the perimeter of the pitch uttering only one sound — 'Herehhhh'. Apparently this translates as 'Get your copy of the Gazette here, fine townsfolk'. This man is an absolute hero, and every time he passes the home fans he gets a cheer and a response of 'Herehhhh', which always makes him smile, and which he always acknowledges with a nod of the head.

The staff in the club shop are excellent, and have plenty of time for away as well as home fans, although in keeping with the town's ambience they do have some particularly garish souvenirs on sale, top of the list being a Sir Stanley Matthews toby jug/tea mug in luminous orange.

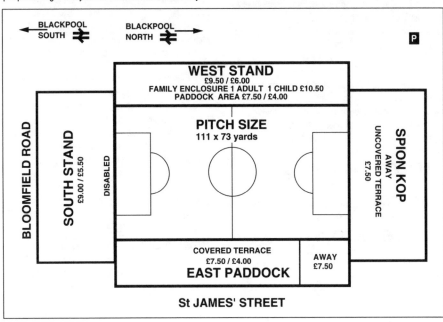

BOLTON WANDERERS

ADDRESS: Burnden Park
Manchester Road
Bolton
BL3 2QR

TELEPHONE No: 01204 389200
TICKET OFFICE: 01204 521101
FAX: 01204 382334
CLUBCALL: 0891 12 11 64
NICKNAME: The Trotters
RECORD ATTENDANCE: 69,912
v Man City FA Cup 5th 18 February 1933 (L 2-4)
CLUB COLOURS:
HOME: Shirts: White; Shorts: Navy Blue; Socks: Navy Blue
AWAY: Shirts: Yellow; Shorts: Blue; Socks: Yellow

KIT SPONSORS: Reebok
MANUFACTURERS: Reebok

GROUND INFO

Bolton adopts an 'eye for an eye' principle as far as supporters' concessions are concerned: ie if the visiting club gives them, then so shall they receive — naturally this fact is worth knowing to save any possible embarrassment if you go on in the ticket office about the cost of ground admission. Similarly if your club offers Bolton family tickets then you will be able to take advantage of the seats in the Great Lever Stand.

The visitors' terrace is uncovered, so it may well be in your best interests to get yourself a seat in the visitors' section of the Burnden Stand. What is not in your best interests is to take your place amongst the home fans who in my experience are not well known for throwing down petals and welcoming supporters with open arms, so if it's raining and the away seats are full, keep quiet or get wet!

CAPACITY: Stands: 8,000; Terrace: 12,800; Total: 20,800

AWAY FANS: Embankment Terrace: 4,300; Burnden Stand: 350; Total: 4,650

DISABLED FACILITIES: There are some 11 places available at the front of the Manchester Road Stand towards the Great Lever Stand. Six of these are allocated to home supporters and five to visiting fans. Disabled fans are admitted free, with helpers paying £8. All places must be pre-booked. There are no matchday commentaries for the blind, nor are there parking facilities for the disabled at the ground.

PROGRAMME: £1.30
An absolute must for all budding players with such

useful tips about the beautiful game such as .... 'Volleying To Score — To do this a player must strike the ball dropping from the air below the bar and between the posts'. Well, that should help bridge the gap between the British game and those technically gifted Europeans! (Although as Bolton did have Robert Fleck on loan the season before last perhaps there was some use for this column.) As if the above wasn't enough, the programme also describes the evacuation siren as a 'Bing-Bong' sound. In an ideal world you feel that the club would be happier broadcasting Clive Dunn shouting 'Don't panic' over the tannoy.

FANZINES:
Come On Feel The Wanderers £1
Tripe 'n' Trotters £1
Both fairly new on the scene. The only Bolton fanzine I've come across *Here We Go Again* seems to have dropped from view (apologies if it is still going strong).

TRAVEL

NEAREST RAILWAY STATION:
Trinity Street (0.5 mile) (0161 832 8353)

NEAREST BUS STATION:
Moor Lane or Trinity Street (01204 391597)
Amongst others, buses 28, 522, and 524 run to the ground

BY CAR:
NORTH: M61 to J5. Take the A676 and follow signs to Farnworth (B653); this will bring you on to the Manchester Road. Once on this road, continue for 0.5 mile and turn left into Croft Lane; the ground is on your left.
SOUTH/EAST/WEST: M62, M61 to J3. When you leave the motorway take the A666 Kearsley by-pass. Then, if the traffic is heavy, continue along the A666 for two miles, then bear left. This will bring you to a junction with Raikes Lane at which you should turn left. Take the first right on to Manchester Road and the second right on to Croft Lane where the ground is on your left. If the traffic is light, take the first exit at the first roundabout on to the A6053 Bolton Road. After 1.25 miles, the road splits in two; take the left-hand lane (B6536 Manchester Road) and after a further 0.75 miles turn right into Croft Lane.

PARKING: There is a large car park behind the visitors' stand where access to — and more importantly if you have won — exit from both the away terrace and the seats can be gained. There is also plenty of on-street parking around. Alternatively take the Manchester Road towards Bolton and try one of the following car parks:
• Trinity Street (Left off Manchester Road, one mile from the ground);
• Breightmet Street (Right off Manchester Road 1.25

miles from the ground);
• Arndale Centre (Straight up Manchester Road 1.25 miles from the ground).

FUTURE DEVELOPMENTS

There are discussions taking place possibly to relocate Wanderers to Horwich (northwest of the town), where there are plans to build a 25,000 all-seater stadium incorporating a leisure and retail complex (the question on all away fans' lips is whether — in order to retain the flavour of Burnden — they will build a supermarket in the away section?), on top of which a further 20,000 seats could be added at a later date if required. If this does not materialise then the current site will be developed with the seating of the Burnden and Manchester Road paddocks and a new stand at the Embankment End. The club's promotion to the Premier may mean it looks to provide temporary seating while the Horwich site is constructed.

OTHER INFORMATION

If you fancy a pre-match pint take note that the pubs around the ground only admit home supporters and the off-licences are forbidden from selling beer on match days. If you bring your own, then don't drink it on the streets as the local authority have introduced an alcohol free zone around the ground and in the town centre.

During the match the two words you are most likely to have shouted at you are not perhaps the ones you would expect, but 'Manchester United', as the Trotters are quite manic about their hatred for their local rivals. Sadly they don't content themselves with questioning the parentage and ability of Giggs, Ferguson, Ince et al, but still insist in wheeling out the old 'Munich' stuff. The 1994/5 season showed us that there were still problems associated with football that one might have reasonably expected to have disappeared, and whilst naturally not on the scale of pitch invasions etc, this does leave a bit of a nasty taste in the mouth.

Having talked about the club's insularity it is only fair to say that it treats its own well and the majority of people who have played for the club are made welcome whenever they return (unlike many other clubs when those they have 'loved' are despised within the twinkling of a transfer fee). Top of the list of heroes is naturally Nat Lofthouse followed a very close second by Frank Worthington, but it is not only the big names whom Bolton remember but also such luminaries as Sam Allardyce, a man whose moniker surely predestined him to play for the Trotters the moment he was christened. Hopefully Wanderers success in the 1994/5 season will mean that the club can hang on to some of their rising stars and add them to the Burnden list of honour.

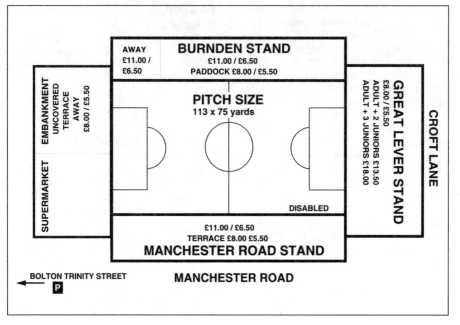

BOURNEMOUTH

ADDRESS: Dean Court
Bournemouth
Dorset BH7 7AF

TELEPHONE No: 01202 395381
TICKET OFFICE: 01202 395381
FAX: 01202 309797
CLUBCALL: 0839 66 44 30
NICKNAME: The Cherries
RECORD ATTENDANCE:
28,799 v Man Utd. FA Cup 6th 2 March 1957

CLUB COLOURS:
HOME: Shirts: Red & Black stripes;
Shorts: White; Socks: White
AWAY: Shirts: Yellow; Shorts: Blue; Socks: Yellow

KIT SPONSORS: Frizzell Financial Services
MANUFACTURERS: Matchwinner

GROUND INFO

The away seating at Dean Court is restricted to the front five rows of A Block and is designated only for families, OAPs and disabled fans.

As visitors, if you are members of your team's family scheme it is worth getting in touch with Bournemouth prior to your visit as they may let you go in their family section with the relevant concessions, but the emphasis here is on getting in touch before you go, and, for that matter, on the word may. The seating is directly in front of an area which the club often uses for school trips so be prepared to have your eardrums assaulted by what, if you shut your eyes, could pass for a schoolboys' international crowd.

The away terrace is surrounded by a large perimeter fence, which from my vantage point restricted the view for the fans (other than those at the very top or the very bottom of it). Perhaps it is the cost of maintenance which means that the club do not see fit to offer away supporters any concessions! However, to be fair, very small children can on occasion slip into the ground with their parents for nothing, and the last time I was at the ground there was a chap walking his dog (admitted gratis apparently) along the gangways at the top of the terrace.

Wherever you are in the ground you can't fail to be impressed by the Army Careers billboard, which shows a Union Jack where the Cross of St George is blue, and that of St Andrew is red! Call me old fashioned but I'd kind of hoped that the Army might have known better.

CAPACITY: Stands: 3,130; Terrace: 7,470
Total: 10,600

AWAY FANS: A Block Stand: 150; Brighton Beach End (uncovered terrace): 2,620; Total: 2,770

DISABLED FACILITIES:

There are spaces for approximately 12 fans in a specially designed shelter by the South Stand. The club states that disabled fans receive complimentary tickets and that helpers have to pay nothing! Pre-booking is required and there are disabled parking facilities at the ground. There are no matchday commentaries available for the blind, although the club is still hoping to introduce them at some point in time.

Bournemouth is one of the few clubs which, if disabled away fans turn up on the day, will let them into the Brighton Beach End, provided they feel there are not likely to be any problems through overcrowding. If you do take this option, expect to pay full whack and accept an adequate view, although you should be all right using the toilets as these are fairly spacious.

PROGRAMME: £1.20.

Lots of half page articles, which given the largish print used, often means they are over before they have had the chance to say anything. Still, on the whole not too bad at all.

FANZINES:

Not the 8502	£1
Exiled!	£1.75

The first of these is quite a size and a good easy read, but as it is on sale in the club shop, don't expect too much controversy!

TRAVEL

NEAREST RAILWAY STATION:

Pokesdown or Bournemouth (01202 292474)
Pokesdown has about one train an hour, so the odds are you will end up at the larger Bournemouth stop. In either case, the number is the same for enquiries.

BUS: Central Bus Depot (01202 673555)

BY CAR:

NORTH and EAST: A338 Wessex Way towards Bournemouth. Turn left off the A338 at the Kings Park exit (signposted Football Traffic). Take the first left at the mini-roundabout into Littledown Avenue (do not take the next exit signposted Kings Park and Parking), then immediately right into Thistlebarrow Road. The entrance to the ground is at the bend of the road.
WEST: A3049 through Bournemouth continuing until you cross the A338 Wessex Way dual carriageway. At the next roundabout turn left into Holdenhurst Road, and at the following roundabout take the second exit into Littledown Avenue. Then as north.

PARKING: There are several large car parks by the ground. Watch out for the nose-to-tail parking in the South Stand Car Park, which unless you get right at the front means you'll undoubtedly spend 20min watching car upon car leave the area while you wait for those behind and in front of you to turn up.

FUTURE DEVELOPMENTS

The club has nothing planned, but continues to review and assess the situation.

OTHER INFORMATION

The club used to be known as Bournemouth & Boscombe; naturally when it was decided to drop one of the names they got rid of the place in which the ground was actually sited in. Consequently, many home fans refer to the club as Boscombe, and those that don't, tend to use the moniker AFCB.

The nearest watering-hole to the ground is the Queens Park which is on the Holdenhurst Road and is only a couple of minutes away, and there are plenty of decent pubs in both Bournemouth and Boscombe. The Seagull, large and cavernous, isn't a bad place to try if there's a group of you, and this can be found half-way down the hill which leads to Boscombe Pier, which could put in a creditable challenge for the dullest pier in Britain competition.

Once you leave the Seagull and head back into Boscombe town centre, the Trocadero is worth nipping into for fish and chips, although there is a mobile food wagon at the ground called Fine Bites which does an excellent (if slightly overpriced) bacon burger, one of the best available outside any stadium. Inside Dean Court, the tea was really strong but not that hot, and the pies were really hot but not very tasty.

The club does seem fairly responsive to fans' needs and questions, although it has encountered postal problems in the past, so if you have a query it is better to phone than write.

Equally, the police seem fairly laid back, and although inevitably there are the occasional problems at the ground, they don't tar everyone with the same hooligan brush, and so treat away fans reasonably.

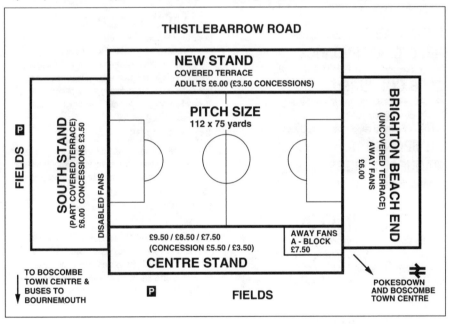

THISTLEBARROW ROAD

NEW STAND
COVERED TERRACE
ADULTS £6.00 (£3.50 CONCESSIONS)

PITCH SIZE
112 x 75 yards

FIELDS

P

SOUTH STAND
(PART COVERED TERRACE)
£6.00 CONCESSIONS £3.50

DISABLED FANS

BRIGHTON BEACH END
(UNCOVERED TERRACE)
AWAY FANS
£6.00

£9.50 / £8.50 / £7.50
(CONCESSION £5.50 / £3.50)
CENTRE STAND

AWAY FANS
A - BLOCK
£7.50

TO BOSCOMBE
TOWN CENTRE &
BUSES TO
BOURNEMOUTH

P

FIELDS

POKESDOWN
AND BOSCOMBE
TOWN CENTRE

BRADFORD CITY

ADDRESS: The Pulse Stadium
Valley Parade, Bradford
West Yorkshire
BD8 7DY
TELEPHONE No: 01274 306062
TICKET OFFICE: 01274 306062
FAX: 01274 307457
CHATLINE: 0891 888 640

The use of the word 'Chatline' to describe the club's recorded information service conjures up some interesting images. Is someone on the other end of the line making lewd suggestions to callers? Does the centre-forward reminisce about the time he was 'pulled-off' at half time?

Fortunately no, the line is just the same as everyone else's — in my view, expensive and not very interesting!

NICKNAME: The Bantams
RECORD ATTENDANCE:
39,146 v Burnley FA Cup 4th 11 March 1911 (D 1-1)

CLUB COLOURS:
HOME: Shirts: Claret and Amber Stripes; Shorts: Black; Socks: Claret
AWAY: Shirts: Blue; Shorts: Blue; Socks: Blue

KIT SPONSORS: Diamond Seal

MANUFACTURERS: Beaver International (snigger, snigger)

GROUND INFO

The 1994/5 season saw the demise (in terms of name alone) of the bizarrely titled Charlie Brown Stand. After much searching the club have managed to strike a deal with new sponsors which allowed the stand to be rechristened with a moniker far more suitable to the gravitas of a football club. Ladies and Gentlemen, let's hear it for the 'HSG Packing Case Stand'!

Away fans are sited in the HSG Stand, and if over 1,800 are expected then they will also be offered the Midland Road Terrace, which otherwise will remain unopened.

The ground is actually on the top of a hill, but strangely has been built in a depression on this. In winter, the slopes leading to the turnstiles are treacherous if there is a bit of snow or ice about, and while, thankfully, the club does lay copious amounts of sand, it is still something to be aware of.

If you go in the HSG you get a decent view of not only the pitch, but also the outskirts of Bradford over the top of the Midland Road terrace. You also get to see the scoreboard, which has a clock counting down the time left in the half. Underneath the figures is the word 'remaining', which is excellent and does help resolve those maddening confusions encountered at other grounds when you look at the clocks and then need to work out whether they mean that five minutes have gone or if there are five minutes remaining!

The tea bar serving the HSG Stand is a bit small, which does lead to queuing. It does fantastic pies though (watch out as these are very, very hot), as well as having on occasions Mexican chilli flan, or some other cosmopolitan dish.

City are rather extravagant on the club mascot front: the City Gent character is OK (bit of a pie eater) but the bantam has to be seen to be believed!

CAPACITY: Stands: 8,098; Terrace: 6,261; Total: 14,359

AWAY FANS: HSG Packing Case Stand: 1,840; Midland Road Terrace (Covered): 855; Total: 2,695

DISABLED FACILITIES: There are 40 places at the front of the N&P Stand, disabled fans and helpers both paying £5.50. Entrance and exit points are good, and pre-booking is not essential (although recommended). The club was trying to sort out a matchday commentary facility as far back as the 1993/94 season, but this still hasn't materialised. No at-ground parking available.

PROGRAMME: £1.20.
Weird. It has the look of a 1950s effort about it (including the teams printed in playing formation). If you can get over the layout you'll find that, whilst not a classic, it isn't too bad.

FANZINES:
City Gent   £1
The voice of Bantam Progressivism is a top-notch fanzine which is worth buying no matter whom you support. All 1994/5 issues were 100 pages, although the editors do state that they make no claims about the quality of the content but hope that readers can find something of interest within the pages. They should have no fears about this as there is plenty to keep home, away or neutral fans occupied for several hours.

TRAVEL
NEAREST RAILWAY STATION:
Forster Square (0113 244 8133 — Leeds Enquiries) Forster Square has a very limited service and it is as well to aim for Bradford Interchange (same telephone number).

NEAREST BUS STATION:
Yorkshire Rider (01274 732237) Too many buses to list stop at Manningham Lane which is just up from the ground. Basically, any Shipley or Saltaire bus will see you right.

BY CAR:

NORTH: A650. Turn left on to the Ring Road then first right by the hospital into Midland Road. The ground is then about 0.5 miles on the right.

SOUTH: M1 to J42, then M62 towards Bradford, exiting at J26 on to the M606. At the end of the M606 take the second left off the roundabout on to the Ring Road (A6177). Take the third exit at the next round-about (in effect turning right) following the signs to City Centre (A614). Turn right at the next roundabout on to the Central Ring Road (A6181), and then turn left at the next two roundabouts. (At the second there is a sign saying 'Local Access Only'; this is you, so don't worry about it.) You then go up a hill (signposted Keighley A650) and at the top of this is a set of traffic lights; go straight over at these and the ground is half a mile on your right.

EAST/WEST: M62 to J26. Pick up M606, then as south.There are signposts to the ground, but not many, and if you are following them continue going straight on at roundabouts, etc until you are positively directed elsewhere, and whoever's navigating can enjoy the relief of seeing an arrow, just when everyone in the car/coach thought they must have missed one and were now lost.

The ground is sited not far from Little Germany, which doesn't have Roads, but rather Strasses. One wonders what sort of person lives in this area; possibly a Yorkshireman who can get his whippets to run on time. (Well, nice to see I didn't fall into the trap of racial stereotyping there eh?)

PARKING: Street parking and car parks by the ground. The car parks aren't cheap at £2.50, but if you do opt for street parking then remember that the ground isn't sited in the nicest part of the city, so be careful where you leave your vehicle.

FUTURE DEVELOPMENTS

None as yet, although if any work is to be done, this may well involve the development of the Midland Road Terrace.

OTHER INFORMATION

Nearest pub to the ground is the Belle Vue, but you're better off either walking a little further down Manningham Lane to Nellie Deans or sticking to the city centre. This also boasts hundreds of curry houses; as a general rule of thumb, the less it looks as if you'd like to eat in the place, the better it will be.

The attitude of the locals towards the team is not overly enthusiastic. The story told by some West Brom fans is that they once saw two kids in the car park who asked them who were playing. When they replied West Brom, they were then asked 'against whom?' this may or not be true, but what I can say for a fact is I have witnessed a home fan going to the club to find out if a match was on or off, and when they were told it had been postponed, replying 'Oh that's lovely'.

The physical signs of the 1985 fire have long since gone, and all there is to show for it is a fairly discreet sculpture on the side of the stand. However, there is still an atmosphere at the ground which can probably best be described as sombre. If you get to the stadium before the main bulk of the crowd, it can be practically oppressive, yet very moving. What happened at Valley Parade seems almost forgotten by many and is often only referred to in passing when mention is made of the Taylor Report (even then, it is inevitably referred to after Hillsborough and Heysel). While it would be obscene to try and 'grade' these disasters into different levels, it is essential that we as supporters never forget that the fire occurred, and that we ensure that clubs are not allowed to forget the lessons of that afternoon.

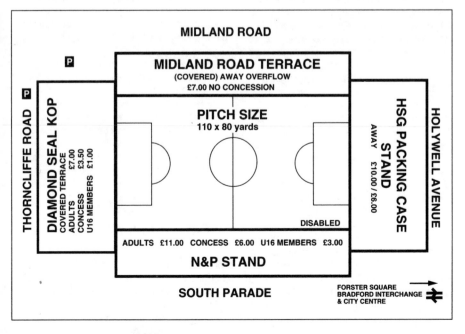

MIDLAND ROAD

MIDLAND ROAD TERRACE
(COVERED) AWAY OVERFLOW
£7.00 NO CONCESSION

THORNCLIFFE ROAD

DIAMOND SEAL KOP
COVERED TERRACE
ADULTS £7.00
CONCESS £3.50
U16 MEMBERS £1.00

PITCH SIZE
110 x 80 yards

HSG PACKING CASE STAND
AWAY £10.00 / £6.00

HOLYWELL AVENUE

DISABLED

ADULTS £11.00 CONCESS £6.00 U16 MEMBERS £3.00

N&P STAND

SOUTH PARADE

FORSTER SQUARE
BRADFORD INTERCHANGE
& CITY CENTRE

BRENTFORD

ADDRESS: Griffin Park
Braemar Road
Brentford
Middlesex TW8 ONT
TELEPHONE No: 0181 847 2511
TICKET OFFICE: 0181 847 2511
FAX: 0181 568 9940
CLUBCALL: 0891 12 11 08
NICKNAME: The Bees
RECORD ATTENDANCE:
39,626 v Preston FA Cup 6th 5 March 1938 (L 0-3)

CLUB COLOURS:
HOME: Shirts: Red/White stripes;
Shorts: Black; Socks: Red
AWAY: Shirts: Blue/White stripes;
Shorts: White; Socks: Blue

KIT SPONSORS: Ericsson Mobile Phones
MANUFACTURERS: Hummel

GROUND INFO

The entrance to the away end is tucked in between a row of houses, and once in the visitors' section you will find it looks like a multi-storey car park basement, with the 'roof' of the terracing actually being the bottom of a tier of seats. There are two big pillars which can block your view, and the toilets are not the nicest you'll ever come across (let's just leave it at that, I'm sure your imagination can fill in the gaps). At £12 a seat it is not the best value for money, and the concession of £9 whilst a nice gesture isn't really much better. The pricing structure in the rest of the ground isn't easy to get to grips with either. It seems to be based on a non-members adult price of £7.80 (nice round figure eh?) and a concession price of £5.50, with other areas having prices added to this tariff (eg the Braemar Stand Block A is £7.80 plus £2, Block B £7.80 plus £3.70 etc.). Given that there are also reductions for members (£1 for adults and concessions), this means that it takes about three years of dedicated study before you can feel fairly confident that you know how much you are going to be charged when you enter Griffin Park.

If you're stuck for somewhere to go, try the Braemar terrace or stands, as the fans around here (unlike the stewards who in my experience tend to adopt a rather superior attitude to those around them and who can be unhelpful and slightly inflammatory) are fine: very much the purveyors of truth, justice and good football, in as much as if anyone, be they from the away team or Brentford, is rubbish and/or dirty, they are quite happy to let them know about it.

The New Stand (don't let the name fool you — this is a terrace, and gets its name from the fact that it is on New Road) has daubed on its roof in massive letters 'Next Time Fly KLM'. Presumably this ace marketing ploy was aimed at catching the attention of people coming in to land at Heathrow. However, call me old fashioned, but if I was going to entrust an airline company with my life, I'm not sure it would be one who painted their advertising slogans on a big piece of corrugated metal!

CAPACITY: Stands: 3,905; Terrace: 9,349;
Total: 13,254

AWAY FANS: Brook Road Stand 636;
Brook Road Terrace: 1,636;
Total: 2,272

DISABLED FACILITIES: There is a disabled area in the Brook Road End which houses about 30 people in total. Both disabled fans and helpers are admitted free of charge (a maximum of one disabled helper per disabled fan). Pre-booking is required, as it is for match commentaries for the blind, which are also free. For the latter of these two services, make sure bookings are made well in advance. There are no parking facilities at the ground.

The good news, however, is that there are no less than two disabled toilets!!! Rather less encouraging is the fact that these are in the Braemar Road Stand.

PROGRAMME: £1.50
Not cheap but quite worth buying. There is a decent enough away team spread, and enough home team news to be interesting without being overly obscure to other than the most die-hard of Bees fans. Added to which there are normally a couple of well above average general interest articles in it which means it can fill the half-time break admirably.

FANZINES:
Voice of the Beehive	50p
Thorne in the Side	50p
Beesotted	80p

Beesotted comes out more regularly than the other two, and is the only fanzine I can think of which is printed in a rectangular format. *Voice of the Beehive* can be the best/funniest of the three on its day, but of the three *VOTBs* I've seen, while two were excellent, one was dire!

TRAVEL
NEAREST RAILWAY STATION:
Brentford (0171 928 5100 — Waterloo Enquiries)
NEAREST TUBE STATION:
South Ealing (Piccadilly Line)
Without wanting to sound like your mother, if you go to South Ealing (turn left as you leave the stadium) watch out when you are crossing the A4! It can be a bit hairy.

BUS: London Transport (0171 222 1234)

BY CAR: NORTH/EAST: Take the A406 North Circular Road (heading west) to Chiswick. At Chiswick Roundabout take the third exit on to Chiswick High Road and continue straight on for 0.75 miles before turning right on to the A3001 Ealing Road. The ground is 0.25 miles on the left.

WEST: M4 to J2. When you leave the motorway there is a set of traffic lights. Do a U-turn at these on to the A4 (heading west). After 0.3 miles turn left into Ealing Road (A3001 and the ground is 0.5 miles on the right.

SOUTH: Take the A205 South Circular Road (heading west) until you cross the Thames; turn left into Kew Bridge Road (A315). Turn right after 0.25 miles into Ealing Road (A3001) and the ground is 0.5 miles on the left.

PARKING: There is street parking around. Otherwise those coming from the north, east or south can take the Ealing Road past the ground and take the second turning on the left into Layton Road where there is a car park. This is also where supporters' coaches park. For those coming from the west, Layton Road is first right after you turn on to Ealing Road. An alternative for those coming from north, east and south is to continue on the A315 for 200yd past the Ealing Road turn; there is a car park on the right. Coming from the west, go past the ground to the bottom of Ealing Road and turn right.

FUTURE DEVELOPMENTS

The club plan to put a roof over the Ealing End of the ground, although they did say that this was not imminent, and that may be delayed in order that they do not simply cover an area which may require development in the short/medium-term future. A further option would be for the area to be closed and redeveloped with a purpose-built stand. The general opinion is that the progression towards all-seater status would be driven by the club's league status and the level of grants available rather than an urgent desire to change the look of the ground.

OTHER INFORMATION

There is a pub on each corner of the ground, and there doesn't seem to be any regulars-only restriction or membership schemes. (Hmmm, is this because the landlords in this area have been specially trained to ensure that there are no problems when away supporters — gasp — have a pint, or does the expression 'supply and demand' ring more bells?) Of the four, the New Inn is my personal favourite, but away fans tend to congregate in a different one every time, so play it by ear.

Inside the ground, the food is OK but every time I've been to Griffin Park there has always been a 'Wanted for Murder' poster stuck up next to the food counter, and what a fine appetite stimulant that is!

At half-time the club has a compère on the pitch whose high-tech method of bringing the fans the latest scores in other matches seems dependent on his mate in the Braemar paddock shouting them out to him. How this other chap resists the temptation to feed him completely bogus half-times is beyond me, but I can but admire his willpower and sense of fair-play.

All in all, Griffin Park is the type of ground where, even given the cost/potential poor view, you'll go away with favourable memories; the fans are friendly and it's easy to get a decent pint.

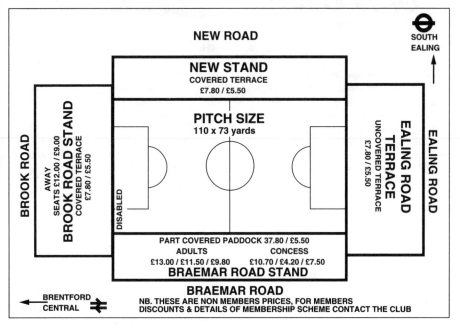

27

BRIGHTON & HOVE ALBION

ADDRESS: Goldstone Ground
Newtown Road,
Hove
East Sussex BN3 7DE
TELEPHONE No: 01273 739535
TICKET OFFICE: 01273 778855
FAX: 0123 321095
SEAGULL LINE: 0891 800 609
NICKNAME: Seagulls
RECORD ATTENDANCE:
36,747 v Fulham Div 2 2 December 1958 (W 3-0)

CLUB COLOURS:
HOME: Shirts: Royal Blue & White Stripes;
Shorts: Royal Blue; Socks: White
AWAY: Shirts: Yellow; Shorts: Yellow; Socks: Yellow
In the past Brighton has not been afraid to experiment
with its kit, as anyone who can remember the horrors
of the 'candy-stripe' shorts will testify. However, perhaps even less popular with the supporters was the
sponsorship deal the club struck with Nobo, thus con-
demning wearers of replica strips to verbal torture from
opposition fans who refused to pronounce the first syllable of the name correctly.

KIT SPONSORS: AKZO Sandtex
MANUFACTURERS: Admiral

GROUND INFO
It is said that a convert to any cause is far more zealous than anyone who has followed it for years, and this
certainly seems to apply to Brighton and price concessions. For a long while it was full whack for away supporters whatever their age. Somewhere along the line
the club had a blinding revelation (perhaps this is not
surprising for a club who once had Clive Walker on its
books) and decided that this was unfair and not only
introduced concessions throughout the ground, but
also joined a campaign to get all other league clubs to
offer concessions as well. Joy shall be in heaven (not
to mention visitors' wallets) over one sinner that repen-
teth etc etc.

Sadly, the fencing around visiting supporters in the
South Stand remains at present which inevitably leads
to a restricted view of the nearest goal. The south side
of the East terrace is allocated to away supporters; this
is spacious but open to the elements, so if the weather
is looking dodgy, consider spending those extra few
quid (or wrapping up extra warm if you prefer to be
able to have a good view of the action).

CAPACITY: Stands: 5,110; Terrace: 11,144;
Total: 16,254

28

AWAY FANS: South Stand Block A: 738;
East Terrace South: 2,517;
Total: 3,255
DISABLED FACILITIES:
There are spaces for 20 wheelchairs, 20 helpers and
38 'others' in the southwest corner of the ground.
Disabled fans are admitted free, though helpers pay
matchday prices.

The standard of facilities is fairly good, with the
notable exception of there being no parking at the
ground. Match commentaries for the blind are available, and the club states that neither this nor disabled
spaces require pre-booking, although it recommends
that it is preferable for the blind to contact the club in
advance.

PROGRAMME: £1.50.
A good section about the visiting team comprising two
pages of general club information, and two pages of
penpics. The rest of the programme is readable
enough, though maybe for £1.50 you'd expect a little
more substance. Obviously the odds are that this will
not apply to many readers, but should you happen to
go to a match which is called off at the last minute,
when you go to the rearranged fixture watch out for the
club's little trick of printing exactly the same programme but with a different front cover.

FANZINES:
Gulls Eye   50p

TRAVEL
NEAREST RAILWAY STATION:
Hove (01273 206755 — Brighton Enquiries)

BUS: Brighton & Hove Bus & Coach Co (01273
821111)/ Brighton Borough Transport (01273 606141)
Hove station is a three-minute train trip from the main
line station at Brighton with a good service between
the two. From Hove station it is a five-minute walk to
the ground, although if the weather is reasonable it can
be better to walk along the sea front from Brighton to
the stadium (stopping naturally to sample the atmosphere in some of the many hostelries along the route).
If you do go for the longer walk and you get fed up
with it, then grab any of the following buses: 3, 5, 5a,
5b, 5c, 7, 29, 90, 91, 96, 229.

Alternatively, there appear to be hundreds of cab
firms who advertise in phone boxes, albeit with strange
names such as 'Fantasy', 'Angel', 'Dominant', etc. But
presumably they have all got the knowledge.

BY CAR:
NORTH: Take the A23 towards Brighton. When on
this road you will come to a place called Pyecombe (or
do you combe to a place called Pyecome?) and two
miles after this, turn right (signposted Hove). After a

mile the road forks; bear left on to the A2038 Nevill Road. In one mile there is a major crossroads, turn left here on to the A27 Old Shoreham Road, and the ground is 200yd on your right.

EAST: Take the A27 through Brighton, following signs for Worthing. This will bring you on to the Old Shoreham Road (A27) and the ground is on the left.

WEST: A24 to A27. Follow signs for Hove and Brighton. This leads you on to the Old Shoreham Road and the ground is on the right.

PARKING: Brighton dog track is on Nevill Road. It has plenty of parking space and is easy to get away from. Alternatively, go into Hove via Sackville Road and take the sixth left (Blatchington Road) and fourth right for Car Park. There is some street parking around the ground.

FUTURE DEVELOPMENTS

The club has been actively searching for a site at which to relocate, although at present it has had about as much luck as the team has; so expect The Seagulls to be staying in Hove (for goodness sake don't call it Brighton otherwise the residents will go right into one) for at least the medium-term. During the summer repairs were scheduled to be undertaken on the East Terrace and it is hoped to have it fully opened for the 1995/6 season.

OTHER INFORMATION

The nearest pub to the ground is the Hove Park Tavern on the Old Shoreham Road, and about 25yd away from this there is a chip shop. There are more pubs in Hove town centre. Inside the ground, the food is OK but the tea tasted grim and had a handful of

sand or something at the bottom of each cup. Try to have the right money with you as inevitably the solitary person serving doesn't have any change.

The Goldstone is one of those grounds which seems to crop up with alarming regularity whenever there are tales of woe being told by away fans about being prevented from taking something into a ground. Among the sinister items rejected by Goldstone stewards so far are:

• A duffel bag with a plastic bottle of lemonade inside it — Reason: suspicious package.

• A bag of shredded 'ticker tape' paper — Reason: can cause mess and mayhem.

• A sausage roll — Reason: the club has its own catering facilities and besides you might throw it at someone.

• A meat pie — as above.

But the top in this category surely goes to the steward who stopped a middle-aged female fan and made her peel the banana she was carrying — Reason: to prove there was no weapon hidden inside it. Heaven knows what Dishy Des Lynam, the housewife's choice and the club's celebrity fan would make of it all.

There have been quite a few changes in the personnel at the Goldstone over the last few months so hopefully along with the new enlightened outlook on under 16s will come a rethink on away supporters.

Finally, any of you reading this with a few bob to spare may be interested in the pitchside advertising hoarding for 'Brighton and Hove Albion Financial Services'... Presumably this has got something to do with the football club which, if my memory serves me correctly, nearly went belly up a couple of years back. It would be interesting to have been a fly on the wall at the inaugural marketing meeting just to see what sort of suggestions were put forward for a catchy company slogan.

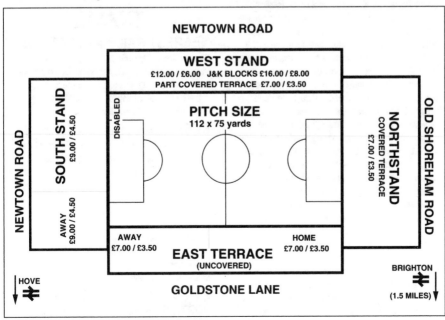

BRISTOL CITY

ADDRESS: Ashton Gate
Winterstoke Road
Bristol
BS3 2TE

TELEPHONE No: 0117 963 2812
TICKET OFFICE: 0117 963 2812
FAX: 0117 963 9574
CLUBCALL: 0891 12 11 76
NICKNAME: The Robins
RECORD ATTENDANCE:
43,335 v Preston FA Cup 5th 16 February 1935
(D 0-0)

CLUB COLOURS:
HOME: Shirts: Red; Shorts: White; Socks: Red
AWAY: Shirts: Black/Green hoops with thin Red
stripe; Shorts: Black; Socks: Black

KIT SPONSORS: Auto Windscreens
MANUFACTURERS: Loki

GROUND INFO

Away fans are sited at the 'Covered End' of the
ground, which deserves a prize if only for being one of
the most accurately described named stands you'll
come across. This is at the opposite side of the ground
to which fans were sited pre-1994/5 season, and the
old uncovered away area ('The Open End') has been
replaced by a new all-seater construction (sadly not
called the Fairly Impressive New Stand, but rather the
Carling Atyeo End, but that's the pressure of marketing
for you) which is allocated for home fans' use only.

The away allocation is more than adequate for the
vast majority of matches. If you do find yourself either
unable to get in, or would prefer a side of the pitch
view then I would recommend you go in the Upper
Williams Stand, which offers an excellent view and has
the advantage over the Dolman Stand of not only
being much newer but also having plastic as opposed
to wooden seats. If you do go into the Dolman, you
can pretty much guarantee that some kid will sit behind
and accidentally kick one of the seats down, but be so
impressed by the loud wooden bang it makes that they
will spend the next 90min banging it up and down (by
the end of the game you will be seriously wondering
what sort of noise the little darling's head would make
if you bounced it off the seats a bit).

The pitch at Ashton Gate is massive enough to
make even the Wimbledon back four sit up and think,
and is easily the longest in the league. The first time
you see it you really notice the difference.

The Covered End offers decent facilities and a
fairly good view of the action, but it is worth avoiding

the first few rows if you can as these aren't quite
raised enough to give you the proper perspective of
the match. Good concessions for visiting supporters.

CAPACITY: Stands: 21,040; Terrace: Nil;
Total: 21,040

AWAY FANS: Covered End: 2,500; Total: 2,500
This can be extended to the whole of the End (capacity
5,500) if demand is sufficient.

DISABLED FACILITIES: There are 50
places for disabled fans, and these are sited at the
Atyeo and the Covered End. Pre-booking is not necessary, but if you do, at least you can stipulate which end
of the ground you want to be in. Admission for disabled
fans is free, with helpers paying £8.50. Parking facilities are available at the ground. The club states that
match commentaries are available but add the rider
that these are for the blind — extending the policy of
stating the obvious past the naming of the stands.

PROGRAMME: £1.30
Still one of the worst in the First Division. Not only was
it thin and too reliant on full-page adverts and pho-
tographs, but the written articles there were in it
weren't that interesting.

FANZINES:
One Team in Bristol   £1
Doubled in price last season but also improved
radically. *The Bountyhunter* and *Take Your Seats*,
which were previously produced, appear to have gone
out of circulation.

TRAVEL
NEAREST RAILWAY STATION:
Parson Street (0117 955 7013 — Bristol Enquiries)
Parson Street is (contrary to popular belief) still open
but the number of trains that stop there is minimal; so
you are better off aiming for Temple Meads, which is
about 1.5 miles from the ground.

BUS: City Line/City Dart (0117 955 7013)
In my experience, the bus drivers in Bristol are
among the worst for pulling out in front of cars at bus
stops; and as you slam on the brakes and your shoulder gets pulled out of its joint by your seatbelt, the driver will rub salt in the wound by either belatedly indi-
cating or giving you a wave to thank you for your 'co-
operation'.

There are no buses direct from Temple Meads to
the ground, and to avoid a longish walk you should
take either an 8 or 9 bus to Broadmead, and then a 21
or a 22 to the ground.

BY CAR:
NORTH/WEST: M5 to J16. Take the A38 (signposted Patchway, Bristol) and keep going along this

road until you see signs for Taunton (A38); follow these and this will take you across the River Avon. Bear left into Winterstoke Road, then turn left into Marsh Road and right into Ashton Road.

EAST: M4, M32 into Bristol City Centre, picking up the signs for Taunton (A38), then as north/west.

SOUTH: M5 to J18. When you leave the motorway, pick up the A4 (Portway), cross the swing bridge and bear left into Winterstoke Road. Then as north.

Whichever way you are going in, watch out for the road signs which seem to change for no given reason, eg one minute you will see a motorway indicated in the left-hand lane, and 20yd up the road it will have miraculously changed to the right-hand lane. (Another favourite is for the signs for a particular area to stop for no obvious reason other than to worry drivers that they have missed their turn-off.)

PARKING: The car park at the ground is for permit holders only; otherwise there is a Do-It-All/Curry's right by the ground which has a decent car park and a Sainsbury's along Winterstoke Road, and plenty of parking on side streets around the ground.

FUTURE DEVELOPMENTS

1994/5 saw the opening of the Carling Atyeo Stand. During the 1995/6 season the old Dolman's Schoolboys' enclosure will be redeveloped to provide additional seating for approx 1,500-2000.

OTHER INFORMATION

The Wedlock and the Rising Sun on Ashton Road are the nearest pubs, and there is a decent Chinese chip shop next to the latter. There is also the Ship & Castle just over the railway crossing on Ashton Vale Road which serves both breakfasts and lunches.

If you decide to go into town, it's worth taking the bus as otherwise it's a bit of a walk. The town itself is a little disappointing, and there seemed — when I was there — to be an atmosphere about the place which at times, especially for night matches, almost bordered on the hostile.

As with many grounds, fans are banned from taking such deadly weapons as umbrellas into the ground, but unlike most places there is actually a little hole in the wall (in which a steward is incarcerated) where you can deposit your brolly for the duration.

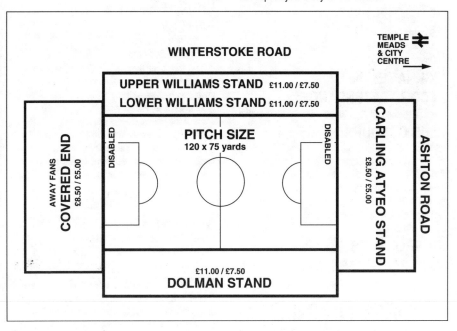

BRISTOL ROVERS

ADDRESS: Twerton Park
Twerton High Street
Bath,
Avon BA2 1DB
(Only on matchdays)

TELEPHONE No: 0117 986 9999

TICKET OFFICE: 0117 986 9999

MATCHDAY OFFICE:
01225 312327

FAX: 0117 986 4030

CLUBCALL: 0891 66 44 22

Although Bristol Rovers currently ground share with Bath City, the office base of the club remains in Bristol. The 0117 numbers above are Bristol not Bath based. If you want to write to the club use the Registered Office address:

BRFC plc,
Acornfields House,
Somerfield,
Keynsham,
Bristol BS18 2DJ.

NICKNAME: The Pirates

RECORD ATTENDANCE:

38,472 v Preston FA Cup 4th 30 January 1960 (D 3-3)

CLUB COLOURS:

HOME: Shirts: White and Blue Quarters; Shorts: White; Socks: Blue

AWAY: Shirts: Green; Shorts: Black; Socks: Black Rovers' home kit remains one of the most pleasing to the eye in the Football League, somehow capturing a flavour of a Corinthian spirit of bygone days. The away kit isn't and doesn't.

KIT SPONSORS: Yet to be announced

MANUFACTURERS: Matchwinner

GROUND INFO

The away terrace is uncovered and if it rains this tends to blow straight into your eyes. However, this is compensated by the beautiful Avon hills and the City of Bath in the distance. Away fans are admitted into the family enclosure, the admission rules for which are that women, juveniles and OAPs can go in alone, but adult males must be accompanied by one from the previous categories. Seating for unaccompanied males is at a premium in terms of both availability and price. £13 for a place in the unimpressive grandstand may be more than your wallet can take, although as a visitor if you choose to go here, so long as you are not overly enthusiastic you shouldn't have too many problems.

CAPACITY: Stands: 1,040; Terrace: 7,903; Total: 8,943

AWAY FANS: Dominion Road Open Terrace: 1,166; Total: 1,166

The figure above does not take account of the several houses overlooking the Bath End of the ground from where, on sell-out days, a fiver can buy you a place on the roof of one of these with a brilliant view of the ground.

DISABLED FACILITIES:

There are 14 places for disabled fans with space for one helper each. Admission is free of charge for both parties, but you must pre-book (use the normal office number). There are no parking facilities for the disabled at the ground which given both the general parking difficulties in the area, and the hilly terrain, can make life difficult. There are match commentaries for the blind, but these must be booked at least a fortnight in advance.

PROGRAMME: £1.30

FANZINES:

Trumpton Times 60p
On The 2nd May 50p

TT is a fairly good read, put together with a passion that has sadly disappeared from many fanzines. The editor can be seen selling it at the Bath End of the ground and is an excellent source of gossip, from which of the Rovers players your side will have to watch out for, to what are the best pubs to head for. As his answer to my first question was, 'None, they're all crap', I can only guess that either I caught him on a bad day, or he is getting very disillusioned with his life.

TRAVEL

NEAREST RAILWAY STATION:

Oldfield Park or Bath Spa (01225 460713)
Oldfield Park is the nearest but as it has only about 15 trains a day stopping there it is probably best forgotten.

NEAREST BUS STATION: Central bus station — Badgerline Buses (01225 464446)
Grab a number 10 Whiteway bus from Bay 10 at the bus station. This is just across the road from the railway station, and will drop you right outside the ground. The journey takes about 10min, but if the traffic is bad (as it often is, especially on the way back into Bath after a match) then it can be just as quick to walk.

BY CAR:

NORTH: A46(T). Turn right on to the A4 London Road (signposted Bath). Follow the A4 until it becomes Upper Bristol Road and then turn left on to Windsor Bridge Road and cross the River Avon. Turn right on to the Lower Bristol Road (A36), and after about one mile turn left into Mill Lane then right into High Street; the ground is on the left.

SOUTH: Take A367 towards Bath and turn left on to the A3062 Frome Road. After a couple of miles the road becomes Whiteway Road; you will see a school on your right, and shortly after this road forks in two. Keep to the right, continuing up Whiteway Road. After two miles there is a park on your right, turn right immediately after this into Shaws Way. Continue until you get to a cross-roads at which you should turn right into Freeview Road; the ground is then a couple of hundred yards on the left.

WEST: A4, A36 (Lower Bristol Road) towards Bath. After two miles turn right into Little Hill, then first left into High Street and the ground is 300yd on the right.

EAST: A4 into Bath until it becomes Upper Bristol Road, then as north.

PARKING: A problem. There is little parking around Twerton Park, and you may find yourself pushed towards Bath city centre (two miles) which isn't very good for getting away from, and a better bet is to head the same distance towards Twerton Hill in order to make good your escape.

FUTURE DEVELOPMENTS

The club are hoping to build a 20,000 all-seater close to the new M49 near the second Severn Bridge which is currently under construction. If everything does get the go-ahead then the stadium could be operating by 1997/8. However, don't hold your breath as nothing is definite and previous plans for a return to Bristol have been thwarted by the City Council. The reason for the last of these refusals was apparently that the site was

considered dangerously near to a chemical plant. This must be very reassuring for the residents living right by it, and is a little ironic as the fans' nickname of 'Gasheads' is derived from the fact that Eastville was right by a huge gas works.

OTHER INFORMATION

Twerton Park is sneered at by both local and visitor alike, and is referred to by many as 'Trumpton'; but in truth, apart from the parking problems, it is a beautiful place at which to watch football. There is a bookies, a Chinese, a chip shop and a pub within 50yd of the ground (although the pub does have limits on the amount of people it can fit in on match days). Inside, the tea is good, the pies indifferent and the toilets a bit bleak. The pre-match entertainment involves an old boy going round with a mike and chatting to fans (even away ones) and reminding people not to swear; although easy to mock, it actually works quite well.

Finally, be warned that the Rovers' fans version of the 1950s hit 'Goodnight Irene' is dreadfully addictive; at best it will be in your mind for weeks afterwards, and at worst you will join in with them as their team scores a last minute winner against you (don't worry what your mates will say, as they'll probably be singing it too).

A different ground, a different experience, perhaps not the best place for league football but I like it and am always treated like a human being there; thus I find it infinitely preferable to some of the other stadia mentioned in this book.

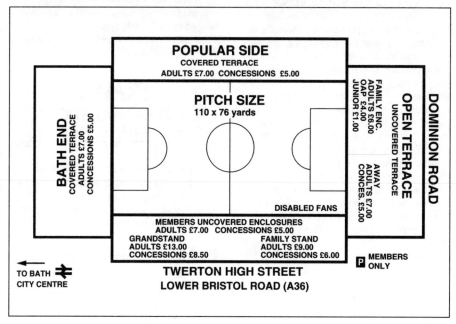

POPULAR SIDE
COVERED TERRACE
ADULTS £7.00 CONCESSIONS £5.00

PITCH SIZE
110 x 76 yards

BATH END
COVERED TERRACE
ADULTS £7.00
CONCESSIONS £5.00

FAMILY ENC.
ADULTS £6.00
OAP £4.00
JUNIOR £1.00

OPEN TERRACE
UNCOVERED TERRACE

AWAY
ADULTS £7.00
CONCES. £5.00

DOMINION ROAD

DISABLED FANS

MEMBERS UNCOVERED ENCLOSURES
ADULTS £7.00 CONCESSIONS £5.00
GRANDSTAND
ADULTS £13.00
CONCESSIONS £8.50
FAMILY STAND
ADULTS £9.00
CONCESSIONS £6.00

🅿 MEMBERS ONLY

TO BATH
CITY CENTRE

TWERTON HIGH STREET
LOWER BRISTOL ROAD (A36)

BURNLEY

ADDRESS: Turf Moor
Brunshaw Road
Burnley
BB10 4BX

TELEPHONE No: 01282 427777

TICKET OFFICE: 01282 427777

FAX: 01282 428938

CLUBCALL: 0891 12 11 53

NICKNAME: The Clarets

For whom 1994/5 was not a vintage year

RECORD ATTENDANCE:

54,775 v Huddersfield FA Cup 3rd 23 February 1924 (W 1-0)

CLUB COLOURS:

HOME: Shirts: Claret and Blue Trim;
Shorts: White; Socks: White
AWAY: Shirts: Yellow with Black pinstripes;
Shorts: Yellow; Socks: Yellow

KIT SPONSORS: Endsleigh

MANUFACTURERS: Mitre

GROUND INFO

The best view at the ground is from the Bob Lord Stand although it may not always be possible to enjoy the facilities (it is easier for visitors to get in here than it is to the non-allocated section of the Endsleigh Stand which is members only, and very much kept that way). Bob Lord was, in case you've forgotten, the controversial chairman at the club and the first in such a position to be given a high media profile, so we've probably got him to thank for the likes of Ken Bates, Alan Sugar, etc. Lord never courted popularity (especially with away fans) but in many places in the town he is still regarded as somewhat of a demigod. He also had the dubious distinction of being a ringer for Lew Grade.

Gone for the 1995/6 season is the magnificent Longside side terrace, which used to house 9,600 home and away supporters and inevitably created the majority of the atmosphere at Turf Moor. At present the club has not announced where away fans will be sited for the 1995/6 season, although it is possible that until the Longside Stand reopens (See Future Developments).

The club states that concessions are not available after 12 noon for a Saturday game, and 4.30pm for a midweek game.

CAPACITY: Stands: 15,185; Terrace: 5,000;
Total: 20,185

The figure above is post-completion of the Longside Stand and assumes that the Bee Hole Lane End terracing remains open.

AWAY FANS: Endsleigh Stand: 810; Total: 810
Housing of away supporters during alterations will be in a section of the Endsleigh Stand; numbers could be restricted.

DISABLED FACILITIES: There are limited places available at the front of the Bob Lord Stand, which is quite open to the elements, and a better bet can be the Cricket Field Stand which has had seats taken out so that 20 wheelchair-bound supporters can be accommodated. There is the normal admission charge for helpers, with disabled fans getting in free. There are 10 seats for the blind near the press box in the Bob Lord Stand at concessionary prices.

If you want to go to Turf Moor the best advice is to either pre-book your space via your own club, or get in touch with the Community Officer at the club (Bob Oates) on 01282 831456.

Match commentaries are available in the Bob Lord Stand and these must be pre-booked.

PROGRAMME: £1.50.
A bit pricey but not too bad.

FANZINES:

Marlon's Gloves	£1
No Nay Never	60p
The Claret Flag	60p

Of the three, *Marlon's Gloves* is by far and away the best, and isn't afraid to stick its head over the parapet now and again. The sellers are always willing to have a chat and they are a good source of gossip, as well as tips on decent pubs etc.

TRAVEL

NEAREST RAILWAY STATION:

Burnley Central (01282 425421)
If your team's supporters have something of a 'reputation', expect to be escorted back to the station and lined up outside until your train arrives. Whilst outside, if my experience is anything to go by, you'll be advised by the police that anyone who steps off the pavement will be 'in trouble', ie given a severe wigging until precisely 20sec after your train has left the station. So be on your best behaviour!

BUS: Central bus station (01282 423125)

BY CAR:

NORTH: Follow the A682 to the town centre and take the first exit at the roundabout (by Ritzy's nightclub) into Yorkshire Street. Continue through traffic signals into Brunshaw Road for the ground.
EAST: A646 to A671 then along Todmorden Road towards the town centre. At the traffic lights turn right into Brunshaw Road.

SOUTH/WEST: Leave M6 at J31 (although this junction can get busy when roadworks are in place) and take the A59/A677 to Blackburn then up the A6119 for the M65. Take the M65 to J10 and on exiting follow NT signs to Towneley Hall. The road goes past the ground.

As Turf Moor lies in a valley and still has its floodlights, they remain the easiest way to navigate yourself to the ground.

PARKING: There is a plethora of streets near the ground although the club advises these can be difficult to park-up in. There is also space for 500+ cars in Fulledge Rec Ground where a hard surface is being laid. Town centre multi-storey car parks are only 5min walk from the ground.

FUTURE DEVELOPMENTS

The development of the Longside into a 7,744-seat stand is due to be completed for Christmas 1995. This will be a two-tier stand which will incorporate executive boxes, as well as shops, restaurants and possibly a cinema complex as well. After which, dependent on the available finance, the club will start work on a 4,840-seater at the Bee Hole Lane End. It is Burnley's avowed intention that the redevelopment of the ground should not be allowed to impact on the playing side of the club, so no dates have been set for when this will take place although it hopes to complete it in a year; there will always be three sides of the ground open.

During the construction of the Longside the ground's capacity will be reduced to around the 13,000 mark and due to the demand from home support as well as potential problems segregating supporters, it is difficult to see where visitors will be able to go apart from the 810 Cricket Field seats currently allocated. Possibly some space could be allocated in one of the wings of the Bob Lord Stand, but nothing has yet been announced. During the construction at the Bee Hole Lane End the capacity will be just over 15,000 and this may still lead to access problems. Also it is considered likely that either a larger section of the Cricket Field Stand or part of one tier of the new two-tier Longside Stand will be made available. On completetion of all the rebuilding, the ground should hold 21,500 seats.

OTHER INFORMATION

For pre-match refreshment try the nearby Wellington or the Park View, both of which serve a decent enough pint. The club intends to introduce its own facilities in the Bob Lord and Endsleigh Stands, which will include betting booths.

Hopefully you will have all the information you need about the club here, as trying to get information about away details over the phone was akin to getting blood out of a stone, though to be fair, once at the ground, the club was a lot more helpful. The club also states that it is introducing a new telephone system which should help.

As with many clubs, the tannoy at Burnley is near impossible to understand, although it is difficult to decide whether this is to do with the acoustics or just the local accent — when speaking with home fans you need to remind yourself that there is only one 'r' in the team's name!

A trip to Turf Moor will probably bring back memories of the good old days for fans of a certain age such as Ralph Coates' wraparound hair at its worst and Leighton James at his best, and although time has not been too kind on the club, it still remains a friendly place where you can enjoy a pint and a chat about football with locals who not only feel passionate about the game but who turn up in sufficient numbers to keep the memories alive.

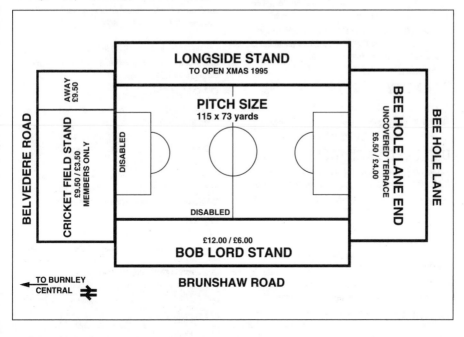

BURY

ADDRESS: Gigg Lane
Bury
Lancashire BL9 9HR
TELEPHONE No: 0161 764 4881
TICKET OFFICE: 0161 764 4881
FAX: 0161 764 5521
CLUBCALL: 0891 12 11 97
NICKNAME: The Shakers
RECORD ATTENDANCE:
35,000 v Bolton FA Cup 3rd 9 January 1960 (D 1-1)
CLUB COLOURS:
HOME: Shirts: White; Shorts: Royal Blue;
Socks: Royal Blue
AWAY: Shirts: Red and Navy Stripes;
Shorts: White; Socks: Red/Navy

KIT SPONSORS: Birthdays

MANUFACTURERS: Le Coq Sportif

GROUND INFO

Cemetery Enclosure is a family stand which admits an adult and child for a combined fee of £9 if they are club members, and £12 if they are not, with each additional child costing £3. Compare and contrast these more than reasonable prices and excellent concessions with the £12 it would cost an adult and child to stand on the Cemetery Road Terrace where there are no concessions for away fans. If you are an away fan travelling with kids then any part of the ground is going to be considerably cheaper than the away terrace, ranging from £6 in the Family Stand, to £2.50 for prime seats on the halfway line in the Main Stand — still it's only (your) money.

CAPACITY: Stands: 12,500; Terrace: Nil;
Total: 12,500 (all-seating)

AWAY FANS: Manchester Road: 2,800;
Total: 2,800 (seats)

DISABLED FACILITIES: There are 20 places for wheelchair-bound supporters in the South Stand. Pre-booking is not required and admission is free of charge for both disabled supporters and their escorts. Match commentaries for the blind are also available as are parking facilities.

PROGRAMME: £1.20.
A real 'bog standard' programme, one of those that you end up buying simply because you always buy a programme at matches, and you'll turn to the away section where you will read that your star striker .... has scored .... goals this season (or had done when this was put together) and was bought from

36

.... for a fee of .... — fill in the blanks and there you have it. With normal managers comments, etc etc, you'll end up wondering why you bothered.

FANZINES:
Where Were You At The Shay? 50p
This is not the most regular of publications, but when it does appear it is well worth a read. Check the date of issue though before coughing up; if it is under three weeks old then it's worth getting, but older than that and it's probably as well to give it a miss.

TRAVEL
NEAREST RAILWAY STATION:
Bury Interchange (from Manchester Victoria — 0161 832 8353)

BUS: Bury Interchange bus station (0161 228 7811) If your journey takes you into Manchester you could enjoy a nostalgic trip on the tram from the City to Bury. From the centre of Bury you can take either a 90 or a 92 bus to the ground.

BY CAR:
NORTH: M66 to J2. Turn right on to the A58 Rochdale Road (signposted Bury) and after 0.5 mile turn left on to Heywood Street (B6219). After another 0.5 mile turn right into Wellington Road. Continue until you get to the T-junction with Manchester Road (A56) at which you should turn left. Turn left again after 0.5 mile into Gigg Lane and the ground is on the right.
SOUTH/EAST/WEST: M66 to J3. Turn left on to Pilsworth Road. After 1.25 miles you will get to a T-junction, at which you should turn right (A56 Manchester Road). A mile later turn right into Gigg Lane.
Alternatively: Leave the M62 at J17 and take the Bury Road (A56) towards the town. After three miles turn right into Gigg Lane.

PARKING: There is plenty of street parking around the ground, otherwise take the A56 Manchester Road towards Bury (ie from north, turn right on to Manchester Road, and from other directions continue straight past the Gigg Lane turning) and either turn right into Keighley Street, where there is a small car park by the Tech, or continuing to the T-junction with Angouleme Road (A58) and within 0.75 mile there are three car parks on your right, the furthest of which is 1.5 miles from the ground.

FUTURE DEVELOPMENTS
Bury used to be the butt of many a visiting fan's jokes with references to Bury/Cemetery End, 'Giggle' Lane, and the fact that one of the most popular songs sung by the locals went 'Tiptoe through the Ceme' to the tune of 'Tiptoe through the Tulips'. Whilst the originality

of the songs may not have improved and southern fans can still do their 'cloth cap' impression on the trams — you can laugh, but they are ecologically sound! — the reopening of the South Stand means the ground is over three-quarters of the way to becoming all-seater. There are plans afoot to finish off the job by converting the Cemetery End and it is projected that this will be, er, undertaken (see? You just can't help making dodgy puns!) possibly in the summer, but certainly for completion in 1996. The club suggests that the approximate capacities during and post-construction will be 11,500 and 12,500. Nothing definite has been decided as to what will happen to away fans during the construction period, expect a further allocation of seats possibly in the Manchester Road End

OTHER INFORMATION

For a pre-match pint try either the Pack Horse or the Staff Of Life, both of which are on Manchester Road, on the right as you leave Gigg Lane. For purveyors of fine cuisine why not sample the delicacy for which the town has won numerous championships, black pudding? If your only ever encounter with BP's is via a

Little Chef breakfast then you are in for a treat (not that there is anything wrong with Little Chef's, yum, yum, yum, I wish I could eat in one every day, honest guv!) and even southerners can enjoy them (provided they don't start enquiring as to what the recipe is).

The club extends a welcoming hand not only to visiting supporters but also to Manchester United reserves and Swinton Rugby League (Macclesfield and Kidderminster take note: ground sharing with a club from a different town appears to be OK if you enjoy playing with funny shaped balls). The zenith of ground sharing was reached in the past by the club being one of the hosts for the Lacrosse World Cup finals. This extensive use of the ground, while being very good news for the club coffers, is not so good for the state of the pitch and although the groundsman does undertake some Herculean efforts, it does tend to achieve quagmire status around the middle of the season.

The town links with football are everywhere, not least of all being that it was the birthplace of Sir Robert Peel, founder of our beloved boys in blue (as in the police, rather than the Scottish national squad).

Finally visitors from rural areas may find the nearby town of Ramsbottom too exciting to resist!

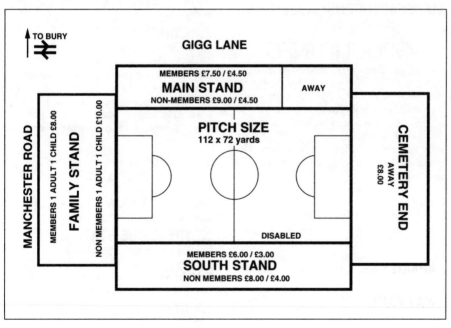

CAMBRIDGE UNITED

ADDRESS: The Abbey Stadium
Newmarket Road
Cambridge CB5 8LL
TELEPHONE No: 01223 566500
TICKET OFFICE: 01223 566500
FAX: 01223 566502
ABBEY UPDATE: 0891 555 885
NICKNAME: The U's
RECORD ATTENDANCE:
14,000 v Chelsea Friendly 1 May 1970 (W 4-3)
CLUB COLOURS:
HOME: Shirts: Amber with Black Sleeves;
Shorts: Black, Amber trim; Socks: Black, Amber top
AWAY: Shirts: White; Shorts: White; Socks: White

KIT SPONSORS: To be advised
MANUFACTURERS: Vandanel

GROUND INFO

The away supporters get good concessions, although the Habbin Stand has got two fairly intrusive pillars which mean that if it isn't raining it is as well to brave the open terrace. The Main Stand isn't officially an away area, but if that is where you want to go then you are unlikely to encounter too many problems, although I can't really see why you'd want to pay an extra £2 to go into what isn't an especially good stand. Still, it takes all sorts.

The Abbey, and especially the Habbin Stand, is acoustically fantastic and simply saying hello to a friend creates the sort of din you'd expect at a Thrash Rock concert, but wait until you've seen the Sunday papers before you brag to your mates about how your team took 'at least 5,000 up there' as you will feel deflated at best when you find out the total crowd was around the 3,000 mark!

Before a visit to the Abbey it is worth brushing up on your country code, as the visitors' entrance is not on the main road, but via a hike through fields negotiating swing gates and stiles! There is a path laid down but as this is about the width of two people you can imagine what it gets like after the final whistle goes, and you're in for a particularly pleasant time if there has been a drop of rain which reduces the fields to marshland very rapidly.

Due to the low walls surrounding the stadium, the gamblers amongst you might like to organise a little sweepstake amongst your friends about how many times you will see the ball hoofed out of the ground. If you were to be unkind about Cambridge's style of play, I'd say between four and eight (please send 20% of your winnings to me c/o Ian Allan Publishing).

CAPACITY: Stands: 3,242; Terrace: 6,425; Total: 9,667
AWAY FANS: Habbin Stand (Seats): 366; South Terrace (Uncovered): 2,876; Total: 3,242

DISABLED FACILITIES: There are six spaces for fans adjacent to the Main Stand, and a further 18 at the Newmarket Road (North Terrace) End of the ground. Disabled fans are admitted free of charge, with helpers being charged £7.

When you phone up to book your place (which you must do), let the club know if you need a place to park, and it will do its best to accommodate you. Space is very limited though, so you might have the pleasure of trying to find on-street parking. There are no match commentaries for the blind.

PROGRAMME: £1.30.
Last season's was an improvement on previous years, and while it is still a bit heavy on the ads, it is more than readable.

FANZINES:
The Abbey Rabbit 80p
This isn't too bad (if you can actually get hold of a copy) and seems to have fairly good relations with the club. There is a large billboard in the ground advertising it, although you may find your eye wandering to the one next to it which is for the Samaritans. 'Depressed? Lonely? Suicidal?' well tough because there's still 20min to go!

TRAVEL
NEAREST RAILWAY STATION:
Cambridge (two miles) (01223 359602)
NEAREST BUS STATION:
Cambridge city centre (01223 423554)
From Cambridge railway station take the Street Shuttle to the city centre (Emmanuel Street), and from there take either a 3 or a 3a to the ground.

BY CAR:
NORTH: A1 then A604 (signposted Huntingdon/Cambridge). Follow A604 until the turn-off for the A14 (old A45 — signposted Felixstowe/Newmarket). Take A14 and continue for 4.5 miles then leave A14 and turn right on to the B1047 (Horningsea Road). After 1.5 miles you get to a T-junction; turn right here on to the A1303 Newmarket Road; go straight over at the next roundabout and the ground is 0.25 mile on the right.
EAST: A14 (ex-A45), as you approach Cambridge turn left on to the A1303 Newmarket Road. Continue for 2.5 miles to the roundabout and go straight over; the ground is 0.25 mile on the left.
SOUTH: M11 to J11. Take the A1309 towards

Trumpington and Cambridge. After one mile turn left on to the A1301, then two miles later turn right on to the A603 Lensfield Road. Turn right after a mile on to the A1303, then right again after one mile for the ground.

NB: This route takes you through Cambridge. If the traffic is heavy, it may be better to take the M11 to J14, pick up the A14 and go from the north.

WEST: A14 (ex-A45) then as north.

Make sure that you have your directions clearly in your mind before you set off, because if you don't and you get lost you've had it! And don't be thinking that you can get out of it by asking a passer-by for directions, because they will either give you a blank stare and tell you that they didn't even know Cambridge had a team, or give you excellent directions...to Cambridge City's ground!

PARKING: There is a (very) small car park behind the Globe PH, but if you're not there early, forget it. Parking is on-street and at a premium; be very careful where you do park as there is a tow-away scheme in operation.

FUTURE DEVELOPMENTS

The club is looking to relocate at some point in the future, which if it aspires to the heights of the league system it will have to do. However, although it may sound defeatist, it is a bit of a shame that the club can't look to consolidate its league status and remain at what, for all its faults, is a very nice 'home'.

OTHER INFORMATION

The news that the Globe 'disco pub' had shut broke the hearts of millions of football fans, who can only hope that one day it reopens (perhaps called the Klinsmann, being that it was such a dive!). If you are looking for sustenance try the Wrestlers, or the Seven Stars up towards the City Centre (about 15min walk), or pay £1 and go in the supporters' bar.

There is a chip shop by the Wrestlers, but if you can stave off your hunger check out the food in the ground where there is a little burger bar which does amongst other things freshly fried bacon in hunks of French Bread, as well as boiling hot tea. The one bad thing about it is the fact that the queues are very, very slow moving.

The toilets are very dark, although you will probably be able to make out the Cambridge Clubcall signs which are on the walls. As these toilets are for away fans, I'm not sure whether they think you are likely to have a spiritual 'conversion' in them or whether it is just misplaced advertising. Either way you will no doubt leave them being impressed at the toilet fresheners hanging in the urinals! Nice touch, boys!

Although you may find plenty to dislike and sneer about at the Abbey, one thing you won't be able to fault is the attitude of the staff at the club. If you need assistance before, during or after a match they appear to be prepared really to put themselves out for you, and if more football clubs could adopt a similar stance, life would be far sweeter.

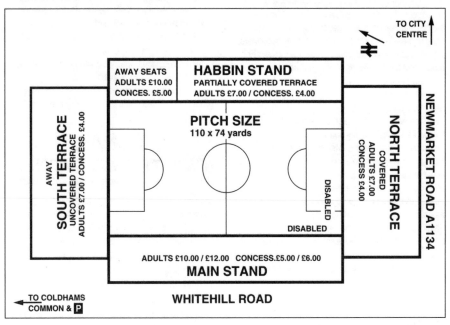

CARDIFF CITY

ADDRESS: Ninian Park
Sloper Road
Cardiff CF1 8SX
TELEPHONE No: 01222 398636
TICKET OFFICE: 01222 398636
FAX: 01222 341148
CLUBCALL: 0891 424 424
NICKNAME: The Bluebirds
RECORD ATTENDANCE:
61,556 Wales v England 14 October 1961 (D 1-1)
57,800 v Arsenal Div 1 22 April 1953 (D 0-0)

CLUB COLOURS:
HOME: Shirts: Blue; Shorts: Blue; Socks: Blue
AWAY: Shirts: Yellow; Shorts: Navy; Socks: Navy

KIT SPONSORS: South Wales Echo

MANUFACTURERS: Bluebird

GROUND INFO

Sadly the scheme that Cardiff were the first to initiate whereby you paid according to the club's league position (and surely if there has to be categorisation of football matches then this is the fairest way to do it) is no longer in operation. However, the fixed prices that the scheme has been replaced by are very fair with good concessions for both home and away supporters.

The possible development of the Grangetown End means that for the 1995/6 season visiting supporters are likely to be initially sited only in the Grandstand with possibly a return to the Grangetown (or at least part of it on reopening).

If you haven't got a ticket for the away enclosure then while I would not say don't go to a game, then at least be aware of certain facts. Many, many people who go to the ground have no hassle whatsoever, come away from the club having had a fine afternoon/evening and are more aware of the steps that the club has taken (on occasion with a seemingly astonishing lack of support from the powers that be) to eradicate the problem. However, if you do go in to the home sections, then its advisable to be careful about what you say (if indeed you want to say anything) as not all the fans will be keeping a welcome in the hillside for you.

The Grandstand has decent facilities although can be a bit tight on the leg room if you're over six feet.

CAPACITY: Stands: 11,100; Terrace: 2,324;
Total: 13,424

AWAY FANS: Grandstand Block A: 539;
Grangetown End: 2,324;
Total: 2,863

DISABLED FACILITIES: The disabled area is situated in the corner of the Popular/Bank Canton Stand and provides space for 20 spaces each for home/away supporters. One helper per disabled fan is also admitted. There are no special parking facilities at the ground.

Matchday commentaries for the blind are available and these, along with disabled spaces, should be pre-booked from one calendar month prior to the match.

PROGRAMME: £1.20

FANZINES:
Bobbing Along	60p
O Bluebird Of Happiness	50p
Watch The Bluebirds Fly	30p
Bluebird Jones	£1
Cover The Grange	50p
The Thin Blue Line	50p
Do The Ayatollah!	50p

A wealth of excellent fanzines which seems just to keep growing. Some come out very regularly and others are more sporadic. A brief line on some of the highlights/lowlights: *O Bluebird* is possibly the best of the bunch even though the print they use is so small and tightly packed that it can be headache inducing. *Do The Ayatollah!* is a (relative) newcomer, and is also well worth a read. The title is derived from the bizarre head beating dance/chant that the home supporters do (the heads which are being beaten are their own I hasten to add). The one disappointment is Bluebird Jones. This is a footballing comic and while it tries hard to say/depict the right things, the storylines are a little bit clichéd and obvious, which is a bit of a disappointment given that the increase in adult comics/graphic novels etc over recent years suggests that this is an area that, given the right treatment, could be very appealing.

TRAVEL

NEAREST RAILWAY STATION:
Ninian Park Halt (from Cardiff Central) (01222 228000)

BUS: Cardiff bus station (01222 396521)
From the bus station catch a City Circle No 1 bus from stand E4 which will drop you right outside Ninian Park. On the way back you'll need to pick up a number 2 (urrgh) from the opposite side of the road.

BY CAR:
FROM ALL DIRECTIONS:
Leave M4 at J33. Take the A4232 for approx 5/6 miles. Leave at roundabout signposted Barry and then turn into Leckwith Road. The car park is on the right.

PARKING: There is a large car park on Sloper Road, and street parking; the latter is not recommended as there are restrictions on all surrounding roads that are rigorously enforced. If when you are approaching the ground you go left at the Cowbridge Road East/Lansdowne Road fork, there are two car parks within a mile or so. To get to these, turn either left into Llandaff Road or, slightly further on, left into Severn Road.

FUTURE DEVELOPMENTS

The plans to convert the Grangetown End to a covered stand have been apparently shelved at present. This doesn't necessarily reflect a lack of ambition at the club following its relegation in the 1994/5 season but is rather an indicator that there remains a degree of uncertainty about who will be at the helm as the Bluebirds progress towards the year 2000. Almost inevitably there has been talk of the club moving into any redeveloped national stadium which is constructed to host the Rugby World Cup finals in 1998, but in reality these are not likely to materialise, if only for the simple fact that it would be difficult to resolve issues such as the length of grass on the pitch, the requirements for which are considerably different for the two sports.

OTHER INFORMATION

If you fancy a pre-match drink (possibly to steady your nerves!) it is as well to stick to the centre of the city rather than anywhere near the ground which can be a bit intimidating, especially for big matches. If you are an away fan and you take one little piece of advice from this book, may I suggest that it would not be to walk into the Ninian (by the ground) with your England replica top on offering to buy pink gins for everyone. One of the most predictable items of the season is that come FA Cup time someone (probably Motty) will wheel out the old chestnut that Cardiff is the only team to take the cup out of England when it beat Arsenal, etc, etc. Cardiff is now one of the few clubs who enjoys the 'privilege' of operating in the English League whilst playing in Wales. Compare this to the situation of Newport AFC, who although 15 or so miles nearer to England, cannot get sanctioned by the Welsh FA (although the courts feel differently) to enjoy any such luxury.

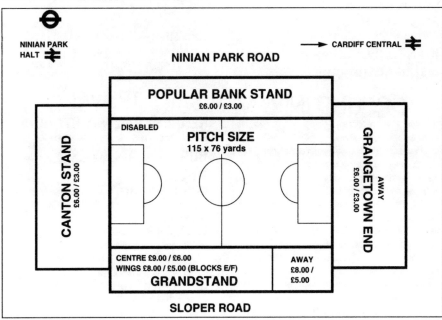

CARLISLE UNITED

ADDRESS: Brunton Park
Warwick Road
Carlisle CA1 1LL

TELEPHONE No: 01228 26237

TICKET OFFICE: 01228 26237

FAX: 01228 30138

CLUBCALL: 0891 12 16 32

NICKNAME: The Cumbrians

RECORD ATTENDANCE:

27,500 v Birmingham FA Cup 3rd 5 January 1957 (D3-3); v Middlesbrough FA Cup 5th 7 February 1970 (L 1-2)

CLUB COLOURS:

HOME: Shirts: Blue, with White/Red markings; Shorts: White; Socks: Blue

AWAY: Shirts: Green, Red/White Stripes; Shorts: Green; Socks: Red

KIT SPONSORS: Conway Vauxhall

MANUFACTURERS: Matchwinner

GROUND INFO

Since the arrival of Michael Knighton as club Chairman some excellent concessionary schemes have been introducedincluding in certain parts of the ground free admission for the under 10s, in what must be one of the only instances known to fans of a 'lift 'em over the turnstiles' policy made official.

Away fans get part of the Petteril End, and there is talk of some of the seats in the East Stand being allocated once the stand is fully open towards the end of 1995. Although the away terrace is uncovered, the place never seems to get as cold as you can experience at Hartlepool and Sunderland (that said, it is recommended that you wear more than a pair of shorts if you are travelling to a midweek fixture in February).

One thing that visiting fans can't fail to hear and be impressed with is the way the home supporters sing their team's name, opting for the 'Glory, Glory' chant as in 'G. G. Man Uni-ted', or 'G. G. Tot Nem Ot Spur' but somehow squeezing in an extra syllable by speeding up the word Carlisle to an almost supersonic rate.

Also, a piece of amazing architecture at the ground is the floodlighting which appears to have been modelled exactly on the radio transmitter which sat on top of the globe at the beginning of the old RKO films.

CAPACITY: Stands: 8,036; Terrace: 9,131; Total: 17,167

AWAY FANS: Petteril End: 1,015; Total: 1,015

DISABLED FACILITIES: There are limited spaces for fans in front of the paddock and admission is by prior arrangement only. The club admits one helper per wheelchair-bound supporter, neither of whom is charged for admission. There are no match commentaries for the blind.

PROGRAMME: £1.20

A couple of general interest articles which are better than average, but otherwise don't expect it to keep you enthralled on your journey home (or even, come to think of it, much past the half-time interval). Some parents may find the adverts contained within the pages a little overbearing — after all football is expensive enough nowadays without kids demanding G & M Monkhouse brown eggs, or to utilise H & E Trotter Waste Services, isn't it?

FANZINES:

So, Jack Ashurst, Where's My Shirt?   50p
Watching From The Warwick   50p

A fair number of 'away trips we have loved' type articles in both publications, but apart from that minor grouse not bad. *Jack Ashurst* probably shades it as the slightly better put together/longer read, but if you can live without the 'bog standard' penpics it is worth considering forgoing a programme and buying both.

TRAVEL

NEAREST RAILWAY STATION:

Carlisle Citadel (1.5 miles) (01228 44711)

BUS: CMS Buses (01946 63222)

BY CAR:

NORTH/SOUTH: Take M6 to J43 then the A69 Warwick Road into Carlisle. The ground is 1.25 miles on the right.

EAST: A69 into Carlisle. After the A69 crosses the M6, the ground is 1.25 miles on the right.

If when you are going home you are on the southbound M6 and you fancy a break, stop at Killington Lake, certainly the most picturesque service station in Britain and arguably one of the nicest in Europe, although accessible only to southbound traffic.

If you intend filling up with petrol for the way back there is only one garage at which you can do this on either side of the road between Brunton Park and the motorway; so if you have time when you arrive it is best to do it on the way into Carlisle because after the match the roads get very choked up.

PARKING: There is a sizeable car park behind the ground which if you turn up early enough you can drive to via the club grounds. However, if you are not in time to do this, drive past the ground about 0.25 mile and turn right into Victoria Drive and right again into St Aidans Road (along which there is street parking). At the bottom of St Aidans Road there is a golf club; drive into here and keep going and the car park is on your right.

There is on-street parking but if you go for this option it is best to park on the motorway side of the ground in order to avoid being held up as the police direct the traffic leaving the club car park on to the main road. Also, if you do park-up by the ground and fancy a walk into town, be warned, it is a fair hike.

FUTURE DEVELOPMENTS

On his arrival at the club Michael Knighton developed a 10-year blueprint which included such issues as the redevelopment of the ground into a 28,000 all-seater, and the attainment of Premiership status. The latter is moving along nicely with promotion to the Second Division last year. As for the former, cards seemed to be played a bit tighter to the chest. There are certainly architect's drawings around for those who want to look at them, but a timetable of events is harder to obtain from a club which becomes slightly coy when asked for details. The first thing to be undertaken was the opening of executive boxes, and currently under way is a development of the East Stand, which will be fully completed containing approx 6,000 seats by late 1995. The capacities given above are after the East Stand has been fully opened. What the following stage of development will be is something the club appears more cagey about, although it is considered that due to the popularity of the Warwick Road End, the Petteril may be the target of the next stage of development.

OTHER INFORMATION

There are a couple of bars by the Main Stand in which away fans are generally welcomed although these do tend to be heaving from the moment they open their doors. The Beehive slightly down the Warwick Road is a better bet, but not always open on match days. Right at the bottom (town end) of Warwick Road is the Crescent, which is large and serves a decent pint, but which has toilets that... ! A lot of the chip shops in the town serve haggis and black pudding in batter, both of which are miles better then anything I found in the ground, where the pies were soggy and the tea luke-warm and weak. However, if you are prepared to go slightly upmarket the club's 'Foxes' restaurant has received many a glowing tribute (phone to pre-book a table).

Generally the stewards and staff at Carlisle are good and will endeavour to assist away fans without making them feel as if they are a nuisance, although tuning into the local Scottish/Geordie/Yorkshire accent takes some doing. One thing that is worth knowing is that although the club, apparently in an attempt to maintain the high level of stewarding, does operate a 'let us know what we do well/badly policy', of all the people I have heard wrote to the club, none got a reply. If you do have any queries about your visit get them sorted out actually at the ground where the atti-tude is much more helpful, and it is not unknown for MK to come and help out if needed. (If you get serious grief why not ask for him in person?)

Older supporters who remember the stuffed red fox that used to be laid on the centre spot before United's games by a man in blue and white top hat and tails (who was, if my memory serves me correctly, a local dustman) will now notice its absence from the field of play. However, if you want to pay a trip down memory lane then just pop into the lobby of the ground where 'Olga' now resides.

Finally, the high water-table at Carlisle means Brunton Park is subject to waterlogging. If there is more than a spit of rain, check the match is still on before leaving home.

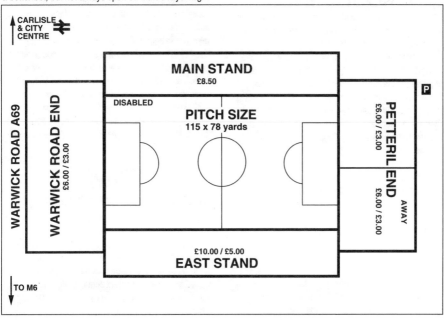

CARLISLE & CITY CENTRE

WARWICK ROAD A69

WARWICK ROAD END
£6.00 / £3.00

MAIN STAND
£8.50

DISABLED

PITCH SIZE
115 x 78 yards

PETTERIL END
£6.00 / £3.00
£6.00 / £3.00
AWAY

P

£10.00 / £5.00
EAST STAND

TO M6

CHARLTON ATHLETIC

ADDRESS: The Valley
Floyd Road, Charlton
London SE7 8EL

TELEPHONE No: 0181 293 4567

TICKET OFFICE: 0181 858 5888

FAX: 0181 293 5143

CLUBCALL: 0891 12 11 46

NICKNAME: The Addicks

Charlton seem to change their nickname as often as some teams (Charlton, for example) change grounds. Perhaps the most interesting is The Addicks, which is thought to be a derivation of the word haddock, and which came about when, in days of yore, one of the Charlton directors owned a fish and chip shop and all visiting team officials were given a free haddock supper by the club.

RECORD ATTENDANCE: 75,031 v
Aston Villa FA Cup 5th 12 February 1938 (D 1-1)

CLUB COLOURS:
HOME: Shirts: Red; Shorts: White; Socks: Red
AWAY: Shirts: White with single Red and Black hoop; Shorts: Black; Socks: White
THIRD: Shirts: Green, Purple and thin White stripes; Shorts: Purple; Socks: Green

KIT SPONSORS: Viglen

MANUFACTURERS: Quaser

GROUND INFO

Entrance to the Valley is ticket controlled, and although away fans do have their own ticket booths by the South Stand, this still inevitably leads to having to queue twice to get into the ground. The view from the South Stand isn't too bad although there are a couple of pillars (as there are in the North and West Stands) and it isn't over generous on leg room. One good thing is that the stand seating everywhere except the West Stand starts from about six feet up, and this means that no matter where you go you get a decent view of the pitch.

If you remember the Valley from a few years back when it had the old banked terracing, then to see a compact all-seater ground can be a bit depressing. If on the other hand you are a Charlton fan who has in the past had to travel to Selhurst Park and Upton Park to see your team, then it's probably the most beautiful sight you could imagine.

The club's attitude to concessions seems to get better and better. Initially it cost visitors £12 to get into the South Stand with no concessions, then in 1994/5 that became £10 with £5 concessions and for this season while adult pricing returns to £12, juniors can now

get in for the more than reasonable cost of £3 (as they can in any part of the ground), and OAPs pay £6. For home supporters the significant savings in members' as compared to non-members' prices mean that, if you intend going more than a couple of times a season, membership is very well worth checking out.

CAPACITY: Stands: 14,986; Terrace: Nil;
Total: 14,986

AWAY FANS: South Stand: 3,073;
Total: 3,073

DISABLED FACILITIES: There are spaces for 20 wheelchair-bound fans with their helpers in the front of the West Stand (north end), and a similar allocation at the back of the East Stand (south end). There is no charge for either disabled fans or helpers, but you must book in advance. Similarly, if you want a parking space by the ground you must pre-book this. The club do offer match commentaries for the blind, and state that whilst pre-booking is not essential, it is recommended.

PROGRAMME: £1.50.
Fairly good, with a couple of decent general interest articles on Division One/football issues.

FANZINES:

The Voice Of The Valley	£1
The Valiants Viewpoint	80p
Remember Remember	50p
Valley Floyd Road	50p

The top one of these was one of the first ever fanzines and did so much to help bring the club back to the Valley that to try and summarise it is impossible. If you are a football fan who has forgotten what a fanzine should be all about, then buy a copy. If you are a Charlton fan, then even if you don't always like what it says (or the people who sell it, some of whom have a touch of the over-inflated ego syndrome) you should really subscribe to it as a vote of thanks. The next two weren't available on my last trip and it was suggested to me that they may not be produced any longer. I don't like criticising fanzines but *VFR* (one issue so far — April 1995) is one of the worst I've come across. A total of 16 very weak pages which should be avoided.

TRAVEL

NEAREST RAILWAY STATION:

Charlton: (0171 928 5100 — London Bridge Enquiries) Although there has been some improvement on the rolling stock serving Charlton with the introduction of the new Class 465 trains, the line is still served by some of the grimmest carriages imaginable, mixing the classic ingredients of ripped seats, graffiti, rubbish and eau de sewage to produce that very special British Rail atmosphere.

BUS: London Transport (0171 222 1234) 177 and 180 buses stop on Woolwich Road which is five-minutes walk from the ground.

BY CAR:

NORTH: A1 into London. At the roundabout by Highbury and Islington tube station go straight over on to the A1200 (signposted Shoreditch). When you reach Shoreditch pick up and follow the signs for Whitechapel, and once there, take the A13 (signposted Limehouse and Tilbury). Turn right to cross the Thames via the Blackwall Tunnel then continue on to the A102/A102(M). After one mile turn left on to the A206 Woolwich Road and then right after one mile into Charlton Church Lane. Take the first left into Floyd Road and the ground is 200yd on the right.

EAST: A2 into London, continuing past Eltham to Kidbrooke at which point take the A102(M) (signposted Blackwall Tunnel). After one mile turn right on to the A206 Woolwich Road, then as north.

SOUTH: M23/A23 into London until you get to Kennington. Turn right on to the A202 Camberwell New Road (signposted Camberwell, Peckham) and carry on for 3.5 miles until the road merges with and becomes the A2. Continue for 2 miles then turn left at the roundabout on to the A102(M). Then as east.

WEST: M4/A4 into Central London. As you approach Hammersmith, turn right following signs for A306 Hammersmith Bridge. Cross the river and continue for two miles then turn left on to the A205 Richmond Road. After one mile this merges with the A3; follow A3 to Kennington and by Oval tube station turn right into Camberwell New Road (A202). Then as south.

NB: When you join the A3, watch out for the one-way system which appears to take you in the wrong direction: you simply take left and right turns (in effect, forming a triangle), and end up on the right road.

PARKING: Some street parking, but watch out because there is a tow-away scheme in many of the roads in the immediate vicinity of the ground. If you want off-street parking then take the A206 past the ground following signs for Woolwich Free Ferry, next to which there is a car park (about 1.5 miles from the ground).

FUTURE DEVELOPMENTS

The West Stand at the ground is due to be extended at some point in the future which will increase the capacity to approximately 16,000.

OTHER INFORMATION

Historically, the club has been very strict about what is and what isn't allowed into the ground. In 1919 one of its own supporters was banned from attending matches because he insisted on bringing in a haddock nailed to a piece of wood, which he waved in the air for 90min. (So remember, kids; fish and football don't mix; leave your scaly companions at home!)

The Watermans Arms and McDonnells are both at the corner of Woolwich Road and Charlton Church Lane, but it's much better to wander down Woolwich Road for about 0.25 miles to the Horse & Groom. Nothing special in terms of décor, it makes up for this by being a good honest boozer with a very friendly landlord and landlady; they also sell matchday programmes here.

For food, the Kebab House on the corner of Floyd Road and Charlton Church Lane does an excellent portion of chips, although its burgers aren't fantastic. Once inside the ground the mince and onion pies aren't bad tastewise even if they do have a tendency to fall to pieces on that long journey between silver tray and mouth.

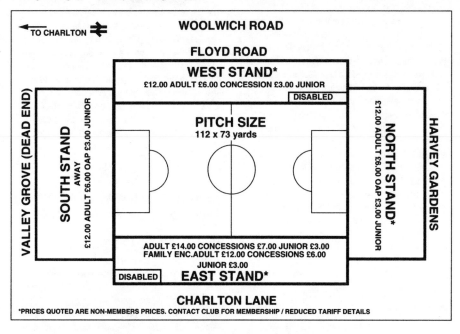

CHELSEA

ADDRESS: Stamford Bridge
Fulham Road
London SW6 1HS

TELEPHONE No: 0171 385 5545

TICKET OFFICE: 0171 386 7799

FAX: 0171 381 4831

CLUBCALL: 0891 12 11 59

NICKNAME: The Blues

RECORD ATTENDANCE:
82,905 v Arsenal Div 1 12 October 1935 (D 1-1)

CLUB COLOURS:
HOME: Shirts: Blue; Shorts: Blue; Socks: White
AWAY: Shirts: Graphite, Tangerine/Navy Trim;
Shorts: Tangerine; Socks: Tangerine

KIT SPONSORS: Coors

MANUFACTURERS: Umbro

GROUND INFO

The category system at Stamford Bridge was mercifully simplified in 1994/5 to a two-category system which can be summarised as:
• Category 'B' — An arm and a leg.
• Category 'A' — An arm and a leg and the shirt off your back.

In truth if you think you've got it hard then pity the poor home supporters who have to try and find that sort of money every other week.

Comfort can be gained from the fact that for their money away supporters do (at present) have the benefit of an excellent along-the-pitch position. True, the wind does tend to bring the rain in on you, and the sun setting behind the West Stand can result in you squinting at the action for the last 45min, but at least there is some cover, unlike home fans who opt for the joy of the temporary South — Shed — Stand (still what can they expect for only £10 or £15?), and as anyone who ever stood on the old North Terrace at the Bridge will testify, at least the East Stand does not sweep back in a huge semi-circle, at the apex of which it appeared that you were about four nautical miles from the action.

The new North Stand at the Bridge is impressive, although if you do want to go in it be aware that the top tier is for members only, and there are also some restricted view seats in it (though the price for these is not similarly curtailed).

CAPACITY: Stands: 28,488; Terrace: Nil;
Total: 28,488

AWAY FANS: East Stand Lower: 1,749;
Total: 1,749

Dependent on whether the club is forced to comply with the 10%/3,000 space regulation for away fans, visitors can either expect to remain here or possibly be accommodated in the upper tier of the East Stand, where 2,500 can be housed.

DISABLED FACILITIES: There are 40 places at the ground for disabled supporters, these being sited in the front row of the East Stand Family Section. In addition, there are some places in the upper tier of the North Stand for club members only. Admission in 1994/5 was £5 Category 'A' and £4 Category 'B' with helpers paying £10 or £8 depending on the match. Visiting supporters are welcome, but tickets should be obtained from their own club. There are no matchday commentaries for the visually impaired, nor now that the temporary South Stand is up against the pitch are there any parking facilities. One area for which the club does deserve praise is that there are actually toilets for both male and female disabled supporters — other clubs please take note; 'disabled' is not a third gender!

PROGRAMME: £2
The most expensive in the League (tell me how surprised you were at this news?). To be fair, it is a decent read for home supporters with the erstwhile Mr Bates never shying away from giving his opinion. However, for visitors it does not offer much other than the standard penpics and usual array of stats.

FANZINES:

The Red Card	80p
The Chelsea Independent	£1
The Cockney Rebel	50p

The first two are perhaps the obvious choices, although The Red Card certainly shades it, adopting a slightly less preachy attitude than the CI. If upsetting those who run the club is a mark of a fanzine, then RC must be in the running as best fanzine in the known universe, and a chat with its editor is an eye-opening affair. Cockney Rebel defies description, a throwback to the office photocopier days of fanzines. The content is unlike any other fanzine I've come across; you'll either love it or hate it, but you should give it a try.

TRAVEL

NEAREST RAILWAY STATION:
Putney Bridge (a long old walk) (0171 262 6767 — Paddington Enquiries)

NEAREST TUBE STATION:
Fulham Broadway (District Line)
When getting on the District Line make sure you get on a Wimbledon train, not one to Richmond, Olympia or South Ealing. The tube does not stop at West Brompton, the station before Fulham Broadway, at weekends, so you want the first stop after Earl's Court.

BUS: London Transport (0171 222 1234)
The number 14 stops directly outside the ground. Alternatively the 91, 295 and 28 stop outside Fulham Broadway.

BY CAR:

NORTH: M1 to J1. Turn right on to the A406 North Circular Road (travelling west). Continue for four miles to Hanger Lane roundabout (or gyratory system to give its full belly-dancing title) and go straight over into Hanger Lane. After two miles you will see Gunnersbury Park and shortly after this is the Chiswick roundabout. Take the second exit here on to the A4. At the next roundabout (Hogarth) take the first exit, which keeps you on the A4 Great West Road. After one mile you reach Hammersmith. Follow the one-way system until you are almost travelling back in the direction you have just come from and turn immediately left into Fulham Palace Road (A219). After 1.5 miles turn left on to the Fulham Road (A304) and the ground is 1.25 miles on you left.

WEST: M4 to J1 continuing straight on to the A4. After one mile you come to Hogarth roundabout, then as north.

SOUTH: A24 into London. At the crossroads with the A214 (by Tooting Bec station) turn left on to Trinity Road. Continue for 1.75 miles then turn left on to the A3. After one mile the road splits into two; take the right-hand lane (Upper Richmond Road) then go right at the next crossroads into Putney High Street (A219). Take this road and cross Putney Bridge, then 0.25 mile later turn right on to the A304 Fulham Broadway and the ground is 1.25 miles on your left.

EAST: A12 to A406 North Circular Road (travelling west). Continue along the A406 until you get to the end of the M1. Then as north.

PARKING: Street parking off the Fulham Road is the only real choice, but be aware that the Fulham Road can be closed by the police just before and/or just after matches.

FUTURE DEVELOPMENTS

At present the club is working on a new underground car park which is due to be finished around December 1995. This will have spaces for 200 vehicles, but is likely to be for permit holders only. It will also include the foundations for the office block, shops, restaurant and hotel the club is to put up. The following stage of development will be the construction of these buildings together with the new (approx. 10,000-seat) South Stand. However, the first change in the stand structure is to be the building of a 2,000-seat corner stand between the North and West Stands which will also serve to make the North Stand 'weatherproof'.

OTHER INFORMATION

A lot of the pubs in the vicinity of the ground have a real 'home only' feel about them, and it can be quieter either to have a drink a couple of tube stops away, or go for a serious 'pose' pub down the King's Road. Alternatively turn right as you leave Fulham Broadway (ie head away from the ground) and if you wander down the road there are a few decent pubs which are hassle-free.

Once in the ground the food is quite good, but at £2.50 for a cheeseburger and £1 for a cup of tea or a Coke, it ought to be.

A final comment about the club stewards, for some of whom it would appear that nothing is too much trouble...and you should see their reaction if you ask them to do something!

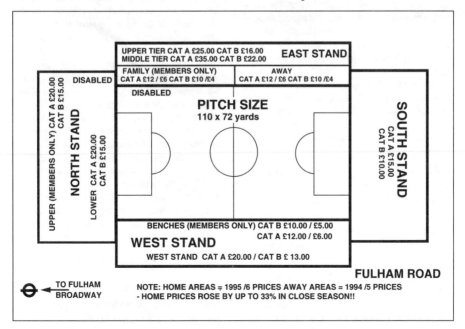

CHESTER CITY

ADDRESS: Deva Stadium
Bumpers Lane
Chester CH1 4LT
TELEPHONE No: 01244 371376
TICKET OFFICE: 01244 371376
FAX: 01244 390265
SPORTSLINES: 0891 66 45 54
NICKNAME: City or Blues
RECORD ATTENDANCE:
20,500 v Chelsea FA Cup 3rd Rep 16 January 1952
(L 3-2 AET). At Deva: 5,638 v Preston North End Div 3
2 April 1994 (W 3-2)

CLUB COLOURS:
HOME: Shirts: Blue & White Stripes;
Shorts: Blue; Socks: White/Blue
AWAY: Shirts: Yellow & Black Stripes;
Shorts: Black; Socks: Black/Yellow

KIT SPONSORS: Corbett Bookmakers
MANUFACTURERS: Matchwinner

GROUND INFO

Within the East Stand there is a family section which
offers the same concessions as the home section of
the West Stand (see Ground Map). Visiting supporters
can phone the club in advance and obtain tickets for
this area with the relevant discount for kids. The club is
apparently reviewing the possibility of offering away
fans concessions but at the moment hasn't decided on
whether to embark on what some might consider a
radical move (well, entering the 1990s can be so trau-
matic!).

The club's current policy on away supporters is all
the more frustrating as it runs some excellent schemes
on occasions for its own fans such as 'kids for a quid',
as well as having a great 'standard' concession in the
West Stand of £2. One can only hope that it will end
up doing the right thing.

CAPACITY: Stands: 3,608; Terrace: 2,392;
Total: 6,000

AWAY FANS: South Terrace: 1,196:
West Stand 600: Total: 1,796
If the away support warrants it, they can be given the
whole of the West Stand, increasing their total seating
allocation to 1,274.

DISABLED FACILITIES: There are 32
spaces for disabled fans which are spread in pockets
along the East and West Stands, with the club having
installed ramps to these at the side of the pitch. Away
fans are admitted although pre-booking is required.

Disabled fans are admitted free, with helpers paying
the standard matchday price. Match commentaries for
the blind are available, but these too should be pre-
booked. There are disabled parking facilities at the
ground; just speak to one of the stewards when you
turn up.

PROGRAMME: £1.20
Not a bad read for either home or away fans.

FANZINES:
Hello Albert 50p
The title refers to the story that when the club played
at Sealand Road, they were one of the first grounds to
have a PA system installed. The announcer on this
used to start every broadcast by saying 'Hello, Spion
Kop! Hello, Albert!'. A decent fanzine firmly based in
the humorous camp.

TRAVEL

NEAREST RAILWAY STATION:
Chester (1.5 miles) (0151 709 9696 — Liverpool
Enquiries)

NEAREST BUS STATION:
Chester Interchange (01244 602666)
Bus 1a runs from the Exchange to the ground every
half an hour, and it's worth being on one as it is a long
walk from the city centre.

BY CAR:
NORTH: M56/A41/A5116 into the city centre. At the
second roundabout take the third exit (in effect turning
right) into St Martins Way (signposted A548
Queensferry). About 0.5 mile later you will pass a car
park on your left. Take the next right after this on to the
A548, Watergate (will the whole truth ever really be
known about this road, and how it brought down the
Nixon presidency?) and travel past the top end of the
dreadfully under-utilised Chester Racecourse into
Sealand Road. Turn left at the traffic lights (this is
where the old ground used to be) into Bumpers Lane,
and the ground is at the bottom of this road.
NB: An alternative route is to come in on the A56. If
you do this, follow A548 Queensferry signs into
Watergate, then as above.
EAST: A51 into Chester. Turn left into Union Street
(A483), and about one mile later at the next roundabout take the third exit into Nicholas Street. After
400yd turn left into Watergate (A548), then as north.
SOUTH: A483 into Chester, taking the first exit at
the roundabout by the castle into Nicholas Street, then
as east.
WEST: A55 to the roundabout with the A483, at
which you should take the first exit (signposted
Handbridge and Chester) on to the A483, then as
south.

PARKING: There is ample parking at the ground, which is free up to one hour before the kick-off. This is designed to get people to arrive at the stadium as soon as possible, but, as with many out of town sites, there is absolutely nothing to do when you get there, especially if you are an away fan and as such considered too much of a pariah to be admitted to the social club. The club recognises that there is a lack of facilities outside the ground, and...plans to install catering outlets by the ground! (Well, I don't know about you, but that swings it for me; I'm setting off now!)

FUTURE DEVELOPMENTS

As the ground was only completed in August 1992, there are no immediate plans for change, although the foundations have been laid to cater for future extensions as and when required. It is the intention of the club to retain the traditional two stands and two terraces for as long as they are allowed to.

OTHER INFORMATION

At one time Chester was reputed to have the most pubs per square mile in Britain. This title has now been relinquished, but there are still enough good watering holes in the city to make a visit there pleasurable.

However, the nearest pub to the ground, the Waterstones by the Racecourse, is still a good 20min walk away. Alternatives you might plump for are the pleasantly named 'Axe' and 'Headless Woman'. If you prefer something a little less gruesome, you can do an awful lot worse then driving past the turn-off to the ground heading away from the City and continuing for 1.5 miles until you get to the rather pleasant Elms.

The city itself is nice enough, and well worth strolling round for a while as it is one of the few 'Olde World' places that has managed to retain its character without simply looking twee and artificial.

Although the majority of the Deva is in England, whisper it softly, but parts of it are in Wales! Surely Alun Evans and his Merry Men should do something about this, perhaps a team from the Konika League should traipse on to the pitch midway through a match and start attacking the Chester goal. Mr Evans take note, because if you fail to address this problem you could be undermining the whole football pyramid in the Principality...

Chester stride on to the pitch to the theme from the 'Big Country' (yes, I know it sounds like the 'Magnificent Seven' but trust me on this one!). Perhaps Elton John's 'Don't Let The Sun Go Down On Me' would be more appropriate, especially if you go into the East Stand as that is what you'll be singing during the second half as you squint madly to try and catch sight of the ball.

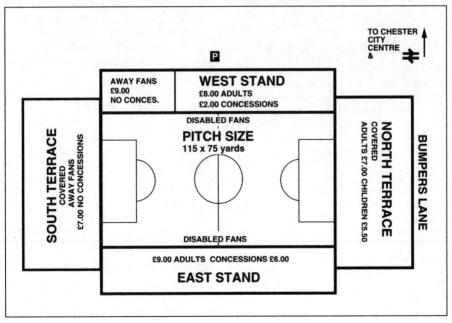

TO CHESTER CITY CENTRE &

P

AWAY FANS
£9.00
NO CONCES.

WEST STAND
£8.00 ADULTS
£2.00 CONCESSIONS

DISABLED FANS

PITCH SIZE
115 x 75 yards

SOUTH TERRACE
COVERED
AWAY FANS
£7.00 NO CONCESSIONS

NORTH TERRACE
COVERED
ADULTS £7.00 CHILDREN £5.50

BUMPERS LANE

DISABLED FANS

£9.00 ADULTS CONCESSIONS £6.00
EAST STAND

CHESTERFIELD

ADDRESS: The Recreation Ground
Saltergate
Chesterfield
Derbyshire S40 4SX
TELEPHONE No: 01246 209765
TICKET OFFICE: 01246 209765
FAX: 01246 556799
CLUBCALL: 0891 12 15 73
NICKNAME: The Spireites

RECORD ATTENDANCE:
30,968 v Newcastle Div 2 7 April 1939 (W 2-0)

CLUB COLOURS:
HOME: Shirts: Blue Red/White shoulder flashes;
Shorts: Blue; Socks: White
AWAY: Shirts: Green & White stripes;
Shorts: Blue; Socks: Blue

KIT SPONSORS:
Home: North Derbyshire Health Authority
Away: GK Group (Ford)

MANUFACTURERS: Matchwinner

GROUND INFO

When I was there, the Main Stand looked very unkempt from the outside, with flaky paint on rusty metal being the order of the day. Inside, the seats are wooden and appear to have been hewn out of the stand itself; you are unlikely to get to half-time before you start shifting from one buttock to another in an attempt to get more comfortable. There is also one large pillar in the away section which can lead to a restricted view.

The facilities are basic, and there tend to be long queues for half-time tea and pies. The gents' toilets are particularly horrible, being of a trough-in-the-floor variety, but just to add a bit of spice, the trough actually encircles the whole floor, and so you have to step over it to enter the toilet. Once inside it doesn't take long to notice both that the trough is fairly shallow, and that the floor seems horribly wet considering there is a roof over it...

The away terrace is open, and to get in you have to queue up outside what appears to be a sandstone castle wall on which is the biggest sign advising 'visiting supporters only' that you'll ever come across.

The club is somewhat lacking in facilities but many visitors find they can forgive this due to its genuinely helpful and responsive attitude to all supporters. Given this, it is even more annoying to report that there are no concessions for away fans.

CAPACITY: Stands: 2,674; Terrace: 6,280;
Total: 8,954

AWAY FANS: Cross Street: 2,300;
Main Stand: 885; Total: 3,185

DISABLED FACILITIES: There are 20 spaces available for home and away supporters by the Saltergate wing of the Main Stand. The club has advised that pre-booking is required for this. Mind you, a steward I spoke to also said that there were no toilet facilities available for the disabled, upon which the wheelchair-bound supporter who was passing queried what they had just used then.

Disabled supporters are admitted free of charge, with helpers paying £7.

There are no matchday commentaries for the blind, and nor are there any parking facilities at the ground.

PROGRAMME: £1.20
This has a nice feel and look to it, although a couple of pages less of adverts and a couple of pages more of football wouldn't go amiss.

FANZINES:
The Crooked Spireite 70p
A real whizz bang of a fanzine and one that will keep you interested no matter who you support. The folk who sell it seem a good bunch and are always prepared to have a chat/laugh. The only grouse is that it isn't on sale before every home match so if you are unlucky you can end up missing out on what is a good read.

TRAVEL

NEAREST RAILWAY STATION:
Chesterfield (01332 257000 — Derby Enquiries)

BUS: Busline: 01246 250450

BY CAR:
NORTH: M1 to J30. Take the A619 from the exit roundabout and continue into the Town Centre where you should pick up signs for Old Brampton. Following this road will bring you on to Saltergate and the ground is on your right.
SOUTH: A61 into Chesterfield. Turn left at the roundabout with the A617 and left again at the next roundabout with the A617 Markham Road. At the following roundabout take the fourth exit into Foljambe Road. At the end of this road is Saltergate and the ground is directly in front of you.
EAST: A617 to Town Centre. Turn left at the roundabout with the A619, then as south.
WEST: A619 into town centre. As you enter the town there is a crossroads with the A632; turn left at this into Old Hall Road and right at the bottom of this road into Saltergate. The ground is 0.5 mile on your left. NB: If you miss the turn into Hall Gate Road, which is easy

50

enough to do, take the first exit at the next roundabout into Foljambe Road, then as south.

PARKING: Chesterfield appears to be a town of about a million car parks, with 18 to my knowledge within 0.75 mile of the ground. One of the best ones to use (if only because it is free, and is probably the closest to the ground) can be found on the left as you drive 0.25 miles along Saltergate past the ground (heading away from the town centre). The pay-and-display car parks tend to be fairly reasonable, costing about £1 for four hours.

FUTURE DEVELOPMENTS

It is probably unreasonable to expect the club to be able to make the 'Rec' into an all-seater stadium, which leaves the obvious option of moving to a purpose-built stadium. The club has acknowledged this and in an end-of-season message to the fans from the splendidly named Chairman, Norton Lea, it was stated that the club would hope to make progress in achieving the aim of finding a new stadium site within the next few weeks.

OTHER INFORMATION

There are quite a few pubs in Saltergate. Those that spring to mind are the Yellow Lion, the County Hotel, the Manhattan and the Barley Mow. The last of these is probably the best, but none of them are all that good and a better bet is to go to the town centre where every other building seems to be a pub, and you are bound to find something that suits your taste. The Saltergate Club by the ground is members only, although dependent on the match you will probably be able to get in (provided you are not in a big group).

There are no chip shops in the immediate vicinity of the ground and the fairly large drum shop which was on the corner has disappeared. However, there is now a piano repairer and tuner; which is great news if you are Richard Clayderman but not so good if you are either Cozy Powell or a hungry football fan! The Saltergate sandwich shop does some hot snacks, and without being fantastic, is probably better than what you can expect once inside the ground.

Two things to check out before the game are:
• the ballboys who form a guard of honour for the teams as they come on to the pitch, then position themselves around the centre circle as the captains toss up, before dispersing like a ripple in a pond to their various points around the ground. Presumably this is seen by the club as giving the occasion the dignity it deserves.

• the club mascot. This is obviously an animal of some sort but just quite what it is meant to be is difficult to discern. A quick straw poll on my last visit bought suggestions of 'a mouse', 'a meerkat', 'a vole', and perhaps most astutely 'a mutant'. The costume appears to have been made out of fuzzy felt but, although the strangest thing of all is that the home fans love it, and its every appearance is greeted by genuinely warm applause.

Finally, no trip to Chesterfield is complete without checking out the Crooked Spire, which dominates the skyline, like something from a fairy tale. Apparently the spire's shape is due to the devil lashing out in rage as he flew over Chesterfield having had a nail driven into his foot by a Bolsover blacksmith who was reshoeing him. Well, either that or the fact that the eight-sided spire was made out of green timber which distorted under the weight of the heavy lead covering.

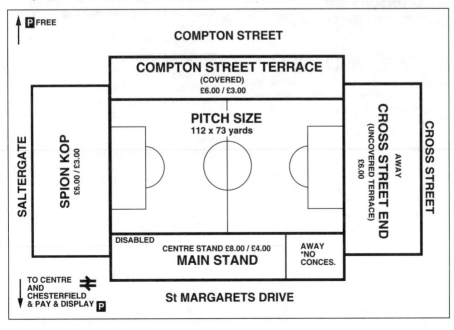

COLCHESTER UNITED

ADDRESS: Layer Road,
Colchester
Essex CO2 7JJ
TELEPHONE No: 01206 574042
TICKET OFFICE: 01206 574042
FAX: 01206 48700
U's LINE: 0891 66 46 46
NICKNAME: The U's
RECORD ATTENDANCE: 19,072 v
Reading FA Cup 1st 27 November 1948 (D 1-1)
Imagine: an FA Cup tie, a massive crowd, the match
nicely balanced, what happens next? Well, on this
occasion the game was abandoned at half-time. For
the stats fans amongst you, the rearranged tie was
played the following Saturday and the U's went down
2-4.

CLUB COLOURS:
HOME: Shirts: Blue and White;
Shorts: Black; Socks: Red
AWAY: Shirts: Red/Black quarters;
Shorts: Black; Socks: Black
However... if the opposition wears black shorts or
socks then the away kit will comprise white shorts or
socks as appropriate, and should the opponents wear
white shorts and Colchester are forced to use their
third kit, then they may wear red socks if appropriate.
Clear? I thought so.

KIT SPONSORS: SGR
MANUFACTURERS: Vandanel

GROUND INFO

Other than Layer Road Terrace 1, the other sections of
the ground detailed below are made available to visiting supporters only if it is deemed there is likely to be
sufficient demand.

The terracing is only nine steps deep, and if you
are anything but dead centre and right at the front,
then you are going to have problems seeing around
one of the corner areas. In addition, the stanchions
which support the roof can also restrict your view.

There are also pillars in the Main Stand, although
these are no worse than you'd find at many grounds.
What you do need to know, however, is that Row E is
directly behind Row D with no elevation, which means
that for a sell out match people in Row E must have a
dreadful view.

As you drive into Colchester there are signs proclaiming that it is Britain's oldest recorded town.
Further investigation shows that it was the Romans
who did the recording, and the entry went, 'Went to
Layerus Roadicus, by Jupiter it's old and run down'.

Good concessions are on offer from the club, who
are always on the lookout for innovative ways to attract
people to the ground. This, combined with a positive
attitude from office staff to stewards, means that, while
the ground is (considerably) lacking in mod cons, a trip
to Colchester can be a very pleasurable thing.

CAPACITY: Stands: 1,147; Terrace: 6,043;
Total: 7,190

AWAY FANS: Layer Road End (Terrace 1): 580;
Layer Road End (Terrace 2): 515;
Main Stand Block A: 247;
Total: 1,342

DISABLED FACILITIES: There are
spaces for six wheelchair-bound fans at the ground,
and although pre-booking isn't essential, due to the
limited availability it is recommended. Unless it is considered dangerous due to the size of the crowd, the
club will consider letting supporters in wheelchairs into
the front of the terrace, although many supporters may
find that this isn't quite wide enough to allow the
wheelchair to be positioned straight on and facing the
pitch. This does result in the minor inconvenience of
making a bad area to watch footie from even worse.
There are special toilet facilities at the ground behind
the main stand.

There is no charge for disabled supporters and one
helper is also admitted free of charge

The club does offer match commentaries for the
visually impaired; contact them direct for full details
and to pre-book a spot. There is space for only one
visually-impaired supporter and helper only; the
remaining two positions are occupied regularly by
home supprters.

No parking facilities are available at the ground.

PROGRAMME: £1.20
A cut above, for the Third Division. There are two
themes that tend to run through the programme: one is
memories of the famous victory against Leeds in the
cup, and the second is the grim reaper. Yes death certainly does seem to play a big part in filling the pages
of the programme, although the tastefulness of this
may be questioned at times,. For example, the notice
about a fan who '...was at our last game, before taking
his life a few hours later. (He was) A man with a sense
of humour'.

FANZINES:
The Blue Eagle   70p

TRAVEL
NEAREST RAILWAY STATION:
Colchester Town (01206 578261)
Slightly further away but with a better service is
Colchester North (01206 564777). Layer Road is really

in the middle of nowhere, so the train station here is not to be recommended unless you like walking.

BUS: Colchester Borough Transport (01206 44449) Either a 4 or a 4a will drop you outside the ground. Alternatively Eastern National Buses 64 and 64a will do likewise.

BY CAR:

SOUTH: A12 towards Colchester town centre until you reach the roundabout with the A604. Take the third exit into Spring Lane and continue along this road as it becomes Church Lane and The Commons until you get to a T-junction. Turn right into Norman Way and go straight over the cross-roads into Boadicea Way. At the bottom of Boadicea Way there is a T-junction. Turn left on to Layer Road and the ground is 0.3 miles on your left.

NORTH/WEST: A45/A12. Take the A1232 Ipswich Road into the town centre. To avoid the one-way system turn left before the castle on to the A1224 Queens Street. At the next major roundabout on to the B1022 Maldon Road. Continue for one mile then turn right into Boadicea Way. Then as south.

PARKING: Street parking. One of the best places to leave your car is by the Shrub End playing fields around Boadicea Way.

As you drive down Layer Road, watch out for some residents-only parking schemes which are not to be trifled with: some of the residents in question are part of Colchester garrison and any out-of-place car is quickly identified and acted upon. Rather than returning to find a ticket, or your car's been towed away, you're more likely to find that your transport home has been reduced to a pile of smouldering metal in a controlled explosion!

FUTURE DEVELOPMENTS

At the time of going to press nothing definite had been announced, but the club had stated its intention to increase the capacity at Layer Road to 8,500 by means of a £100,000 covered stand at the Rainsborowe Road End. The decision to develop this side of the ground was taken after consultation with the fans who were given the chance to state from where they would prefer to watch their football (!!!!!). Due to the fact that the area suggested has been closed for the past two seasons it is unlikely that any work undertaken will have a significant impact on the ground capacity during construction.

OTHER INFORMATION

The ground is a bit out of the way, and it as well to stick to Colchester town centre (especially for food). There are plenty of decent pubs in the town, with perhaps the most welcoming for away fans being the Castle, which has a painted sign outside proclaiming 'Wanderers welcome'. There is one pub near the ground itself, this being the Drury Arms, which serves a decent pint and is well worth a visit.

The range of food on offer is limited to burgers, burgers or burgers all of which tasted equally dreadful. The tea isn't bad especially as you get to add your own milk and sugar, so at least you can be sure of ending up with a strong cuppa.

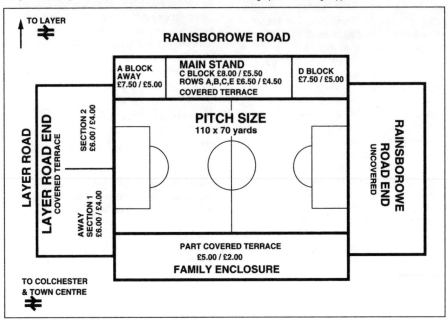

COVENTRY CITY

ADDRESS: Highfield Road Stadium
King Richard Street
Coventry CV2 4FW
TELEPHONE No: 01203 223535
TICKET OFFICE: 01203 225545
FAX: 01203 630318
CLUBCALL: 0891 12 11 66
NICKNAME: The Sky Blues
RECORD ATTENDANCE:
51,455 v Wolves Lge Div 2 29 April 1967(W 3-1)

CLUB COLOURS:
HOME: Shirts: Sky Blue; Shorts: Sky Blue;
Socks: Sky Blue
AWAY: Shirts: Purple and Mauve Stripes with Gold
Pinstripes; Shorts: Purple with Gold Trim;
Socks: Gold with Purple Trim

KIT SPONSORS: Peugeot
MANUFACTURERS: Pony

GROUND INFO

In 1994/5 the club dropped one level of its four-tier pricing system; if it continues to adopt this policy, then by 1996/7 it should be just about comprehensible. However, one thing that will always be a mystery is why visiting supporters pay a pound more than home fans for using the M&B Stand. I'm sure we'd be very interested in the reasoning behind that! Still, at least they give concessions to visiting fans.

On my last visit, the ticket office was the only area of the club staffed by people who didn't seem keen to help. Of course, things aren't helped by the fact that Coventry appear to have invested in a soundproof speaker-grille system. This inevitably leads to situations where you are screaming at the top of your voice 'One for the away end please!' just as a bunch of mean-looking home supporters come in. Funnily enough, this soundproofing appears to be one-way only as you will be able to hear the price quoted for the ticket without any problem at all, though naturally if you've got 15 free minutes on your hands you don't have to acknowledge this fact and can spend an enjoyable time either shrugging your head and putting your hand to your ear, or saying 'My, 15 pence, that is reasonable' — this is not however recommended if the aforementioned group of supporters is behind you!

CAPACITY: Stands: 23,500; Terrace: Nil;
Total: 23,500

AWAY FANS: Mitchell and Butler Stand Upper
Tier: 2,814; Mitchell and Butler
Stand Lower Tier: 1,236;
Total: 4,050

Having had a pop at the ticket office it should be said that Coventry is one of the most organised and helpful clubs for fans in not only the Premiership but the whole of the league. Queries and problems are dealt with promptly and efficiently, and the stewards will go out of their way to help. People often say that as fans we deserve to be treated as customers by clubs, but in truth, there is a lot more to going to a football match than this; after all, do you invest the same time and love in going to Sainsbury's as you do to going to the footie? Of course not! Coventry seems to have got the balance between the fan as a customer and a supporter just about right, which combined with its central location makes for a very easy (if not cheap) away day.

DISABLED FACILITIES: There are 77 spaces for disabled fans confined to wheelchairs with a further 130 seats available to helpers. Ten of the seats have headset facilities which are plumbed into the local hospital radio. The new East Stand is also fully accessible to disabled fans, including the executive areas and lounges; normally home disabled fans go in the East Stand and away disabled fans in the Clock Stand. Telephone the club to pre-book your space. It should be noted that there are no parking facilities at the ground. Admission is £5 for an 'unaccompanied wheelchair'! Helpers pay M&B Stand prices.

PROGRAMME: £1.50

FANZINES: None. It seems very strange that this remains a void. The club certainly isn't lacking in passionate supporters, nor have the fans nothing to complain about with regards to the team. Perhaps they just don't fancy stepping into the media spotlight; after all, it didn't do their ex-boss much good (no, it didn't boss, I agree with you there etc, etc).

TRAVEL
NEAREST RAILWAY STATION:
Coventry (01203 555211)

BUS: West Midland Transport (01203 559559)
BY CAR:
NORTH/SOUTH/WEST: M6 to J2. Take the A4600 (signposted City Centre). Follow this road until it becomes Walsgrave Road. Shortly after this the road forks in two by the Walsgrave Pub; take the left-hand lane and at the next roundabout take the third exit. Continue along Walsgrave Road until you get to a set of traffic lights by a former railway bridge (this has now been demolished and the resulting roadworks will cause disruption for a considerable time). Turn right at these lights into Swan Lane, and the ground is 100yd on the left.
NORTH/WEST: M45/A45 towards Coventry city centre. Turn left on to the A4114 (Allesley By-Pass) and take the third exit at the next roundabout, continuing along the A4114 Holyhead Road (signposted City

Centre). After 1.75 miles turn left on to the Inner Ring Road (A4053), and carry on for 1.5 miles, then turn left into Sky Blue Way (A4600). When this road forks in two, take the left fork into Walsgrave Road, then take a left by the traffic lights under the railway bridge into Swan Lane. The ground is 100yd on the left.

Generally it is quicker for those coming from the south to go via M6 J2 as this is only 2.5 miles from the ground. However, given that the M6 is capable of being as fast moving as a snooker-playing snail on Mogadon, it is worthwhile listening to radio traffic bulletins before you pick your route.

PARKING:
There is a small coach and car park on the opposite side of the road to the Swan Lane turning by the ground, which is good for getting away from. Alternatively head down the A4600 (Sky Blue Way) on to the inner ring road and there are car parks almost immediately on the left or right of this; these are about 1.25 miles from the ground. There is some street parking available, although this is restricted in the immediate ground vicinity.

FUTURE DEVELOPMENTS
The completion of the new East Stand provided the club with its second bash at going all-seater. The club was of course the first English team to have an all-seater stadium back in 1981. This proved unpopular with some supporters, and there was a partial conversion to terracing in the East Terrace in 1983, and fully converted in 1985 after a crowd disturbance when seats were ripped up and used as missiles. Perhaps Lord Justice Taylor missed this point whilst compiling his report!! As every fan could have told him, terracing doesn't cause crowd problems, it's people. Still, its a bit late to be worrying about things like that now.

OTHER INFORMATION
The Sky Blue Tavern (formerly the Mercers Arms) by the ground has home and away bars and is excellent for having a prematch drink with your mates. Other than that, its a bit of a walk to find anywhere to go for a drink. If you walk away from the ground from the visitors' section of the Sky Blue Tavern and bear left into Hamall Lane East (about 5min walk), there is a chip shop which sells reasonable, well-filled chip batches (rolls). This is worth a visit if only to avoid hunting down a food outlet and then queueing interminably for below average grub inside the ground.

Whilst the vast majority of clubs seem only too happy to embarrass their supporters occasionally, Coventry is in a class of its own in this respect. Naturally there's a mascot (a grubby elephant), but the fun really starts with the music. First there is *Sky Blue City* played when the team come out at the start of a match (and at half-time), which is the 1987 Cup Final song, and a cross between Bucks Fizz and Slade. The chorus of 'Go for it, go for it City. Sky Blues — shooting to win' is horribly insidious and will lurk around your consciousness for months afterwards (if you have been to Coventry before, you're probably humming it now — sorry!). Almost as bad is the 'chant', written by one Jimmy Hill to the tune of the Eton Boating Song. The fans have resigned themselves to this and actually sing it of their own volition, and after every Coventry goal the club blast about five bars (played on a whiny electric guitar) out of the PA system.

WOMEN! Fancy a swear? How about acting abusively or throwing missiles? If you do, Highfield Road is the place for you. There are masses of signs telling spectators about unacceptable behaviour but as these are all addressed to gentlemen, presumably you've got *carte blanche* to behave in any manner you choose!

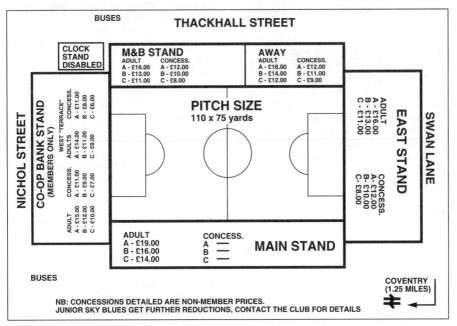

BUSES

THACKHALL STREET

CLOCK STAND DISABLED

M&B STAND		
ADULT	CONCESS.	
A - £16.00	A - £12.00	
B - £13.00	B - £10.00	
C - £11.00	C - £8.00	

AWAY	
ADULT	CONCESS.
A - £16.00	A - £12.00
B - £14.00	B - £11.00
C - £12.00	C - £9.00

PITCH SIZE
110 x 75 yards

NICHOL STREET

CO-OP BANK STAND (MEMBERS ONLY)

WEST "TERRACE"

ADULT	CONCESS.
A - £11.00	A - £11.00
B - £8.00	B - £8.00
C - £6.00	C - £6.00

ADULTS	CONCESS.
A - £14.00	A - £11.00
B - £11.00	B - £9.00
C - £9.00	C - £7.00

ADULT	CONCESS.
A - £15.00	A - £11.00
B - £12.00	B - £9.00
C - £10.00	C - £7.00

EAST STAND

ADULT	CONCESS.
A - £16.00	A - £12.00
B - £13.00	B - £10.00
C - £11.00	C - £8.00

SWAN LANE

ADULT	CONCESS.
A - £19.00	A —
B - £16.00	B —
C - £14.00	C —

MAIN STAND

BUSES

COVENTRY (1.25 MILES)

NB: CONCESSIONS DETAILED ARE NON-MEMBER PRICES.
JUNIOR SKY BLUES GET FURTHER REDUCTIONS, CONTACT THE CLUB FOR DETAILS

CREWE ALEXANDRA

ADDRESS: Gresty Road
Crewe
Cheshire CW2 6EB
TELEPHONE No: 01270 213014
TICKET OFFICE: 01270 213014
FAX: 01270 216320
SPORTSLINE: 0891 66 45 64
NICKNAME: The Railwaymen
RECORD ATTENDANCE:
20,000 v Spurs FA Cup 4th 30 January 1960 (D 2-2)
CLUB COLOURS:
HOME: Shirts: Red; Shorts: White; Socks: Red
AWAY: Shirts: White; Shorts: White; Socks: White
KIT SPONSORS: Boldon James
MANUFACTURERS: Vandanel

GROUND INFO

Hats off to Crewe for the decent concessions offered to one and all. The Gresty Road away terrace has now been converted into a 1,000-seat stand, which will be for the use of away fans. If you prefer a seat along the side of the pitch rather than behind the goal try the main stand (A Block has in the past been used unofficially by visiting supporters). The stand itself is fairly basic with the seating being of the wooden plank variety, and be warned, there are plenty of pillars to contend with. The Synchro Systems family stand affords more comfort and better protection from the elements. In the past away supporters have been welcomed into this stand, with the only regulation that there should be no unaccompanied adult males. However, like the new Gresty Road Stand, as this is behind the goal, there doesn't seem any purpose in going here rather than in the standard away section. If you can't get into an all-ticket match try persuading one of the residents of the houses on the opposite side of Gresty Road to the away turnstiles to let you in as they have a belting view of the ground from their bedrooms! (At least they did prior to the new stand going up.) Be warned, though, if you are forced into asking one of these people for your 'admission'; apparently some charge more for a place in their back bedroom than the club do for a front row seat!

Considering Crewe is (quite rightly) regarded as a passing team the standard of the pitch at Gresty can be a bit of a disappointment. It seems both patchy and uneven and every winter appears to deteriorate rapidly.

CAPACITY: Stands: 4,656; Terrace: 1,136;
Total: 5,792
These are post-opening of the Gresty Road and Popular Side Stands (see Future Developments).

AWAY FANS: Gresty Road Stand: 1,000;
Total: 1,000

DISABLED FACILITIES: There are seven places for wheelchair-bound supporters (plus seven for helpers) in the Family (Synchro Systems) Stand, with a further seven spaces (but none apparently for helpers) in the North (Popular) Stand and for visitors 10 spaces (five helpers) in the Gresty Road (West) Stand. Admission for both disabled supporters and helpers is half price. Pre-booking is essential. The club does provide special parking facilities at the ground and from the 1994/5 season match commentaries for the visually impaired have also been available; these too must be pre-booked. This is an increase of well over 100% on the number of spaces previously available at Gresty Road and represents a confirmation of the club's previously stated intention to ensure that everyone can come and watch football at Crewe (as opposed to certain other clubs which may be full of good intentions but never seem to be able to translate them into action).

PROGRAMME: £1.20
This seems to be an area which the club just can't crack and last season's followed the trend of previous years by being well dodgy!

FANZINES:
> *Super Dario Land!* £1
> *To Work Upon The Railway* 50p

The last time I saw *SDL* it was 70p and only 16 pages long. Surprisingly it had a glossy cover and this must surely only have served to bump up the cost of producing it, and the odds are that Alex fans would prefer a little more content for their cash. *TWUTR* is fairly new to the 'Zine scene' and has been getting fair to good comments made about it, so it may be worth an investment.

TRAVEL

NEAREST RAILWAY STATION:
Crewe (01782 411411)
Unbelievable! One of England's busiest stations and you have to dial a Stoke-on-Trent number for enquiries. If you think this is ludicrous dial 01270 532727 (the actual number of Crewe station) and tell them so!

BUS: Cheshire Bus: Crewe bus station (01270 505350)

BY CAR:
NORTH: M1 to J17. On leaving the motorway take the A534 (signposted Sandbach and Crewe). When approaching the town you will see Crewe and Alsager College on your right; continue for 0.25 miles past this to the next roundabout, at which you should take the

second exit on to the A534 Nantwich Road (signposted to BR station). Take the first left after the station into Gresty Road and the ground is 300yd on the left.

SOUTH/EAST: M1 to J16. Take the A500 (signposted Crewe) then turn right on to the A5020 Weston Road (again signposted Crewe). Continue to the roundabout with the A534 Nantwich Road at which you should take the first exit (signposted BR station), then as north.

WEST: A534. Follow the signs for Crewe and Sandbach. Turn right at the crossroads with the B5071 on to South Street. This then merges after 0.25 mile with Gresty Road and the ground is immediately on the left. NB: If you miss this, drive past the station to the roundabout, do an about-turn and have another go.

PARKING: There are a couple of car parks right by the ground. Alternatively you can try the British Rail long-stay off the Nantwich Road, but this tends to be a bit pricey. There is also plenty of on-street parking in the side-streets off Gresty Road.

FUTURE DEVELOPMENTS

The club has been hard at work upgrading the ground with the construction of a 1,000-seat stand at the Gresty Road End and a 1,700-seat stand along the Popular Side. Provided everything goes to plan, these should be open in August for the start of the 1995/6 season.

OTHER INFORMATION

Take advantage of the decent train link and leave the car at home for this match, because although the ground is away from the town centre, there is no shortage of decent pubs around.

The Royal Hotel and the Crewe Arms both on the Nantwich Road are a fair size, but also worth a visit is the Barrel on the corner of South Street and Nantwich Road, if only because the landlord goes by the name of Michael Crawford! If you go in here do make sure you say 'Oooh Betty' to him because he's probably never heard that one before and is sure to laugh along with you. Also on the Nantwich Road opposite the Royal Hotel is the Golden Chip Shop which serves a delicious meat and potato pie and chips.

If you do end up wandering towards the town, pop in at the newsagent's on Edelston Road which doesn't actually sell papers (or much else) because 'there's no call for it'. Inside the ground the refreshments were fairly limited and for some strange reason away fans always seem to attract suicidal flies to their drinks — if this happens to you don't bother complaining as it will probably be the freshest meat you get on your trip.

The floodlights at Gresty Road are weird, and look like they have been lifted from a motorway repair site (talking of which, there was a British Rail luggage trolley saying 'Do not remove from Crewe Station' at the back of the Family Stand as I left the ground).

In any event, Crewe definitely deserves some kind of award for an inspired piece of economising: they seem to use Coca-Cola corner flags all the time rather than their own (red and white, same difference...).

A final oddity about 'the Alex' is that their club crest consists of a lion playing with what appears to be a ball of wool.

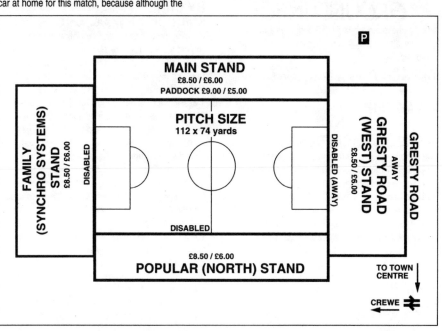

CRYSTAL PALACE

ADDRESS: Selhurst Park
London SE25 6PU
TELEPHONE No: 0181 653 1000
TICKET OFFICE: 0181 771 8841
FAX: 0181 771 5311
CLUBCALL: 0891 400 333
NICKNAME: The Eagles
RECORD ATTENDANCE:
51,801 v Burnley Div 2 11 May 1979 (W 2-0)
The vast majority of this crowd was probably of the
opinion they were watching the dawning of great times
at Selhurst and that the following season the
media-hyped team of the 1980s was going to claim its
place at the top of the then First Division. Sadly, the
press failed to explain to the adoring masses that the
term was actually being used to describe the number
of goals they were expecting them to concede the
following season.

CLUB COLOURS:
HOME: Shirts: Red & Blue Stripes;
Shorts: Red; Socks: Red with Blue Trim
AWAY: Shirts: White; Shorts: White; Socks: White

KIT SPONSORS: TDK
MANUFACTURERS: Nutmeg

GROUND INFO
£14 a game in the Arthur Wait Stand is I'm sure very
good value for money that no right thinking supporter
could begrudge.

CAPACITY: Stands: 26,000; Terrace: Nil;
Total: 26,000

AWAY FANS: Arthur Wait Stand: 2,337;
Total: 2,337

DISABLED FACILITIES: There are
places available in the Arthur Wait Stand and the
Holmesdale Road Stand. Pre-booking for these is
required, as it is for match commentaries. There are
disabled parking facilities available in the stadium.
Disabled season ticket holders are admitted free of
charge as are their helpers. There is a charge for
casual escorts who accompany disabled spectators
who attend on a match by match basis.

PROGRAMME: £1.50
FANZINES:
Eastern Eagle	80p
One More Point	50p
The Palace Echo	£1

Twelve months ago when I was doing a fanzine review,
the two Palace fanzines available were Eastern Eagle

and Eagle Eye. I sneeringly suggested that any
publication that was written for Palace fans in the east
of the country was unlikely to have a massive print run,
or a long life span. Naturally it has gone on to thrive
and prove me absolutely wrong, an error for which I
unreservedly apologise.

From what I can gather, the content of Eastern
Eagle has improved dramatically and it is well worth a
read, although to be honest I haven't seen a copy
recently. I also couldn't get a copy of Eagle Eye on my
last visit to the ground, and it has folded.

TRAVEL
NEAREST RAILWAY STATION:
Norwood Junction, Thornton Heath, Selhurst (0171
928 5100 — Victoria Enquiries)
Norwood Junction is probably the nearest to the
ground, but if you are a person who simply follows the
crowds at the end of the match then don't be surprised
if you end up at one of the other two. Two things you
don't want to do when you are going to watch Crystal
Palace are first to get off the train at Crystal Palace
(unless of course you enjoy five-mile walks), and
second to spend time looking at a tube map wondering
if there is an underground station nearby, as the
answer to this is a resounding 'No!'

NEAREST BUS STATION: London
Transport (0171 222 1234)

BY CAR:
NORTH: M1. Take the A406 North Circular Road
(heading west) to Chiswick Roundabout (just before
you get there you will see Gunnersbury Park on your
right). Take the third exit at the roundabout on to
Chiswick High Road, then first left on to the A205
(signposted Kew). After two miles you reach a
T-junction at which you should turn left (signposted
Putney). Continue until the road merges with the A3,
then a mile later turn right on to the A214 (signposted
Tooting and Streatham). When in Streatham, turn right
on to the A23 Streatham High Road. After one mile
turn left into Green Lane (B273) which becomes
Parchmore Road. At the bottom of the road turn left on
to the High Street. Go straight over at the crossroads
with the A212 into Whitehorse Lane and the ground is
300yd on the right.
EAST: M25, A20 (signposted London) After approx.
four miles turn left on to the A224 (signposted St Mary
Cray). After three miles turn on to the A232 Spur Road
and follow this until you see Shirley Park Golf Club;
then right on to the A215 Shirley Road. Turn right
again at the top of this road, then first left into Spring
Lane (A215). After 1.5 miles turn left on to the B266,
and the ground is 0.5 mile on the left.
SOUTH: A23 into London, following the signs for
Thornton Heath, turn right on to the A235. (NB: to get

to this you need to go through a small one-way system; this is nothing more than an overblown roundabout really). Once on the A235 turn immediately left on to the B266 Brigstock Road which becomes the High Street, then as north.

WEST: M4 to Chiswick, then as north.

PARKING: There is parking for 500 cars at the Sainsbury's car park just off Whitehorse Lane by the ground. There is also plenty of street parking available. Alternatively, drive down the A212 towards West Croydon and park in one of the two Whitgift Centre car parks.

FUTURE DEVELOPMENTS

The completion of the two-tier 8,500 capacity Holmesdale Stand represents the first phase in Palace's current plans.

OTHER INFORMATION

The Clifton Arms on Clifton Road is the nearest pub, but this never seems to be open on match days. In fact, there is a bit of a dearth of decent watering holes in the immediate vicinity (although the Cherry Trees by Norwood Junction railway station is OK), and it may be easier to go somewhere like Streatham, which is within reasonable striking distance (by train/bus) and has a wider choice.

The food in the ground is OK. There is a Chinese chip shop in Whitehorse Road which does a fine sausage in batter and chips.

Crystal Palace has always been a team to lay on entertainment for visiting supporters: in the past it was the sight of the players running out with the word 'Virgin' on their chests, and also a creature that led the team out which, given the club's nickname, one can only assume to be somebody's idea of what an Eagle looks like. (If this is the case then they should either invest in better glasses or lay off whatever illicit substance they have been indulging in.) However, the most bizarre thing ever seen at Selhurst Park was the Fiat 500 they used to wheel out at half-time, at the rear of which was a roller. The back half of the vehicle had such phenomenal weight that it almost used to repair the damage to the pitch... caused by the front half.

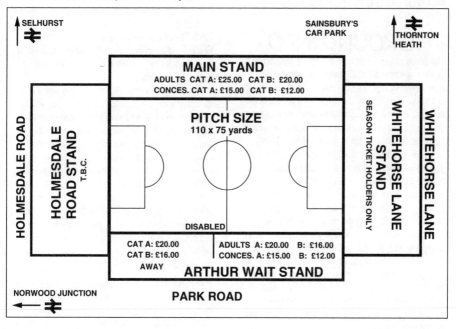

DARLINGTON

ADDRESS: Feethams Ground
Darlington DL1 5JB
TELEPHONE No: 01325 465097
TICKET OFFICE: 01325 465097
FAX: 01325 381377
CLUBCALL: 0891 12 11 49
NICKNAME: The Quakers
RECORD ATTENDANCE: 21,023 v
Bolton Lge Cup 3rd 14 November 1960 (L 1-2)

CLUB COLOURS:
HOME: Shirts: Black & White Hoops;
Shorts: Black, White side; Socks: Black
AWAY: Shirts: Orange with Blue Trim;
Shorts: Blue; Socks: Yellow

KIT SPONSORS: Orange Telecom

MANUFACTURERS: Premier Sports

GROUND INFO

The prices at Feethams rose during the 1994/5 season (a 17% hike from £6 to £7 for terrace admission). However, from a purely comfort point of view it is difficult to see how fans have obtained any benefit from this. Still, the club also offers half-price concessions for both home and away fans, which means an adult and junior can watch a match at just a shade over £10 (although you have got the £50's worth of petrol that you will use in getting there and back to consider...).

The Polam Lane (aka South End) away allocation covers half the terrace behind one of the goals, and sweeps around to join on to the West Stand, the former area offering the better view for supporters.

Feethams is a really bizarre ground which has a cricket pitch behind the Victoria Road End Terrace, which when added to the River Skerne (apparently the dirtiest river in Britain, although you couldn't tell) running behind the East Stand, gives the place a traditional English village feel, especially for matches at the very start/end of a season. Admittedly on a bleak winter's evening with the wind whipping around, the floodlights on the stand can give the place a more of a POW atmosphere.

CAPACITY: Stands: 1,109; Terrace: 5,937;
Total: 7,046

AWAY FANS: Polam Lane End: 830;
Family Stand: 200; Total: 1,030

DISABLED FACILITIES: There are 25 places available in the East Stand Paddock section of the ground, and admission is free to both disabled fans and helpers. Phone the club to pre-book a place. A disabled toilet facility has recently been installed.

PROGRAMME: £1.30
FANZINES:
Mission Impossible

TRAVEL

NEAREST RAILWAY STATION:
Darlington (01325 355111)

BUS: United Automobile Services (01325 468771)

BY CAR:
NORTH: A1(M) to junction with A167 (Great North Road), then follow signs to Darlington Town Centre. Pick up the signs for Northallerton, and this brings you into Victoria Road, then turn right into Feetham. The cricket ground will be directly in front of you and the football ground is behind this.
SOUTH: A1(M) to A66(M). Follow signs to Darlington Town Centre. Take the third exit at the first major roundabout into Victoria Road and then turn into Feethams.
EAST: A67 into town centre, then as north.
WEST: A67 into town centre. Take the third exit at the first major roundabout into Victoria Road and then turn into Feethams.

As you get near the ground you may well see signs 'directing' away supporters. It is probably as well to ignore these as, thanks to certain little scamps from the town, they are often pointing the wrong way — a fact you only get to realise as you've headed three miles down the road and your passenger tells you that they did see a sign pointing back in the direction you've just come from a couple of miles previously, but they didn't like to mention anything. Naturally this prank is very funny at the best of times, but is most enjoyable for fans who have been on the road for over five hours, and who, thanks to the vagaries of the British coning systems, are cutting it a bit fine to get in before kick-off!

PARKING: There is plenty of on-street parking around the ground. If you prefer to go off-street, then there is either a car park in Victoria Road, and also plenty available in the town centre which is about a 10-15min walk away.

FUTURE DEVELOPMENTS

There is still some question as to whether the club are going to stay at Feethams or look for another (out of town?) site. Any improvements to the ground are dependent on the outcome of this decision. It could be argued that the state of the stadium and the (lack of) seating capacity means that the club is on a hiding to nothing if it stays at Feethams and might as well up sticks and go. However, the fans love the ground, and even if there is plenty for away fans to complain about, what cannot be denied is that its looks and surroundings are unique. If they are forced, or choose to move what the hell eh? It will only be another piece of footballing history and tradition down the tubes, and let's be honest, has that really got any place in the modern game; surely balance sheets are far more important?

OTHER INFORMATION

There are plenty of good pubs in the town centre. The Falcion (rather quaintly named after a broad curved sword) is a good bet, as it not only serves Cameron's Strongarm Ruby Red Bitter which is excellent, and a good protector against winter chills etc, but also cheap and filling grub.

Unlike a lot of grounds, away fans are more than welcomed in the Social Club at Darlington; indeed the locals will be only too happy to bend your ear about how this is the worst ever 'Darlo' team that they've seen! The back of the Social Club looks out over the ground, which means that you can really leave it to the last minute before taking your place on the open terraces, although, because of this it can mean that as the captains toss up there is a bit of a mad exodus (or resigned shuffling) away from the bar and there can be slight queues at the turnstiles. If you don't want to run the risk of missing the first couple of minutes, the appearance of the teams from the tunnels really should be your cue to leave.

I'd advise that away supporters eat before the game as the caravan from which food is sold really (and I do mean really) didn't appeal. The club has subsequently reported that the caravan has gone and has been replaced by a modern mobile catering unit. If you want to kill a bit of time on the way home, why not play a word association game and see how long it takes you to get from 'Darlington Food Caravan' to 'Haute Cuisine'; this should be good for at least 200 miles. The toilets are also quite reminiscent of an old air-raid shelter, and to add to the atmosphere they are illuminated by 40W bulbs. Soft paper in the ladies, none in the gents.

Darlington used to be a Quaker town (feel free to make up your own gag about hoping to get your oats here), and is very different from the way that most fans imagine it. Although the locals say that there are no morals in the place any more, that it's dirty etc, it's a lot nicer than a lot of the places you get to visit, and fairly friendly. If you get a chance to wander around the town before the game, Big Chief I-Spy says award yourself five points if you spot the 'Adult' shop which has its opening times written in Olde English Script, making it look like a nice tea shoppe, and 10 points if you spot the house which has the family of Indian gnomes in the garden!

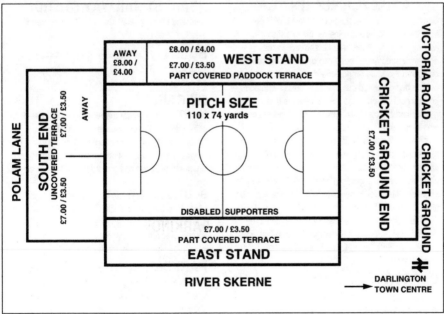

DERBY COUNTY

ADDRESS: The Baseball Ground
Shaftesbury Crescent
Derby DE3 8NB
TELEPHONE No: 01332 340105
TICKET OFFICE: 01332 340105
FAX: 01322 293514
CLUBCALL: 0891 12 11 87
NICKNAME: The Rams
RECORD ATTENDANCE:
41,826 v Spurs Div 1 20 September 1969 (W 5-0)
CLUB COLOURS:
HOME: Shirts: White; Shorts: Black; Socks: White
AWAY: Shirts: Petrol Blue;
Shorts: Petrol Blue; Socks: Petrol Blue

KIT SPONSORS: Puma
MANUFACTURERS: Puma

GROUND INFO

Don't be put off by the sight of the Baseball Ground from the outside as, once inside, the tattiness gives way to a fairly tidy little ground. The away area is OK if not overly spectacular but it can be as well to consider going into the Main Stand, where you can safely go without being pointed out as a stranger. One thing to know though if you do go into this area is that you will get hassled beyond belief...by the lottery-ticket sellers who simply won't take 'no' (or even 'go away or I'll scream') for an answer. If you do succumb to their verbal equivalent of Chinese water torture, do not simply stick the ticket in your wallet and sit down, but either put it half in a strategically placed pocket, or keep it in your hand. The key is however to make sure it can be seen, otherwise the whole process will begin again.

The club has been talking about bringing in concessions for visitors, but the same was true last year, and they never seemed to materialise, so don't hold your breath.

CAPACITY: Stands: 17,665; Terrace: Nil;
Total: 17,665

AWAY FANS: Osmaston Middle/Lower: 3,081

DISABLED FACILITIES: Given that there are 110 spaces for disabled supporters in the Normanton Stand, it is perhaps a little odd that the club insists on pre-booking. There are some parking facilities available at the ground which should also be pre-booked, as should any requirements for match commentaries.

Admission for both disabled supporters and helpers is free of charge.

PROGRAMME: £1.40
Fans who remember the newspaper programme that the club used to produce many moons ago may be disappointed to find that the club has gone all glossy. Make sure you take plenty of change with you though because the sellers never seem to have enough. The programme itself is OK, but nothing more.

Traditionalists may be happy to know that the club still produces an A3-sized paper called *The Ram*, and yes, just like the good old days, you will end up with newsprint all over your fingers, and it will turn to mush given the slightest moisture in the air.

FANZINES:
C-Stander £1
Hey Big Spender £1
C-Stander is written with a fair amount of humour (provided you're not a Forest fan), and still manages to come up with some original stuff. Certainly worth buying if you're a home supporter and it fills a good half hour if you're a visitor.

TRAVEL

NEAREST RAILWAY STATION:
Ramsline Halt (Specials Only) or Derby Midland (01332 332051)

BUS: Derby City Transport (01332 754433)
Take either a 37A or a 39 which leave every 15min from the station to the ground.

BY CAR:
NORTH: Take either the A6 or the A38 towards the city centre then follow the signs for Allenton, Melbourne (A514). After about 0.75 mile you will see a railway bridge. Turn left before the bridge into Shaftesbury Street and the ground is 0.3 mile on your right.

SOUTH/EAST/WEST: Take the ring road (A5111) to the junction with Osmaston Road (A514). Turn towards the city centre and after about 0.25 mile you go over a railway. About 50yd further on turn left into Shaftesbury Street for the ground.

PARKING: There is plenty of on-street parking available around the ground, but there's a problem: the streets around the ground all look remarkably alike and about half-a-dozen people per match go scurrying to the police to tell them that their car has been nicked. The police simply tell them to go and have another look and in 99% of the cases they duly find it where they left it. So it is worthwhile making a note of the road you park in to save potential anxiety and embarrassment.

If you don't trust your memory there are car parks at both the north and south ends of the Osmaston Road (A514), although if you go to the car park signposted for away fans expect a fair walk back to your car, and to somehow be at the back of the queue of traffic leading away from the ground.

FUTURE DEVELOPMENTS

During the 1994/5 season the club gave up on its plans to develop a new all-seater stadium on a 42-acre site at Chadderton Sidings. Instead, and it must be said to the pleasure of many of the home fans, a re-development programme is being undertaken at the Baseball Ground, which will see changes made to the Main, Normanton and Osmaston Stands. The club feels that even during construction the capacity will not fall beneath the figure quoted previously, with the bulk of the major work being undertaken during the close season. The final capacity at the ground, which the club is hoping to achieve by August 1996, is 26,000.

OTHER INFORMATION

The Baseball Hotel by the corner of Vulcan Street and Shaftesbury Crescent is a fairly good pub. It is members-only but members can sign in guests, and you shouldn't have too much of a problem getting someone to do the honours for you — although once inside I wouldn't recommend you either bragging about how your team are going to stuff Derby, or asking them to confirm exactly how many million the club paid for some of its players.

Alternatively away fans may find it preferable to stick to either the Litchurch, which is right by the away fans' car park, or the Jubilee City on Osmaston Road by the turn to the away car park.

There are a couple of chip shops by the ground, though you might find the food rather tepid and over-priced. Inside the tea is belting hot and very strong, but the pies are stodgy and cold; ie, typical football ground fare.

The ground is about a mile from the city centre and if you want a fixed odds bet then it's best to have one there, as there isn't really anywhere around the stadium where you can place it. If you do go to the city centre it can be worth staying around the vicinity for food and drink as there is a wider and better (especially for food) choice.

Derby, like many other clubs, has its own mascot and this is a half-ram, half-man character. But unlike other clubs where the mascots tend to stick to the pitch taking hopeless penalties à la Diana Ross, at the Baseball Ground this chap, who looks like a cross between a creature from Greek Mythology and something you might dream about if you'd eaten a couple of pounds of cheese just before going to bed, walks around the stands frightening the kids (and fighting off the damned lottery ticket sellers).

The Ram makes its presence felt in many other areas around the club, from the home supporters with their 'Sheep Shag Army' banners and the bleating of the theme tune from 'Match Of The Day' to the two scoreboards which in an attempt to spur the players to greater things occasionally display an animation of a ram apparently propelled by its own wind.

The Derbyshire police seem quite well-disposed towards football supporters and are quite willing to share a joke, or help out where they can; the result being that if you act sensibly, that is exactly how you will be treated.

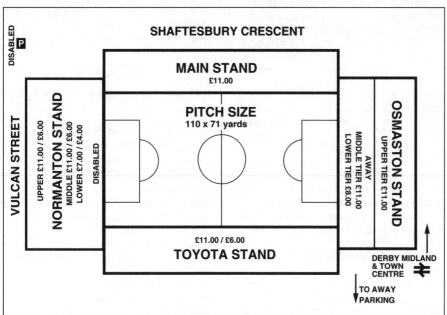

SHAFTESBURY CRESCENT

DISABLED [P]

MAIN STAND
£11.00

PITCH SIZE
110 x 71 yards

£11.00 / £6.00
TOYOTA STAND

VULCAN STREET

NORMANTON STAND
UPPER £11.00 / £6.00
MIDDLE £11.00 / £6.00
LOWER £7.00 / £4.00

DISABLED

OSMASTON STAND
UPPER TIER £11.00

AWAY
MIDDLE TIER £11.00
LOWER TIER £8.00

DERBY MIDLAND & TOWN CENTRE

TO AWAY PARKING

DONCASTER ROVERS

ADDRESS: Belle Vue
Bawtry Road
Doncaster DN4 5HT
TELEPHONE No: 01302 539441
TICKET OFFICE: 01302 539441
FAX: 01302 539679
CLUBCALL: 0891 66 44 20
NICKNAME: Rovers
RECORD ATTENDANCE:
32,149 v Hull City Div 3 North 2 January 1948 (D 0-0)

CLUB COLOURS:
HOME: Shirts: Red; Shorts: Red; Socks: Red
AWAY: Shirts: Blue; Shorts: Blue; Socks: Blue

KIT SPONSORS: Doncaster Star
MANUFACTURERS: Matchwinner

GROUND INFO

Directly opposite the ground is Doncaster racecourse which has got one absolutely magnificent stand. Slightly further down the road is a very futuristic-looking building which houses a leisure centre, and round the back we find the newish Asda, Multiplex, Bowling Alley and large Pizza Hut. These buildings combine to make Belle Vue look a lot worse than it is. Yes it is fairly basic, but if you look at it in a certain way (probably in the dark with the light right behind it), it is beautiful as well, and what is more it's got a bit of character. Mind you, if you look at all the other attractions there are within spitting distance of the ground it is easy to see why, although enjoying somewhat of a renaissance, football will never attract the crowds it did in the 1970s and before, although what sort of future we are breeding for this country when youngsters prefer ten-pin bowling to standing on an open terrace in the middle of winter I just don't know!

The away terrace comes to a dead stop behind one of the goals after which it becomes an overgrown bank, which one of the locals, rather sinisterly referred to as the 'grassy knoll'. If you come away from Donny on the end of a dubious defeat, be sure and keep your eye open for a shadowy figure lurking around. Oliver Stone is said not to be interested.

The single stand doesn't really give an unrestricted view from anywhere as there are two rows of pillars running along its full length. Generally the closer you are to the front the better, but as the second of these aforementioned rows of pillars is set into the paddock area at the front of the stand, even Row A is not ideal. Be careful of the steps in the Stand which are fairly steep, and also be prepared to have to say 'Excuse Me' a lot, as although there are plenty of gangways

going up and down, there are virtually none going from side to side.

CAPACITY: Stands: 7,349; Terrace: 1,259; Total: 8,608

AWAY FANS: Asda End: 1,204; Total: 1,204
Although there are no official seats allocated to away fans, you will not have too many hassles if you want to go into the Main Stand. If you do want to sit down it may be advisable not to travel in your team's colours as the stewards aren't overly keen on having away shirts in this area. To be fair, if you insist on wearing them, although you may be asked to move, you are unlikely to be told to do so (subtle difference). Doncaster has invested time and effort into training its stewards, which is commendable given the fact that the club doesn't have cash to throw around. The difference with other clubs is not fantastic, but it is noticeable, and if you need help, they will endeavour to do their best to give it to you.

DISABLED FACILITIES: There are places for 14 fans and helpers. Pre-booking is not required, and there is plenty of parking right by the ground. There are no match commentaries available for the blind.

PROGRAMME: £1.20

FANZINES: The old Rovers fanzine *Raise The Roof* was not on sale on my last visit, and as it no longer appears in the *When Saturday Comes* listings I can only presume it has folded, which is a shame as it was always readable and good value at 60p. If it is still going, it's worth checking out.

TRAVEL
NEAREST RAILWAY STATION:
Doncaster (01302 340222)
NEAREST BUS STATION: South bus station (0114 276 8688 — Sheffield Travel Line) Either a 55 or a 56 from the bus station will take you to opposite the ground. These leave every 10min.

BY CAR:
NORTH: A1, A638 towards Doncaster town centre. Follow the A638 past Doncaster railway station (Trafford Way). There are then three large roundabouts; go straight across the first two, and then left on to the A18 (Carr House Road) at the third. A mile later there is another large roundabout at which you should turn right on to the A638 Bawtry Road (dual carriageway) and the ground is on your right.
SOUTH: M1 or A1(M) to M18. Exit at J3 on to the A6182 (signposted Doncaster), and continue for approximately three miles until you get to a roundabout with the A18. Turn right at this roundabout on to Carr House Road, then as north.

WEST: A635 until the road merges with the A638 (York Road). Continue along this road until you pass the railway station, then as north.

EAST: M180 to M18. M18 to J3, then as south.

PARKING:
There is a large car park at the ground, plus plenty of street parking around Hyde Park (although you may consider the walk from London a little tiring). The A638 is a dual carriageway so rather than trying to cut across the traffic you are far better to drive past the ground to the next roundabout (0.25 mile, if that) and do a 180° turn there. If you turn right at the roundabout, and then right again, you will find yourself by a large Asda which has its own (free) car park and cheap petrol station.

FUTURE DEVELOPMENTS

Towards the end of last season all hell broke loose at Donny regarding the stadium, with the club stating that it would fold if the council did not let it move out of Belle Vue to a purpose-built ground. Everything seemed to quieten down a bit and then the club announced that it would have to lay everybody off unless it got a new ground. When your own manager (Sammy Chung) describes your ground as a shit-hole (a bit harsh) then you know you've got problems. The council appear to be trying to resolve the situation and there is talk of a new stadium being opened for 1996/7, but one feels there is a still lot of water to pass under this particular bridge yet.

OTHER INFORMATION

There are not too many pubs around the ground but in the town centre is the White Swan which apparently has the tallest bar in Britain. For food you can't do much better than the locally made pies on sale inside the ground which are served with mushy peas instead of gravy, and with the option of putting mint sauce on as well. The only problem with the food at Belle Vue is that they can be a bit disorganised; on one of my last visits there was no food in the stand until about five minutes before kick-off. I asked one of the stewards why and was informed that 'some bugger forgot t'keys to t'tuck shop' and when t'tuck shop opened nobody got any onions with their burgers as the same daft bugger had forgotten to bring anything to serve them with.

If you go to Doncaster on a day when there is a race meeting, go early and place a few bets before you leave, because you can get a cracking view of the racecourse (or at least part of it) standing by the Bawtry Road. Whilst watching the racing if you are in luck the football club may start its pre-match music selection and you can be transported back to a time when people thought kaftans were an acceptable item of clothing, as tracks such as 'Tubular Bells' are belted out of the PA. I don't know if the DJ is the same chap who does the match announcing, but if he is, he ought to get a medal for honesty (or short-sightedness) as after a scrambled goal there will often be a crackle of static, a pregnant pause and the comment 'Goal for Rovers, scored, we think, by...'

Finally whatever Belle Vue's problems, one thing you can't fault it on is the way in which the teams come out — as the ground luxuriates in the sensual pleasure of having not one but, count 'em, two tunnels; one for each team!

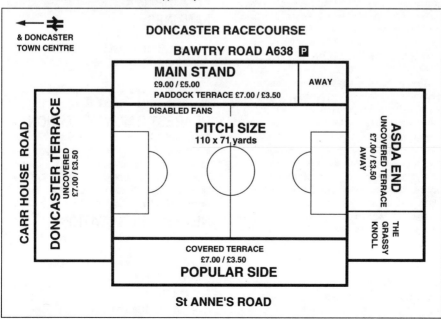

EVERTON

ADDRESS: Goodison Park,
Goodison Road,
Liverpool L4 4EL
TELEPHONE No: 0151 521 2020
TICKET OFFICE: 0891 12 15 99
(Recorded Information)
FAX: 0151 523 9666
CLUBCALL: 0891 12 11 99
NICKNAME: The Toffeemen
RECORD ATTENDANCE:
78,299 v Liverpool Div 1 18 September 1948 (D 1-1)
Goodison Park also holds the English record for a mid-
week league match when in 1957 72,077 watched the
game versus Manchester United.
CLUB COLOURS:
HOME: Shirts: Blue; Shorts: White;
Socks: Black/Blue Hoops
AWAY: Shirts: White with Grey markings;
Shorts: Black; Socks: Black
KIT SPONSORS: Danka
MANUFACTURERS: Umbro

GROUND INFO

The resiting of away fans in the Bullens Road Stand
was greeted with sighs of relief all round the country
from people who thought the club might just lay seats
in the old Park Road End terrace, a place which used
to offer one of the worst views in football as the game
was watched at ground level (although this did mean
you could assess which footballers had the nicest
ankles).

The 1994/5 season appears to have seen the
dropping of the two-tier pricing category, but before
you give a big thumbs up to Everton it's worth noting
that as none of the prices have ended up below the old
'premium prices' (and in the vast majority of cases,
prices rose on the previous premium level) it is fair to
say that every game at Goodison is now category A.

If you are a neutral, or haven't got a ticket for the
Bullens, then check out the top balcony of the Main
Stand, although remember not to toss anything over
the front — even an empty sugar sachet — as you are
so far up that by the time it hits some poor soul underneath it will have gained the weight of a large concrete
block.

The stewarding at Goodison tends to lie on the
strict side of fair. As well as the traditional banned
objects such as umbrellas, cans, (but never guns if you
notice), is the most heinous of objects — the beach
ball. I assume that the majority of readers will have
seen the problem with this item, but just in case you

haven't let me illuminate you: 'You might throw it on to
the field of play, thus disrupting the game'.
Appreciation of sarcasm isn't one of the stewards'
strong points either, as the comment that as it was
made of plastic, it could also be very dangerous and
lead to suffocation if it landed on a young child's head
was simply met with a sage nod and agreement.

CAPACITY: Stands: 40,000; Terrace: Nil;
Total: 40,000

AWAY FANS: Bullens Stand Lower: 1,500;
Bullens Stand Upper: 1,200;
Total: 2,700

DISABLED FACILITIES: There are 40
places for disabled fans by the Park Stand. The majority of these are held by season ticket holders. However,
the club does ensure that some tickets are available
for visiting fans and these are distributed on a first-
come first-served basis. The best way to try and
assure yourself of getting one of these is contacting
the club as soon as the fixture list comes out, and then
again about a month before the fixture is played. There
are match commentaries available for the blind, which
must be pre-booked, although there are no parking
facilities at the club.

From conversations I have had with fans who have
used the facilities at Goodison, whilst they may not be
the best in the country, the club is very good at sorting
out things like tickets, etc, unlike other places where
even if you have pre-booked you end up travelling not
quite knowing whether you're going to get in or not.

PROGRAMME: £1.50
FANZINES:
When Skies Are Grey	60p
Speke From The Harbour	70p
Gwladys Sings The Blues	70p

TRAVEL
NEAREST RAILWAY STATION:
Kirkdale (0151 709 9696 — Lime Street)
In truth you will probably find it as easy to get a bus or
cab from Lime Street. If you were thinking about walking it from Lime Street, be warned that the 'Just down
the road' that you'll be told the ground is fails to
include the vital words 'four miles'.

NEAREST BUS STATION:
Central bus station (opposite Lime Street station —
0151 709 8600)
Numbers 30, 92 and 93 run from the centre to the
ground.
BY CAR:
NORTH: M6, M58, M57 to J4, picking up signs for
Liverpool A580 (Lancashire Road/Walton Hall Avenue
East). After about three miles you will see Walton Hall

Park on your right, and shortly after this there is a large intersection with the A5058. Go straight across and then straight on until you see Anfield cemetery. Turn right by the cemetery into Gwladys Street and the ground is 300yd on the left.

SOUTH/EAST: M62. Turn right off the M62 on to the A5058 Queens Drive (signposted Knotty Ash, and as such ideal time to treat everyone to a terrible impression of a 'Diddyman' or crack a Ken Dodd/tax-man gag). After about 3.5 miles you get to an intersection with the A580; turn left here and continue until you see Anfield Cemetery, then as north.

PARKING: If when you are coming down Walton Lane you take the first left past Anfield Cemetery into Priory Road, and continue for 0.3 mile (past Stanley Park), there is a large car park on the corner of Priory Road and Utting Avenue. Be warned, you will get old waiting to get out of this after a match. Otherwise you can try street parking, but keep an eye out for residents-only parking areas.

FUTURE DEVELOPMENTS

The opening of the 6,500-seat Park Stand in 1994/5 represents the end of developments for the moment at Goodison. If you haven't been to the ground for a while you may be nicely surprised (given that it has had very little publicity) at how impressive it has turned out. The Goodison Megastore, with over 5,000sq ft of retail space is due to open in November 1995.

OTHER INFORMATION

If you are looking for a decent pub which serves good food and where away fans are not simply tolerated, but positively welcomed, try the Elm Tree (5min from the ground). The landlord is prepared to cater for coach parties, and if you pre-book will even provide a cooked breakfast on arrival. There are plenty of decent fish and chip shops on Goodison Road compared to the food inside the ground which always seems to be luke-warm and take ages to be served.

Everton take the field to the theme from 'Z Cars', but from enquiries I made nobody seemed to know why. (This is about the only problem I had on my last visit, and the club seemed clued up to dealing with [both home and away] supporters' needs.) Plenty of people were happy to have a guess (Sergeant Lynch in the series was a big Everton fan, Newtown was meant to be Goodison etc, etc) but the general consensus was that 'It's tradition'; very illuminating!

One tradition that the club discontinued is the practice of the Toffee Lady throwing Everton Mints to the crowd. This will not bother the majority of the away fans as she used to give them a very wide berth, and no wonder: inevitably when she did give them some, the mints came winging back to her at a rate of knots.

The signing of Daniel Amokachi and Earl Barrett in 1994/5 makes it seem that some things are changing for the better at Goodison, albeit rather slowly. Ironically one of the club's biggest heroes Dixie Dean was once called a 'black bastard' by a fan as he left the pitch due to the fact that he had a swarthy complexion, whereupon he promptly lumped them one (supposedly to the commendation of the local constabulary)! This story may or may not be true, but thank goodness footballers don't do that nowadays!

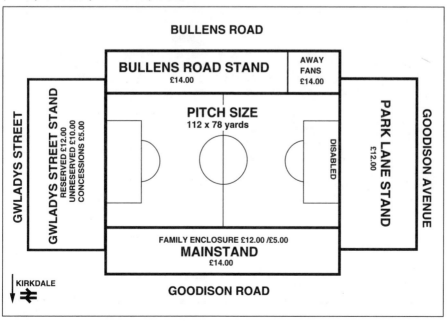

EXETER CITY

ADDRESS: St James Park
Exeter
Devon EX4 6PX
TELEPHONE No: 01392 54073
TICKET OFFICE: 01392 54073
FAX: 01392 425885
CLUBCALL: 0891 44 68 68
NICKNAME: The Grecians
All together now: What's a Grecian Urn? About seven bob a week if he's lucky (God bless Sid James, Kenneth Williams, Hattie Jacques et al).

RECORD ATTENDANCE: 20,984 v Sunderland FA Cup 6th Rep 4 March 1931 (L 2-4)

CLUB COLOURS:
HOME: Shirts: Red/White Stripes Black trim; Shorts: Black/White/Red; Socks: Red
AWAY: Shirts: Blue and White Stripes; Shorts: Blue; Socks: Blue

KIT SPONSORS: To be confirmed

MANUFACTURERS: Matchwinner

GROUND INFO

The pricing structure at the ground means that away fans pay £1 more than home supporters for uncovered behind the goal terracing, and the same price as home supporters who opt for the along-the-pitch view of the famed Cowshed. There are concessions in the St James Road, provided that Exeter will receive (or have received) them from the visiting club. It can be a bit tricky to get concessionary tickets for the Grandstand, but the stewards are together enough that if necessary (other than for big matches) visiting supporters can go through the home supporters' turnstiles in the Main (Grand) Stand and then wander across to the away supporters' seating areas. The view from the seats isn't too bad, but watch out for some of the seats which have extra strong springs in them, and thus are capable of catapulting a cup of tea/programme/coat put on to them as you get yourself comfortable about eight or nine rows back (and almost inevitably on to the the lap of the meanest looking person in the ground).

St James fills up very late, and if you get to the ground before 1pm the streets are so deserted of life that it can become a bit of a worry as to whether there is a match taking place at all, or whether it has been called off, is being played on Sunday etc, etc.

CAPACITY: Stands: 1,690; Terrace: 8,496; Total: 10,186

AWAY FANS: St James Road: 960; Grandstand: 220; Total: 1,180

DISABLED FACILITIES: There are 12 places for disabled supporters who, along with their helpers, are admitted free of charge. The club recommends that these are pre-booked. However, there are no parking facilities at the ground other than for brief (and I do mean brief) dropping off/picking up, which is a bit of a trial. There are no match commentaries available for the blind.

PROGRAMME: £1.50
So-so (although the club says it was voted No 2 in the country recently), buy it if you feel like helping the club out with a few extra quid, but not if you are looking for any interesting/decisive comment.

FANZINES:
The Exe Directory 50p
In Exile 60p

The Exe Directory isn't a bad fanzine and is worth the investment, even though it does come over as getting a bit star-struck when interviewing people involved with the club. The apparent desire to encourage strong links with the club does mean it can be a bit toothless on occasion.

In Exile is a fanzine put together by London-based Exeter fans, and is absolutely essential reading if you follow the team from afar, but in truth this doesn't really offer that much for non-City fans, or those who are in the position to be able to get to every match.

TRAVEL

NEAREST RAILWAY STATION:
St James Park Halt, Exeter St David's, Exeter Central (01392 433551)
St James Park Halt is, as the name suggests, a tiny stop just outside the ground. The service there is such that it is likely that you will end up at one of the two other stations, which are a fair walk from the ground.

BUS: EWN Buses (01392 427711)
Take note that the Paris Street bus station has now apparently closed. There are no buses that run directly to the football ground, but any letter 'N' bus will take you to the city centre from where it is about a 5-10min walk.

BY CAR:
NORTH: M5 to J30. Follow signs to Exeter City Centre, this will bring you on to Sidmouth Road which then becomes Heavitree Road. When you get to a large roundabout take the fourth exit (in effect you will be turning right) on to Western Way. At the next roundabout take the second exit on to Old Tiverton Road, then immediately left into St James Road. The ground is 100yd down this road.
EAST: Take the A30 into Exeter, this brings you on to Heavitree Road, then as north.

SOUTH: A38 into Exeter, following the City Centre signs until you hit Western Way, then as north.
WEST: A30 to A377 (signposted Exeter). Follow the signs to the City Centre until you pick up Western Way, then as north.

PARKING: There are three car parks in close proximity to the ground, two off Western Way and one by the Old Tiverton Roundabout. The best bet for off-street parking however is the Dix's Field multi-storey off Paris Street, which is 25yd from the Western Way/Heavitree Road roundabout. From here it is only about 0.5 mile to the ground walking up Western Way.

FUTURE DEVELOPMENTS

In April 1995 the Board put the club up for sale for £750,000. The club was then £1.2 million in the red, but hoped to clear the debt by selling the ground for development and relocating to a (further) out of town site. Last season saw numerous rumours regarding who would be running the club, and where it would be playing come, if not this season, then certainly the next. However, at the time of going to print all of these have come to naught, the club is in administration, and all efforts are on survival rather than development.

The away end (St James Road) is currently under-going redevelopment. The club expects it to be reopened by Christmas 1995.

OTHER INFORMATION

Exeter is a strange place; one half of it is filled with tourists looking up at buildings going 'Gosh, isn't that quaint' and is all a bit twee, and the other half is a throwback to 1960s precinct architecture of which there are rows of houses all painted in different colours, which fail to give the place the air of cheeri-ness they might if they were, for example, on a sea front. Guess which side of the city the football ground is in?

Pubs in the vicinity of the ground include the Fiddlers Pie in Sidwell Street, the Duke of York on the corner of Sidwell Street and York Road, and the Horse and Dray in Blackboy Road. The nearest one to the ground is the Brook Green which isn't too bad.

If you go to the 'nice' part of the city there is the Ship, of which Sir Francis Drake once said 'Next to mine own ship, I dost love the Ship in St Martins Lane most'. Which just goes to prove although he was a great British naval hero, he knew nowt about what makes a decent pub.

If you're making a weekend of it, the staff at the Tourist Information Centre are very good at finding decent places for fans to lay their weary heads at a cost of about £15 for B&B. Alternatively, you could buy a tiny cube of 'real Devon fudge' for about the same amount.

The meat and potato pasties at the ground appear to have been made by a delinquent fourth-former, and consist of masses of pastry which crumbled to the touch, and ended up everywhere but in the mouth; which in a way was a blessing as the tea was so dreadful I was glad I didn't have to drink all of it to wash down my food.

As mentioned previously, times are tough at St James Park. Things have apparently got so bad that burglars who broke into the ground, causing over £300 of uninsured damage, got away with a mighty haul of £3. To try and prevent a recurrence the Administration Manager offered any would-be thieves the keys of the club so that they could look round to realise there was nothing worth nicking there!

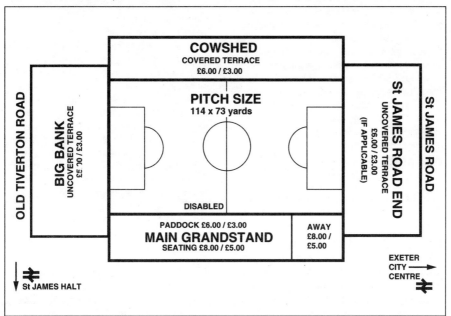

COWSHED
COVERED TERRACE
£6.00 / £3.00

PITCH SIZE
114 x 73 yards

OLD TIVERTON ROAD

BIG BANK
UNCOVERED TERRACE
£6.00 / £3.00

DISABLED

St JAMES ROAD END
UNCOVERED TERRACE
£6.00 / £3.00
(IF APPLICABLE)

St JAMES ROAD

PADDOCK £6.00 / £3.00
MAIN GRANDSTAND
SEATING £8.00 / £5.00

AWAY
£8.00 /
£5.00

EXETER CITY CENTRE →

St JAMES HALT

FULHAM

ADDRESS: Craven Cottage
Stevenage Road
Fulham
London SW6 6HH

TELEPHONE No: 0171 736 6561
TICKET OFFICE: 0171 736 6561
FAX: 0171 731 7047
CLUBCALL: 0891 44 00 44
NICKNAME: The Cottagers

It should be noted that Fulham's nickname is derived from the Craven Cottage, which is a listed building at the corner of the ground.

RECORD ATTENDANCE:
49,335 v Millwall Div 2 8 October 1938 (W 2-1)

CLUB COLOURS:
HOME: Shirts: White, Black collar and cuffs; Shorts: Black; Socks: White. Red/Black trim.
AWAY: Shirts: Red and Black halves; Shorts: White; Socks: Black

KIT SPONSORS: G.M.B
MANUFACTURERS: Vandanel

GROUND INFO

The Putney End is high on Fulham's list of areas to develop, not least because it is apparently collapsing in on itself, which explains why various parts of it are taped off. The Riverside Stand offers a decent view, though space for (official) away fans is at a premium.

Although the Cottage is not necessarily 'all that' as the locals would say, it does give you a chance to enjoy some very nice chanting, with occasional bursts of 'Y Viva El Fulham' (remember Fulham's Cup Final Song??) and even more spectacularly 'Edelweiss'. One thing that the club's fans should be praised on is the lack of bad language; after all, where else could you expect to here someone singing 'and we don't give a stuff whoever you may be'?

CAPACITY: Stands: 5,119; Terrace: 9,850; Total: 14,969

AWAY FANS: Riverside Stand Z Block: 470; Putney Terrace: 1,930; Total: 2,400

DISABLED FACILITIES: There are places for 15 wheelchairs in a covered area along the touchline of the Main Stand. Pre-booking is not essential, and admission is free for disabled supporters and £7 for helpers. It appears that match commentaries are no longer available. There is very limited off-street parking at the ground.

PROGRAMME: £1.50

Good value for money, with both a decent section on visiting teams and (normally) a couple of good well-written general interest articles.

FANZINES:
There's Only One F In Fulham £1
Where's Ara 60p

Apart from being the sauciest thing many people will hear on their visit to the ground, *TOOFIF* is a damned good read and has a nice balance of humour/campaigning/moaning. Well worth the investment.

TRAVEL

NEAREST RAILWAY STATION:
Putney Bridge (0171 262 6767 — Paddington Enquiries)

NEAREST TUBE STATION:
Putney Bridge (District Line)

If going on the tube, make sure you get a Wimbledon train. Give yourself a good 15min to walk from the station through Bishop's Park to the ground. NB: Watch out at night matches because the park gets locked at about 8pm. This means either you have to do some fence scaling or have an even longer yomp back.

BUS: London Transport (0171 222 1234)

BY CAR:
NORTH: M1 to J1. Turn right on to the A406 North Circular Road (heading west). Continue for four miles until you get to the Hanger Lane roundabout. Go straight over on to the A406 Hanger Lane. After two miles you will see Gunnersbury Park, and shortly after this is the Chiswick roundabout. Take the second exit on to the A4 and at the next roundabout (Hogarth) take the first exit, continuing along the A4 Great West Road. After one mile you will get to Hammersmith; follow the one-way system until you are heading back in the direction from which you have just come, and turn left on to the A219 Fulham Palace Road. After one mile turn right into Inglethorpe Street, at the bottom of which you should turn left into Stevenage Road and the ground is 100yd on the right.

NB: If you miss Inglethorpe Street, no worries; the next six turnings (as well as the four previous ones) will bring you on to the Stevenage Road.

WEST: M4 to J1 continuing straight on to the A4 (heading east). After a mile you will reach the Hogarth Roundabout, then as north.

EAST: A12 to A406 North Circular Road, continuing till you get to the end of the M1, then as north.

SOUTH: A24 into London. At the crossroads with the A214 (by Tooting Bec station) turn left on to Trinity Road; after 1.5 miles turn left on to the A3. One mile later the road splits in two, take the right-hand lane (Upper Richmond Road) then right at the next crossroads into Putney High Street. Continue across Putney Bridge, then after 0.75 miles turn left into Findlay Street, at the bottom of which turn right for the ground.

PARKING: Street parking off Stevenage Road. There is a veritable warren of streets around this side of the ground, and it's very much a case of driving around till you find a place.

FUTURE DEVELOPMENTS

Until the club has sorted out the issue of the freehold of the ground there is little work that can be done in improving it. Undoubtedly when developments do occur there will be problems due to the fact that not only is the Cottage a listed building, but so is part of the Main Stand. About once a year there is usually talk about a ground share with Chelsea or QPR, but expect the club to stay put, and possibly finance changes through the sale of some of the land for property development.

OTHER INFORMATION

There aren't any pubs right by the ground, although there are plenty of good pubs down by the river (not so good if you are visiting on a bleak January evening).

If you get bored with the match you can while away some time by playing 'spot the celebrity'. Jimmy Hill is always down there, but keep the eyes peeled for other such luminaries as 'Diddy' David Hamilton, the Dad from the Oxo adverts, Sharon Duce, and of course latest additions, actor Hugh Grant ('Four Weddings and a Funeral') and his girlfriend Elizabeth Hurley (I wonder if she'll be wearing that dress? Oooh I can hardly wait!).

There is a definite 'we shall overcome' spirit at Fulham which you'd be hard pressed to find at a lot of other places. Like any fans the supporters love their team, but it is equally important for them that guests (which is how they view away fans) think highly of their club, and if you've got any problems or queries don't be afraid to ask. Always a good day out.

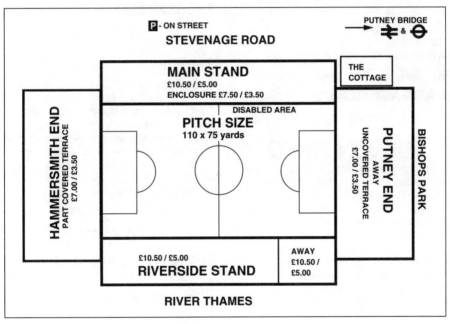

GILLINGHAM

ADDRESS: Priestfield Stadium
Redfern Avenue
Gillingham
Kent ME7 4DD
TELEPHONE No: 01634 851854
TICKET OFFICE: 01634 576828
FAX: 01634 850986
GILLS HOTLINE: 0891 800 676
NICKNAME: The Gills
RECORD ATTENDANCE:
23,002 v QPR FA Cup 3rd 10 January 1948 (D 1-1)
The record attendance actually occurred while
Gillingham were a non-league club, as they lost their
league status in 1938, and did not recover it until 1950.

CLUB COLOURS:
HOME: Shirts: Blue; Shorts: White; Socks: Blue
AWAY: Shirts: Red; Shorts: Red; Socks: Red
KIT SPONSORS: Cannon Tool Hire
MANUFACTURERS: Spall

GROUND INFO

The away terrace is uncovered, so on wet and windy
days you may wish to take advantage of the 100 seats
available to visitors in the Main Stand (actually, as the
terracing is stuck in the corner of the ground and does
not offer a fantastic view of the pitch, you may wish to
consider going in the stand even if it is 90° in the
shade). However, to do this would mean missing out
on the joys of the 10ft x 8ft snack bar where 'take
away drinks are available'. I dread to think what might
happen if all 1,800 of your team's travelling army said
they would prefer to eat in!

The impact of the Bradford fire disaster was that,
quite rightly, in my opinion, several stands were either
condemned or shut down. One of those that was
ripped down was the Gordon Road Stand at Priestfield,
which was reputedly the oldest stand in the league.
Now only an empty space remains as tribute to its
passing.

It is very encouraging, given the club's financial
plight, that it sees fit to give away fans concessions,
and also that prices for visitors mirror those for home
fans in all areas. Mind you, you should expect to be
pestered by loads of people asking you to buy 'Save
The Gills' merchandise ranging from car stickers to the
club itself. Before you let your irritation get the better of
you, ask yourself what you would do in their place.

CAPACITY: Stands: 1,225; Terrace: 9,197;
Total: 10,422

AWAY FANS: Redfern Avenue Corner Terrace:
1,800; Main Stand: 100;
Total: 1,900
It should be noted that the capacity of many areas of
the ground is under review; thus these figures may be
subject to some fluctuation.

DISABLED FACILITIES: There are 56
places available (including helpers) at the front left of
the Main Stand. These are available at no cost to
home supporters but visiting fans may find themselves
having to pay £3. The words of the trusting official who
divulged this information were 'I'd rather you didn't put
that in the book' and that the system is 'fair though,
isn't it?'. I think we can safely take it that the comments 'OK then mate I won't', and 'Yes, very' do not
apply.

PROGRAMME: £1.30
The layout, printing and content of this leave quite a lot
to be desired (other than a deceptively good front
cover).

FANZINES:
*Brian Moore's Head (Looks Uncannily Like
The London Planetarium)*   £1
The title of this august publication probably provides
more reading than the whole of the programme. Whilst
the fanzine has undoubtedly benefited from the publicity it obtained from the reference to ex-Gills Director
Moore's shiny dome, it has to be said that there is a lot
more to it than a wacky title. One of the earliest
fanzines and still one of the best.

TRAVEL

NEAREST RAILWAY STATION:
Gillingham (01732 770111)

BUS: Maidstone & District Buses (01634 832666)

BY CAR:
FROM ALL PARTS: M2 to J4. When you leave
the motorway, follow the signs for the A278
(Gillingham). At the third roundabout turn left on to the
A2. After 1.5 miles, turn right on to Nelson Road
(A231). Just after the bus station turn into Gillingham
Road, passing the Livingstone Arms and the ground is
on the right.

If you think Gillingham is the back of beyond, then
spare a thought for the home fans. Their 'local' derby
in 1994/5 was against Colchester!

PARKING: The car park at the ground is not for
us humble supporters, which means street parking.
This is not plentiful; the side streets fill up quickly and
can be a nightmare to get away from due to their nar-
rowness and the fact that they are all double parked,
so you may find it easier to park-up in the town centre.

Midweekers take note — street parking is for permit holders only Monday-Friday 8am-10pm.

FUTURE DEVELOPMENTS

The club is considering relocating within the Medway area, but this is unlikely to occur within at least another four or five years. With this in mind, as well as its current financial plight, don't expect any significant changes to the ground for the next couple of seasons.

OTHER INFORMATION

A decent pre-match pint can be found at either the supporters' club bar, or the Cricketers on Toronto Road. If you decide to go into town (a good 15min walk) then the Golden Belle or the Britannia, both of which are right by the station, are worth a visit. If you are looking for food then the Circus Fish Bar, up from the ground, is sizeable and popular. Alternatively, slip back to the 1970s and pay a visit to the Wimpy in the town centre. Inside the ground the pies etc are above average and the tea is good and strong (and even comes with a lid so you don't end up spilling half of it as you head back to your seat/terrace position). Mind you, the highlight of the visit for any sweet-toothed fan has got to be the amount of penny chews that the club sell. Not only will these give you a quick sugar high (although the refreshers are about a tenth of the size they were when I was a kid) but they are almost guaranteed to remove that loose filling that you've been worrying about.

Gillingham is twinned with the Japanese towns of Yokosuta and Ito. There are two stories to explain this:
1: The Japanese have invested heavily in Gillingham,
2: A Gillingham man by the name of Will Adams once landed his aircraft by chance in Japan — how on earth do you land your aircraft 'by chance' in Japan? — and promptly became a local ruler and sumo wrestler. Incredibly, given his sense of direction, he later founded the modern Japanese navy!

Veterans of away travel who have suffered wrong turnings, wrong grounds and short cuts that weren't, swear that his descendants can be found to this day driving away coaches to their various destinations (eventually) up and down the country.

Gillingham is indisputably Kent's finest Football League team, if only due to the fact that it is Kent's only Football League team. Given this, and the fact that the club can still pull in the crowds (10,425 for a cup match with Sheffield Wednesday last year), it is difficult to see from where its problems have arisen. Hopefully everything will resolve itself to the club's satisfaction, but I can't help feeling that things might have been a lot easier now if it had paid more attention to things while they had more room to manoeuvre.

One final unanswered question: just who are the lads in sharp suits who keep popping up around the ground? They dress like the Mafia, but I can't just can't see Vito Corleone and his chaps eating pies on a Priestfield Terrace (no imagination, that's my problem).

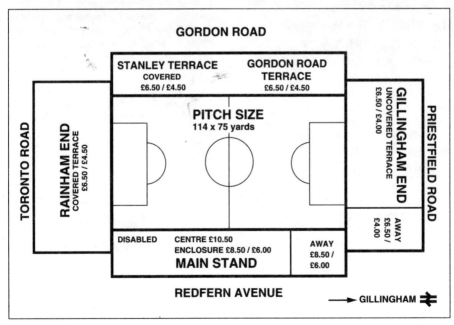

GORDON ROAD

STANLEY TERRACE
COVERED
£6.50 / £4.50

GORDON ROAD
TERRACE
£6.50 / £4.50

PITCH SIZE
114 x 75 yards

TORONTO ROAD

RAINHAM END
COVERED TERRACE
£6.50 / £4.50

GILLINGHAM END
UNCOVERED FINEST TERRACE
£6.50 / £4.00

PRIESTFIELD ROAD

AWAY
£6.50 /
£4.00

DISABLED

CENTRE £10.50
ENCLOSURE £8.50 / £6.00
MAIN STAND

AWAY
£8.50 /
£6.00

REDFERN AVENUE

→ GILLINGHAM ⇄

GRIMSBY TOWN

ADDRESS: Blundell Park
Cleethorpes
Humberside DN35 7PY

TELEPHONE No: 01472 697111

TICKET OFFICE: 01472 697111

FAX: 01472 693665

MARINERS' HOTLINE:
0891 555855

OK, let's get this over right from the start: the good people of Grimsby are obsessed with two things in life. One is Harry the Happy Haddock (about which more later) and the other is the football trivia question 'Which football club never wins/plays at home?'. The answer of course being Grimsby because they play in Cleethorpes. This question is supposed to baffle and amaze you, but because it is as old as the hills, does not. (The fact that there is no such place as Port Vale, and therefore they too satisfy the equation, is the ideal balloon bursting antidote to use when you are asked this question on your trip.)

Apparently there could be more fun and games in the future as there has been talk of uniting the two towns under the moniker of Cleeby (although as this story was told to me by someone who professed to be 'half Dane, half Grimsby' and who had long since left the area, add a pinch of salt to the idea).

NICKNAME: The Mariners

RECORD ATTENDANCE: 31,651 v Wolves FA Cup 5th 20 February 1937 (D 1-1)

CLUB COLOURS:
HOME: Shirts: Black and White stripes; Shorts: Black; Socks: White
AWAY: Shirts: Red & Blue stripes; Shorts: Blue; Socks: Red

KIT SPONSORS: Ciba

MANUFACTURERS: Diadora

may be as well to pre-book tickets for the Main Stand, as you shouldn't have too many problems with the stewards on the day (provided you have a little decorum). This can be done by credit card (5% surcharge) up to two weeks in advance of a game.

Check out the spectacular floodlights which are painted red, white and black and look as if they belong about three miles out to sea. Maintaining the nautical theme, the club stride out on to the pitch to a stirring rendition of 'Anchors Aweigh' ah ha me hearties!

CAPACITY: Stands: Approx. 8,700; Terrace: Nil; Total: Approx 8,700

AWAY FANS: Osmond Stand: 1,800 approx. In 1994/5 away fans were allocated 632 seats, and 1,350 standing places in the Osmond Street end. The figure given above is an estimate as to what this will increase after conversion in the summer to all-seater.

DISABLED FACILITIES: There are 30 spaces for wheelchair-bound fans in the Main Stand. These tend to be allocated to home fans but call the club and you may be able to pre-book yourself a place. Matchday commentaries for the blind are available; again contact the club before you travel. There are no parking facilities at Blundell Park for the disabled.

PROGRAMME: £1.50
Could try harder, but not dreadful. The club occasionally produces the *Mariners Independent* (Ahem) *News* which is a free paper, and as such fairly good value for money. It's OK for home fans, but for away supporters offers nothing more than providing something to wrap your chips in.

FANZINES:
Sing When We're Fishing   50p
A better read than both the above. Well put together with a good mix of the amusing and the abusing. The club hate it so much that ex-manager Buckley once 'blasted' them in the local press for having a pop at then Town goalie Rhys Wilmot, which is always a good sign.

GROUND INFO

The close season saw the development of the remaining terraced areas of the ground which presumably means an end to having your chants drowned out by the home fans stamping their feet on the wooden floor of the Pontoon End. The Osmond Stand offers a fairly decent view although the fact that the club have consistently failed to offer concessions remains a bugbear as does the fact that not only does the club welcome them to home fans, but in 1994/5 they paid £1 less for a seat in the stands, including the Main Stand which offers a side, rather than a behind the goal view. A tad naughty *n'est ce pas*? If you are travelling with kids it

TRAVEL

NEAREST RAILWAY STATION: New Clee station (specials only); Cleethorpes (01302 340222 — Doncaster Enquiries)
New Clee halt is right behind the ground, but you'll probably find yourself at Cleethorpes which is right by the sea front and has a bizarre Disney-type clock spouting out of it. Slightly less appealing is the fact that the station bar is called 'The Number 2'.

NEAREST BUS STATION:
Grimsby City Transport (01472 241568)
Take either a 3F, 8X or 9X from the town to the ground.

BY CAR:

NORTH/WEST/SOUTHWEST: M180 to the junction with the A180 (this is at the end of the motorway). Follow the signs to Grimsby and Cleethorpes. After a while you cross the docks and come to three roundabouts in quick succession. At the third of these (this marks the end of the A180), take the second exit. You will cross over the railway and come on to the Cleethorpes Road (A1098). This becomes Grimsby Road as you approach Cleethorpes. Continue on this road until you see a drive-through McDonald's which is directly in front of the ground.

SOUTHEAST: A1, A46. Continue along the A46, following the signs for Cleethorpes town centre, until you get to a T-junction-come-roundabout, signposted Town Centre to your right and Immingham/Grimsby/M180/A180 to the left (you should also see a memorial hall on your left). Turn left here (on to the Grimsby Road) and the ground is about a mile on your right.

PARKING: There is plenty of parking on both sides of the Grimsby Road outside the ground, as well as loads of side streets. There is also a McDonald's drive-through outside the stadium which has a smallish car park (just tell them you are driving-through very very slowly). If you want a public car park you are best off going into Cleethorpes town centre.

FUTURE DEVELOPMENTS

Having said that there are going to be changes in the Pontoon and Osmond Street Ends, both of which are scheduled for completion by August 1995, it should be noted that there are still plans to possibly relocate, although these appear to be very much in the early stages of review.

OTHER INFORMATION

As promised, more data about the natives' obsession with 'Harry the Happy Haddock': first, their love of the fish is based on the fact that Cleethorpes is the land of a million chip shops, 90% of which serve better fish and chips than anything you will find elsewhere. If you want to treat yourself, go to Steels Corner House for an out-of-this-world (if slightly pricey) experience. Because it is a sit-down place, it is always packed to the rafters on a Saturday, and getting a table can be a drawn out affair (but well worth it). If you prefer eating while you walk, try Hobsons which is right by the ground. Secondly, it was the sight of thousands of Mariners waving their blow-up inflatable Harry's that epitomised for many the inflatables' craze a few years ago. Whatever happened to all those blow-up haddocks?

There aren't many pubs around the ground as the area seems to specialise in 'hotels' — an ideal excuse for, as Basil Fawlty would say, keeping the riff-raff out! Stick to the town centre where the choice is wider. The Queen Victoria by the station is as good as any, and is about 20-30min walk to the ground. If you want to stay overnight and sample the delights of Cleethorpes' nightlife, expect to spend about £10 for a decent B&B.

Inside the ground the food (served from a 'café' no less!) is above average but suffers in comparison with what you can get outside. The tea is hot, strong, and comes in a decent sized cup.

The exit signs at Grimsby depict a person running away, but that's probably a bit hard on the club, especially since last season there has been a considerable and very welcome change in its attitudes towards the fans (its own as well as visitors), concessions excepted. Perhaps they just didn't like fish...

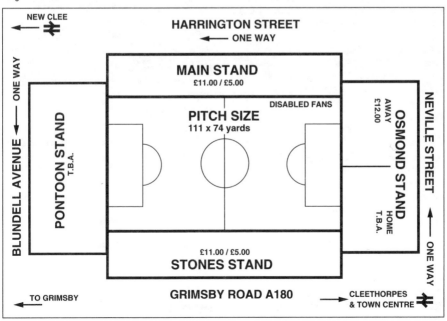

HARTLEPOOL UNITED

ADDRESS: Victoria Park
Clarence Road
Hartlepool TS24 8BZ

TELEPHONE No: 01429 272584

TICKET OFFICE: 01429 272584

FAX: 01429 863007

CLUBCALL: 0891 66 44 47

NICKNAME: The Pool

After their formation in 1908 the club were known as Hartlepools United, but in 1968 they not only lost an 's' but also the 'United'. In 1977 they refound the United, which had fallen down the side of the armchair, but sadly the missing 's' remains unaccounted for and it can only be assumed that it was thrown out with the newspapers by mistake.

RECORD ATTENDANCE: 17,426 v
Manchester Utd FA Cup 3rd 5 January 1957 (L 3-4)

CLUB COLOURS:
HOME: Shirts: Blue and White;
Shorts: Blue and White; Socks: Blue
AWAY: Shirts: Red and White;
Shorts: Red; Socks: Red

KIT SPONSORS: Cameron's Brewery

MANUFACTURERS: 1908 Gold

GROUND INFO

1995/6 sees a move for away fans from the Town End to the Rink End. However, if you prefer to position yourself down the side of the ground, rather than behind the goals then you can expect to remain unaccosted in the Millhouse Stand which offers a decent view of the pitch, but sadly (or otherwise) with the construction of the Cyril Knowles Stand no longer will you be able to while away a pleasant 90min watching the trawlers go off to sea.

The newish seating at the Rink End was installed at the expense of the Pool's most noisy and loyal fans who found themselves exiled and quieter. This gave matches an almost funereal feel on occasion, but it did mean that if away fans put their minds to it, it wasn't too hard to make themselves heard for their team. The resiting of home supporters into the Town End may mean a change to this, especially given that they should have a roof to aid their vocal efforts (See Future Developments).

Legend has it that one of the club's old managers was so poorly paid that he used to run a poultry business at the ground on the side, with the result that fans used to find themselves ankle deep in feathers and guano; the remains of which, it is said, are still discernible today.

If there is a heaven, then somewhere in it Cyril Knowles will be looking down with a big smile on his face at the Stand named in his honour by the 'Pool. It's not the biggest in the world but running along Clarence Road it not only provides a decent view of the pitch for its inhabitants, but also gives a bit of protection for the people in the Millhouse Stand from the biting North Sea wind. Before it was built, Hartlepool had a three-sided stadium; now it's been made complete by the man who loved the place. A brilliant gesture by the club for a man for whom no one who he ever met seems to have a bad word. Nice one!

CAPACITY: Stands: 3,946; Terrace: 3,390;
Total: 7,336

AWAY FANS: Rink End: 717; Total: 717
Given that the maximum capacity in the Town End used to be 1,255, the club may increase this for certain matches.

DISABLED FACILITIES: There are 20 places between the Rink End and the Millhouse Stand of the ground, and a further 14 places in the Cyril Knowles Stand. Admission is £5 for both disabled supporters and their helpers; pre-booking is not required. Match commentaries are available, but there is no specific at ground parking. If you are offered the option of which of the two places you would prefer to enter, may I recommend that you go for the Cyril Knowles Stand as not only should it have adequate toilet facilities — something that was (and as far as I know still is) sadly lacking in the Rink End Enclosure — but also it will resemble something more like a place where you can watch footie, as opposed to the Rink End which appears to have been designed with the sole aim of getting you through any nuclear strike that might occur during your visit.

PROGRAMME: £1.30
Little substance to this programme, and unfortunately what there is isn't really worth reading.

FANZINES:
Monkey Business   £1
Put together by some good old boys who love their club but are not blind to the limitations of the team, ground or town. Excellent gallows humour, and if you like a good hanging then this is for you.

TRAVEL

NEAREST RAILWAY STATION:
Hartlepool Church Street (0191 232 6262 — Newcastle Enquiries)

BUS: Hartlepool bus station (01429 267085)

BY CAR:
NORTH: A19(T) then left on to the A179 (signposted

Hart and Hartlepool). Continue along Hart Road towards the town centre until you reach a crossroads between Hart Road, Middleton Road and Raby Road; turn right into Raby Road. As you drive down Raby Road you will see a swimming pool; 300yd past this turn left into Museum Road, and then left again into Clarence Road. The ground is on your left.

SOUTH/WEST: A689 into Hartlepool town centre. You will see a shopping centre and 100yd past this there is a large intersection. Continue straight past the new marina development (on your right with Asda on your left). Left at the following roundabout and then left at the traffic lights on to Clarence Road.

PARKING: There is a car park on the Raby Road side of the ground and a large car park by the shopping centre. Also plenty of on-street parking available.

FUTURE DEVELOPMENTS

Following the completion of the Cyril Knowles Stand in May 1995 work was undertaken during the summer sprucing up the Town End Terrace (including the addition of a roof!) which will increase the capacity from 1,255 (Town End 1: 492; Town End 2: 763) to approximately 2,000. This should be completed by the start of the 1995/6 season and the figures given for 'capacity' above are post-completion of this work.

OTHER INFORMATION

M O N K E Y H A N G E R S ! During the course of my research for this book I came across a story of mindless violence. I feel I would be cheating you if I did not relay it to you, but be advised, it is not for the squeamish! Still with me? We'll don't say you weren't warned

... Many moons ago when England was at war with France a ship was wrecked off the coast of Hartlepool. The only thing that washed ashore was a live monkey. The people of Hartlepool saw the monkey and were much afeared, as they thought it was a Frenchman — so they arrested the monkey and took it into the town where they tried it as a spy. Mistaking the ape's grunts for French, they decided it was guilty as charged, and without further ado… the monkey was hanged! Such shameful behaviour must not be forgotten, and in memory of the poor innocent creature, whenever you are in the town, or see anyone from the town be sure to shout 'You hung the monkey!' at them. (If you want to practise, watch Coronation Street and shout it at Des Barnes, who is, in real life, a monkey hanger!)

The Mill House in Raby Road and the Corner Pin by the side of the ground are the nearest watering holes. The majority of pubs in the town centre aren't all that appealing, especially if you're a woman where (almost unbelievably) you will find that you will not be served in certain bars! Nor is this disgraceful sexism particularly good news for the men, who are consequently expected to get every round in.

Make sure you get some food before you enter the ground, as the pies on my visit were rather tepid and stodgy and the tea virtually undrinkable. Still, at least it is not a health hazard to go into the toilets which are clean and have soft paper!

It's worth putting your fixed-odds bets on before leaving home, as it's nearly impossible to find a nationwide bookies either around the ground or in the town.

Even with the construction of the Cyril Knowles Stand a bitter wind whips across the ground from the North Sea and it is generally considered that the ground is the coldest in the league, so be sure to ask your Mum if she can dig out an old balaclava before you go to try and save your nose from frostbite.

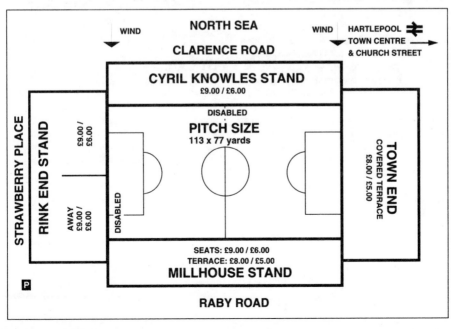

HEREFORD UNITED

ADDRESS: Edgar Street
Hereford HR4 9JU
TELEPHONE No: 01432 276666
TICKET OFFICE: 01432 276666
FAX: 01432 341359
BULLS BULLETIN: 0891 555 808
NICKNAME: United
RECORD ATTENDANCE: 18,114 v
Sheff Wed 4 January 1958 FA Cup 3rd (L 0-1)
CLUB COLOURS:
HOME: Shirts: White with Black stripes;
Shorts: Black; Socks: Black
AWAY: Shirts: Red/Black;
Shorts: Black; Socks: Black
During the 1994/5 season the club ditched their 5D
stereogram home shirt, but introduced an away top of
noteworthy garishness. It's hard to know where to start
with what is obviously meant to be a fashion item,
other than to say that in my opinion, it makes
Jean-Paul Gaultier look understated, and it's horrible.

KIT SPONSORS: Sun Valley
MANUFACTURERS: Palinni

GROUND INFO

In 1994/5 the away terrace had the massive fences
that gave it the nickname of 'The Cage' taken down.
As it sweeps in a semicircle away from the pitch, you
lose a bit of atmosphere. The seats in Block E of the
Len Weston Stand are beginning to look a little worn,
and also because of the design do not really allow fans
to see what is going on down the nearest touchline.

It is very disappointing that there are no concessions for away supporters, especially as pricing struc-
tures have been innovative in the past. When you consider that an adult and child can get into the home terracing, buy a programme and still have change from a
tenner, it is hard to consider what more it could do to
try and persuade the good people of Hereford to come
to Edgar Street. Admittedly the ground looks rather
tatty and the facilities are not brilliant, but the club
appears to be in a chicken and egg situation in that to
develop these areas it needs income, which fans generate, but the fans aren't coming.

CAPACITY: Stands: 2,897; Terrace: 6,123;
Total: 9,020

AWAY FANS: Blackfriars Street End: 1,477;
Len Weston Stand Block E: 500;
Total: 1,977
The capacity given for the Blackfriars Terrace includes
an area of overspill in the Len Weston Paddock.

DISABLED FACILITIES: There are eight
places for wheelchair-bound supporters in front of the
Merton Meadow Stand. Admission costs are likely to
be reviewed during the summer, so contact the club
before you go and to book your place. There are specific car parking facilities for the disabled. Match commentaries are provided by the local Lions Club.

PROGRAMME: £1.50
A very strange and, it must be said, rather poor offering. There are four pages on the visiting team, which
do seem to go further than the normal penpics.
However, there is little for home fans to get their teeth
into. Well over 50% of the programme is given over to
adverts and the printing style and layout is not reader
friendly. A much enlarged new programme is being
produced in full colour for the 1995/6 season.

FANZINES:
Talking Bull   60p
This is now available from the club shop and is a good
example of a traditional fanzine, although it has spread
its wings slightly and on occasions looks at football
issues in general, not just the goings on at Hereford.
Better at discussing/complaining than humour, it's
worth buying instead of the programme every time.

TRAVEL

NEAREST RAILWAY STATION:
Hereford (01452 529501 — Gloucester Enquiries)

BUS: Midland Red West (0345 212555)
There are no buses from the station to the ground, and
if you walk along the roads it's a 1.5-mile journey.
However, turn right through the Archway as you
approach the city, and you will just about halve your
journey.

BY CAR:
NORTH: A49 into Hereford. As you enter the city
you will see the racecourse on your right; shortly after
this the road bears left and is called Newtown Road;
take the second left into Edgar Street (still the A49)
and left into Blackfriars Street after 0.25 miles.
EAST: M50 to J2, then A417 (signposted Ledbury)
until you pick up the A438 to Hereford. Shortly after
you enter Hereford, the road forks; take the right fork
(Folly Lane) and after 0.25 miles turn left on to
Aylestone Hill (signposted railway station). After 0.75
miles there is a major junction at which you should turn
right (Blue School Street). Turn right at the next roundabout into Edgar Street (A49) and right 0.25 miles later
into Blackfriars Street.
SOUTH: A49 into Hereford. Continue on A49 following signs for Leominster. This brings you to Edgar
Street; continue along this until you see the ground on
the right.
WEST: A438 into Hereford, when you are in the city

centre turn left on to the A49 (signposted Leominster), this brings you on to Edgar Street and the ground is on the left.

NB: Whatever way you approach the city the best thing to do is to follow signs for the Cattle Market which is adjacent to the ground.

It's also worth knowing that getting into Hereford involves driving along miles of winding roads where overtaking is almost impossible. Your fun is increased by a local bye-law that these roads must have either a tractor or a 98-year-old couple doing 10-15mph along them. Although you may be tempted to take your life in your hands to get past them, it really isn't worth the risk; a couple of miles up the road there will be another hold-up. When you actually get to Hereford things don't improve and the city centre's a nightmare — allow a good 20min to traverse it.

PARKING: There is parking for 1,000 cars next to the ground, there are also several car parks within spitting distance. There is some on-street parking around but due to the fact that the ground is in the city centre do not be tempted to park illegally as there are plenty of traffic wardens about. Probably the best car park to use is the Cattle Market which allows you to be at the front of the queue when its time to leave.

FUTURE DEVELOPMENTS

Nothing concrete; there is a need for improvement at the ground, but unofficial sources suggest that the cost of these may make it more feasible for the club to relocate to an out of town site, especially as the City Council encourage retail developments to be undertaken in the centre rather than on greenfield sites, thus making Edgar Street an attractive target for a buyout.

The club states that nothing will occur within the next 12 months after which it will either renovate or relocate.

OTHER INFORMATION

If you like pies, you'll love Hereford. The best place to go is Heggies on Widemarsh Street (one minute from the ground) which does a brilliant variety of pies and 'sub' sandwiches. If these are not the best pies you'll come across in your travels, then they are certainly amongst the top five. If you prefer fish and chips then the Dolphin Fish, Chip and Kebab shop isn't bad. Inside the ground is a different matter with long queues but little choice.

If you fancy a pre-match pint then there is a huge choice. The club's Sportsman's bar is open to away supporters, and the Newmarket is by the Cattle Market car park. For a better choice, try Widemarsh Street and either the Old Harp (Banks) or the Wellington (M&B). Mind you, instead of your normal pint why not try some of the local 'King Offa' Cider. Available from the Cider museum (which is not only frighteningly sited right next to the eye hospital, but which also has what appears to be 100yd or so of metal disembodied intestines outside it) this weighs in at about 8.5% proof and so should be handled with care. It should be noted that drinking it, or any other alcohol on the streets of Hereford is an offence. On big match days a Herefordshire Bull is walked around the ground. Almost inevitably at some point on its trip it gets 'excited' or chooses to relieve itself. Naturally it's too much to ask visiting fans to turn a blind eye or treat the creature with the reverence it deserves. However, if you think you've got a bad job, spare a thought for the poor bloke who has to walk the animal!

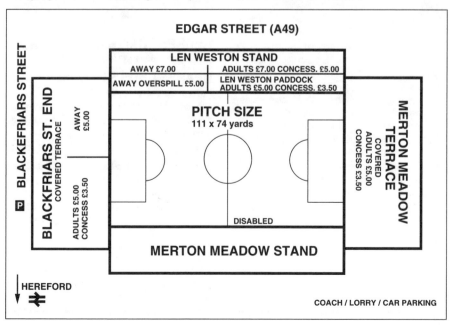

EDGAR STREET (A49)

BLACKEFRIARS STREET

LEN WESTON STAND
AWAY £7.00 — ADULTS £7.00 CONCESS. £5.00
AWAY OVERSPILL £5.00 — LEN WESTON PADDOCK ADULTS £5.00 CONCESS. £3.50

BLACKFRIARS ST. END
COVERED TERRACE
AWAY £5.00
ADULTS £5.00 CONCESS £3.50

PITCH SIZE
111 x 74 yards

MERTON MEADOW TERRACE
COVERED
ADULTS £5.00
CONCESS £3.50

DISABLED

MERTON MEADOW STAND

HEREFORD

COACH / LORRY / CAR PARKING

HUDDERSFIELD TOWN

ADDRESS: The Alfred McAlpine
Stadium, Leeds Road
Huddersfield HD1 6PX

TELEPHONE No: 01484 420335

TICKET OFFICE: 01484 424444

FAX: 01484 515122

CLUBCALL: 0891 12 16 35

NICKNAME: The Terriers

RECORD ATTENDANCE:

67,037 v Arsenal FA Cup 6th 27 February 1932 (L 1-2)
At Alfred McAlpine Stadium: 19,600 Rugby League
Regal Trophy Final 28 January 1995; 18,775 v
Birmingham City Div 2 6 May 1995 (L 1-2)

CLUB COLOURS:

HOME: Shirts: Blue & White Stripes;
Shorts: White; Socks: White
AWAY: Shirts: White and Black;
Shorts: Black; Socks: White

CLUB SPONSORS: Panasonic

MANUFACTURERS: Glory Years (Super League)

GROUND INFO

Much has been said about the club's new stadium, and for good reason — the design is simply breathtaking. As you drive towards the town it looms up from out of nowhere, dwarfing the terraced houses that lie near to it, but appearing to stand guard over them. Be warned that if you are driving to the ground for the first time it is very easy to become so entranced that you can nearly end up ploughing into the car in front of you as it stops at one of Huddersfield's many sets of traffic lights. I would recommend you take a camera (but as you can probably tell by now I am a sad, lonely obsessive), simply because you'll curse yourself on a missed opportunity, as you won't be able to describe it to your mates back home. If you are an away fan and you want to obtain the best effect, sit about half-way down, as right at the front you can be slightly exposed to the rain if the wind is blowing through the gap between the stands, and if you are right at the back, while you still have an excellent view of the pitch, you don't really get to appreciate the other stands.

CAPACITY: Stands: 19,600; Terrace: Nil;
Total: 19,600

AWAY FANS: South Stand: 4,000; Total: 4,000
It's good to report that the club has not got 'above itself' with the opening of the new stadium; the staff there are still friendly and helpful and visitors get excellent concessions. One bone of contention is the fact that now it is attracting large crowds it really ought to get the entrance sorted out. In my experience, the turnstiles seem a bit inefficient, and you can expect to queue upwards of 30min on a bad day, especially if you are a cash payer. This is annoying and may well lead to tempers fraying.

DISABLED FACILITIES: There are over 200 places for disabled supporters and these are sited in all areas of the ground. Pre-booking is required for the elevated platform of the John Smith (Kilner Bank) Stand and the two elevated platforms for away supporters in the Gardner Merchant (South) Stand; the capacity for each of these areas is 16 wheelchairs — a total which can be easily reached for certain games. There are no requirements to book for spaces in the Main Stand. Admission is half the price of whatever area you go in for both disabled fans and their helpers. Hospital Radio is utilised to provide match commentaries; this applies only to the visually-impaired and must be pre-booked. The club advises that reserved parking for disabled supporters has been fully utilised. However, with the abundance of parking around the stadium this shouldn't present too much of a problem.

PROGRAMME: £1.20
The programme does try hard, but somehow doesn't quite reach the grade you'd expect or hope, although it's a lot better than the previous season's which was the ultimate triumph of style over content. Really it's one for home fans and collectors only.

FANZINES:

Hanging On The Telephone 50p

TRAVEL

NEAREST RAILWAY STATION:

Huddersfield (01484 533481)

NEAREST BUS STATION:

Huddersfield Central (01484 423389)
The stadium is a bit of a trek from the town centre and the railway station. If you are walking allow yourself a good 20min to get from one to the other.

BY CAR:

NORTH/EAST/WEST: Leave the M62 at J25 and take the A644 and A62 following the signs for Huddersfield. About a mile away from the town centre you will suddenly see the stadium on the left (MIND THAT CAR!). Turn either into Bradley Mills Road and then right after 0.25 mile into Kilner Road, or take the following left into St Andrews Way and left after 0.25 mile into Stadium Way.

SOUTH: Leave the M1 at J28 and follow the A637/A642 to Huddersfield; at the ring road follow the signs for the A62 (Leeds). Once on the A62 continue until you see at least two car prangs which means you are getting very close to it. Then turn right into St Andrews Road and left into Stadium Road, or next right into Bradley Mills Road and right into Kilner Road.

The fact that on the A62 there are permanent snow warning lights and the council seems to undertake annual maintenance on these in about mid-August in order that they aren't caught out by an early snap of bad weather are reasons enough for you to:

A: make sure you wrap up warm

B: make sure that there's plenty of grip on your tyres

C: ensure that your AA/RAC membership hasn't expired and if it has to put a couple of blankets (and about three months supply of food) in your boot. Well, maybe I'm exaggerating, but if I am, be warned, it isn't by a lot and the roads can get very tricky in winter.

PARKING:
There is ample car parking at the ground and in the side streets around it, although departing from these can get a bit hairy, and you may wish to park on one of the other roads off the A62 and walk up to the ground. Although this will probably take you 10-15min each way you could end up saving yourself a lot of time come 4.45pm/9.30pm.

One thing that seems to have disappeared from previous visits is the supporters' club cabin that used to be on the corner of the old car park. A brilliant place to pop in and enjoy a cup of tea, away fans were always welcomed, provided they were prepared to have a chat and gossip about football, life and the general state of the universe. I wasn't able to find out what had happened to it when I went up to the new ground, and I only hope that the club have found a place for it within the confines of the McAlpine.

FUTURE DEVELOPMENTS
Currently the ground is open on three sides only. Completion of the North Stand is anticipated for May 1996 dependent on the construction contract. On completion the stadium capacity of this area will be 25,000.

OTHER INFORMATION
There are quite a few pubs in the town centre, but these are of variable quality and a fair walk to the ground so you are best off sticking to Ricky's which is on the Leeds Road (any veterans among you may remember this as the Waggon & Horses). It looks garish and a bit of a dive, but once inside, while it could never be described as luxurious, you can enjoy a pint in a very nice and relaxing atmosphere.

The chip shops on Leeds Road can run out of chips from about 1pm onwards. Instead try Snax on the corner of Bradley Mills Road which sells delicious corned beef pasties. These are so hot that if you buy one at 2.30pm stick it in your coat pocket, and it will act as central heating until half-time when it may just be cool enough to eat. Burning the roof of your mouth is one thing you don't really have to worry about with the food inside the ground. The chips I had were only half cooked, and my mate's pie was disgusting and cold. So bad in fact that neither of us could bring ourselves to finish it (and having been round the 92 it is a source of somewhat perverted pride that I consider that I'll snaffle just about anything).

The majority of football fans I have spoken to during the course of assembling this book will, like myself, admit to being traditionalists, happy with two stands and two terraces (put cover over one of the terraces and people are ecstatic), but like it or hate it the Taylor Report is here to stay; as this is the case it is superb that there are clubs as forward-thinking as Huddersfield which are prepared to stretch the boundaries of stadia design. If you haven't been to the ground then get along there, you won't be disappointed and as a departing gift for those of us raised in the old fashioned way, the architects have not gone for lighting built into the stand but have stuck with floodlights... marvellous!

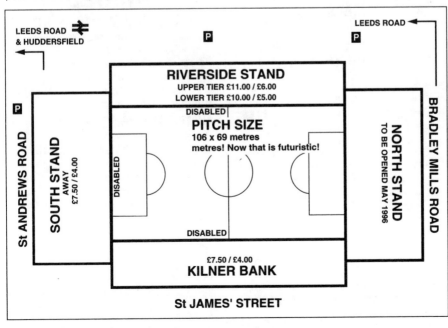

LEEDS ROAD & HUDDERSFIELD

P · P · LEEDS ROAD ←

P · St ANDREWS ROAD

RIVERSIDE STAND
UPPER TIER £11.00 / £6.00
LOWER TIER £10.00 / £5.00

DISABLED

PITCH SIZE
106 x 69 metres
metres! Now that is futuristic!

DISABLED

SOUTH STAND
AWAY
£7.50 / £4.00

DISABLED

DISABLED

NORTH STAND
TO BE OPENED MAY 1996

BRADLEY MILLS ROAD

£7.50 / £4.00
KILNER BANK

St JAMES' STREET

HULL CITY

ADDRESS: Boothferry Park
Boothferry Road
Hull HU4 6EU
TELEPHONE No: 01482 351119
TICKET OFFICE: 01482 351119
FAX: 01482 565752
CLUBCALL: 0891 66 45 50
NICKNAME: The Tigers
RECORD ATTENDANCE: 55,019 v Man
Utd FA Cup 6th 26 February 1949 (L 0-1)

CLUB COLOURS:
HOME: Shirts: Amber and Black;
Shorts: Black; Socks: Amber and Black
AWAY: Shirts: Green and White*;
Shorts: White; Socks: Black
In answer to the questionnaire I sent out the club rather enigmatically, while answering every other question I set, failed to mark a reply for what colour the away shirts were. Possibly a slip of the pen on their part, or could it be that we are going to see a new revolution in replica kits with that old schoolboy favourite 'skins'? And before you scoff and say impossible, don't forget that there has already been one radical change in kit design which emanated from Boothferry Park, with the introduction of the tiger design shirts. These had the proud claim to fame that the black 'tiger' markings on each top were unique, and were remarkably the club's best ever replica top seller.

KIT SPONSORS: IBC
MANUFACTURERS: Super League

GROUND INFO

Away fans have an allocation of 530 seats in the West Stand which are basic, but OK. The club does not encourage visitors to go in the South Stand, but if that is where you so desire to put your weary body then you are unlikely to get too much grief.

The away terrace divides into two sections — the North Terrace which is a fairly narrow strip behind the goal that backs on to a supermarket, and the North East Section which sweeps up around the corner and joins (surprise, surprise) on to the East Stand. The view from this section isn't particularly good and it's worth avoiding if you can, especially if there is likely to be a big crowd at the match.

The West Stand has a family section where the pricing is £8/£4, thus a saving of £3 for a parent and child on the normal prices. As with the South Stand, don't expect to be encouraged to go here, but neither will you be banned.

CAPACITY: Stands: 5,495; Terrace: 9,501;
Total: 14,996

AWAY FANS: West Stand: 530; North Terrace: 1,560; North-East Terrace: 1,400; Total: 3,490

DISABLED FACILITIES: Wheelchair facilities for 15 fans are available in-between the South and East Stands; bookings are not always necessary depending on the match, but better safe than sorry. There are match commentaries available, and these should be pre-booked, as should a parking space which the club will organise for you. Disabled fans are admitted free of charge, with helpers paying £7.

PROGRAMME: £1.30
Over the last couple of seasons the Hull programme has got steadily better, with more general interest stuff. It's worth buying, but if there isn't a seller around I wouldn't necessarily go on a long hunt for it.

FANZINES:
On Cloud Seven	50p
Tiger Rag	£1

It's a bit difficult to keep track of the City fanzines; first there was the excellent *Hull, Hell and Happiness,* which disappeared a couple of years back, and then *Look Back In Amber* mysteriously dropped out of view. *On Cloud Seven* holds the flag admirably for the old guard, and *Tiger Rag* is a promising newcomer. However, by the time you read this it may well be all change again, so wait and see what is available when you get up there.

TRAVEL
NEAREST RAILWAY STATION:
Hull Paragon (1.75 miles) (01482 223710)
Hull Paragon is the city's main station and if you are making your own way up then aim for getting to Paragon and either walking or catching a bus the rest of the way. Boothferry Halt, which used to serve the stadium, is now no longer used

NEAREST BUS STATION:
Central bus station (01482 27146)
The bus station is right by Hull Paragon. The best bus to catch is a 66, of which there are three an hour, and which drops you opposite the ground. There are extra buses back to the station on match days, and these pick up from the away fans/supermarket end of the ground.

BY CAR:
NORTH: A1 to A1079 Hull turn-off. Follow City Centre signs until you reach the A63. Head towards Leeds on the A63 till you reach Anlaby Road. A mile down Anlaby Road you will reach a roundabout, the first exit from which takes you on to Boothferry Road for the ground.

SOUTH: M1, M18, M62. Leave the M62 and turn on to the A63 (signposted Hull). About a mile further on there is a large hotel which serves a decent pint, and football fans provided they aren't too unkempt. Pop in here and if your team have travelled up on the night before you may well bump into them in reception area (or bar!). By the hotel the road forks in two — take the left fork. About half a mile further on is the Humber Bridge roundabout. Take the first exit and 1.5 miles down the road is a roundabout, the first exit of which is Boothferry Road.

WEST: M62, then as south.

EAST: If you can drive across the North Sea you can find your own way to the ground.

PARKING: There is a car park by the ground, which belongs to the club; it is, however, pass only.

For those of you who hold truthfulness above all other virtues there are plenty of on-street parking places, at which you may be approached by a youngster with a new version of the 'look after your car for you mister' routine which goes 'clean your car for you mister'. Once you look at the liquid (which may or may not have once been clean water) in his bucket you'll blanch at the idea of him coming anywhere near your wheels, and send him swiftly on his way — good idea, poor execution!

Two local schools — Francis Askew and Eastfield — are utilised to provide car parks. Each are about 5min walk from the ground and are signposted.

FUTURE DEVELOPMENTS
Nothing planned at the moment.

OTHER INFORMATION
The pubs round the ground can sometimes be closed on matchdays, and I've always availed myself of the hostelries in the city centre; take your pick as they are all pretty much the same.

If this is your first visit to Hull then I'm afraid that you have missed a treat as until a couple of seasons ago you could see, the wonderful spectacle of the Hull team taking the field not to the pounding drums of Tina Turner and 'Simply The Best' nor the horns of the theme from Rocky, but that anthemic classic of the 1970s... 'Tiger Feet' by Mud. One can only presume that someone who had never heard the track thought they were doing the club a mega favour by finding a track with the club's nickname in it, or that the club's record buyer was a secret Grimsby Town fan. Whatever the truth, the Hull players did not join in with the spirit of the event by partaking in a quick burst of the Tiger Dance seen on countless 'Top Of The Pops', but simply shuffled around looking embarrassed with their heads slightly bowed in an attempt to block out the visiting fans laughing in utter disbelief. No wonder the club has now resorted to using the theme from 'Rocky' and 'Simply the Best'.

The club has a very positive attitude to fans, both home and away, which comes from the Chairman down. It also likes to hear from fans about their experiences at the club, so if you've got anything to say (good or bad) drop them a line, so they know what they're doing well or otherwise.

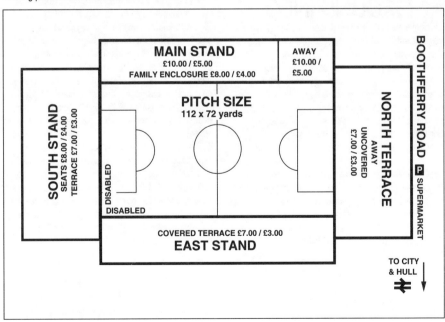

IPSWICH TOWN

ADDRESS: Portman Road
Ipswich
Suffolk IP1 2DA
TELEPHONE No: 01473 219211
TICKET OFFICE: 01473 221133
FAX: 01473 226835
CLUBCALL: 0839 66 44 88
NICKNAME: Town
RECORD ATTENDANCE:
38,010 v Leeds FA Cup 6th 8 March 1975 (D 0-0)
CLUB COLOURS:
HOME: Shirts: Blue; Shorts: White; Socks: Blue
AWAY: Shirts: Red; Shorts: Black; Socks: Red
Although the craze for old-style kits has spawned some visual horrors, it has to be said that Ipswich have over the last couple of seasons looked better than it has done for many years. If you doubt the validity of this, just check out a picture of the Ipswich FA Cup winning team, which is a sea of dodgy haircuts, polyester, and fake satin shorts, all apparently about one size too small.

KIT SPONSORS: Fisons
MANUFACTURERS: Umbro

GROUND INFO
The atmosphere both inside and outside the ground is very relaxed, and if the away section is sold out you can go pretty much anywhere without having too much hassle. For preference try the Churchmans Stand which is like an unofficial family enclosure. On occasions (but not always) the police have been known to move away fans in the Churchmans into the proper sections of the Portman Stand at no extra cost, but don't expect this to be the case for every match.

One thing I have never managed to get sorted out is any concessionary tickets at Portman Road; apparently they did exist for away fans in 1994/5 although they hadn't the year before. I'm not quite sure what the club's policy will be this season, but if you encounter any problems then, on quieter days, it may be worth having a word with one of the stewards to see whether they'll let you buy children's tickets for the Ipswich section of the Portman Stand but either go in through the visitors' entrance, or transfer across once you're in the ground.

CAPACITY: Stands: 22,539; Terrace: Nil;
Total: 22,539

AWAY FANS: Portman Stand Upper Tier:
2,300; Total: 2,300
Not got a ticket? Well don't despair. The touts which

can be seen outside Portman Road for big games tend not to be fairly new to the game, and unlike those who you may meet outside other grounds (one of whom I once saw eat a £25 ticket on the premise that 'word'll get around that I'm not a haggler') they tend to get a bit nervous as kick-off time approaches, and by the time the match is two minutes old it's like the first day of the January sales. If you really want to do their heads in, mention after you've bought a ticket that touting is illegal (and of course now that it is I'm sure none of us has seen one during the 1994/5 season) and that you feel you may have to report them to the relevant authorities.

DISABLED FACILITIES: There are 35 spaces in the Pioneer Stand which are divided 30 for home, and five for away supporters. You must have a helper with you for 'safety reasons'. Pre-booking is essential, as it is if you want a match commentary. Admission prices are £9 for helpers, but free for disabled fans. No car parking facilities are available at the ground.

PROGRAMME: £1.30
Last season's can best be described as cheap and cheerful. It would get you through the half-time break, but not much further.

FANZINES:
Dribble	50p
Those Were The Days	50p
A Load Of Cobbolds	50p
Without A Care In The World	50p

Generally Ipswich don't have what you would describe as a fervent support (although I appreciate all Town fans will beg to differ with this view), but instead of banding together, zealous supporters have split into a number of factions which means plenty of fanzines but no cohesion. Each of the aforementioned has got plus points about it, but it's difficult to pick one that stands head and shoulders above the rest. Perhaps a merging of titles would see a 'must buy' arise from the current situation, although this being said, *Those Were The Days* does incorporate *'Blue'*, a previous Town publication, and it would be difficult to say that this had radically improved. If you go on the right day, you may have four new titles being waved at you, and then the next home match nothing. Take your pick if there are some new issues out but otherwise it may be as well giving them a miss.

TRAVEL
NEAREST RAILWAY STATION:
Ipswich (01473 693396)
NEAREST BUS STATION:
Ipswich Buses (01473 250500)

BY CAR:

NORTH/WEST: Take the A14 (ex-A45) and follow the signs for 'Ipswich West Only'. As you come to Ipswich you will see a large Post House hotel by which there is a set of traffic lights; go straight over at these and then turn right into West End Road. Turn right into Portmans Walk and the ground is 0.25 miles on the right.

SOUTH: A12, then take the A1214 following signs for Ipswich West until you get to the lights by the Post House hotel, then as north.

PARKING: There are car parks in both Portmans Walk and Portman Road, plus on-street parking in the vicinity of the ground.

Any trip to Ipswich is notable for the hospitality of the people, but maybe this is best illustrated by the very friendly girls you see on and around Portmans Walk, who will peer into your car and wave in a jovial manner at you especially if you are a single male, and are going to a night game!

FUTURE DEVELOPMENTS

None; the development of the ground is complete for the current time. Having said that, although the club has spent millions in developing the ground (including more than £350,000 on refurbishing toilets by the end of the 1995/6 season), I still thought some of the toilet facilities were an utter disgrace.

OTHER INFORMATION

The nearest pub to the ground is the Drum & Monkey on Princes Street, although there are bars inside Portman Road (or parts of it anyway). If you wander further afield then for the most part the pubs you will come across will be friendly and amenable, although as with any town there are always one or two to be avoided. From past experience, you should be able to identify these fairly easily as they will be the ones with the boarded up window and the unofficial bouncer on the door whose one word of English is 'Yeah?' In so far as food is concerned, there are plenty of mobile sellers around the ground but no good chip shops. As such, it is probably as well to wait until you get inside the stadium, where the pies are well above average and tongue-burningly hot, and as well as all the normal paraphernalia you'd expect to find being flogged, there are also 7in pizzas... and I think you'd have to agree that Italian food is so much more technically gifted than ours, isn't it?

The PA at Portman Road is manned by one of those overexcitable chappies who is desperate to try and whip the fans up into a passionate frenzy before kick-off. The home and away fans simply pour derision on his efforts and attitudes are probably best summed up by a woman of about 70 whose reaction to being asked to 'put her hands together for the team' simply suggested to her neighbour that 'im daft bugger shouldn't be let out annoying people like that'. Quite.

A trip to Portman Road is 99 times out of 100 a pleasurable experience, with possibly the only minor annoyance being that the aisles and exits always seem to be blocked by stewards and police, all of whom seem far more intent on watching the game to let the little task of ensuring that you can get through to get your half-time cuppa 5min early distract them.

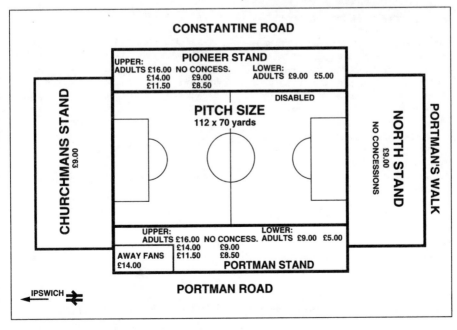

CONSTANTINE ROAD

PIONEER STAND

UPPER:
ADULTS £16.00 NO CONCESS. LOWER:
£14.00 £9.00 ADULTS £9.00 £5.00
£11.50 £8.50

DISABLED

PITCH SIZE
112 x 70 yards

CHURCHMANS STAND £9.00

NORTH STAND £9.00 NO CONCESSIONS

PORTMAN'S WALK

UPPER:
ADULTS £16.00 NO CONCESS. LOWER: ADULTS £9.00 £5.00
£14.00 £9.00
AWAY FANS £11.50 £8.50
£14.00

PORTMAN STAND

PORTMAN ROAD

IPSWICH

85

LEEDS UNITED

ADDRESS: Elland Road
Leeds LS11 0ES
TELEPHONE No: 0113 271 6037
TICKET OFFICE: 0113 271 0710
FAX: 0113 270 6560
CLUBCALL: 0891 12 11 80

The ticket office number is for credit card bookings only, and Leeds United Ticket Call is the number the club ask you to dial for enquiries (yes I know this is a premium rate number, and you'll have to wait ages to hear the bit you want to know, but for goodness sakes don't be so selfish, where would it all end if the ticket line spent time assisting the fans — really!).

NICKNAME: None
RECORD ATTENDANCE: 52,892 v
Sunderland FA Cup 5th Rep 15 March 1967 (D 1-1)

CLUB COLOURS:
HOME: Shirts: White; Shorts: White; Socks: White
AWAY: Shirts: Green and Blue Stripes;
Shorts: Green and Blue; Socks: Green and Blue
The big question is whatever happened to those very fashionable elasticated 'tie-ups' which had the players numbers on? Also, how come you can buy an away shirt for a very reasonable (if probably not exactly kosher) £12 from a street vendor outside the ground?

KIT SPONSORS: Thistle Hotels
MANUFACTURERS: Asics

GROUND INFO

The actual ground looks quite impressive from the outside but once in the away section you find that there are five pillars within a very short space, thus pretty much guaranteeing a restricted view wherever you sit. The East Stand has a shopping mall and plenty of eating and watering holes, the longest cantilever in Europe, and is a very good place to go if you're a neutral (or are suffering from laryngitis and won't be able to cheer your team on). A word of advice though: unless you have been training for a marathon stick to the Lower Tier, as it is a heck of a climb to the top, and if you are at the very top of the stand make sure you take your oxygen and glasses with you.

Many of the fans feel that the developed stadium lacks the passion of the old ground and have rechristened it 'Bland Road'. This is true to a degree, but only to the extent that if you were a Christian in Roman times then getting thrown to five lions was better than getting chucked in with six.

A nice touch, and quite typical of the club, is the renaming of the old Geldard End after the side's most successful manager, the late Don Revie.

CAPACITY: Stands: 40,000; Terrace: Nil;
Total: 40,000

AWAY FANS: South East Corner: 2,200;
Total: 2,200
Given the FA's new regulations regarding minimum ticket allocations, this may be extended, if appropriate, to incorporate a further 800 South Stand seats.

DISABLED FACILITIES: There are spaces for 40 wheelchair-bound supporters and 40 helpers along with 80 ambulant spaces in the West Stand Paddock. In the North Stand there are spaces for 25 wheelchair-bound supporters and helpers along with 58 ambulant spaces. The South West Corner offer accommodation for 34 wheelchair-bound supporters and helpers, 30 blind supporters and helpers and 13 ambulant. Radio coverage is available for the blind. Disabled supporters have access to their own lounge. Escort tickets cost £11 for an 'A' category game and £10 for a 'B'. Facilities should be pre-booked.

PROGRAMME: £1.50
One of the best programmes going for home supporters (it even has pull-out posters for the kids), although there still remains something of a Jonah tag to it, as home players who are featured within its glossy pages have an alarming tendency to be injured, dropped or sold. The focus, however, is very much on the club, and visitors will probably not get too much out of it.

FANZINES:

Marching Altogether	50p
The Hanging Sheep	60p
The Square Ball	£1
Till The World Stops	50p

A bunch of high class fanzines. *Marching Altogether* especially has done a lot to try and remove racism from the ground (more it can be argued than the club itself), and while it is not backward in coming forward to express its views, it does so in a way which isn't overly preachy or holier than thou. There is a lot more to these than tub thumping though and they all have more than their fair share of good writing.

TRAVEL

NEAREST RAILWAY STATION:
Leeds City (0113 244 8133)

BUS: Swinegate bus station (0113 245 1601)

BY CAR:
NORTH: A58 or A61 into the city centre. follow the signs for, then get on to, the M621. After 1.5 miles on the motorway leave at the junction with the A643, and take this road at the exit roundabout for Elland Road and the ground.
SOUTH: M1 to J47. At J47 take the M621. Continue for one mile to the junction with the A6110. Leave the

motorway and take the A6110 for Elland Road and the ground.

EAST: A63 or A64 into the city centre. Pick up signs for the M621, then as north.

WEST: M62, M621 to junction with the A643, and then as north.

PARKING:
There is parking for 1,000 vehicles opposite the ground in Wesley Street. This fills up very quickly on matchdays, so if you want to use it then arrive early. As the attendants cram as many cars as is humanly possible in the available space, it can take an absolute age to escape after the match. A second car park can be found at the bottom of Wesley Street by the shopping centre.

There is some on-street parking, but the good people of Yorkshire seem obsessed by certain names, and thus you get Noster Grove, Noster Hill, Noster Place, Noster Road, Noster Street, Noster Terrace and Noster View all adjacent to each other. So make sure you pay attention to the second part of the name of the street you park in unless you want a very frustrating half hour after a match tracking down your car.

FUTURE DEVELOPMENTS

A general tidy up in preparation for the European Championships, but no major projects.

OTHER INFORMATION

If you're a visitor and you've got your club's replica top on it can be as well to avoid the Peacock which is just outside the ground, and instead make your way to the city centre and any one of the numerous pubs that serve a hand-pulled pint of Tetleys. The United Fisheries just down the road from the Peacock does a fine fish and chips, but there are massive queues from

about two hours before kick-off. Unless you are of Yorkshire descent or have a very strong stomach, avoid the local delicacy of pie and peas — the pie is pork, and served hot, which for some reason makes it fairly appalling. If you don't care about your teeth, there is a mobile van which dispenses a fine array of sweeties near to the ground. Inside Elland Road the away catering facilities consist of a small basic hut just by the entrance, from which it takes ages to get served (if you do decide you want something, get it before going to your seat if you want to avoid a second climb up a veritable Everest of stairs — same is true for the toilets). You can actually see the catering facilities offered to home supporters in the rest of the South Stand which are palatial in comparison, but even if there is no one queuing at them don't expect the stewards to let you go through and quickly use them, as it's more than their job is worth.

Talking of stewards it is fair to say that they have one of the worse reputations in the country. I'm afraid in my experience it is easy to see why; their attitude towards away fans is deplorable, and if you've got a problem either put up with it, or sort it out yourself, because you won't get much help from these people.

The fans too have somewhat of a reputation, and certainly there are some things that will make you ask yourself questions (the father buying his young son a woollen hat with the legend 'Munich 58' embroidered on it is a prime example). However, it is worth remembering that bad news sells better than good news, and these are the same people who had a whip round in a pub when a visiting fan had his wallet/train ticket/match ticket stolen and was on for a long hitch-hike home without seeing the game. To be honest they are not likely to welcome visitors with open arms and a kind word, but neither are they the monsters that some might have you believe they are.

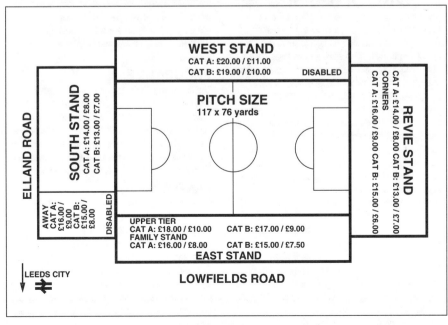

WEST STAND
CAT A: £20.00 / £11.00
CAT B: £19.00 / £10.00   DISABLED

PITCH SIZE
117 x 76 yards

SOUTH STAND
CAT A: £14.00 / £8.00
CAT B: £13.00 / £7.00

AWAY
CAT A: £16.00 / £9.00
CAT B: £15.00 / £8.00

DISABLED

ELLAND ROAD

REVIE STAND
CAT A: £16.00 / £9.00 CAT B: £15.00 / £6.00

CORNERS
CAT A: £14.00 / £8.00 CAT B: £13.00 / £7.00

UPPER TIER
CAT A: £18.00 / £10.00   CAT B: £17.00 / £9.00
FAMILY STAND
CAT A: £16.00 / £8.00   CAT B: £15.00 / £7.50
EAST STAND

LEEDS CITY

LOWFIELDS ROAD

LEICESTER CITY

ADDRESS: City Stadium
Filbert Street
Leicester LE2 7FL
TELEPHONE No: 0116 255 5000
TICKET OFFICE: 0116 291 5232
FAX: 0116 247 0585
CLUBCALL: 0891 12 11 85
NICKNAME: The Foxes
RECORD ATTENDANCE:
47,298 v Spurs FA Cup 5th 18 February 1928 (L 0-3)
CLUB COLOURS:
HOME: Shirts: Blue; Shorts: Blue; Socks: Blue
AWAY: Shirts: Gold; Shorts: Gold; Socks: Gold
KIT SPONSORS: Walkers Crisps
All together now 'Welcome home. Welcome. Come On In. Now learn your script'. For anyone who hasn't heard Leicester's favourite son on Radio 5 live, tune in; it just goes to prove that Gary may have never been booked, but he can certainly read very slowly.

Actually, the worst thing about the damned Leicester tops is that I inevitably see one of their fans wearing one when I'm on holiday, and despite the fact that I are on a beautiful sun-kissed island with not a care in the world I desperately want to get back to Blighty for a packet.

MANUFACTURERS: Fox Leisure

GROUND INFO

The abiding memories of yesteryear were the crushes that occurred as I tried to get into the ground, then when I got on the terrace I seemed to surge over every inch of it, until the final whistle blew and I was once more swept along with the crowd until I popped out on to the street like a cork from a bottle. When I was young I used to love the adrenalin rush that this caused (and to be fair it didn't only happen at Leicester but it's here where my memories are most vivid), and then Hillsborough occurred and I realised just what could have happened. I hate the concept of all-seater stadia, but if you look at Leicester now, with no fear or squash involved in getting into a ground where you get a decent view of the action, then you can't help but thinking that the game has come a long way.

Sitting in the visitors section in the East Stand you can't fail to be impressed by the Carling Stand opposite, but if you look closely you will see it doesn't quite seem to join on to the South Stand, and when it rains the wind swirls around that corner and gives the home supporters a bit of a soaking. Which just goes to prove that there is still a way to go yet. (Mind you if the team you support is putting up a hapless performance, it can provide the only bright spot of the day.)

CAPACITY: Stands: 22,526; Terrace: Nil;
Total: 22,526
AWAY FANS: East Stand Block U: 745;
East Stand Block T: 1,121;
Total: 1,866
If there is sufficient demand from away supporters they will also be allocated 1,174 seats in the South Stand (Blocks R and S) taking the total capacity to 3,040. It is difficult to know what to make of Leicester at times.

The majority of people involved with the club do try and help away fans, and you get the feeling that they are glad to see you there. However, then the club spoil the whole effect by not offering concessions, and when I enquired of a steward why this was the case their reaction was one of 'If you don't like it you know what you can do', and I got the feeling that if I had said anything more I would have run the risk of being thrown out of the ground.

Having talked to other fans it seems that I am not alone in having experienced the odd problem, which only serves to undermine the good work that the club have done, and if you encounter it, it will leave you with a bit of a nasty taste in the mouth.

DISABLED FACILITIES: This is a real area of improvement at the City Stadium, and gone are the days when the club couldn't accommodate away (and for a time even home) supporters. Now there are 75 spaces available at the ground, 34 in the Carling Stand, 24 in the South Stand Lower Tier, and 17 in the East Stand Block T for away fans. The standards of all these facilities are pretty good. The club were hoping to have introduced a matchday commentary facility for the 1994/5 season, but sadly as yet this hasn't materialised. There is no charge for disabled supporters, but helpers pay £10. Spaces should be pre-booked.

Note, there are no parking facilities at the ground for disabled fans.

PROGRAMME: £1.50
The cost stayed the same in 1994/5 as it had for the previous season, but the quality improved dramatically. Loads to read, ranging from a good piece on the visiting team (about six pages in length!), which steers well clear of just reproducing the old penpics to an interesting one page European round-up. Certainly in the top three of programmes, if not the number one itself.

FANZINES:
The Fox	£1
Filbo Fever	70p
Where's The Money Gone	£1

Both *The Fox* and *Filbo Fever* are old stagers and a good read. *Filbo Fever* especially has done a hell of a lot of campaigning towards educating the club to the fans' needs and the fans to their responsibilities to the club. *WTMG* is a new fanzine, and not one I could lay my hands on when I last visited the ground, so I can't really comment.

TRAVEL

NEAREST RAILWAY STATION:
Leicester (0116 248 1000)

NEAREST BUS STATION:
St Margaret's bus station (0116 251 4155)

BY CAR:
NORTH: A46 through Leicester city centre following the signs for Rugby. This will bring you on to Welford Road. (Don't be tricked into following fans who appear to be travelling in a different direction to you, as they are likely to be going to see Leicester Rugby Union Club whose stadium is on Welford Road.) After a while you will see a cemetery on your left. Turn right by the cemetery into Almond Road, then right at the T-junction into Aylestone Road, and immediately left into Brazil Street. At the bottom of Brazil Street turn right into Burnmoor Street and the ground is on the left.

NB: If you are coming down the M1 leave at J22, follow the signs for Leicester City Centre and Rugby, then as above.

EAST: A47 into the city centre, follow the signs for Rugby, then as North.

SOUTH: M1 to J21, and pick up the A46 as you leave the motorway. Continue along this road till you cross the railway, then just under a mile later turn right into Upperton Road and cross the Grand Union Canal. Turn right into Eastern Boulevard, then left into Filbert Street.

WEST: M69. Follow the signs for Leicester City Centre and Rugby, then as north.

PARKING:
There is a car park between the ground and the canal, or plenty of on-street parking. If you are coming from the north/east/west there is a car park off Almond Road, and if you are coming from the south there is one off Upperton Road. Neither of these is too far from the ground.

FUTURE DEVELOPMENTS
None planned at present.

OTHER INFORMATION
The two pubs nearest to the ground are the Turnstile and the Victory which serve Everards. If they aren't your cup of tea (and they may not be), there are plenty of alternatives between the city centre and the ground, as well as the normal assortment of eateries.

At the start of a match you almost expect a crowd of hunt saboteurs to take to the field and start causing havoc amongst the Leicester players who emerge to the tune of the 'Hunting Song.' It does seem strange that a team who go by the nickname of the Foxes would be thought to be inspired by this, which is hardly music to the ears of their animal counterparts. Perhaps it is the manager's idea of a way of making them run faster.

For stats fans, Leicester with all their semi-final and play-off defeats finally managed to exorcise their Wembley hoodoo in 1994. However, they remain one of only eight championship runners-up who have never actually won the title, and are eighth in the list of most relegated clubs.

Finally, remember Basil Fawlty and 'Don't mention the Germans'. Replace Leicester for Cleese and Brian Little for the Germans, and you have a useful maxim to adhere to unless you want your ear severely bent!

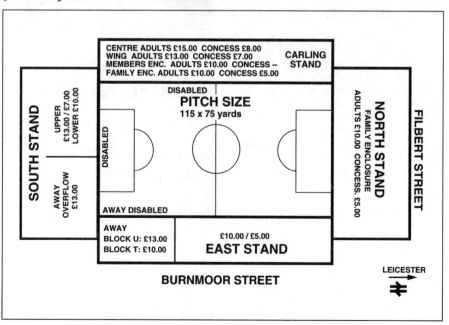

LEYTON ORIENT

ADDRESS: Leyton Stadium
Brisbane Road, Leyton
London E10 5NE

TELEPHONE No: 0181 539 2223

TICKET OFFICE: 0181 539 2223

FAX: 0181 539 4390

CLUBCALL: 0891 12 11 50

NICKNAME: The O's

RECORD ATTENDANCE: 34,345 v

West Ham FA Cup 4th 25 January 1964 (D 0-0)
Leyton Orient are a team with a bit of an identity crisis. They came into the world as Glyn Cricket and Football Club, but five years later Glyn went home and took his bat with him, so they became Eagle FC which they stuck with for two long years. The moniker of Clapton Orient was used between 1888 and 1946, after which they became Leyton Orient for 20 years. They then had 21 years of being plain Orient, before reverting to Leyton Orient in 1987. If this reverse trend continues the club should be back to having GC&FC on their shirts by 2085!

CLUB COLOURS:

HOME: Shirts: Red with White Designs;
Shorts: Red; Socks: Red
AWAY: Shirts: Yellow with Royal Blue Designs;
Shorts: Royal Blue; Socks: Royal Blue

KIT SPONSORS: Acclaim

MANUFACTURERS: Olympic

GROUND INFO

The whole of the pitch at Leyton seems sunken, so even if you are at the front of the terrace you get a feeling of looking down on the action, and a good view of the match. It is a bit of a shame that a club which has as positive attitude to away supporters as Leyton haven't seen fit to take down the South Terrace fencing. Hopefully it won't be too long before this is remedied. The lack of covering on home and away terracing does lessen the atmosphere a bit, especially as both ends are quite large and there is a tendency to spread yourself out. Mind you if you want to get a bit of noise going, check out the Main Stand which is acoustically excellent.

You may find your attention wandering slightly due to a distinctly unpleasant aroma. This is one of the rare occasions when the cause is unlikely to be down to your neighbour's consumption of two burgers and half a dozen pints, but is more likely to be attributable to the 'Waste Disposal' works which are less than 0.25 mile away. Talking of waste disposal, the toilets on the away terrace have only got half a roof, but then terrace is also uncovered.

CAPACITY: Stands: 7,113; Terraces: 9,920.
Total: 17,033

AWAY FANS: Main Stand: 900.
South Terrace: 3,247.
Total: 4,147

DISABLED FACILITIES: There are covered spaces for 12 wheelchair-bound fans with their helpers at the front of the North Terrace on the Main Stand side. There is no charge for disabled fans or helpers, but limited spaces means you must pre-book.

There are no special parking facilities at the ground, but the police are generally OK about drop-offs and pick-ups and if necessary may let you access the roads around the ground which are closed on matchdays. Home fans should also note that the club offer a mini-bus pick-up service. Contact the club directly regarding matchday commentaries.

PROGRAMME: £1.50

FANZINES:

Leyton Orientear	80p
Frankly Speaking	50p
Pandamonium	60p

Any of these are better than the official programme. *The Orientear* probably shades it if only because it appears to be produced more regularly, is more established, and seems to be closer to what is actually happening at the club — meaning not only that its campaigning tends to get better results, but also that the club have on occasions talked to it before doing things that will affect the supporters! *Frankly Speaking* also includes some excellent non-league material, especially about local side Dagenham and Redbridge, and is worth buying for this alone.

TRAVEL

NEAREST RAILWAY STATION:
Leyton Midland Road (0171 928 5100)

NEAREST TUBE STATION: Leyton
(Central Line) — Turn right as you leave the tube station for the walk to the ground.

BUS: London Transport — 0171 222 1234

BY CAR:
NORTH: M11 into London. At the end of the M11 turn right on to the A12 (signposted Wanstead). Continue for 1.25 miles, going straight over at the roundabout, then 0.25 mile later turn right into Church Lane. Turn left at the T-junction with Grove Green Road, bearing left after 200yd on to the one-way system (still Grove Green Road). After 0.75 mile turn right into Leyton High Road. Take the fifth left (Osborne Road) which will take you to the stadium.
EAST: A12 into London via Gidea Park and Wanstead. Then as north.

SOUTH: A23 to A205 (South Circular Road) turning right on to A205 (signposted Tulse Hill). Follow signs for Woolwich then turn left on to the A207 Shooters Hill Road. After 1.5 miles turn right on to the A102(M) and continue on this road through the Blackwall Tunnel. Once through the tunnel carry on for 1.5 miles then turn right on to the A11 (signposted Leytonstone). A quarter of a mile after Maryland station turn left into Chobham Road, and after a further 0.25 mile turn right into Major Road. A mile later turn left into Osborne Road at the bottom of which is the ground.

WEST: M40/A40 into London. Turn left on to the A406 North Circular Road (signposted Willesden/Hendon) and continue along the North Circular via Finchley, Wood Green, Edmonton and Woodford. Just after South Woodford turn right at the roundabout on to the A113 Chigwell Road (if you cross the M11 you've gone too far). After 1.75 miles you get to a major roundabout; take the third exit on to Leytonstone Road (A11) and 0.25 mile later turn right into Church Road. Then as north.

Warning: apparently there are some fairly major road developments around Leyton. So expect delays.

PARKING:
There are some car parks off the A11 which are a fair walk to the ground, you avoid the congestion at the end of the match. A better bet is on-street parking. There are numerous streets around the ground which you can use, and only the roads immediately next to the ground are designated no parking by the police.

FUTURE DEVELOPMENTS
A tricky one. The club did have major redevelopment plans for the completion of a 16,000 capacity, all-seater stadium at Brisbane Road by 1997. This included a new car park and the pitch running from east to west rather than the present north to south. However, during the 1994/5 season Chairman Tony Wood was forced to put the club up for sale at £5 — a price which Barry Hearn eventually found too appealing to resist (although for that bargain price he did also get to pick up the club's debts). Certainly, the rebuilding of the West Stand seems to hang in the balance. In this close season the club is spending upwards of £75,000 renovating and modernising toilet facilities on the West Stand and South Terrace.

OTHER INFORMATION
The nearest pub to the ground is the Coach & Horses on Leyton High Road, which is good, but because its the only one in the vicinity does tend to get packed.

Inside the ground all the previous catering arrangements are set to change. The club reports that from next season a major catering company will be taking over all aspects of food and drink provision on match-days; a good bet for food is the kebab/chip shop on Leyton High Road which also charges less than the club's £2.50 for a cheeseburger and a hot drink.

One memory that I can guarantee you will take away with you, if you visit early in the season, is the O's entrance to the field which is undertaken to the gladiatorial strains of… 'Tijuana Taxi' by Herb Alpert! This sounds so much like the beginning of 'It's A Knockout' that you half expect the teams to emerge wearing giant costumes and having buckets of water thrown over them — if only! According to the club, 'Tijuana Taxi' will be phased out during the early part of the season. All being well, the new broom in Barry Hearn will sweep the club clean of its hand-to-mouth existence, although hopefully any progress on this front won't be made at the expense of the hospitality shown towards visitors by everyone at the club, which traditionally makes Leyton an enjoyable day out.

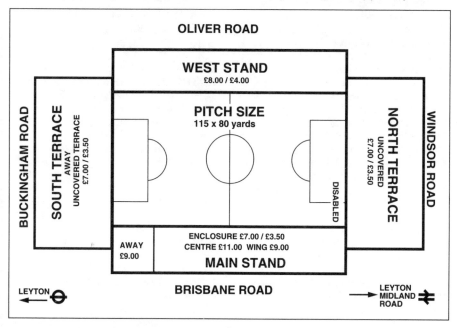

OLIVER ROAD

WEST STAND
£8.00 / £4.00

PITCH SIZE
115 x 80 yards

BUCKINGHAM ROAD

SOUTH TERRACE
AWAY
UNCOVERED TERRACE
£7.00 / £3.50

NORTH TERRACE
UNCOVERED
£7.00 / £3.50

WINDSOR ROAD

DISABLED

AWAY
£9.00

ENCLOSURE £7.00 / £3.50
CENTRE £11.00 WING £9.00
MAIN STAND

LEYTON

BRISBANE ROAD

LEYTON
MIDLAND
ROAD

LINCOLN CITY

ADDRESS: Sincil Bank Stadium
Lincoln LN5 8LD
TELEPHONE No: 01522 522224
TICKET OFFICE: 01522 522224
FAX: 01522 520564
IMPSLINE: 0891 66 46 66
NICKNAME: The Red Imps
RECORD ATTENDANCE: 23,196 v
Derby Lge Cup 4th 15 November 1967 (L 0-3)

CLUB COLOURS:
HOME: Shirts: Red, two White stripes, Black sleeves; Shorts: Black; Socks: Red
AWAY: Shirts: Green, two purple stripes, Black sleeves; Shorts: Black; Socks: Green
Two noteworthy things about the Lincoln kit; firstly, they don't have numbers on their shirts but rather on their shorts (the white stripes do make it look as if they have got 11 number 11s on the pitch), and secondly the away kit is vile. When asked, the club did say that they were very likely to revert to numbering for 1995/6, but didn't mention anything about the latter, and some would say more serious, issue.

KIT SPONSORS: Lincolnshire Echo
MANUFACTURERS: Admiral

GROUND INFO

Away fans have been sited in the South Park End of the Linpave Stand since its opening in March 1995. The good news is that at the tail-end of last season Lincoln started offering away fans concessions to go in this stand, something they had failed to do when visitors were sited in the South Park Stand. However, before you start throwing your hats in the air and proposing toasts to the good health of those running the club, it's worth knowing that the reduction for away concessions was £2 which took admission prices to £6 for kids, while home fans could get into the same stand for a pound. Fortunately, in my experience, some of the stewards could see that this was sheer lunacy, and if you had a word with them, they would sort you out to go in the home turnstiles, so that you could pay a quid for under 16s but then ensure you were free to walk down and sit with your friends.

Mind you, if you think you've got it bad... In the 1994/5 season when Lincoln played Crystal Palace at Selhurst in the FA Cup 3rd round, Palace wanted to reduce the admission price for home and away supporters from their, oh so reasonable, £15 to £12 for adults and £6 for kids. However, they were thwarted by Lincoln who appealed to the FA that normal Premiership prices should be charged, and who

successfully got admission for their own (and Palace) fans hiked up to £20 (reduced to £14 on appeal).

CAPACITY: Stands: 10,000; Terrace: 975;
Total: 10,975
AWAY FANS: Linpave Stand: 1,600;
Total: 1,600
This was the maximum offered during the 1994/5 season. Given that the segregation of the excellent new stand means that there is a large part of it unused in segregating the fans, it may be that away fans are resited into the South Park Stand, which would seem a more obvious choice, and offers seating for approx 1,200.

DISABLED FACILITIES: There are 102 spaces in the Linpave and South Park Stand. Admission for disabled supporters is free of charge although helpers may pay standard match prices in 1995/6. You should pre-book your seat; at the same time advise the club if you require a parking space. No match commentaries are currently available for the blind.

PROGRAMME: £1.20
FANZINES:
Deranged Ferret 75p
Although this does look rather grim (very reminiscent of a parish magazine) it is an excellent read. Interestingly enough the programme looks good, but can you guess what kind of a read it is?

TRAVEL
NEAREST RAILWAY STATION:
Lincoln Central (01522 539502)

BUS: Central bus station (01522 525312)
BY CAR:
NORTH: A15 into Lincoln city centre until you cross the River Witham. About 250yd further on, turn right on to the A57. Continue until you pass the railway station then turn left on to the B1262 High Street (signposted Newark A46). Carry on until you go under a railway bridge, then take the next left on to Scorer Street. Take the second right (not the first right into Sincil Bank) into Cross Street, and the ground is at the bottom of this road.
EAST: A46 or A158 into Lincoln city centre following the signs for A46 Newark. This will bring you on to the High Street. Then as north.
SOUTH: A1, A46. Follow signs for Lincoln South and City Centre, this brings you on to the High Street. Continue until you see the Miller's Arms pub on your left (this is by a pelican crossing) and take the next right into Scorer Street. Then as north.
WEST: A46 into Lincoln. Go through the city centre

following the signs for A46 Newark. This will bring you on to the High Street. Then as north.

PARKING: There is a car park in Cross Street next to the ground, as well as some street parking in the vicinity. For other car parks you need to go into the city centre, which is a bit of a walk, but doesn't get too clogged up at the end of matches.

FUTURE DEVELOPMENTS

The opening in March 1995 of the £1 million Linpave Stand which seats 5,700 means that there is seating on all four sides of Sincil Bank. There is still a small area of terracing at the Stacey West End of the ground which could be transformed into seating easily enough, but expect the ground to stay as it is until such a time as the club reach the higher echelons of the league.

OTHER INFORMATION

Sincil Bank is definitely one of the grounds where it is better to eat inside than out. The nearest chip shop to the ground is on the corner of Scorer Street and Cross Street; directly opposite this is a pet shop, and both establishments sell fish. I just think maybe if they had a rush at the chippie one day, well... Besides, the pies and sausage rolls inside the ground are made by a local butcher's and are excellent — hot, well filled and with a delicious pastry. What is more, in the St Andrews Stand they are served by a couple of charming old girls who treat every male customer under 40 like the prodigal son returning home from the wilderness! They make a terrific cup of tea as well.

The city centre has numerous good pubs. Nearer the ground you can enjoy a pint in either the Miller's Arms (John Smiths) or the George & Dragon; the latter is the bigger of the two, but the Miller's tends to have a better atmosphere. Both pubs are on the High Street just by the Scorer Street turning. A better bet though is to walk down Sincil Bank towards the town, at the end of which is the Portland Arms; this is a free house that serves an excellent pint in a good and relaxed ambience. If you can't be bothered walking then try the bar at the back of the South Park Stand — mind you, be warned, cheap it isn't!

The dug-outs at Lincoln are only really big enough for three, which often provides, especially on wet days, for wonderful pre-match entertainment as the visiting team's substitutes realise this fact. There tends to follow:

- 1 A go-as-fast-as-you-can-without-breaking-into-a-run competition;
- 2 A jostle-your-neighbour-for-position competition;
- 3 An all-out race, elbows, fists, anything-goes type scrap for a place in the dry and warm.

If you take your camera to grounds with you then ... you are sad, but it's also worth noting that Lincoln offers a wonderful photo-opportunity. If you go to the bottom of the South Park Stand, on the Linpave Stand side and look up, you will see the Cathedral beautifully framed in the gap between the Linpave Stand and the Stacey Park West Stand. Enter this into as many competitions as you can as it has got prize-winning shot written all over it (please send 10% of your winnings to me via the publishers).

Ultimately Lincoln is a place of highs and lows, great food, good view and generally friendly people. However, it never quite hits the heights of 'great away day', and this is even more frustrating than normal, because it's easy to see that with a little more thought and effort from the club it could easily become one of the 'must' trips of the season.

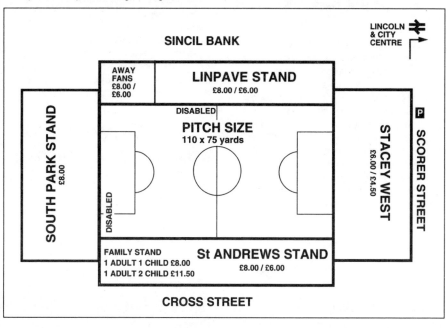

LIVERPOOL

ADDRESS: Anfield
Anfield Road
Liverpool L4 0TH
TELEPHONE No: 0151 263 2361
TICKET OFFICE: 0151 260 8680
FAX: 0151 260 8813
CLUBCALL: 0891 12 11 84

The club does take credit card bookings on 0151 263 5727, and states that tickets can be booked up to 19 days in advance. It is suggested that you don't leave it much later than this if you want to pay this way as the single line tends to be virtually always engaged, and getting through is on the very irritating side of difficult.

NICKNAME: The Reds
RECORD ATTENDANCE: 61,905 v
Wolves FA Cup 4th 2 February 1952 (W 2-1)

CLUB COLOURS:
HOME: Shirts: Red; Shorts: Red; Socks: Red
AWAY: Shirts: Green and White Quarters;
Shorts: Green; Socks: White

KIT SPONSORS: Carlsberg... probably!
MANUFACTURERS: Adidas

GROUND INFO

Anfield being one of the grounds that visiting supporters tend to put on their list of 'must sees' the away allocation of 1,600 isn't always going to be enough. If you don't have a ticket anywhere else in the ground is equally safe/risky. There are obstructed views in the Main Stand, which means that the Centenary Stand (the Old Kemlyn Road Stand) is probably the best bet, though watch out for the steep steps leading to this stand which slows down entry and exit.

Many of the fans consider that the atmosphere at the ground has lessened now the Kop has gone all-seater. Although funnily enough you don't hear too many opposition keepers who still have 12,000-odd voices behind them questioning their ability agreeing with this. In an attempt to maintain the tradition of the Kop, the famous flagpole is being put up at the club forecourt, and in an attempt to leave tradition behind, the new stand has accessible toilets in it which means an end to 'hot legs', a situation which arose on the old Kop where due to the lack of gangways, going to the toilet was impossible, and you went where you stood (the hot legs belonged to the person in front of you). Try it now, and you can expect to receive very short shrift from the local constabulary.

The club is continuing with the standard/premium match differential, with £1 addition on the cost of adult tickets. It's impossible to say what the extra charge is

for children as there are no longer concession prices. To be fair, the club does offer an adult and child combined ticket which works out (for standard matches) at an excellent £5 for the child in either the Anfield Road or Kop Stand, but it really should consider extending this for 'unaccompanied kids'.

CAPACITY: Stands: 41,000; Terrace: Nil;
Total: 41,000

AWAY FANS: Anfield Road End: 1,600;
Total: 1,600

DISABLED FACILITIES: There are 27 places available for disabled supporters in the Kop and Main Stand, which although representing a 69% increase since the opening of the Kop Stand is still way too little. Tickets are generally purchased on a season ticket basis; if you phone up the club you may be able to get a place but do not count on it. If you are to get a space, pre-booking is essential. There are match commentaries for the blind, and also disabled parking facilities at the ground. Once again pre-booking is required for these facilities. Should you be lucky enough to get a space expect to be charged standard admission prices for the section you get into.

PROGRAMME: £1.50, available inside and outside the ground.

FANZINES:
When Sunday Comes   50p
Our Days Are Numbered   £1
All Day And All Of The Night   £1

When Sunday Comes is a nice combination of humour and campaigning, even if the printing isn't the best you'll ever come across (there again are fanzines supposed to be £2 glossies?), and probably shades it as top fanzine. Our Days Are Numbered seems to have peaks and troughs being alternately excellent, and well, not very good at all; a chancy buy, but can be worth it. ADAAOTN is put together in Ireland, and I've not seen a copy so can't comment.

TRAVEL

NEAREST RAILWAY STATIONS:
Kirkdale (0.75 miles)
Lime Street (four miles) (0151 709 9696)
Lime Street is the main city station. Once there either take a local service to Kirkdale, bus it, grab a cheapish cab, or be prepared for a long walk.

BUS: Central bus station (0151 709 8600)
From Lime Street or the city centre, any 17 bus (17a, 17b etc) will take you to Utting Avenue which adjoins Anfield Road. To get back to the station either grab a bus from Utting Avenue, or, depending on the size of away support, you may find buses awaiting you by the Anfield Road exits. Be warned; the buses can drive

directly on to the platform at Lime Street leaving you to be herded on to a train and straight home. Bad news if you fancied an evening in the city (and worse if you drove up).

BY CAR:
NORTH: M6 to J28, then follow signs for A58 to Liverpool. Keep going until you hit Walton Hill Avenue. You will then pass Stanley Park, after which turn left into Anfield Road.

SOUTH/EAST: M6/M62 until you reach the end of the motorway. Turn right on to the A5058 (Queens Drive). After three miles take a left into Utting Avenue. One mile further on turn right at the Arkles PH into Anfield Road.

WEST: Go through Mersey Tunnel (toll) into city centre. Follow the signs for Preston (A580), this will take you into Walton Hall Avenue, and you will see Stanley Park in front of you. Just before you reach this, turn right into Anfield Road.

PARKING: There is a large car park by Stanley Park which takes an age to get out of and which is apparently for permit holders, although this never seems a great problem. Alternatively you can park by Everton FC on the other side of the park. Street parking is also available but much of this is residents-only. If you do find a side street to park in, you will almost certainly be accosted by young Scouse street-waifs suggesting that you give them a quid to 'mind your car, La'. Answering 'no' of course gives accent (not to mention possibly your wheels and stereo) away.

FUTURE DEVELOPMENTS
None.

OTHER INFORMATION
If you fancy a drink near the ground, there are three pubs which are always open on match days: the Albert (behind the Kop), the King Billy and The Arkles (both on the Anfield Road). Of the three the Albert is probably the best bet as it serves a reasonable and cheap pint of Tetleys; The Arkles is on the route from the coach park to the ground. The King Billy has to be mentioned simply because when I told a (non-attending) Liverpool fan about it I had to endure a lecture on how it showed that Liverpool remembered their greats. After about 10min I realised that there had been a slight error in judgement by my opposite number and explained (gently of course) that it wasn't named after Mr Shankly but a certain King William of Orange... People either love Liverpool or they hate it; there seems to be no in-between. Whatever camp you fall in, any trip to Anfield should incorporate a visit to, and some reflection at, the Hillsborough Memorial which is 50yd down Anfield Road from the visitors' entrance. The names on the wreath-bedecked shrine are those of ordinary football fans, men and women who went for a day at a football match and who never came back. Which one of us doesn't know in our heart of hearts that the tragedy could have easily occurred at any ground, and that it is only by the grace of God that the memorial isn't somewhere else with our own name upon it. We shall never forget.

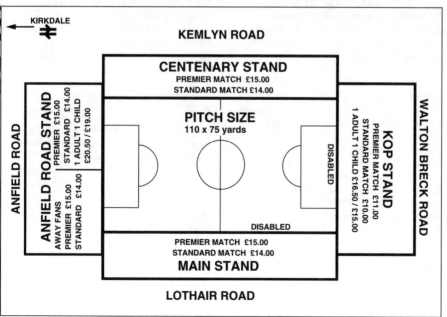

LUTON TOWN

ADDRESS: Kenilworth Road Stadium, 1 Maple Road Luton LU4 8AW

TELEPHONE No: 01582 411622

TICKET OFFICE: 01582 416976

FAX: 01582 405070

CLUBCALL: 0891 12 11 23

NICKNAME: The Hatters

RECORD ATTENDANCE: 30,069 v Blackpool FA Cup 6th Rep 4 March 1959 (W 1-0)

CLUB COLOURS:

HOME: Shirts: White and White/Blue sleeves with White/Orange trim; Shorts: Blue with White and Orange trim; Socks: Blue and White hoops with Orange trim

AWAY: Shirts: Black and Orange vertical stripes, Black collar with Orange trim; Shorts: Black with Orange stripe down the side; Socks: Black with Orange turnover

KIT SPONSORS: Universal Salvage Auctions

MANUFACTURERS: Pony

GROUND INFO

The remnants of Luton's ill-fated 'Members only' scheme are still prevalent. Tickets for the away sections of the ground are not on sale on the day of the match and are available from the visiting club's ticket office only. Membership schemes are still in place around the rest of the stadium although anyone can apparently can buy tickets for the Main Stand priced at £11.50/£5.50 on matchdays. An alternative to this is to persuade a home fan to take you into the ground as a guest.

So many people beat the ban in the past it is hopefully just a matter of time before all regulations are rescinded. Still, just to reiterate, inhabitants of Beds, Bucks, and Herts can become members without any problems. People from other areas may be refused membership; eg if you live in Wallsend don't apply for membership a fortnight before a cup-tie with Newcastle!

The away entrances in Oak Road are literally tucked in between two rows of terraced housing, and to get to this you may well find yourself having to negotiate the 'atmospheric' alleyway that is Beech Hill Path. It is right in the middle of this alleyway that the entrance to the executive boxes is situated — lucky old box holders!

The Oak Road Stand is multi-pillared, so expect to get some kind of obstruction; just keep your fingers crossed that you won't have a goal obliterated.

CAPACITY: Stands: 10,017; Terrace: Nil; Total: 10,017

AWAY FANS: Oak Road Stand: 2,257; Total: 2,257

DISABLED FACILITIES: There are 32 spaces for wheelchair-bound supporters, and admission to this area is free for disabled supporters, while helpers pay normal matchday prices. Pre-booking is essential, as it is for the match commentary facility. There are no parking facilities at the ground. However, I was advised by the police that they don't mind disabled fans being dropped off outside. This of course is especially good news if you've driven yourself to the match as presumably you can drop yourself off, then get back in your car, spend 20min driving around looking for somewhere to park and then take another enjoyable half-hour manoeuvring over the cracked paving slabs on your way back to the stadium.

PROGRAMME: £1.50. Fairly thick, and a good read for home supporters although visitors may find it a very quick read.

FANZINES:

Mad As A Hatter   50p

TRAVEL

NEAREST RAILWAY STATION:

Luton (01582 27612)

Supporters who travel by special (and sometimes those who travel on normal) services can expect on occasion to be met by the police who will take them by bus directly to the ground where they will be put straight into the stadium. The same happens at the end of games (except obviously the other way round).

BUS: Luton & District Transport (01582 404074) There are plenty of buses to the ground, and the best place to catch them is on Upper George Street (very handy for the Duke Of Clarence, see OTHER INFORMATION). Any Dunstable bus will do the trick, numbers include 20, 22, 23, 31, 37, 38, 68, 69... Dividend forecast is low.

BY CAR:

NORTH/WEST: M1 to J11. Take the A505 (signposted Luton), this brings you on to a one-way system which you should go round following signs for Dunstable (ultimately you will find yourself travelling back in the direction you have come from, but on a different road). Turn left into Oak Road and the ground is on your left.

SOUTH: M1 to J10. Follow the signs for the town centre, then turn left on to the Inner Ring Road, and keep going straight until this becomes the Dunstable Road. Continue under the railway bridge and after about 0.25 mile turn left into Oak Road for the ground.

EAST: A505 following signs for Luton and town centre until you get to the Inner Ring Road, turn left on to this, then as south.

PARKING: There is a car park by the ground, but this is for permit holders only and almost impossible to talk your way into. There are a maze of roads around the ground where you can park (if you can find a space), or alternatively try the Sainsbury's car park just off the Dunstable Road. There are further car parks by the Arndale Centre, but be prepared for a bit of a delay getting away after a match as the one-way system can get very congested.

FUTURE DEVELOPMENTS

The lease at Kenilworth Road expires in 1996 and the club has been looking to relocate. Initially a site was earmarked in Milton Keynes, but this was developed as a hockey ground. Enter Town chairman David Kohler, and his modestly-named Kohlerdome. The artist's impression of this £30 million (funding is also being received from Whitbread PLC) 20,000-seat stadium is impressive (if you like buildings which resemble giant ladybirds). It promises to be the country's first indoor stadium (apparently the FA and Football League have been approached and approve the idea of this in principle) with a removable pitch à la Pontiac Silverdome in Chicago (but which can be laid in 6-8hr rather than three days), and direct access to the M1 at J10. If it gets off the ground it will be unlike anything previously seen in Britain, but it's difficult to know how long the construction of the aforementioned beast will take — certainly as the club are only at the stage of lodging a planning application with the Borough Council, one must suppose it won't be ready by the time the lease at Kenilworth Road runs out. Expect the club to try and seek an extension on this, or possibly

even ground share (Watford would seem the obvious — if not universally popular — choice).

OTHER INFORMATION

There are no pubs in the vicinity of the ground. Nelson's Flagship is about the nearest and is tucked in the corner of Sainsbury's car park (about half-way between the town centre/station and the ground). A better bet is to go to the Duke of Clarence on Upper George Street: leave the Arndale Centre at the Burger King/C&A exit, head towards the statue and you can't miss it. The pub is open all day and can have a very good atmosphere for away fans. From here it is about 20min to the ground.

Further evidence that the club is becoming more responsive to the needs of fans is shown by the fact that golfing umbrellas can now be taken into Kenilworth Road. There are of course, a few rules to observe...

- • 1 They must not be waved around (fair enough)
- • 2 They must not be pointed at anyone (no complaints)
- • 3 They must not be put up (ah...)

It's worth noting that smoking is banned in (and under) the Main Stand; break this rule and you will be ejected.

Luton has always been an innovative club: the membership scheme; the plastic pitch. However, one thing that didn't get the publicity it deserved was the legendary incident when after a bid of £1.25 million for the club's striker Lars Elstrup the then chairmen announced that Luton was in the position where it did not have to sell their best players. Sadly for the club, Mr Elstrup then decided he wanted to go home, and headed for BK Odense who captured his heart by also offering him a job as a bank teller.

And how much did Luton get for him? (Clue: it wasn't £1.25 million).

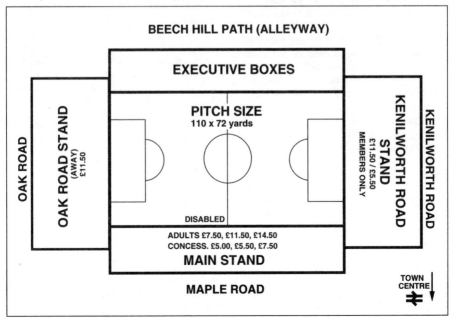

BEECH HILL PATH (ALLEYWAY)

EXECUTIVE BOXES

OAK ROAD

OAK ROAD STAND (AWAY) £11.50

PITCH SIZE
110 x 72 yards

DISABLED

ADULTS £7.50, £11.50, £14.50
CONCESS. £5.00, £5.50, £7.50

MAIN STAND

MAPLE ROAD

KENILWORTH STAND
£11.50 / £5.50
MEMBERS ONLY

KENILWORTH ROAD STAND

KENILWORTH ROAD

TOWN CENTRE

97

MANCHESTER CITY

ADDRESS: Maine Road
Moss Side
Manchester M14 7WN
TELEPHONE No: 0161 224 5000
TICKET OFFICE: 0161 226 2224
FAX: 0161 227 9418
CLUBCALL: 0891 12 11 91
NICKNAME: The Citizens
RECORD ATTENDANCE:
84,569 v Stoke FA Cup 6th 3 March 1934 (W 1-0)
There is some dispute over this fact as some claim there was a higher attendance for a postwar match involving Manchester United who had been bombed out of Old Trafford and did not return till 1949. Not surprisingly City can't support this (!) and no precise records are available, although the club did say there was a crowd of 80,771 for United's 1-1 draw with Bradford Park Avenue in 1947 which they thought was the biggest the Reds had ever got.

CLUB COLOURS:
HOME: Shirts: Sky Blue;
Shorts: White; Socks: Sky Blue
AWAY: Shirts: Red and Black Stripes;
Shorts: Black; Socks: Black

KIT SPONSORS: Brother
MANUFACTURERS: Umbro

GROUND INFO

It is difficult to know whether to applaud or abuse City for their 'Obstructed View' prices. After all there are an awful lot of grounds where there are obstructed views but where you get charged full whack, but on the other hand, who wants an obstructed view?

The Kippax and Umbro stands are very impressive from the outside, although the second of these is a bit of a monstrosity once in the ground — mind you, given the sponsors' creativity with some of the kits they have designed in the past, presumably City fans biggest fear is that they will return each season to find it painted a more gaudy colour than before. If you are a supporter who prefers grounds to be uniform then you may find Maine Road to be a disappointment. However, it does have to be said that by, apparently, designing each stand as a separate entity the club have managed to retain some degree of varying personality between each of the constructions. Whatever your standpoint, it is harder to work out the purpose of the corrugated metal between the executive boxes and the main structure.

Not everything has changed at Maine Road; 'Big Helen' the bell-ringer who sits in the corner of the North Stand, remains omnipresent. To the visitor the bell seems like an amusing and novel way of rallying the troops, but spare a thought for the person who sits in front of her week in, week out. How they have resisted the temptation to take that bell and...is a tribute to their patience and serenity.

CAPACITY: Stands: 32,000; Terrace: Nil;
Total: 32,000

AWAY FANS: North Stand Blocks S,T,U: 2,500;
Total: 2,500
The club is looking to extend this to 4,000 spaces, again all within the North Stand, if demand necessitates.

DISABLED FACILITIES: There are 48 spaces for wheelchair-bound supporters and their helpers in the Umbro Stand, together with eight spaces (plus eight helpers) in the front of the Main Stand for visitors. Permits for all 48 are given out at the start of the season but are rarely all utilised, so a call could reap a bountiful reward. Away supporters should contact their own clubs to pre-book their places. Disabled supporters are admitted free, but there is a charge for helpers.

Despite the fact that there are no matchday commentaries for the blind, the club can be rightly proud of their facilities in this area, with good clean accessible toilets and staff with an attitude that means if you want to travel on your own and you need a hand, then you should have no problems.

PROGRAMME: £1.50
Rather bizarre. On first, second and even third glance this looks to be a bit nightmarish, but when you get past the small print and the cramped layout it is actually a very good read. It is also one of the few programmes which has given space to supporters who it appears can disagree with the official club viewpoint (though not necessarily overly vehemently). The bloke who puts this together is called Dave Wallace and is the club's 'fan on the board', and while you may want to praise City for this step, my own thoughts go to his family as their home phone number is published in the programme so fans with any queries can ring him directly and be sure that someone is dealing with the issue. Absolutely top man.

FANZINES:
Blue Print	50p
Electric Blue	£1
King Of The Kippax	£1
This Charming Fan	50p

Of the four, *King Of The Kippax* is the best established and best read, with a good mix of humour and frustrated, seething, powerless anger, which we can all relate to. However, *Electric Blue* seems to be gaining more and more fans and is well written and worth the investment.

TRAVEL

NEAREST RAILWAY STATION:

Manchester Piccadilly (0161 832 8353)

BUS: Chorlton Street bus station (0161 228 7811) A 99 and a 111 drop off on Lloyd Street South which is 2min walk from the ground.

BY CAR:

NORTH: M61, M63 to J9. Take the A5103 Princess Road (signposted Manchester) and after about three miles you will see Alexandra Park on your right. Turn right at the next crossroads after the park into Claremont Road, and then right again after 0.5 mile into Maine Road.

EAST: M62 to J17. Take the A56 Bury New Road into Manchester. Follow the signs for Manchester Airport then turn left on to the A57(M) (following the signs for Birmingham). Turn left on to the A5103 Princess Road and continue for 1.5 miles, then turn left into Claremont Road (if you go past Alexandra Park you've gone too far). Turn right after 0.5 mile into Maine Road.

SOUTH: M6 to J19. Follow the A556 to Stockport till you pick up the M56. Continue to J3, then take the A5103 (signposted Manchester), then as north.

WEST: M62/M63, then as north. Alternatively M56, then as south.

NB: Maine Road is in the Moss Side area of Manchester which is not among John Carter's top-ten holiday hotspots. Some locals advise that you shoul not drive through without having locked your windows, although it is hard to tell whether this might be just a touch of paranoia/scare the 'foreigners'.

PARKING: There is some parking around Platt Lane and Platt Fields Park. To get to these continue past Maine Road and turn instead into Yew Tree Lane. At the first major crossroads turn left on to Platt Lane

for the park. There is also on-street parking, but don't expect any sympathy from the police if you return to find bits/all of your car missing. Finally, many of the local schools open their gates to cars (at a price).

FUTURE DEVELOPMENTS

The completion of the Kippax means a rest for the moment from major developments at the ground. The club instead is turning its attention to the smaller, yet equally important from a fan's point of view, issues such as more ticket windows being available, increasing staff and obtaining a new computer system, as well as the more noticeable introduction of two giant scoreboards/screens during the close season.

OTHER INFORMATION

Given the area the ground is in, most visitors will find it a more rewarding experience to trip to the city centre, rather than try to find food and drink locally, although the Parkside on Lloyd Street South isn't too bad (provided you can get in) and opposite is a good chip shop. If you do decide to wander then there are some excellent places to check out and if you are into Chinese food then there's a treat in store, as the city houses the largest Chinese population in Europe and there are some supreme restaurants around.

Probably the abiding memory that you'll take home with you is City's dislike of United which is obsessive. This is a bit of a shame as the people and fans are generally friendly and helpful, but you can't help feeling that they will not fully realise the massive potential there is at the club until they focus all their efforts on their own affairs and achievements rather than their neighbour's, in much the same way as Everton did when they stepped out of Liverpool's shadow in the mid-1980s.

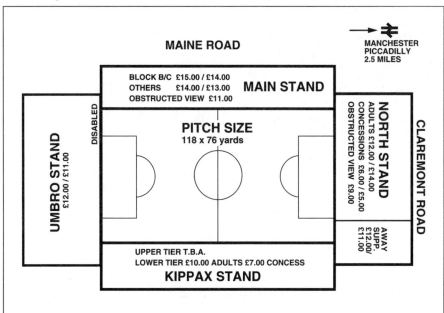

MAINE ROAD

MANCHESTER PICCADILLY 2.5 MILES

BLOCK B/C £15.00 / £14.00
OTHERS £14.00 / £13.00
OBSTRUCTED VIEW £11.00

MAIN STAND

PITCH SIZE
118 x 76 yards

DISABLED

UMBRO STAND
£12.00 / £11.00

NORTH STAND
ADULTS £12.00 / £14.00
CONCESSIONS £6.00 / £5.00
OBSTRUCTED VIEW £9.00

AWAY SUPP. £12.00/ £11.00

CLAREMONT ROAD

UPPER TIER T.B.A.
LOWER TIER £10.00 ADULTS £7.00 CONCESS

KIPPAX STAND

MANCHESTER UNITED

ADDRESS: Old Trafford
Sir Matt Busby Way
Manchester
M16 0RA
TELEPHONE No: 0161 872 1661
TICKET OFFICE: 0161 872 0199
FAX: 0161 876 5502
CLUBCALL: 0891 12 11 61
NICKNAME: The Red Devils
RECORD ATTENDANCE:
76,962 Wolves v Grimsby FA Cup Semi 25 March 1939 (w 2-1)
CLUB COLOURS:
HOME: Shirts: Red; Shorts: White; Socks: Black
AWAY: Shirts: Black; Shorts: Black; Socks: Black
THIRD: Shirts: Blue and White Stripes;
Shorts: Blue and White; Socks Blue and White
All the above are subject to change due to either any amendments in FA regulations or the need for a new left back.
KIT SPONSORS: ~~Benetton~~; Sharp
MANUFACTURERS: Umbro

GROUND INFO

FA legislation that clubs should provide visiting supporters with 3,000 spaces or 10% of capacity was apparently met head on by United who requested that the allocation to visitors of 2,000 in L-Block should be discontinued and replaced by nothing. To be fair this is due to the reduction in capacity arising from the reconstruction of the North Stand (see Future Developments).

However, this means that as a visitor/neutral you will find it very difficult to get inside the ground as any tickets not taken by season ticket/league match ticket book holders are offered to the club's members, of which there are over 125,000. If you desperately want to get into the ground then just turn up as there always seems to be a few touts around (it will cost about £45 for a run of the mill match) who the Criminal Justice Act has had precisely no effect on, but there again you didn't think it would, did you? Don't bother trying to haggle as demand always outstrips supply.

Perhaps you could spend your journey home wondering just how they get their tickets.

If you do get into the ground you will find that the hooligan elements from the 1970s and 1980s have disappeared, although, when I visited, in places they seem to have been replaced by stewards with a holier than thou attitude which is guaranteed to get one's back up in double quick time.

CAPACITY: Stands: 34,000; Terrace: Nil; Total: 34,000
AWAY FANS: Block L: 2,000; Total: 2,000
DISABLED FACILITIES: 32 spaces are available at the front of the South East section, with one helper per disabled fan admitted. There is no charge for either disabled supporters or helpers. Places tend to be pre-booked via a season ticket, and if you're planning on going you must contact the club in advance (and be mighty lucky). Manchester United Radio (1413 AM) provides a full match commentary.

PROGRAMME: £1.50
This will keep you in touch with all the comings and goings at the club (well its marketing department anyway). With its gatefold posters, kids love it, but if you're over 15 you may well not. One very interesting (if not particularly relevant) piece was 'Story of the European Cup' which ran in programmes throughout last season.

FANZINES:
Red Issue	£1
Red News	£1
United We Stand	£1
Northern Exposure	£1
Blackburn Reds	50p
Walking Down The Warwick Road	50p
Red Attitude	50p

Red Issue is the biggest selling fanzine in the country but you won't find it in WSC listing due to it being banned for its vitriolic attacks on other clubs such as Leeds/Liverpool, and also its comments on those running its own club. To be frank if you read one issue you may well love it (provided they are not getting the knives into your team), but it gets a bit 'samey' after a while. If you don't think it will be your cup of tea, then simply don't buy it, and go for the less controversial but equally good read of *United We Stand*.

TRAVEL
NEAREST RAILWAY STATION:
Old Trafford (0161 832 8353).
The station is behind the South Stand, and can be got to via Oxford Road in the city centre.

BUS: Aytown Street (0161 228 7811)
Grab any bus in the city centre which is bound for Stretford.

BY CAR:
NORTH: M61, M63 to J4. On leaving the motorway take the A5081 (signposted Manchester). Continue on the A5081 for 2.5 miles, then turn right into Sir Matt Busby Way (formerly Warwick Road), and first right into United Road.
SOUTH: M6 to J19, then follow the signs for A556 Stockport. This will lead you on to the A56 to

Altrincham. When in Altrincham continue to follow the signs for A56 Manchester for six miles, then turn left into Sir Matt Busby Way, and after 0.5 mile left again into United Road.

EAST: M62 to J17, then take the A56 Bury New Road (signposted Prestwick/Manchester Airport/Manchester) into Manchester, following the signs for 'South' and then Chester. When the road becomes Chester Road (still A56) continue for two miles then turn right into Sir Matt Busby Way and left 0.5 mile later into United Road.

NB: This route takes you through Manchester city centre. If you'd prefer to avoid this, continue along the M62 to the M63, then as north.

WEST: M62 to M63, then as north.

PARKING: There are quite a few car parks in the vicinity of the ground, the biggest being the 1,200 capacity one at Old Trafford Cricket Ground. This can be found at the opposite end of Sir Matt Busby Way to the football ground. Sadly the 900+ car park at White City has been redeveloped into a tenpin bowling centre and thus offers a much reduced capacity. There are a couple of car parks off the A56 Chester Road, and plenty of on-street opportunities around.

FUTURE DEVELOPMENTS

Demolition work started on the North Stand at the end of the season; it will be replaced by a three-tier 25,110 seater which will rise up 150ft in the air, have the largest cantilevered roof in Europe, and take the capacity at the ground to 55,300. This is scheduled to take under a year and will be ready for the European Championships in May 1996. (More excitingly, there are also rumours about the club building another tier on to the megastore, which will increase its capacity to provide merchandise to previous undreamt of levels!)

OTHER INFORMATION

Following the club's lead, the majority of pubs around the ground are either members only or expect patrons to buy a football lottery ticket before going in (funnily enough these never seem to be drawn while I've been still in the pub). A much better choice is the nearby Railway Club where you can be signed in as a guest (this is easy enough to sort out), and you can enjoy a pint for just over £1 together with a decent bite to eat. Alternatively stick to the city centre where there is an excellent choice, and grab a cheap cab to the ground.

Your first trip to Old Trafford will no doubt leave you with a whole host of feelings: disappointment when you look at the ground from the outside, and a touch of awe once inside (if you get that far). You will also probably feel disillusioned at how gullible people can be and also how street vendors and the club play on this loyalty, as well as possibly a little bit jealous of the fact that ultimately it means the club can spend £7 million on a new centre-forward. Like it or loathe it, Manchester United have developed into the Walt Disney or McDonalds of the football world; they are that big *and* they are powerful, which is fair enough... provided that their growth does not mean the death of clubs in the lower divisions, because if it does then football will pay a heavy price, and what it gets in return will not have a 'cute' 'Fred The Red' logo on it.

One final comment; without wanting to pass judgement, I would need to be very, very thirsty before I put another can of 'Champions' (to be fair to United they are changing the name of this) Cola to my lips again (8-10 days in the Sahara might just do it), although it is apparently much better in a can than it is in its draught format (!!!).

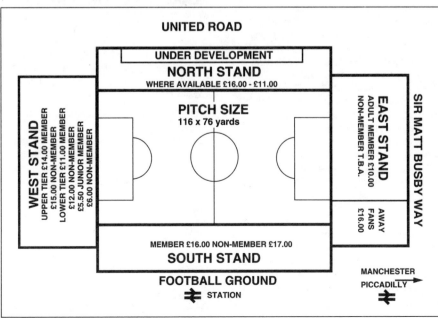

MANSFIELD TOWN

ADDRESS: Field Mill Quarry Lane
Mansfield
Notts NG18 5DA
TELEPHONE No: 01623 23567
TICKET OFFICE: 01623 23567
FAX: 01623 25014
CLUBCALL: 0891 12 13 11
NICKNAME: The Stags
RECORD ATTENDANCE:
24,467 v Nottingham Forest FA Cup 3rd 10 January 1953 (L 0-1)

CLUB COLOURS:
HOME: Shirts: Blue and Amber Stripes;
Shorts: Blue, Amber Trim; Socks: White
AWAY: Shirts: Green, Purple Trim;
Shorts: Green, Purple Trim; Socks: Purple

KIT SPONSORS:
Abacus — Lighting For Sport
MANUFACTURERS: Scholar

GROUND INFO

Away fans are admitted into the Chad Family Stand by prior arrangement only and for Stags fans wishing to use the facility there is an annual membership fee. If you are taking more than one child, contact the club for details of extra discounts available. The stand takes it name from the local paper whose motto of 'More Local Sport Than Any Other Paper — And That's The Truth!' is accurate if not particularly inspiring or surprising.

While some may grumble that the terracing at Field Mill is a bit pricey for adults, and that it is unfair to charge away fans the same as home fans as the home terracing is covered, at least Mansfield do offer the visitors concessions, and what concessions they are! £3 for a child is excellent and deserves to be praised. If the weather is bad then it is as well to try out the West Stand, which at a £2 premium for adults and children can be worth it. The good news is that the only pillars in it restrict the view of home and not away supporters.

The stewarding at the ground is good without having any airs or graces; one commendable point is that the stewards will try to help and will undertake the necessary action before a drama becomes a crisis. The police adopt a fairly no nonsense approach, which some may feel spills over into bloody-mindedness but, in truth, they will only mess fans around if the fans are perceived as causing problems, otherwise you'll be left pretty much to your own devices.

CAPACITY: Stands: 2,903; Terrace: 4,130;
Total: 7,073

The sharp-eyed among you will notice that the two figures do not add up to the total. This is because the total also includes 40 disabled spaces and the club are obviously a bit unsure whether these should be categorised as stand or terrace spaces.

AWAY FANS: Quarry Lane End Uncovered
Terrace: 947; West Stand: 500;
Total: 1,447

DISABLED FACILITIES: There are 40
spaces for disabled fans in the 'Bishop Street Disabled Stand' (the club's words not mine). Admission for disabled supporters is free, and it is £8 for helpers. Pre-booking is not required. Although there is no specific disabled parking facilities at the ground, I have heard that if you phone them up before your visit, they may be able to work something out, as the car park can get a bit cramped and is not the easiest place around which to manoeuvre a wheelchair, you can but ask. No matchday commentaries are available.

PROGRAMME: £1.20
Over 12 full pages of adverts (out of 32) plus many more half and quarter pages is fantastic news for the club's marketing department, but not so good if you are actually buying the thing for a read.

FANZINES:
Follow The Yellow Brick Road   £1
A much better read than the programme... if you can get hold of a copy.

TRAVEL
NEAREST RAILWAY STATION:
MANSFIELD !! (01302 340222 — Doncaster Enquiries) HALLELUJAH!! Yes, it's true, a railway station is due to open in Mansfield around August/September time which is about 10min walk from the ground (if that), so it's goodbye to Alfreton & Mansfield Parkway and that lovely 40min bus trip to the town centre. Let me hear you say 'Yeah!'

BUS: Rosemary Street bus station (Mansfield) (01494 441561)
Just in case anything untoward happens to the beautiful, fantastic and generally terrific new Mansfield station, you'd better know that there are four buses every hour from Alfreton & Mansfield which you should take from Station Approach.

BY CAR:
NORTH: M1 to J29, then take the A617 to Mansfield. After about 6.5 miles you will see the civic theatre on your right. Take the next right into Rosemary Street (if you drive all the way past the civic centre, you've gone too far), and follow Rosemary Street past the bus station where it becomes Belvedere Road, and then Portland Street (A60). After 0.5 mile, turn right into Quarry Lane and the ground is

300yd on the right.

EAST: A617 into Mansfield until the road is intersected by St Peters Way (dual carriageway). Turn left into St Peters Way and continue to the bottom of the road, then left again into Portland Street. Take the third right into Quarry Lane and the ground is 300yd on the right.

SOUTH/WEST: M1 to J28, then follow the A38 (Sutton Road) into Mansfield. As you approach the town centre you will pass the Victoria Hospital. Take the third right after this into Belvedere Road, then as north.

PARKING: There is a large car park by the ground which appears to be a bit of a free for all, and so there is more than a fair chance of getting blocked in. Don't expect the attendants to help, as in my experience they will be far too busy talking to their friend to worry about a silly little thing like your car! Alternatively there are a couple of superstores on the A60 (obviously not that you should use their car parks unless you intend purchasing items from them — oh no, that would be very naughty!) or a car park just off Belvedere Street, as well as some on-street parking.

FUTURE DEVELOPMENTS

There are no ground developments planned. However, the club is considering a move to a new stadium, and work may possibly have started on this in the summer, presumably aiming towards a move in 1996/7.

OTHER INFORMATION

Before the game, try what must be the expert summariser's dream, the Early Doors, which is about 200yd away. Be warned though, this themed American diner is not the cheapest place in the town at which you can have a pint, and a better bet can be the Plough (next to Safeways) or the Victoria in the town centre.

The food inside the ground is a bit iffy with my pie being a bit cold and gristly. Outside Field Mill other than a KFC, you need to take a 15min walk into the town centre for nourishment. If you do decide to stretch your legs, then check out Pie's Plaice for some rather tasty chips with gravy.

Once in the ground, you can't fail to see the Save Our Stags posters. While you can't deny the fans are fighting for a good cause, the use of the wording on some of the posters is slightly questionable, such as stating that the fans of Aldershot and Maidstone 'Let their clubs die'. I'm sure they didn't just sit there idly while it happened, and Mansfield need to be careful that while they are, quite rightly, rallying the troops, they do not inadvertently alienate the supporters of other clubs who can be a great assistance in times of hardship.

One thing you will definitely not be impressed with are the Town's ball boys, some of whom appear to be wonderfully lazy, and unless the ball goes straight to their feet will stare indolently at the teams and stand their ground, until one of the player's frustration gets the better of him and he runs and gets the ball himself.

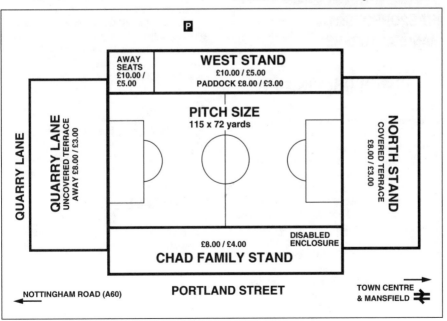

MIDDLESBROUGH

ADDRESS: Cellnet Riverside Stadium, Scott's Road Middlesbrough Cleveland TS3 6RS

Scott's Road was the address of the site office during the construction of the ground. However, a new (and as yet unnamed) road leading from Scott's Road to the stadium will be built during the summer, and it is likely that the name of this road will form the first line of the club's address.

TELEPHONE No: 01642 819659*
TICKET OFFICE: 01642 815996*
FAX: 01642 820244*
LIVEWIRE: 0891 42 42 00

* Note that these are the old Ayresome Park numbers and as such may not be transferred to the new site.

NICKNAME: Boro

RECORD ATTENDANCE:
53,596 v Newcastle Div 1 27 November 1949 (W 1-0)

CLUB COLOURS:
HOME: Shirts: Red; Shorts: White; Socks: Red
AWAY: Shirts: Jade/Hunter Green Stripes; Shorts: Green; Socks: Jade/Hunter Green

KIT SPONSORS: Dickens

MANUFACTURERS: Errea

GROUND INFO

The club quit Ayresome Park, its home for 92 years, at the (emotional) end of last season. The new ground — which at 30,000+ seats is the biggest of the new stadia opened in Britain post-Taylor — was constructed by Taylor Woodrow, and should be fully open by the end of August 1995. The design of the stadium is such that on three sides it is joined by corner stands, (North, South, East) and the West Stand is a separate construction, much as an old style Main Stand. The name of the new ground, Riverside Stadium, was chosen by the club's fans in a referendum at the end of last season. (The 'Cellnet' addition was a financial decision!)

The West Stand is a two-level construction, will hold just under 9,000 and also contain 'support services' (which apparently will be over three levels??) including dressing rooms, club shop, executive boxes, hospitality areas, press room, etc.

Surprisingly, given the inclemency of the local weather, one of the things that those involved with the construction of the stadium were keen to promote was the fact that they undertook a 'sun study' which involved establishing the latitude and longitude of the ground and daily sun paths generated, which led to

translucent panels being introduced into the roof on the South and West Stands. Hopefully this will see an end to those dreadful November days when you can hardly see to drive your car home having spent 90min squinting into the ferociously hot sun.

One thing that doesn't look like changing is the fact that visiting supporters will still be next to home supporters, and although things did improve during the 1994/5 season, all too often away fans in the old South East Corner were still on occasion subject to 90min of having their parentage and sexual preferences queried (almost inevitably this used to be by really young fans in the East Stand whose parents would be with them laughing along at junior's exploits).

CAPACITY: Stands: 30,500; Terrace: Nil; Total: 30,500

AWAY FANS: Nothing confirmed at the time of going to press, although this is likely to be around 3,000 places in the South End of the ground.

DISABLED FACILITIES: There will be over 200 viewing positions/seats available for disabled supporters which will be sited at pitch level in all stands, at the hospitality level in the West Stand and at high level in the South and East Stands (a bit different from Ayresome Park where there were 30 disabled places stuffed in the northeast corner of the ground). The club has in the past provided matchday commentaries and designated parking facilities and there is no cause to doubt that this will still be the case. Boro do charge for both disabled supporters' and helpers' tickets, and this is likely to remain the case at the new stadium. Get in touch with the club direct to find out just how much closer to your visit.

Although in the past it hasn't always been necessary to pre-book spaces, the club recommends that you do so. As it is likely that it will take the club a while to bed down into the new stadium, I would not leave anything to chance and get in touch with them up to one calendar month before your proposed visit.

PROGRAMME: £1.50
A very good programme for home fans, well put together with plenty of information stats and good overall readability. However, away fans may find it too insular, concentrating as it does on everything Boro, rather than football/divisional issues in general.

FANZINES:
Fly Me To The Moon £1
FMTTM is not the thickest of fanzines, but comes out regular as clockwork, and probably will have more of interest to your average non-Boro fan than the official offering, especially if you can live without the standard two pages of fairly obvious comment about 'today's visitors' (a significant portion of which is taken up with a 'they played for both clubs' section).

NEAREST RAILWAY STATION:

Middlesbrough (0191 232 6262 - Newcastle Enquiries) This apparently is the nearest 'busiest' station according to the exceedingly helpful British Rail assistant who further helped the cause by adding, 'but there might be a nearer one... possibly'. Further investigation indicated there wasn't, and at just over 0.75 mile away from the ground it is easily walkable.

BUS: Middlesbrough bus station (01642 244166)

BY CAR:

SOUTH: Take A19, to A66. Head towards Middlesbrough on the A66 (M'boro By-Pass) at the second major roundabout take the first exit then bear right into Bridge Street (this is signposted town centre, and the opposite way would take you on to the B1272). This becomes Bridge Street West, Dock Street, and then Scott's Road off which is the ground.

WEST: A66, then as south.

NORTH: Either — A19, A1032 (Cross river by Tees Bridge), then left on to the A66. Take the first exit at the next major roundabout and bear right into Bridge Street, then as south.

Or — A178/A1046, cross the Tees by the Transporter Bridge. Take the second left on to Commercial Street which leads to Scott's Road and the ground.

NB: If you have any hassle just head for MIDDLE-HAVEN DOCKS and you can't miss it.

PARKING: There will be a large number (but I'm afraid exactly how many or even a rough estimate is naturally a secret) of parking spaces at the ground. However, it is likely that these will be permit holders only so try and find a street to park on. City centre car parks 20 min walk.

FUTURE DEVELOPMENTS

Expect a period while bits and pieces get finished off, and the club get bedded down, but apart from that obviously nothing major.

OTHER INFORMATION

From the 'You Can't Please All The People All The Time' Department. It was reported in April 1995 that the club lost sponsorship with British Gas valued at £10,000 a season because the new stadium was constructed out of German materials rather than from steel from the Lackenby Plant at Redcar, five miles from the ground.

However, possibly more upset by the move would have been the chap who had the red paint franchise at the ground, as the Ayresome Park motto could have been 'if it stands still, paint it red'. It actually made you wonder if the club wanted to play in a different colour kit.

Given that the club have upset one of the local industries, it might have been considered suspicious that during the construction of the stadium a gun shell was discovered. However, after due consideration it was identified that this was nothing worse (??) than a World War 2 navy shell, filled with concrete.

Any 'interesting fact' fans will no doubt be fascinated to know that the first ever half-time scoreboard was introduced by Boro in 1902, and the first ever score that was shown on it was when the crowd at a reserve match were informed that the first team were leading in their away match. Zzzzzz...

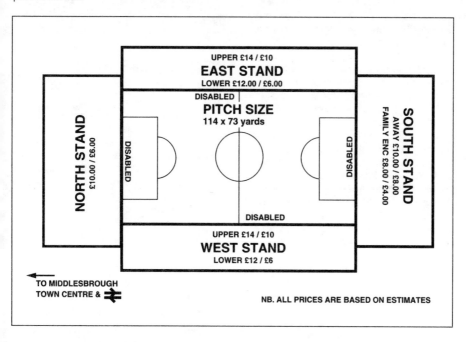

NB. ALL PRICES ARE BASED ON ESTIMATES

MILLWALL

ADDRESS: The Den
Zampa Road
London SE16 3 LN

TELEPHONE No: 0171 232 1222
TICKET OFFICE: 0171 231 9999
FAX: 0171 231 3663
CLUBCALL: 0891 400 300
NICKNAME: The Lions
RECORD ATTENDANCE:
48,672 v Derby FA Cup 5th 20 February 1937 (W 2-1)
At The New Den: 20,093 v Arsenal FA Cup 3rd
10 January 1994 (L 0-1)

CLUB COLOURS:
HOME: Shirts: Blue with White Sleeves;
Shorts: Blue; Socks: Blue
AWAY: Shirts: Green and White Halves;
Shorts: Green; Socks: Green

KIT SPONSORS: Captain Morgan Rum
MANUFACTURERS: Asics

GROUND INFO

To call the new ground the 'Ibrox of England' may be a little over the top, but it certainly seems to have been modelled along these lines, and is a very impressive stadium with facilities to match. Prior to the game, at half-time, and again at full-time, you can have a beer and watch TV. In fact the club are aiming for a situation whereby fans turn up at 11am and go home at 7pm (except for evening matches naturally) and thereby ease the five to three congestion that occurs at many grounds. (The extra income the club earns from the fans drinking inside the stadium has nothing to do with it then?) The only minor criticism is that it is slightly cramped for leg-room.

Don't be fooled into thinking that the nice new stadium means nice new fans. True, some of the supporters feel a little out of place having been used to the comforts of the old Den and seem a little ill at ease and unhappy with their new surroundings, but when you come down to it the atmosphere can be just as hostile and intimidating; and incidentally, unlike the old ground where you had a fair idea of where you were most likely to avoid grief, in the new ground there isn't that kind of identity! (My first visit there was straight from work with me in a suit with a briefcase, and I ended up in a different section to the one I thought I was going in. I blended in like a chameleon in a kilt — a very relaxing night that was!) Stick to your own sections in all but the most important of circumstances.

Having warned you, it must be said that Millwall is not a war zone; sadly for 'big' matches there may be

trouble, but that is true of a lot of grounds. For the vast majority of people, going to the new Den is no more 'dangerous' than going to any other ground, and it is a lot more comfortable than a lot of other places.

CAPACITY: Stands: 20,146; Terrace: Nil;
Total: 20,146

AWAY FANS: North Stand: 4,000; Total: 4,000
If the away team does not have a large following this may be restricted to the East Side of the North Stand which has a capacity of 1,000.

DISABLED FACILITIES: There are 78 places in the West Stand Lower Tier, with one helper admitted per disabled fan. Disabled fans are admitted free of charge, with helpers paying £10.

Commentaries for the blind are available. If you wish to avail yourself of the facilities, the club would prefer that you pre-book, at which time you can also sort yourself out a parking space.

PROGRAMME: £1.70
FANZINES:
The Lion Roars   £1
No-One Likes Us   £1
Worth buying if only for their latest comments (which tend to be none too complimentary) about one Mr Danny Baker.

TRAVEL

NEAREST RAILWAY STATION:
South Bermondsey (0171 928 5100)
This is about 0.5 mile from the ground and has a very frequent service to and from London Bridge.

NEAREST TUBE STATION:
Surrey Quays (East London Line)

BUS: London Transport (0171 222 1234)
The tube station is about 1.5 miles from the stadium, and the trip takes you under some very spooky railway arches around which seems to hang a permanent fog, and out of which you can easily imagine someone belting out screaming that Jack the Ripper had struck again. As such, BR is probably the best choice of public transport.

BY CAR:
NORTH: Leave the M1 at J2 and follow the City/A1 signs then pick up signs first for Shoreditch, Whitechapel, and finally 'Ring Road'. Continue over Tower Bridge and take the first exit at the roundabout on to the A2. Follow the A2 New Kent Road and after four miles turn left at the Canterbury Arms pub into Ilderton Road, then follow Surrey Canal Road into Zampa Road for the ground.
SOUTH: A20, A21 into London. At New Cross follow the signs for City/Westminster into Kender Street, and

follow Avonley Road till you get to Surrey Canal Road, then as north.

WEST: From M4 follow the South Circular (A205) following signs for Clapham, City, A3, then Camberwell, New Cross, Rochester until you get to the junction with Kender Street (which is on the left). Turn into Kender Street, then as south.

EAST: A2 to New Cross, then as south

PARKING: There is car parking available in Juno Way by the ground; alternatively there is some street parking available.

FUTURE DEVELOPMENTS

Nothing planned.

OTHER INFORMATION

With the facilities offered inside the ground, there isn't much need to stray further afield. If you prefer the pleasures of the pub, then the Cliftonville is one of the closest, although there are plenty to choose from. As with all grounds there are some that are probably best worth avoiding if you've got colours on, but suffice to say, I didn't wander into every one with a replica top on to see what the reaction would be. The food inside the ground is well above average — as are the prices charged for it.

Without wanting to sound hackneyed and clichéd, the club has done a lot of work in promoting its role in the community, and a family spirit amongst the fans. To a degree this has worked: everybody seems to know everybody else, and it can be argued that this is what a football club should be all about, local people supporting their local team. As I said before Millwall isn't a no-go zone, and shouldn't be considered as such (after all, it is ages since the fans threw a grenade on to the pitch, and even then it was a dud), and the new stadium is well worth a visit.

Finally, as if the rest of the football world needed any proof that Millwall are a bunch of Godless heathens, it comes as little surprise to report that the first ever English Sunday match was played at The Den in 1974, against those other well-known sinners, Fulham.

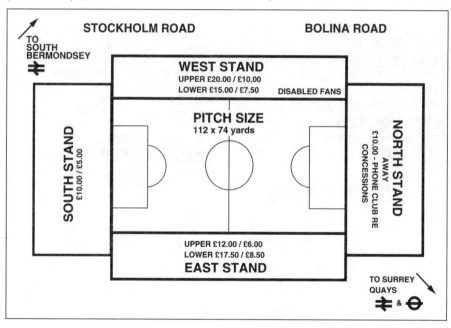

STOCKHOLM ROAD   BOLINA ROAD

TO SOUTH BERMONDSEY

WEST STAND
UPPER £20.00 / £10.00
LOWER £15.00 / £7.50   DISABLED FANS

PITCH SIZE
112 x 74 yards

SOUTH STAND
£10.00 / £5.00

NORTH STAND
£10.00 - PHONE CLUB RE
AWAY
CONCESSIONS

UPPER £12.00 / £6.00
LOWER £17.50 / £8.50
EAST STAND

TO SURREY QUAYS

NEWCASTLE UNITED

ADDRESS: St James' Park
Newcastle upon Tyne
NE1 4ST

TELEPHONE No: 0191 232 8361

TICKET OFFICE: 0191 261 1571

FAX: 0191 232 9875

CLUBCALL: 0891 12 11 90

NICKNAME: The Magpies

RECORD ATTENDANCE:

68,386 v Chelsea Div 1 3 September 1930 (W 1-0)
The club holds two records for attendances in England; these being the highest attendance for a friendly match — 44,480 v Liverpool in 1948 — and the highest attendance for an abandoned match — 63,480 v Swansea in the FA Cup in 1953, which was halted after 8min play.

And should you ever think you have a hard time at work, spare a thought for whichever poor soul had to tell that lot 'No Refunds'.

CLUB COLOURS:

HOME: Shirts: Black and White Stripes; Shorts: Black; Socks: Black
AWAY: Shirts: Blue; Shorts: Blue; Socks: Blue

KIT SPONSORS: Newcastle Brown Ale — Scottish and Newcastle Breweries

MANUFACTURERS: Adidas

GROUND INFO

Last season well over 90% of the available spaces went to season ticket holders, and as these were naturally on offer initially to existing holders, it has become somewhat of an 'inheritance' to have a relative with a season ticket (although whether the actual holders can sleep soundly with the knowledge that half their kin are probably planning their untimely demise is another thing). There have been some mutterings about the club pricing themselves out of the market (though they are certainly not the most expensive club to watch in the Premier), and with the extended capacity in 1995/6 it may be possible that the odd seat will be available in advance, if not on the day. However, for the most part expect it to be a struggle to gain admission (especially if the club start the season well), and over the last couple of seasons if you haven't had a ticket it has been as well to stay at home. If you happen to have a spare ticket on the other hand then spend a pleasant week or so leading up to the match deciding who you want to be forever in your debt, and then offer it to them.

St James' transformation is bewildering, and if you haven't been there for a few years be prepared to be stunned when you get inside. It is quite easy to see

that the £29 million the club is reputed to have spent in renovating the place has been well invested. Mind you, your enjoyment of the ground's architectural splendour may be somewhat diminished if you are in the back row of the Leazes or the Gallowgate and you can only make out the pitch as a green blur

CAPACITY: Stands: 38,000; Terrace: Nil; Total: 38,000

Although there had been some talk of the ground eventually holding 46,000 the figure above is apparently the final capacity, and represents an increase of 2,358 on 1994/5 capacity.

AWAY FANS: Sir John Hall Stand
East Corner: 813; Total: 813

With the new regulations regarding away fans, who it is now stated should be given 10% of the ground's capacity or 3,000 seats, it would seem that the above is likely to change, although my queries about how Newcastle are going to comply with this regulation were met by a rather brusque 'Don't know' and a statement that the club is waiting for the official ruling to come through (??). It may be that a return to the East Side of the Gallowgate is forthcoming, but wait and see. In a way you can't help feeling sorry for the club if it is forced to comply with this rule as it will mean that in effect the last amount of rebuilding in the ground has only resulted in it securing an extra 171 places for their own fans (based on 38,000 — 3,000 away compared to 35,642 — 813 away 1994/5).

DISABLED FACILITIES: There are spaces for 116 disabled fans. Admission is half the standard price for wheelchair-bound supporters and full price for helpers. However, to get one of these places is like chasing the elusive pot of gold, with the majority being allocated on a seasonal basis, but you can always contact the club to try and obtain a place. Match commentaries for the visually impaired are also available.

PROGRAMME: £1.50

Fluctuates from excellent to very parochial from one week to another.

FANZINES:

The Mag	£1
The Number Nine	50p
Talk Of The Toon	£1
Half Mag Half Biscuit	£1
The Giant Awakes	£1
Toon Army News	£1
United	50p

A veritable feast of literature for supporters of the team. *The Mag* is far and away the best of the bunch, well put together (though an irritating A4 size), with a good blend of humour, reportage and, where necessary, tub thumping. The others are much of a muchness, although it is probably fair to warn that the last copy of *United* I saw (admittedly about 18 months ago) was certainly in questionable taste in places.

TRAVEL

NEAREST RAILWAY STATION:
Central station (0191 232 6262)

NEAREST METRO STATION:
St James' (behind Gallowgate)

BUS: Gallowgate or Haymarket bus stations (0191 232 4211)

BY CAR:
SOUTH: A1(M). Turn left on to the A6115 (signposted Felling). Straight over at the first roundabout, then right where it is signposted Tyne Bridge (A6127). Cross over the bridge (according to Geordies 'always a thrilling moment') then left at the next roundabout into Mosley Street. Take the third right into Groat Market and go straight on over the next two roundabouts. After the second of these turn left into Leazes Park Road and left again into Strawberry Place.

NORTH: A1 into Newcastle and follow the signs for Hexham until you get to Percy Street. Turn right into Leazes Park Road and right again into Strawberry Place.

WEST: A69 into Newcastle leading on to the West Road, continue until you reach Newcastle General Hospital. Immediately after the hospital there are some traffic lights; turn left at these into Brighton Grove, then right after 0.25 mile into Studley Terrace. After a further 0.25 mile this merges with Barrack Road. Left at next roundabout (still called Barrack Road) and the ground is on the left.

EAST: A189 to A193 (signposted Newcastle City Centre). After you cross the motorway (A6127) turn left into Haymarket (by the Metro Station). This becomes Percy Street, then as north.

PARKING: There are at least half a dozen car parks within 0.25 mile of the ground (the most convenient being the one on Barrack Road) and two in St James' Park itself, directly behind the ground.

There is limited on-street parking but it's probably best to stick with the off-street!

FUTURE DEVELOPMENTS
None.

OTHER INFORMATION
There is a popular myth that Geordies are brilliant sports and love to see skill. This may be true, but don't travel up thinking that if your team should whack the Toon 4-0 (!!?) and you go into a pub with your replica top on you will be warmly congratulated on your performance. If you are an away fan, avoid pubs like the Strawberry which are just by the ground and instead stick to the city centre. It might also be wise to find something to eat in Newcastle, as inside the ground the food is OK but nothing more.

One of the best things about St James' is that the development has done nothing to dampen the noise and passion of the fans, which on a first visit is almost frightening to witness, it is so intense. Perhaps the worst thing is that the club seems to have forgotten that only a couple of years ago they were getting about 12,000 for some games, and as the prices rise the people who have supported the club through thick and thin are in danger of being squeezed out in order to make more and more profit.

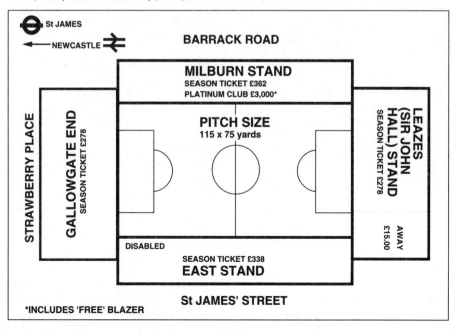

NORTHAMPTON TOWN

ADDRESS: Sixfields
Upton Way
Northampton NN5 4EG
TELEPHONE No: 01604 757773
TICKET OFFICE: 01604 588338
FAX: 01604 751613
SOCCERLINE: 0839 66 44 77
NICKNAME: The Cobblers
RECORD ATTENDANCE:
24,523 v Fulham Div 1 23 April 1966 (L 2-4)
At Sixfields — 7,461 v Barnet Div 3
15 October 1994 (D 1-1)

CLUB COLOURS:
HOME: Shirts: Claret; Shorts: White; Socks: Claret
AWAY: Shirts: White; Shorts: Claret; Socks: White

SHIRT SPONSORS: Lotto UK Ltd
MANUFACTURERS: Lotto UK Ltd

GROUND INFO

Sixfields is a massive improvement on the County Ground, but let's be honest, a shoe box would have been a massive improvement on the County Ground! Away fans are sited in the South Stand which offers a decent unrestricted view. It is worth noting that you are expected to use the toilets by the West Stand, and if you happen to be sitting in the east side of the stand, you will have to walk all the way across to the other side of the ground rather than use the ones 20ft away by the corner of the East and South Stand, and quite right too. Good honest hard-working home supporters don't want you polluting their urinals, you never know what they might catch! The South Stand mirrors the North Stand where the home fans are in all but one key area and that is concessions. Although there are no general concessions for away fans, the club's policy is to encourage better use of its family enclosures in the East and West Stands and away fans are welcome to take advantage of the concessions available in these areas. For 1995/6, the prices for the West Stand family enclosure are: Adult £7.50; Tandem (ie adult and one child) £10; Tricycle (ie adult and two children) £12; and, concession £4.

One can but salute the Northampton commercial department, which has managed to get the original family enclosure at Sixfields, which is just about as far away from the seaside as you could get, sponsored by Butlins. There are now two family enclosures, one in both the East and West Stands.

CAPACITY: Stands: 7,650; Terrace: Nil;
Total: 7,650 (all seated)

AWAY FANS: South Stand: 944; East Stand: 432*; Total: 1,376
* If sufficient demand (overflow area).

DISABLED FACILITIES: There are 80 disabled spaces which are sited in all areas of the ground, including the South Stand. Also available is a raised concourse on the East Stand which is provided with a lift and assistance from stewards. As from the 1995/6 season there will be a combined price of £8 for admission for one wheelchair-bound fan and one helper (£4 for the wheelchair-bound fan and £4 for the helper). If you want to go to the match on your own, expect to pay for admission. The club prefer places to be pre-booked, as they do for match commentaries which will also become available for the 1995/6 season. There are 70 specially designated disabled parking spaces for which you must pre-book, although if you don't there is enough general parking space for this not to be a problem.

PROGRAMME: £1.50
A million times better in 1994/5 than the previous season's effort, which was one of the worst in the league. Sadly this improvement still only leaves you with an average take it or leave it publication. However, at least they are moving in the right direction which hopefully bodes well for this season, and it should be half-decent by the turn of the century.

FANZINES:
What A Load Of Cobblers   £1

TRAVEL
NEAREST RAILWAY STATION:
Castle station: (01908 370883 — Milton Keynes Enquiries)

BUS: Greyfriars bus station (01604 751431)
As well as the normal services (including a 28 from the railway station), there is a shuttle service (100) on match days from the County Ground to the new stadium. In addition Park and Ride Service B drops off two minutes from the ground.

BY CAR:
NORTH/WEST: M1 to J16. Take A45 (signposted Northampton/Duston). After approx. 3.25 miles there is a roundabout; take the fourth exit on to Upton Way for the ground.
SOUTH: M1 to J15a, then A43 (signposted Northampton) to A45 Northampton Ring Road. Bear left (signposted Daventry) at second roundabout, then take first exit into Upton Way and the ground is immediately on the left.
EAST: Either A43 or A428 to A45. Once on the A45, follow signs for Daventry until you pass the Rugby Ground (Franklin Gardens). At the second roundabout

after this, take the first exit into Upton Way for the ground.

No matter which way you are coming from, the ground is very well signposted.

PARKING: There is free on-site parking at Sixfields with six overflow car parks to take the strain on busy days.

This a major step forward from the club's County Ground days when fans were forced to use the maze of nearby streets, and better still, the club appear to have avoided the problems encountered at other purpose-built stadiums such as Walsall, where the lack of exit roads means at least a half-hour wait before getting away.

FUTURE DEVELOPMENTS

None.

OTHER INFORMATION

Behind the North Stand is a huge grass bank which if, for whatever reason, you can't get in to the ground itself, offers a decent free view of most of the pitch. However, where it really comes into its own is during the 10min period 2.55-3.05 when late-arriving fans

have the opportunity to use it as a shortcut to the ground. Inevitably, a large proportion of those who go for it end up somersaulting, bouncing and sliding down its muddy sides… splendid entertainment.

The ground forms part of a leisure complex, part of which is the Washington Square pub, which is designed like a Swiss chalet, thus making it blend right into its alpine surroundings. Away fans are welcomed, but it does get busy on matchdays. For food there is a McDonalds, Little Chef, Burger King, American Diner and Deep Pan Pizza by the ground, as well as an MGM Multiplex for that oh so reasonable popcorn. Inside, away fans have a metal table which has a very limited choice, but from which the tea is on the hot side of warm, and where you will get served fairly quickly.

All clubs, especially those in the lower divisions, have their unsung heroes, but at Northampton they seem to have more than most. The best thing about the club is that even in its darkest days it always had time for the fans, both of the home and away variety. If you have a problem, let the club know and it will try to help out. Given this attitude one can almost (but not quite) forgive it for its lack of a general concessions policy, and hope that 1995/6 brings another trophy to stick alongside the cup on display which commemorates 'The Cobblers' historic 3-2 victory at Shrewsbury on 8 May 1993 ensuring their league status'. (I don't think winning it got them a place in Europe though.)

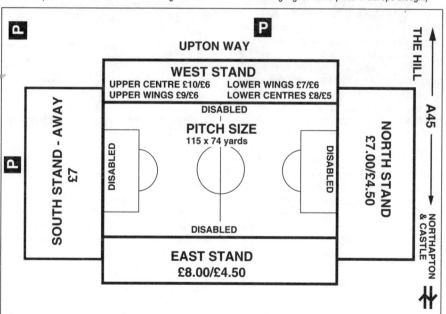

NORWICH CITY

ADDRESS: Carrow Road
Norwich
Norfolk NR1 1JE
TELEPHONE No: 01603 760760
TICKET OFFICE: 01603 761661
FAX: 01603 665510
CITY LINE: 0891 101 500
NICKNAME: The Canaries
RECORD ATTENDANCE:
43,984 v Leicester FA Cup 6th 30 March 1963 (L 0-2)
CLUB COLOURS:
HOME: Shirts: Yellow; Shorts: Green; Socks: Yellow
AWAY: Shirts: Tartan; Shorts: Blue with Tartan trim;
Socks: White
KIT SPONSORS:
Norwich & Peterborough Building Society
MANUFACTURERS: Mitre

GROUND INFO

The away section of the South Stand looks a bit tatty but at least it does offer a good view of the pitch and has plenty of leg room. To be honest there aren't that many spaces for away supporters, and although this can be extended if required, this doesn't always happen. If you haven't got a ticket, then try the Barclay End which is both cheap and safe enough.

Inside the ground away fans have the benefit of what can be best described as a train waiting room. This comprises a food serving area and a couple of TVs. Whilst not being fantastic it is a hell of a lot more than you get at some places. The pies in the ground (Breckland Farm) are in the running for the tastiest you will come across, being deep and well-filled with meat. The only trouble is that the club never seems to have them heated enough so when you bite into them they have a bit of a nasty tepid feel. The hot drinks are average in both heat and taste.

CAPACITY: Stands: 21,836; Terrace: Nil;
Total: 21,836

AWAY FANS: South Stand F Block: 334;
South Stand G Block: 692; South
Stand H Block: 715; Total: 1,741

DISABLED FACILITIES: There are 115 spaces for wheelchair-bound fans in a purpose-built area by the South Stand, with both disabled fans and their helpers being admitted free of charge. Pre-booking of this facility is not compulsory but the club does advise it. If you do book a place, have a word with the club while you are on the phone and it will also sort out a parking space for you. There are no official facilities

for match commentaries for the blind, but all Norwich's home matches are commentated on the medium wave, frequency 1602.

PROGRAMME: £1.50
On first sight the programme looks to be a cracker; there are plenty of general interest items and something about the combination of yellow and green makes it very appealing to the eye. When you actually start to read it though it somehow fails to deliver the goods. For the life of me I cannot pinpoint why this is, but after 10min or so I almost felt as if I couldn't be bothered with it. Having said all that, it is still better than the majority of Premier League programmes. (I seem to keep contradicting myself here, but when you buy it you may well see what I mean.)

FANZINES:
The Citizen	50p
Liverpool Are On The Tele Again	£1
A Fine City	50p
Ferry Cross The Wensum	50p
I Can Drive A Tractor	50p

Rakes of fanzines, but often the sellers aren't prominent around the ground. *A Fine City* is apparently produced in that well known Norfolk stronghold, Darlington! *ICDAT* was new in 1994/5 and got fairly good reviews from home fans although I've never seen a copy. *The Citizen* and *Liverpool* are both well above average, with *Ferry* nipping closely at their heels.

TRAVEL
NEAREST RAILWAY STATION:
Norwich (0.5 mile) (01603 632055)
BUS:
Eastern Counties Omnibus Co Ltd (01603 788890)
Your trip to Carrow Road can be fairly dire if you are relying on public transport, especially for night matches when the vast majority of 'last trains to' are before 9pm. Equally, there are no buses that drop off outside the ground, although this is apparently under review.

BY CAR:
NORTH: A140. Turn left on to the A47 Outer Ring Road (signposted Yarmouth). Whilst on the A47 the road changes names as follows — Mile Cross Lane, Chartwell Road, Mousehold Lane, Heartease Lane and Harvey Lane. At the bottom of Harvey Lane turn right into Thorpe Road. After 0.3 mile turn left into Carrow Road. Cross the railway and continue along Carrow Road as it bears right, and the ground is on the left.
SOUTH: A11. Turn right on to the A140 and continue for one mile until you get to the junction with the A146 at which you should turn left (signposted Norwich). Continue for a further mile then turn on to the A1054. After 0.25 mile you will see Carrow Road, into which you should turn, the ground being 0.25 mile further on.

WEST: A47 Outer Ring Road (signposted Yarmouth) and continue along this road until it becomes Martineau Lane. At the roundabout with the A146 take the second exit into Bracondale, then first right into King Street and the second right into Carrow Road. Go over Carrow Bridge (crossing the River Wensum) and the ground is on the right.

EAST: A47 into Norwich, then as north.

Actually finding Carrow Road can be one of life's great frustrations. In my experience, if you ask a passer-by for directions they will either look at you very blankly, as if the very fact that Norwich had a football team had escaped them, or, and I'm positive this is part of some mean-spirited plot hatched by the people of Norfolk that is designed to keep the city free of visiting supporters, they will send you in the exact opposite direction to the one you want. To make matters worse, there is a McDonalds that everyone uses as a point of reference in their instructions, but which I'm sure must be on castors because no matter which way you are facing the first phrase that you'll always hear is 'No, my booty, you want to be on the other side of the road, then carry on till you see the McDonalds...'. After about the 10th attempt I can only suggest you abandon your vehicle and get a cab!

PARKING: Carrow Road is not in the nicest part of the city so you may be best off avoiding street parking in the immediate vicinity of the ground. Nearest car park to the ground is the Riverside which is opposite the City Stand, but it can be tricky to get out of. A better bet can be found off Thorpe Road towards the city centre — once you've crossed the Wensum, take the second left into Mountergate, and there is a multi-storey with 750 spaces on your right.

NB: If you are going to an all-ticket match at Carrow Road without a ticket, avoid Riverside as a police checkpoint is set up at the top of the road leading from it, and anyone without a ticket will not be allowed to get through.

FUTURE DEVELOPMENTS

Nothing of any significance, but if the club find they have a few quid to spare they could do with sprucing up the South Stand a bit.

OTHER INFORMATION

If you are looking for watering holes, or places of worship, then Norwich is for you with its claim of having a different pub for every day of the year, and a different church for every Sunday. The nearest pubs are the Clarence Harbour (which is by a decent chip shop) on Kerrison Road, and the Kingsway on the corner of Carrow Road, but if you have the chance to go into the city centre, there are some great places to discover.

There are plenty of stewards and police around the ground, the majority of whom are laid back and helpful. However, one can always find an exception, and legend tells of a steward refusing to let a fan (away of course) take a carton of orange into the ground as they might 'Urinate in it and throw it at someone'. Words fail me!

Hopefully 1995/6 will see the re-emergence of the PA blasting out a quick burst of 'Another One Bites The Dust' when Norwich score. Sadly this didn't always happen last season (the music that is, even Norwich managed one or two goals). I say sadly, as while it signified that you'd let one in, at least you had the consolation of seeing the Norwich fans starting to do the Gladiator hand-movements, then remembering where they were and looking all embarrassed about the whole affair.

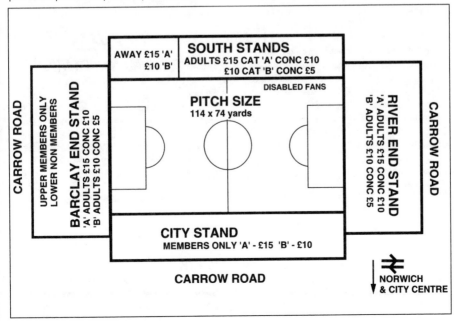

113

NOTTINGHAM FOREST

ADDRESS: The City Ground
Nottingham
NG2 5FJ

TELEPHONE No: 0115 952 6000
TICKET OFFICE: 0115 952 6002
FAX: 0115 952 6003
CLUBCALL: 0891 12 11 74
0115 952 6016

The second of these numbers gives match and ticket news, and rather disgracefully is available at standard rates, as opposed to the 39/49p a minute premium rate. There must be the question as to whether the club could possibly face a charge of disrepute for openly displaying an attitude of not squeezing fans dry; scandalous!

NICKNAME: The Reds, Forest
RECORD ATTENDANCE:
49,945 v Man United Div 1 28 October 1967 (W 3-1)

CLUB COLOURS:
HOME: Shirts: Red; Shorts: White; Socks: Red
AWAY: Shirts: Yellow; Shorts: Blue; Socks: Yellow

KIT SPONSORS: Labatt's
MANUFACTURERS: Umbro

GROUND INFO

The opening of the Trent Stand during the 1994/5 season saw the completion of the conversion to an all-seater stadium, and if your memories are of the tatty old City Ground of the 1980s, then you are in for a pleasant surprise. The Bridgford Stand is comfortable enough and offers an unrestricted view, though if you are seated in the lower tier watch out for occasional cups of tea heading your way from above.

If you are walking to the city after a match it is as well to walk round via the Colwick Road rather than opting for the pathway behind the Trent Stand which can get very congested. However, if you do choose to go this way then put your mind at rest, the locals are far less likely to give you a compulsory swimming lesson by tossing you into the Trent than they were in football's real bad old days.

CAPACITY: Stands: 30,569; Terrace: Nil;
Total: 30,569

AWAY FANS: Bridgford Stand Lower Tier:
4,800; Total: 4,800

This is the maximum allocation in this stand, which may be sectioned if there is not sufficient demand. You can't complain about the allocation, although for some matches there do appear to be difficulties getting through the turnstiles which don't always seem to be plentiful enough, and if you're not careful you can end up missing the first five minutes. NB: Away tickets can be purchased from the outlets by the Executive Stand, but once again expect to queue.

DISABLED FACILITIES: There are 37 spaces in the Bridgford Stand, with disabled fans being admitted free of charge and helpers paying £14. The shortage of spaces mean that it can be a bit difficult to get in, you must contact the club to (try to) pre-book a space, and at the same time you can arrange a parking place. The club do not provide match commentaries for the blind.

PROGRAMME: £1.50
Tries hard but fails to come up with the goods. Mention this to a seller and you may find yourself on the end of a 'Yes, but it's one of the cheapest in the Premier' type comment. Hmmmm!

FANZINES:

The Tricky Tree	50p
The Almighty Brian	70p
Forest Forever	50p
Garibaldi	£1

The Tricky Tree is an excellent read which will not only outlast the programme but is also much more interesting than it. In the past allegations have been levelled at it from other fanzines that because it was available from the club shop it was toothless. From my own experience I have always found that it is prepared to be controversial if it has to, but the links with the club do mean that it gets its hands on some important information for fans, and whilst it would be naïve to say that it helps shape the way the club think, at least they get their opinions across. Well worth buying.

TRAVEL

NEAREST RAILWAY STATION:
Nottingham Midland (01332 257000 — Derby Enquiries)

When leaving the ground you will see a massive sign apparently pointing the way to the station. Ignore this as it is directing you in the exact opposite way to the one which you want to be going in. Presumably the sign is there to persuade away fans that the route march that the Nottinghamshire Police are about to take them on is really in their interest (and if you want to see the back streets of Nottingham then they're right, it is!).

BUS: Victoria Centre bus station (0115 924 0000)

BY CAR:
NORTH: M1 to J26, then the A610 into Nottingham until you see signs for Melton Mowbray and Trent Bridge. Follow these signs on to the A606 and continue until you cross the river. Then take the second left

into Radcliffe Road and the second left again for Colwick Road.

EAST: A52 Radcliffe Road into Nottingham following the signs for Trent Bridge. As you approach the City/Trent Bridge there is an intersection of six roads; bear left (still Radcliffe Road), then take the next right for Colwick Road.

SOUTH: M1 to J24. Take the A453 (signposted Nottingham South) and continue into Nottingham following signs for Trent Bridge (do not cross the river by Clifton Bridge). As you enter Nottingham the A453 (Wilford Lane) is crossed by the A60 Loughborough Road; turn left on to the A60 (signposted Trent Bridge), just before Trent Bridge turn right on to Radcliffe Road then left on to Colwick Road.

WEST: A52 into Nottingham, then follow signs for Melton Mowbray and Trent Bridge (A606). Cross the river, then as north.

There are plenty of signs in Nottingham saying 'Football Grounds' which take you within about 0.5 mile of both Forest and County. However, when you get this close instead of detailing how to get to each ground they disappear completely, leaving you to your own devices.

PARKING: There is a decent car park at the ground behind the Executive (East) Stand, and on-street parking around and about. Alternatively, take the Radcliffe Road (heading eastwards away from Trent Bridge) for 200yd to a large intersection, go straight across into Holme Road and there is parking on the left.

FUTURE DEVELOPMENTS

The completion of the Trent Stand was the final stage of the rejuvenation of the City Ground. There are rumours (but no more) that the club may at some point in the future implement a proposed plan to develop a three-tier Main Stand which would add 3-5,000 on to the capacity.

OTHER INFORMATION

The food on offer at Forest improved slightly during last season. However, it is still not a patch on what is available at Meadow Lane (perhaps in the spirit of brotherly love County could give Forest the address of their pie suppliers), and the club still has to understand that wrapping dodgy food in paper emblazoned with the club colours does not improve its taste. You are left with the distinct feeling that Neil Webb didn't get to look as well developed as he is on the club's cuisine (perhaps among Shelley's myriad skills, she's also a cordon bleu chef). Outside the ground is just as bad, and I once consumed the worst chips I've ever had from a shop in the Radcliffe Road. They had a sign up saying that they sold Shire pie, which must surely have been a spelling error.

If you want a pub near the ground the Trent Bridge Inn (or TBI as it's known) is about the best on offer although it is probably as well to stick to the city centre where the Trip To Jerusalem is worth a visit.

Without wanting to sound like Mary Whitehouse, Forest is definitely not the ground to go to if you don't like swearing! Everyone from about the age of 18 months up seemed to have the vocabulary of a seasoned matelot, so if you are easily offended fill your ears with cotton wool, although this will also mean you'll miss the battle cry which booms out as Forest take the field, namely the 1950s version of Robin Hood. Stirring stuff eh? The idea of Stuart Pearce in doublet and hose is one that even the most hard bitten of fans would feel queasy about (perhaps it was that that put me off my food!).

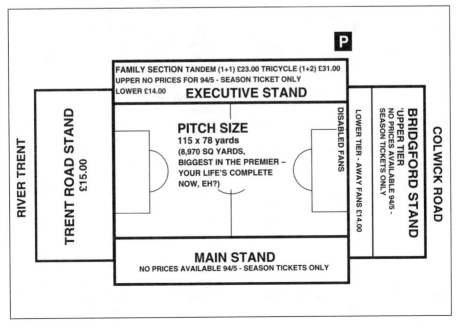

FAMILY SECTION TANDEM (1+1) £23.00 TRICYCLE (1+2) £31.00
UPPER NO PRICES FOR 94/5 - SEASON TICKET ONLY
LOWER £14.00

EXECUTIVE STAND

RIVER TRENT

TRENT ROAD STAND £15.00

PITCH SIZE
115 x 78 yards
(8,970 SQ YARDS,
BIGGEST IN THE PREMIER –
YOUR LIFE'S COMPLETE
NOW, EH?)

DISABLED FANS

LOWER TIER - AWAY FANS £14.00

'UPPER TIER NO PRICES AVAILABLE 94/5 - SEASON TICKETS ONLY

BRIDGFORD STAND

COLWICK ROAD

MAIN STAND
NO PRICES AVAILABLE 94/5 - SEASON TICKETS ONLY

NOTTS COUNTY

ADDRESS: Meadow Lane
Nottingham
NG2 3HJ
TELEPHONE No: 0115 952 9000
TICKET OFFICE: 0115 955 7210
FAX: 0115 955 3994
CLUBCALL: 0891 88 86 84
NICKNAME: The Magpies

RECORD ATTENDANCE:
47,310 v York City FA Cup 6th 12 March 1955 (L 0-1)

CLUB COLOURS:
HOME: Shirts: Black and White Stripes;
Shorts: White; Socks: Black
AWAY: Shirts: Tartan;
Shorts: Black/Tartan; Socks: White
When County announced their new away kit at the end of the 1993/4 season the world held its breath. Were we going to see a whole new meaning to the word garish? Were County going to spend their away days stomping round England looking like a hideous cross between Lena Zavaroni and Andy Stewart?

Sadly (??) no, the County away kit was a muted rather than mutated affair, although unless the Government has been messing around with boundaries more than I was aware, it's still difficult to see what inspired the choice.

KIT SPONSORS: Harp Lager

MANUFACTURERS: Mitre Sports

GROUND INFO
If you haven't been down to Meadow Lane for a while then you're in for a big surprise. The opening of the Derek Pavis Stand for the 1994/5 season means it has been completely transformed from the dump it once was into a really tasty stadium with excellent facilities for home and away supporters alike. What's more, they even started the work before the Taylor report was issued!

There is plenty of leg room, and although there are a couple of pillars in the Kop Stand you'll be mighty unlucky if you get a bad view. Plenty of toilet facilities are available for both sexes, and the food counters are manned by staff who aren't averse to speaking to people and don't even mind selling food! If you add that to the generally friendly and helpful stewards and office staff, it all adds up to a very pleasant day out (even if the majority of these people do mention as an aside that they are really Forest fans!).

The only thing that really irritates is the lack of concessions, which appears to fly in the face of everything else the club is working towards achieving. Part of the

Old County Road Stand (now referred to as the Jimmy 'we are legion' Sirrel Stand) can be used as an overflow for away fans if demand warrants it, although this is not something the club is particularly keen to do, and it does not actively promote it.

The Meadow Lane Stand is a family stand and is strictly out of bounds to away fans. If you go in and are sussed, you will be asked to leave (well actually not so much asked, more ordered).

CAPACITY: Stands: 20,300; Terrace: Nil;
Total: 20,300

AWAY FANS: Kop Stand: 5,438; Total: 5,438
If the club do allocate a section of the Jimmy Sirrel, this is Block X and it can cater for up to 1,200, but guess what? Block X is £2 more than the rest of the stand, which, although making it the same price as the Kop Stand, is still a bit out of order.

DISABLED FACILITIES: There are spaces for up to 100 disabled fans and these are sited in the Family Stand, the Derek Pavis Stand and the Jimmy Sirrel Stand (hmmm, what area of the ground is missing...). The club does ask that you pre-book your place, and whilst on the phone you should also be able to sort out a parking space as well.

Admission is free for disabled supporters, with helpers paying full price. The club previously considered that the development of the Derek Pavis Stand would lead to better facilities for the blind. However, from the information they supplied post-construction it appears that the number of spaces available has reduced from two to nil.

PROGRAMME: £1.30
What there is is good, but the abundance of adverts means that there isn't a great deal of substance to it.

FANZINES:
Flickin' 'N' Kickin	50p
The Pie	50p
No More Pie In The Sky	50p
The Better Half	50p

Collaboration is the name of the game with two of the County fanzines, although the elements that come together are a bit weird. *Flickin'* combines those two intrinsically linked subjects Notts County and Subbuteo, and *NMPITS* adds Stockport County (presumably it's the shared last name that does it, but if this is the case, why aren't Derby included in the equation?). I occasionally have surreal dreams about someone who loves Notts, Stockport and Subbuteo going to Meadow Lane, and finding they've only got 50p to their name; which would they buy? What trauma!!!

Well, actually if they took my advice they'd buy *The Pie*. To call it brilliant doesn't do it justice. Informative and very, very funny, it's easy to see why it is County's most established fanzine. It even manages to keep the virulence about Forest down to a minimum.

TRAVEL

NEAREST RAILWAY STATION:
Nottingham Midland (01332 257000 - Derby Enquiries)

BUS: Victoria Centre bus station (0115 924 0000)

BY CAR:
NORTH: M1 to J26. Take the A610 into Nottingham until you see signs for Melton Mowbray and Trent Bridge. Two hundred yards before the river, turn left into Meadow Lane (if you miss this turning, take next left into Quayside Close — again before the river — and turn back on to the London Road). The ground is 200yd on the left.

EAST: A52 Radcliffe Road into Nottingham, following the signs for Trent Bridge. As you approach the city centre, there is a large intersection; bear left (still Radcliffe Road). Shortly after this there is a T-junction; turn right (signposted Trent Bridge) and cross the river. The second left is Meadow Lane.

SOUTH: M1 to J24. Take the A453 (signposted Nottingham South) and continue towards the city following signs for Trent Bridge (do not cross the river by Clifton Bridge). As you enter Nottingham, the A453 Wilford Lane is crossed by the A60 Loughborough Road; turn left on to the A60 (signposted Trent Bridge), cross the river and take the second left into Meadow Lane.

WEST: A52 into Nottingham picking up signs for Melton Mowbray and Trent Bridge (A606). Then as north.

PARKING: There is a car park in Cattle Market Road (turn left just past the ground, and then next right), and also some on-street parking in the area.

However, a third option which is especially good for those coming from the south and east is to park by Forest's ground and walk across the Trent Bridge to Meadow Lane.

FUTURE DEVELOPMENTS
None.

OTHER INFORMATION
The pies at the ground are worth a trip to Meadow Lane by themselves, especially at half-time on a bleak winter's afternoon. When the crowd get going on a Saturday, it is difficult to work out whether the chant of 'Come on you Pies' is a reference to the team's nickname or a plea for half-time to come along so that more face-stuffing can take place. The meat pies actually have a secret ingredient: meat! Now the secret is out, I suppose all grounds will be copying them (I don't think). Last season saw the range extended to cover meat & potato, beef & onion, steak & kidney and chicken & mushroom.

Now all the club has to do is something about the other food, which was bleak, and invest in spoons for the hot drinks, longer than the ones it currently has, which entail you plunging your fingers into scalding (!?) liquid in order to stir the sludge of sugar at the bottom of your cup.

If you fancy a pint before the match, the Trent Navigation and the Magpie on Meadow Lane are the nearest to the ground, with the Navigation being quite welcoming to away supporters. Alternatively the city centre has a wide choice.

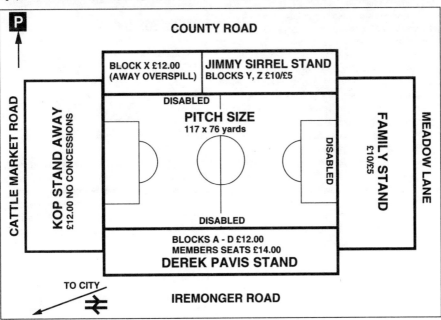

OLDHAM ATHLETIC

ADDRESS: Boundary Park
Oldham
OL1 2PA
TELEPHONE No: 0161 624 4972
TICKET OFFICE: 0161 624 4972
FAX: 0161 652 6501
CLUBCALL: 0891 12 11 42
NICKNAME: The Latics
RECORD ATTENDANCE:
47,671 v Sheffield Wednesday FA Cup 4th
25 January 1930 (L 3-4)

CLUB COLOURS:
HOME: Shirts: Blue; Shorts: Blue; Socks: Blue
AWAY: Shirts: Tangerine and Blue;
Shorts: Blue; Socks: Tangerine

KIT SPONSORS: J. D. Sports
MANUFACTURERS: Umbro

GROUND INFO

The Lookers Stand and the George Hill Stand have members only sections which means if you can't get a ticket for the away end you are limited to where you can go (although the slapping of pockets and the 'I'm sure I had my membership card when I left home' routine may open a few doors).

Those of you who haven't visited Boundary Park for a while may have stayed away as a result of your previous visit! You probably parked in the muddy car park, climbed and slipped your way up the muddy hill to the ground, where you paid through the nose to stand on an uncovered mud heap watching the players wallow around in the mud. How times have changed. True the car park is still dire, and Boundary Park is still not the cheapest of grounds to get into, but at least now away fans get to sit in the cantilevered Rochdale Road Stand which is far and away the best part of the stadium, offering decent views of the pitch, reasonable facilities, and most importantly given the inclemencies of the weather in Oldham, a roof. It also contains a little paddock at the front of it where you can dance a jig of joy when your team score (you just want to be on the end of season video don't you, you sad person). Having said that, the last activity is probably not recommended, as some of the stewards at the ground (who are probably a bit fed up with it now) can be a little bit overzealous if you do.

In general, paddock dancing excepted, the police and stewards operate a softly softly approach, and although they will act if they perceive an individual is becoming overly rowdy, they manage to do so without acting in an inflammatory manner. It is also worth

noting that they don't expect away fans to behave like monks, and chanting and cheering is not frowned or acted upon.

CAPACITY: Stands: 13,544; Terrace: Nil;
Total: 13,544

AWAY FANS: Rochdale Road Stand: 1,843;
Total: 1,843
This can be increased according to the volume of the away following to a maximum of the whole of the Rochdale Road End which holds 4,583.

DISABLED FACILITIES: There are 40 spaces in the Rochdale Road and Seton Stands. Disabled fans are admitted free of charge, with helpers paying £9. Pre-booking is required. There are car parking facilities at the ground, which are well used. This islocated close to the entrance on a tarmacadamed surface in an area patrolled by the police. Ramps are laid for access to this area.

The club no longer has match commentaries for the visually impaired because when it did have the service 'no one took advantage'. If we apply the same principle, then one wonders if as you read this someone is walking around the club going 'fire extinguishers, now let me see, we've never used them, that means we might as well get shot of them!'.

PROGRAMME: £1.50
The programme has a good visitors' section as well as having a nice newsy feel to it. This combined, with the excellent layout, make it a worthwhile addition to the collection.

FANZINES:
Beyond the Boundary   80p
Good value for money; a nice mix of the funny and the serious, and normally a couple of excellent cartoons.

TRAVEL
NEAREST RAILWAY STATION:
Oldham WERNETH (0161 832 8353)
The railway station is about 1.5 miles from the ground, which is a long enough walk in itself, especially as by some quirk of nature, it doesn't seem to matter what direction you are walking in, you always seem to be going uphill. However, this will appear to be a mere stroll in the park if by some mistake you end up going to Oldham MUMPS which is about three days by foot from Boundary Park.

BUS: West Street bus station (0161 228 7811)

BY CAR: From everywhere (all roads lead to Oldham!): M62 to J20, then take A627(M). Then, dependent on how the traffic is moving, either:
• continue along this road for 2.5 miles to a large roundabout, at which you should take first exit on to

A633 Broadway. Then first right off the Broadway into Hilbre Avenue, the ground is at the bottom of this road. Or:

• at the roundabout, take the second exit on to Chadderton Way; after 0.5 mile turn left into Boundary Park for the ground.

Whichever way you go, any male between the ages of 15-25 should please avoid going for the 'Carry On' style gag of stopping the car and asking female 'Here, love, how do you get to Oldham?' Rather than the comic reply of 'Buy me a drink, and ask a bit nicer', you are likely to get your head knocked off.

PARKING: The Lookers Stand car park at the bottom of Hilbre Avenue has space for 1,000 cars. There is some off-street parking in the vicinity of the ground, but if you want alternative off-street parking then you really need to travel into Oldham town centre, which is a fair trek and also difficult to get away from after the match. At the club car park watch out for the stewards who say you will not be blocked in and then as soon as you are out of sight guide the next car about 3cm in front of you; excellent if you want to make a quick getaway after the match. There is also a car park with 125 spaces situated 100yd behind the Rochdale Road end with a charge of £1.

FUTURE DEVELOPMENTS

The ground is all-seater but a new 'super' stand is planned to replace the Lookers Stand. This, when opened, will take capacity at the ground to approx. 23,000. However, at the moment the club are unable to say exactly when this project will be completed.

OTHER INFORMATION

For pre-match refreshment try the White Hart and the Old Grey Mare on the Rochdale Road, where away fans are welcome. Not so at the Clayton next to the ground, which is members only. The chip shops seem to close at 1.30 on matchdays, but there are plenty of mobile snack bars around the ground, which like the facilities inside the stadium, serve edible, if not exactly tasty or exciting fare.

While the facilities (car park excepted) have improved beyond all recognition at Boundary Park, the pitch has got steadily worse since the club reverted to grass. Still, before you criticise too much, it's worth remembering that in 1900 Oldham became the first parliamentary seat of Sir Winston Churchill, whose 'We shall fight them on the beaches' speech may well have been inspired by a visit to the local ground one late January afternoon.

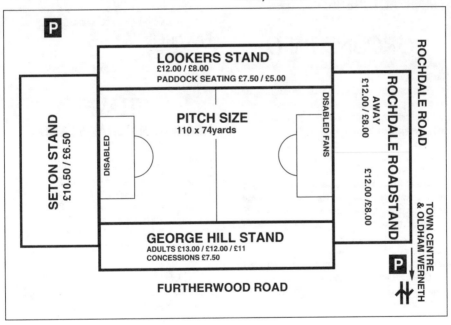

OXFORD UNITED

ADDRESS: The Manor Ground
London Road
Headington
Oxford OX3 7RS
TELEPHONE No: 01865 61503
TICKET OFFICE: 01865 61503
FAX: 01865 741820
CLUBLINE: 0891 44 00 55
NICKNAME: The U's
RECORD ATTENDANCE: 22,730 v
Preston FA Cup 6th 29 February 1964 (L 1-2)

CLUB COLOURS:
HOME: Shirts: Yellow/Navy;
Shorts: Navy; Socks: Navy
AWAY: Shirts: Red/Black;
Shorts: Black; Socks: Black

KIT SPONSORS: Unipart

MANUFACTURERS: Manor Leisure

GROUND INFO

'Velcome to Stalag Luft Manor Ground, Resistance Is Futile!'

Yes, just when you thought those days were gone when being an away fan meant being treated like a common criminal, the good old U's bring them back with a vengeance. In my experience, the moment you approach the ground and see the large number of police and stewards, and the fact that your every move is being videoed, you know you are in for a long day.

The first 10 rows of the Cuckoo Lane terracing are rendered virtually unusable by the tall perimeter fence. In order that no one is excluded from what appears to be the club's maximum irritation policy, a girder with a video camera on top has been placed by the away end goal; this means those at the top of the terrace need to keep moving around if they want to catch all the action.

On the brighter side 1994/5 saw a reduction from three categories of match to two, and the club do offer away concessions, but only if the tickets are purchased from the visiting club's ticket office. The club is also proud of the fact that the stewards have been on an official training course. Naturally this is to be heartily recommended, even if I found it hard to notice the difference in their attitude at first (or even 17th) glance.

The Cuckoo Lane End is uncovered and behind it are numerous large trees. While this does give the ground a rather picturesque quality, it does mean that given the slightest breeze you'll have leaves winging past your ears all afternoon. This becomes particularly annoying if it is raining when, due to an as yet unexplained law of nature, the human neck becomes a magnet for wet foliage. Seriously, although the club does spend a lot of money clearing them up, if you're at the match on a blowy, wet day, enough can have fallen during the game to make walking down the terracing treacherous, so watch your step.

CAPACITY: Stands: 6,769; Terrace: 2,803;
Total: 9,572

AWAY FANS: Cuckoo Lane Terrace: 2,107;
Cuckoo Lane Stand West: 108;
Cuckoo Lane Stand East: 434;
Total: 2,649

DISABLED FACILITIES: There are 20 spaces for wheelchair-bound fans in the Main Stand. Admission is £5 for disabled fans and £7/£8 dependent on the match for helpers. Pre-booking is required, and rather splendidly the club says it can also sort out a parking space. No match commentaries are available.

PROGRAMME: £1.30
Plenty of articles of interest to both sets of fans, with the emphasis on trips down memory lane. Anyone who hasn't been to the ground for a while and who remembers previous offerings will be pleasantly surprised!

FANZINES:
Raging Bull   70p
Plenty of raging, no bull! A good read.

TRAVEL
NEAREST RAILWAY STATION:
Oxford (01865 722333)

BUS: Gloucester Green bus station (01865 711312) There is an excellent bus service to the ground. From the railway station the easiest way is to walk up to the High Street and catch either a 20, 21, 22, 280 or 595, any of which will drop you right by the ground. After matches, go to London Road (see map) where buses destined for the city centre appear virtually every 10min.

BY CAR:
NORTH/EAST: M40 to J8. Take the A40 (signposted Oxford and Headington) and continue to a roundabout with the A420 London Road. After 0.75 mile turn right into Osler Road, then next right into Cuckoo Lane, and the ground is on the left.
SOUTH: Either the M40 to J8 then as north/east, or the A34 towards Oxford until you get to the A423 Southern By-Pass on to which you should turn right. At the second roundabout, take the first exit on to the A4142 Eastern By-Pass. Continue for four miles until you get to a roundabout with the A40/A420 and take the first exit on to the A420 (signposted Oxford/Headington). Then as north/east.

WEST: A40. Shortly after you pass Barton there is a roundabout with the A420 and the A 4142. Take the third exit on to the A420 (signposted Headington), then as north/east.

PARKING: A real nuisance. Many of the surrounding streets are coned off, and because the ground is on the outskirts of the city there are no convenient multi-storeys about. The club does say that one can use the club car park at Headington, a few minutes walk away from the ground, otherwise an idea can be to go into the city, park by the railway station and get a bus to the ground.

When you return from the match, a bit of local knowledge can save on the parking: first, check whether the attendant is in his hut (often this is not the case on a Saturday) but if he is, go to the railway station and buy a single to Islip (about 80p) with car park token. As a 'rail user', your cost of parking is instantly reduced by over two-thirds. Expect some sarcastic comments from the BR staff when you do this, but they made the rules and it's well worth it for the saving you make.

FUTURE DEVELOPMENTS

The club has been trying to get away from the Manor Ground for years, but in the past every time a possible site was found the City Council seemed to come up with a plausible reason why they couldn't have it. However, the club has recently proposed Minchery Park as the site of the 15,000 all-seater stadium and this appears to have been given the council's blessing. If everything goes to plan the £15 million project will open either on Boxing Day 1996, or for the start of the 1997/8 season.

OTHER INFORMATION

One map of Oxford lists 72 places of interest in and about the city. Sadly, but perhaps not surprisingly, the Manor Ground is not one of them. Anyone with an interest in the arts should check out the Ashmolean Museum, which is arguably the best if not in the country then certainly outside London. Another good thing about Oxford is the wide range of food it offers; there are hundreds of places, and these seem to change with a great rapidity. If you like Chinese, you could do an awful lot worse then try the Opium Den which is on the way to the city from the railway station. In both pubs by the ground, the Royal Standard and the Britannia, away fans are welcomed. Both are excellent and worth a visit, but if you are going to stick to one then make it the Standard, simply because it does better food. Try a pint of Morrell's College Ale if you come across it; it's wild stuff. Make sure you don't confuse your experience of the club's attitudes with that of the locals who are generally happy to welcome visitors and chat over the meaning of life and the spiralling cost of transfers over a pint or two.

For a half-time snack get queuing early, because service was really slow on my visit. When you get to the counter the odds are that you will hear but not see who is serving you, as the hut from which the food comes is rendered opaque by the volume of smoke produced within. And when you do get served you may wonder why you bothered. Still, at least the toilets are clean.

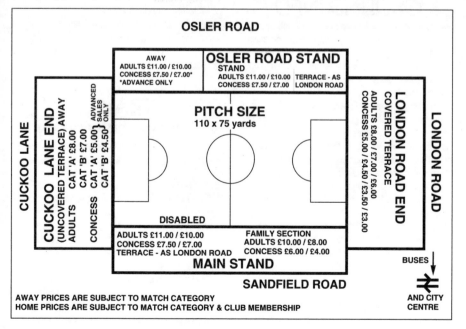

PETERBOROUGH UNITED

ADDRESS: London Road Ground
Peterborough
Cambridgeshire
PE2 8AL

TELEPHONE No: 01733 63947
TICKET OFFICE: 01733 63947
FAX: 01733 557210
CLUBCALL: 0891 424 300
NICKNAME: Posh

RECORD ATTENDANCE:

30,096 v Swansea Town FA Cup 5th 20 February 1965 (D 0-0)
Those of you who like conspiracy theories can't fail to notice that civil rights leader and closet Posh fanatic Malcolm X was assassinated on this day. Coincidence or something else? Spike Lee was unavailable for comment.

CLUB COLOURS:

HOME: Shirts: Royal Blue;
Shorts: White; Socks: White with Royal Blue Hoops
AWAY: Shirts: Red; Shorts: Red; Socks: Red

KIT SPONSORS: Thomas Cook
MANUFACTURERS: Netz Sportswear Ltd

GROUND INFO

Having previously been applauded for not only offering, but positively encouraging away fans concessions, Peterborough must have felt that this sort of publicity was not the sort of thing with which they wanted to be associated with and withdrew them during the 1994/5 season. Thanks.

The Moyes terracing is covered and is of the type that allows away fans to get a good atmosphere going with the minimum of effort. However, the toilets (unpleasant, dark and dank), catering facilities (over-priced drinks and lukewarm pies) leave a lot to be desired, as does the stewarding which in my own experience starts somewhere around bloody-mindedness and finishes up around positively antagonistic. Praise, where praise is due; the people in the ticket office are friendly enough, but it does pale into insignificance when you spend a proportion of the afternoon being hassled for no apparent reason and when you ask why you are being requested to move, stop leaning on a wall, etc you get the response 'Because I told you so...'

The home supporters also take advantage of their covering to create quite a noise, but what always surprises is the fact that one of the London Road End's favourite chants is 'We're the middle, we're the middle, we're the middle of the road'; every time you hear this

you always hope that if this is really the case they will follow it up by doing a couple a verses of 'Chirpy Chirpy Cheep Cheep' but sadly they never do.

CAPACITY: Stands: 4,950; Terrace: 5,500;
Total: 10,450 Stands: 9,950;
Terrace: 6,350; Total: 16,300.
The second set of figures are those for after the opening of the Glebe Road Terrace (see FUTURE DEVELOPMENTS) but the club states that these are approximate capacities. The new stand should have no effect on away fans (other than if you are in the the Main Stand Block A, when you will probably stare wistfully across at it and wonder if they've got a better view than you).

AWAY FANS: Moyes Terrace: 3,350;
A Stand: 889; Total: 4,239

DISABLED FACILITIES: There are 10 places for wheelchair-bound fans in the London Road Enclosure; the club states that pre-booking is required. Disabled supporters and their helpers pay £4.50 each. The club does provide matchday commentaries for the blind, and there are parking facilities for the disabled at the ground, for which the club should also be contacted.

PROGRAMME: £1.20
Not a brilliant programme, but good value for money; it will see you through the half-time break.

FANZINES:

The Peterborough Effect £1
As with the programme, nothing spectacular, but it keeps going along quietly improving with age. The main grouse has got to be that it can be a bit hard to get hold of.

TRAVEL

NEAREST RAILWAY STATION:

Peterborough (0116 248 1000 — Leicester Enquiries)

BUS: Peterborough bus station (01733 54571)

BY CAR:

NORTH/WEST: A1, then take the A47 towards the city centre. Turn right at the roundabout on to the A1260, and then take the second turning to the left on to the A605 Oundle Road. Continue for just under two miles until you get to a roundabout; take the third exit on to London Road, and the ground is on the left.
SOUTH: A1 to the roundabout with the A15. Take the London Road (signposted Peterborough A15) going under the flyover and over two railway bridges. You then get to a large intersection at which you should turn left (continuing along London Road) and the ground is immediately on the right.
EAST: A47 through Eye, and pick up signs for

Peterborough City Centre. Once in the city centre follow signs for Whittlesey (A605); this will take you across the River Nene and on to London Road. Continue along London Road and the ground is on the left. There is good signposting for 'Football car parks' around the city, which although they end up taking you around the houses a bit, do at least get you there.

PARKING: There is a leisure centre next to the ground where you can park, and also a car park on the Oundle Road (left at the roundabout as you are driving towards the ground) which is only about 300yd away. Alternatively, there is ample parking in the city centre. The police traffic control after a match seems to involve a competition as to who can make the longest jam. Give yourself a good twenty minutes to get away unless you leave five minutes early.

FUTURE DEVELOPMENTS

The Glebe Road terracing is being redeveloped and this should be open for business in October 1995. The capacity in this area after development is estimated by the club at 5,000. The latest information from the club states that until the rebuilding is finished, the total capacity of the ground will be made up of 4,975 seats in the old main stand, terracing for approx 3,000 at Moyes End (away fans) and terracing for approx 2,700 at the London Road Enclosure.

OTHER INFORMATION

There are a couple of good pubs on London Road, namely the Bridge and the Wag & Bone. The second of these is kitted out with sofas and armchairs and it is like having a pint in someone's living room. There is a reasonable burger caravan as you make your way into the ground at which you can buy traditional footie foods such as plastic walking sticks filled with Smarties (you just try getting them past the stewards though who may well treat them like some kind of terrorist threat). Given the quality of the food inside the ground, stock up before you go in.

The PA at London Road is bizarre, being so loud as to be virtually incomprehensible and with an announcer who sounds like someone giving a bad speech at a wedding. The advert that is broadcast for the clubcall facility is little more than white noise (appropriately enough!). However, what is unique about it is that it seems to be on the same frequency as the bingo club that is next to the ground, which means that on odd occasions you will hear the numbers being called out. Not too bad for the football fans, who at worst are going to be a little perplexed as they look for the player with the squad number 'six and eight', but spare a thought for the poor bingo player who is one number away from the jackpot, hears 'Number 10' called out and jumps up crying house only for the words 'playing up front for Posh today, Ken Charlery' to be tagged on the end.

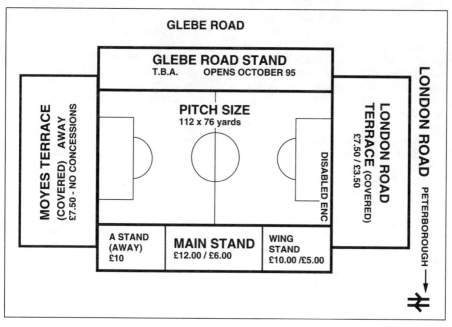

PLYMOUTH ARGYLE

ADDRESS: Home Park
Plymouth
Devon PL2 3DQ

TELEPHONE No: 01752 562561

TICKET OFFICE: 01752 562561

FAX: 01752 606167

CLUBCALL: 0839 44 22 70

NICKNAME: The Pilgrims

RECORD ATTENDANCE:
43,596 v Aston Villa Div 2 10 October 1936 (D 2-2)

CLUB COLOURS:
HOME: Shirts: Green and Black Stripes; Shorts:
Black; Socks: Black with Green top
AWAY: Shirts: Yellow; Shorts: Green; Socks: Green
and Yellow

KIT SPONSORS: Rotolok

MANUFACTURERS: JSW

GROUND INFO

To stand at the away (Barn Park) end at Home Park
means exposing yourself to the elements as there is
no cover, although there is a marvellous aesthetic
quality about the place — as you leave the ground the
banking has been made into a thick rockery. If the
weather is inclement and you're not into 'Gardeners'
Question Time' and the marvellous world of herba-
ceous borders, go into the Grandstand. If you do go
into the Barn Park End, the exit is via the Lyndhurst
Stand.

There are no concessions for away fans on the terrace, though you can get a discount if you go in the
Grandstand.

The Lyndhurst Stand is popular for home supporters and offers very good leg room. It is also acoustically impressive and the fans certainly can (and do) get
some noise going from this area, which due to the lack
of away cover (and the fact that you may feel like
you've travelled half-way round the globe to get to
what is not only the most southerly, but also the most
westerly ground in Britain) can make your efforts
sound rather feeble.

CAPACITY: Stands: 9,000; Terrace: 10,675;
Total: 19,675

AWAY FANS: Barn Park End: 2,640;
Grandstand Wing: 200;
Total: 2,840

DISABLED FACILITIES: There are 70
spaces available in the Devonport End, with one helper
admitted per fan. There is no charge for disabled supporters, but helpers pay £5.50. Visitors are welcome

but should pre-book their space. The club car park has
disabled parking facilities. Matchday commentaries for
the blind are available in the Grandstand. These must
be pre-booked.

PROGRAMME: £1.30

FANZINES:
Rub Of The Greens   50p
Way Out West   60p

Rub Of The Greens is a decent enough read, although
if you have travelled by train it would be more than
optimistic to expect it to keep you amused for the
whole of the journey home. ROTG also appears to be
produced from Bristol, and if someone is commuting
from there to Plymouth every other Saturday then they
deserve some kind of a medal (and should invest in
shares in BR when it becomes privatised).

TRAVEL

NEAREST RAILWAY STATION:
Plymouth North Road (01752 221300)
On my last visit to Home Park, I got chatting with
someone who told me what, if it is true, is one of the
finest stories of footballing frugality you are likely to
come across. Apparently, during the early 1980s a
washing powder was running a scheme whereby if you
bought their product you could obtain free tickets
(this bit is definitely right, I used it myself). Plymouth,
not one to look a gift horse in the mouth, purchased
enough of the aforementioned cleaning material in
order to send the first team on an away trip that season! (Strange perhaps, given that they must have had
so much washing powder that they still chose to air
their dirty laundry with reference to Peter Shilton in
public last season.)

BUS: Bretonside bus station (01752 222221)
Buses 20F, 42F and 37F stop directly outside Home
Park.

BY CAR:
NORTH/EAST: M5 to J31 (final junction), then
take the A38. Turn left on to the A386 (Tavistock
Road) — this road branches into two, keep to the left
(signposted Plymouth). Just over a mile on the left is
the ground's car park which has space for 1,000 cars.
WEST: Take the A38, turn right on to the A386
(Tavistock Road), then as north/east.

Yes, I know it's miles from everywhere (Most
Westerly League Ground in England, etc.), but at least
you only have to go there once in a season. Pity the
poor devils who support Argyle and have horror jour-
neys every other week.

PARKING: As stated earlier, there is a large car
park adjacent to Home Park, which is ideal only if you
have got the rest of the weekend to fritter away. The
cars are parked nose-to-tail and inevitably you will be

parked around people who amble across to the vehicles 20min after the match. This will then mean that you get badly clogged up in the local traffic, where you can spend a pleasant 5min getting yourself into a panic as to whether the local kids throwing stones at the cars at the lights are going to use your vehicle for target practice.

There is some street parking around but even this is no guarantee that you will be speedily on your way home.

FUTURE DEVELOPMENTS

The finalised details of any future developments are not available at present. The away end may well stay as it is for the foreseeable future, although there is the possibility of some nice geranium shrubs being planted for the 1995/6 season.

OTHER INFORMATION

You'll be lucky to get into the supporters' club bar in the ground and it is as well to take the 10min drive into the busy city centre to find a decent watering-hole. Mind you, the speed of service in many of the places left a lot to be desired.

Inside Home Park itself the pasties are above average as is the tea and Bovril, so you've got no excuse for not stocking up on those carbohydrates before the long journey home.

For your entertainment the club opccasionally provides a group of dancing girls, namely the 'Pilgrims Gazelles' (I bet female readers can hardly wait to go now). Gazelle-like they are not! and they display a fantastic lack of enthusiasm for what they are doing. It's clear that they don't want to be there and the fans don't particularly want them there, so why bother? (Late news is that the Gazelles have all been 'shot' and so will not feature in 1995/6.)

You also can't fail to be impressed by the advertising van which drives round and round the pitch before the game advertising a local eatery which seems to serve half a cow, sheep, pig and lamb all for £9.95.

The club quite rightly regards itself as being friendly and accessible, and perhaps it would be more appropriate to call the ground Homely Park.

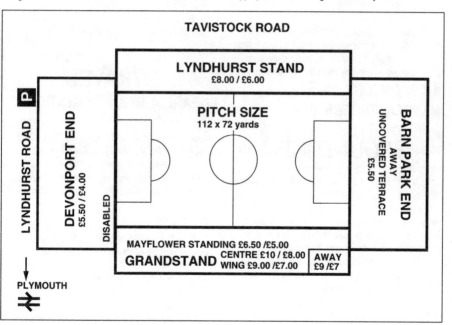

TAVISTOCK ROAD

LYNDHURST STAND
£8.00 / £6.00

PITCH SIZE
112 x 72 yards

LYNDHURST ROAD

P

DEVONPORT END
£5.50 / £4.00

DISABLED

BARN PARK END
UNCOVERED TERRACE
AWAY
£5.50

MAYFLOWER STANDING £6.50 /£5.00
GRANDSTAND CENTRE £10 / £8.00
WING £9.00 /£7.00
AWAY
£9 /£7

PLYMOUTH

PORT VALE

ADDRESS: Vale Park
Burslem
Stoke-on-Trent
ST6 1AW
TELEPHONE No: 01782 814134
TICKET OFFICE: 01782 814134
FAX: 01782 834 981
CLUBCALL: 0891 12 16 36
NICKNAME: The Valiants
RECORD ATTENDANCE: 50,000 v
Aston Villa FA Cup 5th 20 February 1960 (L 1-2)

CLUB COLOURS:
HOME: Shirts: White; Shorts: Black; Socks: White
AWAY: Shirts: Yellow/Black;
Shorts: Yellow; Socks: Black
Port Vale replica shirt sales received a phenomenal
boost when it was revealed that Robbie of 'Take That'
was a Valiant. The club was inundated with orders from
young girls. What will happen following his departure
from the group who knows, and in fact, who cares?

KIT SPONSORS: Tunstall Assurance
MANUFACTURERS: Mizuno

GROUND INFO
There are plenty of signs warning visitors that if they
enter 'home' areas of the ground that they will be ejected, and this policy is adhered to. Equally there are
numerous signs telling home fans that if they enter the
away sections of the ground they too will be ejected.
Presumably this has thwarted the plans of any Vale
supporter to leave the Railway Paddock, where they
can sit for £8.50 and £6.50 concessions, and join the
visiting supporters in the new all-seater Hamil Road
End for £9 and no concessions.

Having made adverse comment about the lack of
away concessions, it is only fair to mention that in
1994/5 the club de-segregated the family stand which
means that visitors can either take advantage of prices
of £7 and £4.50 to sit, or £6 and £3.50 to stand.

The view from the Hamil Road End isn't bad, and
at least you are under cover. Also, the new toilet and
refreshment facilities, while not being the biggest,
aren't bad either.

CAPACITY: Stands: 12,442; Terrace: 10,025;
Total: 22,467

AWAY FANS: Hamil Road Terrace: 4,715;
Main Stand Block C: 1,066;
Total: 5,781
The family section holds a total of 1,090 in a split
between terraces and seats.

DISABLED FACILITIES: There is a special stand called, wait for it... The British Coal
Opencast Disabled Stand. Perhaps not surprisingly, it
is more commonly referred to as the Specialist Stand.
This holds a total of 72 fans and admission is £4, with
helpers being charged. The club also offers matchday
commentaries for the blind and an area for disabled
fans to park. All these facilities should be pre-booked.

PROGRAMME: £1.50

FANZINES:
The Memoirs Of Seth Bottomley £1
One of the earliest fanzines produced, although not
one of the most frequently appearing. Rather gratify-
ingly the people who put it together have gone for
quality rather than quantity of writing. *TMOSB* is a
none-too-handy A4 size and is reminiscent of the old
'on the office photocopier' fanzines. However, it is also
an excellent read, with emphasis on humour. Well
worth buying ahead of the programme and it can be
purchased at the club shop; a real 'don't miss'.

TRAVEL
NEAREST RAILWAY STATION:
Stoke Central (01782 411411)

BUS: Potteries Motor Transport (01782 747000)
Sometimes abbreviations work, and sometimes they
don't. Plastering PMT all over your buses and bus
stops most definitely falls into the second category.
If you decide to risk it, a 452 will drop you off on Hamil
Road by the stadium.

BY CAR:
NORTH: M6 to J16 and follow the signs for Stoke
(A500). Turn left when you see the signpost for
Tunstall (A527). This brings you to a roundabout; take
the second exit into Newcastle Street which later
becomes Market Place. When you get to a major
crossroads turn left, and about 300yd further on turn
right into Bycars Road. Next left is Bycars Lane and
the ground is on the right.
SOUTH/WEST: M6 to J15, then take the A500
(signposted Stoke). Follow this road for approximately
4.5 miles then turn right on to the A527 (signposted
Tunstall), then as north.
EAST: A52 into Stoke. Follow the signs into Burslem,
this will bring you on to Waterloo Road (A50). Go
straight over when you get to a major crossroads and
about 300yd after this turn right into Bycars Road, then
as north.

PARKING: There is parking by the away end in
Hamil Road. Alternatively, just after you go through the
major crossroads there is a car park on the left which
is about 600yd from the ground.

FUTURE DEVELOPMENTS

At the time of going to press, nothing has been cast in stone as the Hamil Road End has been turned into an all-seater stand (holding 3,500).

OTHER INFORMATION

For any 'Motty' types amongst you, let me explain how the geographically non-existent Port Vale obtained its name. The Port comes from all the canal ports from which pottery was transported, and the Vale comes from the Vale Inn pub side out of which the club was founded. Initially called Burslem Port Vale, the club dropped the Burslem when they moved to Hanley. When they returned to Burslem they couldn't be bothered to change the name back (or something like that) and, hey presto, Port Vale remains its moniker to this very day...You at the back there, have you fallen asleep? This is interesting stuff!

Local pubs include the Vine on Hamil Road (excellent) and amongst others the Sagger Makers Bottom Knocker in the town centre, which is great if you can't resist going in so-so pubs with silly sounding names.

The locals are some of the friendliest I've encountered on my travels and they give the impression that they care about what you think about the team, the ground and them. If you fancy a chat about football, or need some help during your visit, then these are among the best fans to turn to. And no! I am not a closet Port Vale or Take That fan! (Honest!!)

A few tips for your visit:when I went to a night match, the outside of the ground was very poorly illuminated, except for one part at the back of the Lorne Street terrace where there was a floodlight which shone directly into myr eyes. Bring a davy lamp, and some shades.

Also essential is plenty of change, as it seems that no one at the ground, ie programme sellers, car park attendants or turnstile operators is given a float of more than 50p.

If you get a chance, check out the club shop, not only for your copy of *Seth Bottomley*, but also to see if you can see anyone furtively picking up the Port Vale temporary tattoos!

Finally, don't be fooled into thinking that you can buy a ticket from the ticket office — this is for match-day complimentaries and away match sales only

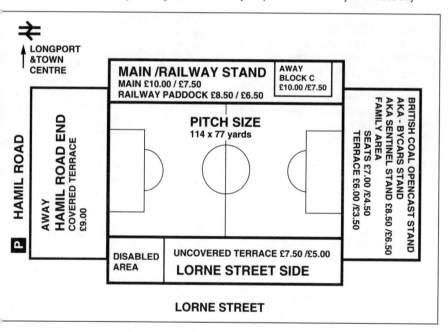

LONGPORT &TOWN CENTRE

HAMIL ROAD

P

AWAY
HAMIL ROAD END
COVERED TERRACE
£9.00

MAIN /RAILWAY STAND
MAIN £10.00 / £7.50
RAILWAY PADDOCK £8.50 / £6.50

AWAY
BLOCK C
£10.00 /£7.50

PITCH SIZE
114 x 77 yards

DISABLED AREA

UNCOVERED TERRACE £7.50 /£5.00
LORNE STREET SIDE

BRITISH COAL OPENCAST STAND
AKA - BYCARS STAND
AKA SENTINEL STAND £8.50 /£6.50
FAMILY AREA
SEATS £7.00 /£4.50
TERRACE £6.00 /£3.50

LORNE STREET

PORTSMOUTH

ADDRESS: Fratton Park
57 Frogmore Road
Portsmouth
Hampshire PO4 8RA

TELEPHONE No: 01705 731204

TICKET OFFICE: 01705 618777

FAX: 01705 734129

CLUBCALL: 0891 12 11 82

NICKNAME: Pompey

RECORD ATTENDANCE:
51,385 v Derby FA Cup 6th 26 February 1949 (W 2-1)

CLUB COLOURS:
HOME: Shirts: Blue; Shorts: White; Socks: Red
AWAY: Shirts: Red and Black halves;
Shorts: Red; Socks: Black

KIT SPONSORS: Goodmans

MANUFACTURERS: Asics

The club's response to Premier League players having their names on their shirts was for them to stick 'Pompey' on the back of all of theirs. The story goes that one reporter (probably seconded from cricket duty that day) was foolish enough on seeing a player wearing one to express surprise and delight at Portsmouth finding someone with the club's nickname as a surname!

While we're on the subject of replica shirts, do you think they come with the word 'Pompey' already on their back? Good guess! But as the club shop was only too happy to say at the time, it would only cost £3 to have it put on. Oh well, that's all right then.

GROUND INFO

Perhaps the best architectural feature about Fratton Park is the Tudor-style fronting proclaiming the date 1898 which is when the club was founded, and not as you may believe when the final bit of renovation was done to the ground. The away end is open and thus leaves you exposed to a biting wind coming off the sea. Even if you try and get some protection by going in the South Stand it can be freezing, and a trip isn't complete without thoughts of one of the works of the city's most famous sons, that being Dickens' 'Bleak House'.

Fair concessions for one and all.

CAPACITY: Stands: 12,500; Terrace: 6,762;
Total: 19,262

AWAY FANS: Milton End: 1,980; D Section
South Stand: 1,200; Total: 3,180

In previous seasons away fans have been allocated the whole of the Milton End (capacity 4,620) if demand

called for it. However, until the Fratton Park Stand opens (see FUTURE DEVELOPMENTS) then this may not be the case in 1995/6.

DISABLED FACILITIES: There are spaces for 30 disabled supporters at the front of the Fratton Road Terrace, with the construction work expect to be shunted possibly to the side of the South Stand. Disabled supporters are admitted free, with helpers paying 'a seasonal charge' which presumably means either the club are going to look at the sky and say 'looks like winter is coming on, that's £5' or that you're going to have a very expensive trip for a one-off match. In reality expect to pay standard terrace prices. Pre-book your place.

There is no parking at the ground, which is not good news at all. Continuing with the slightly surreal, I was advised by one source last year that the club was considering introducing match commentary for the deaf! Sadly neither this, nor any facilities for visually impaired supporters were forthcoming.

PROGRAMME: £1.50
Not bad. Not cheap.

FANZINES:
Frattonise   50p
Blue and Wight   50p

Much of a muchness, and both a reasonable way to pass a bit of time. *More Dead Wood Than The Mary Rose* has been defunct for longer that it existed, but still warrants a mention for the title alone.

TRAVEL

NEAREST RAILWAY STATION:
Fratton (01703 229393 — Southampton Enquiries)

BUS: Red and Blue Admiral (01705 650967)

BY CAR:
NORTH: A3(M), A27 Westbound (signposted Fareham), M275. At the end of the M275 take the third exit at the roundabout into Kingston Crescent. Continue to the T-junction, then turn right into Kingston Road. After 0.75 miles turn left into St Mary's Road, and at the next roundabout take the fourth exit (Milton Road). At the next roundabout take the third exit into Alverstone Road (which becomes Specks Lane) and the ground is on your right.
EAST: A27, M275, then as north.
WEST: M27 to M275, then as north.

PARKING: How bad is it finding a parking space in Pompey? Here's a clue: the players have to use a factory yard which is away from the ground!

There are car parks in Pompey city centre, which are about 1.5 miles away from the ground, and also or the sea front, which is nearer to the stadium but puts you on the wrong side of the traffic come the time you want to leave. Alternatively there is good street parking off Milton Road, but this does fill up very quickly, not least of all by inconsiderate residents wanting to park outside their houses.

Don't be tempted to park on double yellow lines, or by cones, or indeed anywhere that you might be deemed to be causing an obstruction, as the Hampshire police tow away faster than the Wimbledon defence.

FUTURE DEVELOPMENTS

A fiasco. Fratton Park was 75% terrace, and although many people love the ground for what it is, the club knew that their best bet for meeting the requirements of the Taylor Report was to relocate. It picked a site at Farlington which it was going to call Parkway (possibly because it was going to feature parking for more than 4,000 cars). This would be a 22,500-capacity fully can-tilevered ground. While the club waited for the OK to go ahead it naturally didn't want to spend any cash on Fratton Park, and then on 15 December, Whitehall, (where they really have their finger on the pulse of Portsmouth) via the DOE said no go, as the new stadium would be a threat to wildlife! (self-same reason they banjaxed Southampton). Consequently the club is now undertaking the arduous task of converting Fratton Park to an all-seater stadium, the first stage of which will be the opening of a 4,600-seat stand at the Fratton End of the ground in November 1995. The figures given in the capacities above are pre the opening of this stand. No news yet as to whether the club will get a further extension on being allowed to keep their terracing open, but as sanity prevailed last year, one can only keep fingers crossed for more of the same.

OTHER INFORMATION

Days after you've been to the ground you will find yourself humming the Pompey chimes, which has the catchy insistence of a Bananarama song. In fact if I just write the words 'Play up Pompey, Pompey Play up' it should probably be enough to have you singing for at least 20min.

The openess of the ground doesn't affect the atmosphere; in fact the chants seem to bounce of the sea breeze and return much magnified. This also means that when you eventually manage to park your car in a far distant spot of Hampshire you will probably be able to hear the singing and think you are only a minute or so away from the ground — wrong!

Probably the nearest pub to the ground is the Shepherd's Crook on the corner of Goldsmith Avenue and Winter Road (down which is a decent chip shop and a Chinese), although the Milton Arms and the White House aren't a million miles away. Some of the pubs can be very much 'home' affairs, and similarly the sea front can get a bit hairy on a Friday and Saturday night. Portsmouth is probably one of the few places which can actually get away with calling one of its streets 'The Hard'. If in doubt there are numerous pubs on Kingston Road which are worth a visit and are a bit calmer. Inside the ground, the food is OK, but be prepared to queue, especially in the South Stand where the narrow corridors make half-time crushes a speciality.

DID YOU KNOW? Terry Fenwick, the manager at Portsmouth, sent every female member of staff at Fratton Park a long-stemmed rose on Valentines Day? What a gent!

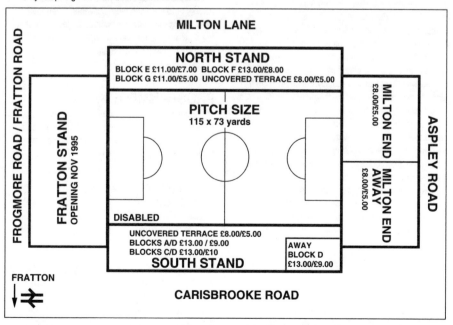

MILTON LANE

FROGMORE ROAD / FRATTON ROAD

NORTH STAND
BLOCK E £11.00/£7.00 BLOCK F £13.00/£8.00
BLOCK G £11.00/£5.00 UNCOVERED TERRACE £8.00/£5.00

FRATTON STAND
OPENING NOV 1995

PITCH SIZE
115 x 73 yards

MILTON END
£8.00/£5.00

MILTON END AWAY
£8.00/£5.00

ASPLEY ROAD

DISABLED

UNCOVERED TERRACE £8.00/£5.00
BLOCKS A/D £13.00 / £9.00
BLOCKS C/D £13.00/£10
SOUTH STAND

AWAY
BLOCK D
£13.00/£9.00

FRATTON

CARISBROOKE ROAD

PRESTON NORTH END

ADDRESS: Lowthorpe Road
Deepdale
Preston PR1 6RU
TELEPHONE No: 01772 795919
TICKET OFFICE: 01772 795919
FAX: 01772 653266
CLUBCALL: 0891 660 220
NICKNAME: The Lilywhites
RECORD ATTENDANCE:
42,684 v Arsenal Div 1 23 April 1938 (L 1-3)

CLUB COLOURS:
HOME: Shirts: White and Navy;
Shorts: Navy; Socks: White and Navy
AWAY: Shirts: Red and Navy;
Shorts: Navy; Socks: Red and Navy
THIRD: Shirts: Yellow and Blue;
Shorts: Yellow; Socks: Yellow and Navy

KIT SPONSORS: Baxi
MANUFACTURERS: Footy

GROUND INFO

The news of the development of the West Stand brought sighs of relief from visiting supporters all around the country, as the old monstrosity had over 20 pillars, meaning that it was indeed a lucky man who could go into there and leave saying they had not had a restricted view. Sod's law meant that you inevitably got a pillar right in front of one of the goals and had to spend half your time either leaning over the person next to you or craning your neck to impossible angles. Added to the fact that you actually went in through a door marked exit, and also its rickety wooden nature, it would take a phenomenal traditionalist to shed any tears (other than those associated with great joy) over its demise. At the time of writing, the club has not decided what section of the ground visiting supporters will be allocated, but if you can put your hand on your heart and say that you think they will still get 1,900 places in the new West Stand, then one can only assume you are the type of person who watches the national lottery every week and expects to win.

Educated guesswork seems to suggest that away fans will be allocated a proportion of the Fulwood (Town) End partially covered terrace and possibly some places in the Pavilion Stand, although until the West Stand reopens, seating will be at an absolute premium in the ground so don't hold your breath on the latter part of the equation coming true.

In 1994/5 Preston introduced a 'Pay As You Play' scheme, as pioneered by Cardiff City, whereby if the club were in the top seven of the division adults paid a

£1 premium (those away fans we discussed earlier, who are sure they are going to be given a place in the new West Stand, would probably describe this as getting a £1 discount if the club were lower than 7th). While cynics may point to the fact that Preston was among the bookies' favourites for promotion at the start of the season, perhaps this is one instance when we shouldn't be overly cynical as we all know there are no cast-iron guarantees as to how well a club will do, and at least it meant that if the club struggled, the financial burden would be relieved slightly. What is definitely worth praising is the fact that the club offer matching concessions for away fans to those given to home supporters.

CAPACITY: Stands: 1,068; Terrace: 9,173;
Total: 10,241

AWAY FANS: Pavillion Paddock: 650;
Total: 650
See future developments for further information regarding the modernisation of the ground.

DISABLED FACILITIES: There are approximately 20 places available in front of the West Stand Paddock. Nobody knows what the impact of the developments will be, so it's probably as well to be safe than sorry and take a hard hat along with you. Disabled fans are admitted free, with helpers paying £6.50 or £5.50 dependent on the club's position. There are match commentaries available for the visually impaired, or rather there were, for as the club says at present this is 'unfortunately broken, the blind need personal radio', (much more convenient than them fixing it, I suppose). There is no specific parking area for the disabled, but the club car park is large enough, and close enough to the West Stand for this not to present too big a problem. The club states that pre-booking isn't necessary, but I would.

PROGRAMME: £1.30
There normally is at least one informative article in here that rises above the rest, and this being the case it certainly puts it in front of a lot of club programmes. Nothing spectacular, but alright..

FANZINES:
Vernon's Two Left Feet	£1
Pie Muncher	£1
Deepdale Rudge	50p
Preston's Pride and Joy	£1

Two of the club's fanzines bit the dust in 1994/5, namely *Sleeping Giant* and *Tommy Who?* Three fanzines probably would have been one too many, but into the void stepped PP&J which is produced by the club's Independent Supporters Association. Certainly this isn't a bad publication, but the good stuff (and there is very good stuff in all of them) is too thinly spread, and there are definite signs of padding in places. Another minor irritant is the fact that there are so many fanzine sellers, there are occasions when you spend a fruitless 10min going up to the wrong people in search of the official programme.

TRAVEL

NEAREST RAILWAY STATION:
Preston (01772 259439)

BUS: Preston bus station (01772 263333)

BY CAR:
NORTH: M6 to J32, M55 to J1. Take A6 (signposted Fulwood and Preston) and continue until you pass the Royal Preston Hospital and Moor Park. Immediately after you have past Moor Park, turn left on to St Thomas's Road (if you miss this the next left into St George's Street is as good). At the T-junction turn left into Deepdale Road, and the ground is on your right.

EAST: A59 towards Preston, and as you approach the town take the second exit at the roundabout into Blackpool Road. Continue for 1.5 miles until you get to the crossroads with the A6063 Deepdale Road; turn left on to this road for the ground.

SOUTH: M6 to J31, then take the A59 towards Preston. After one mile take the second exit at the roundabout into Blackpool Road, then as east.

WEST: M55 to J1, then as north.

PARKING: There is a large car park in front of the West Stand which can hold 600+ vehicles. Alternatives are either on-street parking, which is plentiful along Deepdale Road, or to drive into the town and park at the Fishergate Shopping Centre car park. This is right by the railway station and is convenient for numerous decent pubs. If you want to get a taxi to the ground from the station, you should get change from £3.

FUTURE DEVELOPMENTS

The talk of either rotating the pitch 90° or moving to a different location both seem unlikely to materialise. If the club is to stay at Deepdale then the redevelopment process is likely to be a fairly long one. This is being kicked off with the development of the west side of the ground and the construction of a new 7-8,000-seat stand. This is scheduled (hopefully) to be opened in the third week of December 1995. During construction the capacities will be reduced to approximately 1,500 seats and 9,500 terrace places. The new stand may possibly open in two stages, although nothing has been officially announced yet. During construction it is considered most likely that away fans will get 1-2,000 places in the Fulwood End, and possibly 100 or so seats in the Pavilion Stand. Segregation may prove to be a problem (in terms of logistics rather than perceived trouble) and at the time of going to print, the club was reviewing a number of other possibilities.

OTHER INFORMATION

There are a couple of good pubs around Deepdale although Legends, which is right by the ground and incorporates a night-club and a pool hall, is not the most hospitable of places for visiting fans. The County Arms on the corner of Deepdale Road and Ribbleton Road looks rough but isn't too bad, and the Hesketh Arms on the way in from J31 is always worth a visit.

Preston's away following include drummers, bell-ringers and various other percussion players, but fear not because these people often leave their instruments when they go to Deepdale, meaning you can leave your earplugs (and Anadin) at home.

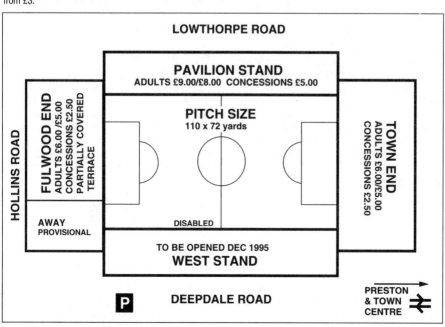

LOWTHORPE ROAD

HOLLINS ROAD

PAVILION STAND
ADULTS £9.00/£8.00 CONCESSIONS £5.00

FULWOOD END
ADULTS £6.00 /£5.00
CONCESSIONS £2.50
PARTIALLY COVERED
TERRACE

PITCH SIZE
110 x 72 yards

TOWN END
ADULTS £6.00/£5.00
CONCESSIONS £2.50

AWAY
PROVISIONAL

DISABLED

TO BE OPENED DEC 1995
WEST STAND

P DEEPDALE ROAD

PRESTON
& TOWN
CENTRE →

QUEENS PARK RANGERS

ADDRESS: Rangers Stadium
South Africa Road
Shepherds Bush
London W12 7PA

TELEPHONE No: 0181 743 0262

TICKET OFFICE: 0181 749 5744

FAX: 0181 749 0994

CLUBCALL: 0891 12 11 62

NICKNAME: The R's

RECORD ATTENDANCE:
35,353 v Leeds Div 1 27 April 1974 (L 0-1)

CLUB COLOURS:
HOME: Shirts: Blue and White Hoops; Shorts: White with Blue trim; Socks: White
AWAY: Shirts: Red with Black trim; Shorts: Red with Black trim; Socks: Red

KIT SPONSORS: Compaq

MANUFACTURERS: Rangers Clubhouse

GROUND INFO

Lesson number 842 in translating commentator-speak into real English is the expression 'Loftus Road is a compact little ground'. What this actually means is that you can find yourself crammed sardine-like into your seat, spending 90min with your knees up by your ears.

The view from the upper tier of the School End is reasonable, and although the lower tier isn't brilliant, the low roof does have good acoustic qualities, which means a good sing-song is always in order.

Other than that, probably the best thing about the ground are the stewards, who are arguably the most helpful and polite in the Premiership. Where else do you get called Sir?

The club operates a membership scheme which costs £12 for adults and £6 for juveniles. Adult members can buy tickets at £8 for B games and £10 for A games. Junior members get a 50% reduction on admission prices.

CAPACITY: Stands: 19,074; Terrace: Nil; Total: 19,074

AWAY FANS: School End: 3,100; Total: 3,100
NB: If demand requires it, the club will make available a section of the Ellerslie Road Stand (capacity about 480) and part of the old West Paddock in the South Africa Road Stand (capacity about 750) for away fans. However, it should be noted that the club did state that it is considering a possible resiting of away fans during the 1995/6 season, although where and when this would be, it could not say.

DISABLED FACILITIES: There are 20 places for wheelchair-bound supporters, seven of these are given to QPR season ticket holders and the remaining 13 are up for grabs — get in quickly. The season ticket holders go in Block A of the West Paddock of the South Africa Road Stand, and visiting supporters are in Block X of the Ellerslie Road Stand. Admission is free of charge for disabled supporters and their helpers. There are match commentaries and also parking facilities available. Phone up the club and they will sort you out.

PROGRAMME: £1.50

FANZINES:
In The Loft	£1
A Kick Up The R's	£1
Beat About The Bush	£1

TRAVEL

NEAREST RAILWAY STATION:
Paddington (0171 262 6767 — Paddington Enquiries) This is miles away from the ground, but you can pick up the tube from here.

NEAREST TUBE STATION: Shepherds
Bush — Hammersmith & City Line. White City — Central Line
These are closer, but still not what you might call on top of the ground. White City is perhaps the more convenient of the two.

NB: There is another station called Shepherds Bush on the Central Line, the stop before White City. This is even further away from the ground, but does set you down in a better area for pre-match food and drink.

BY CAR:
NORTH: M1, then turn right on to the A406 (signposted Neasden). After three miles turn left on to the A404 (signposted Harlesden). 1.75 miles later bear right into Scrubs Lane, and after a further 1.25 miles you will see White City. Take the first right after White City into White City Road (if you go past BBC TV you have gone too far), and then first left into South Africa Road. The ground is 0.25 mile on the left.

EAST: A12, A406, then A503. At the end of the A503 follow signs for Oxford to bring yourself on to the A40(M). After two miles, branch left off the A40(M) to join the M41 (signposted The West). At the roundabout take the third exit for the A40, then left on to the A4020 Uxbridge Road (signposted Acton). 0.25 mile later turn right into Loftus Road.

SOUTH: A3, and turn left by reservoirs at Putney Heath on to the A219 Tibbets Ride/Putney Hill. Continue along this road for 1.5 miles (crossing Putney Bridge) then bear left for Fulham Palace Road, still the A219, signposted Hammersmith. Once in

Hammersmith, follow the one-way system until you turn left on to the A219 Shepherds Bush Road. (If you go past a big hotel on your left, you have gone too far and will need to follow the one-way system round again.) Continue for 0.75 mile then turn left on to the A4020 Uxbridge Road (signposted Acton) and 0.25 mile later turn right into Loftus Road.

WEST: M4 into Chiswick, then continue along the A4. At Hogarth roundabout take the first exit on to the A4 Great West Road (signposted Hammersmith). Follow the one-way system, then as south.

PARKING: There is an NCP at White City which you will pass if you are coming from the north. For those coming from other directions, instead of turning into the Uxbridge Road continue along the A40 past the BBC TV Centre and the car park is on your left. There is also reasonable street parking about.

For a real exercise in futility, try and talk your way into the BBC car park. No chance!

FUTURE DEVELOPMENTS
None planned.

OTHER INFORMATION
Whilst it is true that visiting fans sit in relative security in any part of the ground, a closer look at certain facts might lead one to think twice about QPR's friendly, easy-going and naïve image.

There's the categorisation of matches, the fact that certain seats are over double the normal price for big games, the lack of juvenile concessions for visitors... Hell, it's as bad as the rest of them! To be fair to the club, it does always seem prepared to try and help with any problems or enquiries.

The only pub near the ground is the Springbok which, true to the QPR experience, is a place where home and away fans can mingle. The pub is not that big, but the police don't seem to mind people taking their drinks into the square which is just outside.

This square also houses a bookies and an above average chip shop, which I strongly recommend you visit as inside the ground there are always massive queues to get food. And when you do make your purchase you may wish you hadn't; on my visit the first word in the phrase 'Hot Dog' was a clear breach of the Trades Descriptions Act. (Funnily enough I've never heard anyone suggest that this is also the case for the second word!)

A very, very interesting fact (so interesting, indeed, that I hope you are sitting down) is that QPR have had more home grounds than any other league club (14). You may now be wondering why, if this is the case, they opted to stay at Loftus Road.

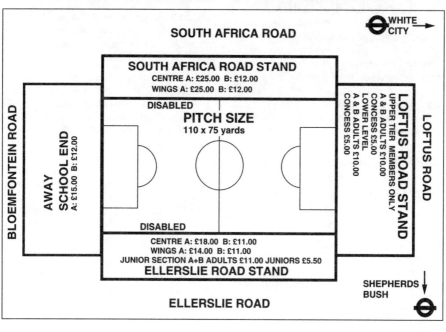

SOUTH AFRICA ROAD

WHITE CITY

SOUTH AFRICA ROAD STAND
CENTRE A: £25.00 B: £12.00
WINGS A: £25.00 B: £12.00

DISABLED

PITCH SIZE
110 x 75 yards

BLOEMFONTEIN ROAD

AWAY SCHOOL END
A: £15.00 B: £12.00

DISABLED

CENTRE A: £18.00 B: £11.00
WINGS A: £14.00 B: £11.00
JUNIOR SECTION A+B ADULTS £11.00 JUNIORS £5.50
ELLERSLIE ROAD STAND

ELLERSLIE ROAD

LOFTUS ROAD STAND
UPPER TIER MEMBERS ONLY
A & B ADULTS £10.00
CONCESS £5.00
LOWER LEVEL
A & B ADULTS £10.00
CONCESS £5.00

LOFTUS ROAD

SHEPHERDS BUSH

READING

ADDRESS: Elm Park
Norfolk Road
Reading RG3 2EF
TELEPHONE No: 01734 507878
TICKET OFFICE: 01734 507878
FAX: 01734 566628
CLUBCALL: 0891 12 1000
NICKNAME: The Royals
RECORD ATTENDANCE: 33,042 v
Brentford FA Cup 5th 19 February 1927 (W 1-0)

CLUB COLOURS:
HOME: Shirts: Blue and White Hoops; Shorts: White;
Socks: White
AWAY: Shirts: Red; Shorts: Red; Socks: Red

KIT SPONSORS: Auto Trader
MANUFACTURERS: Pelada

GROUND INFO

Away fans are sited on the open West Terrace. This is really quite strange as it has walls jutting out at peculiar places on it. These walls have fencing attached to them which can lead to a restricted view especially on the rear left hand side. The Norfolk Road Stand is OK but as it is only about a dozen rows deep and away fans only have a small section of it, get there early if you want to be sure of a seat. The away terrace has concessions to encourage more away families as does the away seating area.

CAPACITY: Stands: 2,242; Terrace: 11,816;
Total: 14,058

AWAY FANS: Norfolk Road Stand 'A': 342;
Reading End: 2,832; Total: 3,174

DISABLED FACILITIES: There are places for 16 wheelchair-bound supporters and helpers in the Norfolk Road Stand Block 'E'. Eight seats are also available to provide match commentary for the visually impaired. Admission is £5 for wheelchair-bound supporter; this price also includes admission for the helper. There are no parking facilities at the ground.

PROGRAMME: £1.50
A sizeable tome, the first article in which is called 'Entree'. If the club continued the culinary terminology then the away section would have to be called 'mint that you get with your coffee' in that what there is is nice, but it's not really enough to get your teeth into and it always leaves you wanting more.

FANZINES:
Heaven 11   50p

A strange offering which ranges from some excellent to some truly awful articles. Examples of the former include its away day guide (though obviously it isn't as good as this book!) and some of the stuff they have done with reference to the need for a new ground/ground development. As for the dodgy pieces, well the four pages of fantasy league are of no interest to anyone not in on the game, and the predictive match report joke wears thin after about one paragraph, and by the end of page three is very dull. That being said, I've seen a couple of copies and it is improving and provides a decent 45min read.

TRAVEL

NEAREST RAILWAY STATION:
Reading West (01734 595911)
This is about 10min from the ground. However, it is not the main station in Reading which is sited in the town centre. It is absolutely pointless asking anyone how far the station is from the ground as anyone you question has a different answer, ranging from '10 min max' to 'If you set off now you should be there for Tuesday'. In truth it is 20min at a jog, and 30 if you walk.

BUS:
Reading bus station (01734 594000)
Take a 33, 34, or 35 from the town centre to the ground. After-match congestion may well mean it is quicker for you to walk back.

BY CAR:
NORTH: A423, A4074, then A4155 following signs for Reading. Once on the A4155 you cross the Thames (albeit not at one of its grandest points) and the road becomes Caversham Road. Continue along this road until you get to the second large roundabout, where you should take the third (ie right) exit (signposted Newbury A4). Then take the third turning on your right into Russell Street/Tilehurst Road and the ground is about a mile on your right.

EAST/WEST: M4 to J12. Turn into the A4 (signposted Reading) and after about 3.5 miles turn left on to Liebenrood Road, then right on to Tilehurst Road. The ground is on your left.

NB: If you are coming from the east you will no doubt be told by someone masquerading as a friend to leave the M4 at J10. Ignore them, as by going to J12, although you travel slightly further, you cut out Reading town centre which can really slow you down.

PARKING: A bit of a problem. There are small car parks at the church on Tilehurst Road, at the top of Kensington Park (this connects the Oxford Road to Norfolk Road), or half-way down Liebenrood Road where there is a small turning on your left which takes you into Prospect Park. There is a signposted park-and-ride scheme from Prospect School — follow signs on A4. On-street parking is very restricted and early arrival is essential.

FUTURE DEVELOPMENTS

If you judged them on the ground development work they had undertaken, then the board at Reading must have had little confidence in the club staying in the First Division never mind progressing into the Premier. The ground is a three-sided terrace and no improvements were undertaken in 1994/5, nor has any work on a new stadium at a different site started. At the time of writing it is odds on that the club will move, and the favourite for where this would be is Smallmead which is just off the Basingstoke road and home to the town's Speedway team and dog track. As the club was promoted to the First Division only in 1994 it still has until August 1997 to go all-seater. Expect the ground to stay very much as it is this season, although among some of the more bizarre schemes that have been tossed into the ring is that they might play 'big' games at a 'London ground', or they might ask the FA for a permanent exemption to retain terracing.

OTHER INFORMATION

There are plenty of pubs on the way to the ground, but as you get nearer these become more rare. The Three Guineas by the railway station and the Hobgoblin on Oxford Road are both good meeting places. The Spread Eagle is on the corner of Norfolk Road right by the ground and is normally open before the match, however entry is to recognised members only.

Food is more of a problem. There are no decent chip shops around the ground, and if you want to eat before you go in, stick to getting something from one of the myriad places on Oxford Road (where there are a couple of excellent curry houses). The food in the ground is below average, and the hot dog I had last season lay heavily on my stomach for ages. The tea looks horrible, but doesn't taste too bad, although last season it went from being one of the hottest in the league to being a fairly tepid affair.

Actually getting into the ground is no mean achievement as quite often you are subject to a fastidious search by the Thames Valley Police and/or the stewards. This is a real empty-all-your-pockets job, and one of the last times I was at the ground both my pen and a packet of chewing gum I had were picked up and 'examined' by a PC. Oh, and don't try to take banners or flags into the ground because they too are a big no-no.

There is a notice in the toilets serving the away terrace that reads: SERIOUS WARNING — This is private property, all toilets have been renovated for the comfort of supporters. Any person who misuses or defaces this property will be prosecuted and banned from Elm Park. YOU HAVE BEEN WARNED!' What, you might wonder, causes such strong words: are we talking hand-crafted porcelain à la Highbury? Well, not exactly, more like a rusty metal gutter. Still, the ivy growing down the wall through the gap where the roof doesn't quite join does give a certain ambience.

If you listen carefully during the warm-up you'll hear the club playing a 'team' song 'Sing for the Royals (La La La La La)'. This horrid sub-disco record is dreadful even for its genre, and you can only be grateful that the club doesn't play it loud.

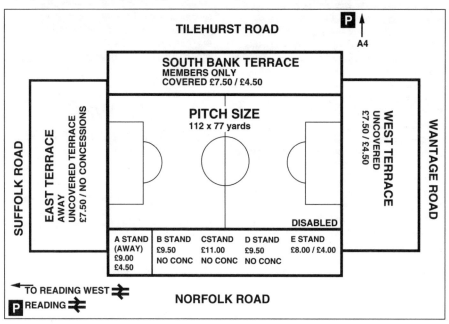

ROCHDALE

ADDRESS: Sandy Lane
Spotland
Rochdale
OL11 5DS

TELEPHONE No: 01706 44648
TICKET OFFICE: 01706 44648
FAX: 01706 48466
DALE NEWSLINE: 0891 555 858
NICKNAME: The Dale
RECORD ATTENDANCE: 24,231 v

Notts County FA Cup 2nd 10 December 1949 (L 1-2)

CLUB COLOURS:

HOME: Shirts: Blue with White/Red Flashes;
Shorts: Blue; Socks: White
AWAY: Shirts: Green with narrow Black Stripes;
Shorts: Black with Green Side
Socks: Green with Black and White Top

KIT SPONSORS: Carcraft
MANUFACTURERS: Glory Years

GROUND INFO

Brilliant concessions for visitors at the ground... provided you want to sit down. It will be interesting to see whether any relocation of away supporters due to redevelopment work results in a simultaneous review of the price strategy in the area they are moved to. Raise your hats in mighty salutation to the person who decided on the pricing for the family stand which although not very cheap for adults at £8 is a fantastic £1 for accompanying children.

Rochdale has shared its ground with the town's rugby league team, Rochdale Hornets, for the past four years, in a move that saw the club receive £0.5 million and helped finance the Main Stand, the floodlights, and will also go some way to meeting the costs of the new Pearl Street Stand. However, the twin use does mean that the pitch (or mudflat as it could be better described) is laid waste from fairly early on in the season. If you support a team that likes to play a passing game on the deck, prepare yourself for a very long afternoon/evening.

CAPACITY: Stands: 2,054; Terrace: 4,601;
Total: 6,655

AWAY FANS: Pearl Street End: 1,166;
Main Stand: 250; Total: 1,416
Both these sets of figures will be subject to change during 1995/6, see Future Developments.

DISABLED FACILITIES: There are 14 places for wheelchair-bound supporters and 25 spaces for what the club describes as advocates (my dictionary defines this word as one who pleads for another in a Scottish Court — but I think they probably mean helper). Disabled supporters are admitted free of charge but succulent pear-shaped fruits (no, that's something else isn't it?) pay £8. These facilities are sited in the Main Stand and offer a very good view of the action. Match commentaries for the blind are available, and there are special parking facilities at the ground. Contact the club in advance to pre-book your place.

PROGRAMME: £1.20

This programme is always capable of throwing up the odd classic, whether it's a full page photo with caption 'Mark Stuart's (Rochdale forward) 25 yard free kick heads for goal' on a page entitled 'Incredible But True', or John Dawson's guide to sports injuries 'No 11 the dislocated shoulder...Recognition factors — Severe pain' — illuminating stuff eh?

The programme has in the recent past won the divisional programme of the year, but I'd be very surprised if it held on to its title, although for all that, it is not too bad.

FANZINES:

Exceedingly Good Pies £1
EGP seems to be developing into a better and better fanzine. 1994/5 issues were of a continually improved standard to the previous season's which swung between brilliant and dire. Mind you, there was also a 100% price rise, and you can't help but feel that there should be somewhere that fans could vent there feelings about how footie is costing them more and more...

TRAVEL

NEAREST RAILWAY STATION:

Rochdale (0161 832 8353)

BUS:

Baillie/Smith Street bus station (0161 228 7811)
The station is quite a way from the ground, with the bus station about half-way between the two. If you don't fancy walking take either a 436, 460 or 461 to Spotland.

BY CAR:

FROM ALL DIRECTIONS: M62 to J20, turn left on to the A627(M) and take the second exit at the second roundabout into Roch Valley Way. A mile later turn right into Willbutts Lane.

PARKING: There is plenty of on-street parking to be found but make sure you leave yourself pointing in the right direction for when you want to leave otherwise you will cause yourself untold grief trying a three point turn in the very narrow streets.

FUTURE DEVELOPMENTS

The Pearl Street End is due to be converted into a 2,600-seat stand. The proposed completion date is late 1995. This will make the club's capacity 8,089 with seats for 4,654. During the construction period away fans may well be moved into the Willbutts Lane Terrace although nothing definite has been decided on. If this does occur expect to get approx 1,000 spaces.

OTHER INFORMATION

If you fancy a pre-match pint, the Radcliffe Arms is on the corner of the ground and is fairly welcoming (though not the cheapest place you'll ever imbibe at). Mind you, if the signboard is an accurate depiction of ex-Dale chairman Fred Radcliffe, I reckon he could have given John Merrick a run for his money! Also worth a call is the Cemetery Hotel on Bury Road which has an excellent selection of beer, and the Church which is just behind the Pearl Street End. There are also plenty of good pubs in the town centre which are very welcoming.

As far as food is concerned, Cockleys fish and chip shop outside the ground on Willbutts Lane is good but a bit small and thus you can have a fair queue for your food. Tragically the food inside the ground took a massive nosedive last year, and from being arguably the best pies in the country, the offering, while still being fairly meaty, was served at a nasty tepid temperature. Sort it out Dale, thousands of carbohydrate-addicted fans are depending on you!

Rochdale's claim to fame is that it has given the world Gracie Fields, Lisa Stansfield and the Co-op but we can surely forgive them for that. You'll probably find this quite easy as 90% of the population are the friendliest and kindest you could hope to meet. The club will go out of its way to solve any problems you have and you'll never be stuck for someone to have a chat with over a pint. If all away days could be like this then life would be a lot easier.

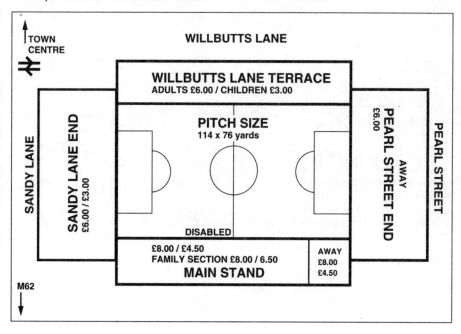

ROTHERHAM UNITED

ADDRESS: Millmoor Ground
Millmoor
Rotherham S60 1HR

TELEPHONE No: 01709 562434

TICKET OFFICE: 01709 562434

FAX: 01709 563336

MILLERS CHATTERBOX LINE:
0891 66 44 42

NICKNAME: The Merry Millers

RECORD ATTENDANCE: 25,149 v

Sheffield Wednesday Div 2 26 January 1952 (D 3-3)
The club programme states the biggest crowd is
25,000 for the above match and a match in December
1952 against Sheffield United, but what do they know!

CLUB COLOURS:

HOME: Shirts: Red with White sleeves;
Shorts: White; Socks: Red

AWAY: Shirts: Yellow; Shorts: Black; Socks: Yellow

KIT SPONSORS: Parkgate Retail World

MANUFACTURERS: Matchwinner

GROUND INFO

The ground looks very tatty from the outside, but once
in through the turnstiles it is a lot better. The entrance
to the away terrace is via the high-walled Millmoor
Lane which is very thin and thus dreadfully congested
pre and post match, although this might not play on
your mind as much as the signs opposite warning of
asbestos roofs. The cover over the away terracing is
ideal for chanting beneath, and you'll probably feel like
having a bit of a shout when you find that visiting supporters do not get the concessions that the home ones
do.

The ground is in a very industrial setting with a
scrap metal merchant who specialises in dismantling
trains behind the visitors' end, and the region is very
obviously connected with coal mining. (Younger readers may wish to ask their parents what a coal mine
was at this stage — if they answer 'A place where
trouble-makers used to congregate' then it's my sad
duty to have to tell you that you might have been sired
by a member of the Tory cabinet.)

CAPACITY: Stands: 4,486; Terrace: 7,047;
Total: 11,533

AWAY FANS: Railway End Terrace: 3,125;
Millmoor Lane Stand: 1,094;
Total: 4,219

DISABLED FACILITIES: There are 12
places in the Millmoor Lane Stand family section.

There is no cost for either disabled supporters or their
helpers, although the club does stipulate that this is
true only if there is one helper per disabled fan, so if
you were planning on organising a coach trip and aiming on making a few bob by claiming that everyone
was with you, then I'm afraid your devious plans have
been thwarted. There is disabled parking at the
ground, which together with your place should be pre-
booked. No match commentaries are available.

PROGRAMME: £1.20

1994/5's was much better than previous seasons'
offerings, although some of the 'humour' in the Vice
President's article may be considered slightly questionable by some.

FANZINES:

Mi Whippet's Dead	50p
Windy and Dusty	60p
Moulin Rouge	80p

The second of these tomes is produced out of London
and thus has naturally got a heavy 'exiles' feel about it,
and you won't find yourself tripping over sellers of the
other two at the ground.

TRAVEL

NEAREST RAILWAY STATION:
Rotherham Central (01742 726411)

BUS: Rotherham bus station (01742 768688)
If you don't fancy the 0.5 mile or so walk from the centre to the ground, either a 137 or an X78 will save your
legs.

BY CAR:

NORTH/WEST: M1 to J34. Take the A6109
Meadow Bank Road (signposted Rotherham) and continue for just over a mile until you get to a roundabout
with the A629. Turn right at this roundabout on to the
Wortley Road (A629), then take a right at the next
roundabout on to Masbrough Street. The fourth left is
Millmoor Lane and the ground is on your left.

SOUTH/WEST: (Yes! Yes! I know it says west
above as well, but I couldn't decide which route you
were likely to take so I decided to put both down and
let you take your pick!) M1 to J33. Turn on to the A630
(signposted Rotherham) then left at the next roundabout on to Bawtry Road (A631). Straight over the next
roundabout and you will be back on the A630 Canklow
Road (signposted Rotherham and Canklow). 1.5 miles
later, turn left (by the White Rose) on to the Old
Sheffield Road. Turn left again at the end of this (short)
road, then right at the roundabout on to the A630
Centenary Way. Left at the next roundabout on to
Masbrough Street, then as north/west.

NB: Meadowhall Shopping Centre is situated at
J33 of the M1 so if the game coincides with a busy
shopping period it can be better to go to J34 and follow

the directions from the north.

EAST: (But definitely not west). A631 into Rotherham until you get to a roundabout with the A6021 Wichersley Road. Take the A6021 and go straight over the next roundabout. A mile later turn left into Hollowgate; this becomes Alma Road, at the bottom of which you should turn left on to the A630 Canklow Road and then immediately right on to Old Sheffield Road, then as south (and dammit west as well!).

PARKING: You can park at the club car park, but it is a bit of a shenanigans to get into it. You are not allowed to drive in the front entrance (that would be far too easy) as only players and directors are allowed to use this. Instead, turn away from the ground (opposite the car park entrance) and follow the small side road by the bridge. Turn left through the railway arches and this brings you into the tradesmen's entrance. There is also some street parking around.

FUTURE DEVELOPMENTS

The club keeps muttering about doing something at the Railway End, but nothing concrete has been decided.

OTHER INFORMATION

For a pre-match pint why not try the club's own club, the Tivoli. If you have ever been to Copenhagen try to spot the difference between the Tivoli Gardens there and the one in Rotherham. The astute amongst you may come up with the odd one or 63,000 or so (not least of which is that beer is a lot cheaper in Rotherham!). If you don't fancy this, either the Moulders or the Travellers Rest (best for away fans) on Masbrough Street will do the trick. For food Julia's Millmoor café opposite the ground is good, but a bit small. If the queue's too long, wait till you get inside and enjoy an excellent Pukka Pie.

If you bank on listening to those half-time scores as they come in over the tannoy, pay a trip to the doctors before you go to get your ears syringed and in full working order. Even if you do take these precautions you may still never know the second half of the Arsenal 0 ... score due to it being drowned out by extraneous noise — such, on my visit, as the person next to you breathing.

The locals are welcoming enough to visitors, but it's got to be said, if there was ever a championship for complaining about the team you support then the people of Rotherham would be up there amongst the big boys. Whether they are really this discontented, or whether it's just a cunning ruse to get you to buy them a pint and/or not take the rise out of them if you win, is difficult to tell, but either way after listening to them tell you of their woes for half an hour or so you'll be in such a depressed state that even a Leonard Cohen tape would be a pick-me-up.

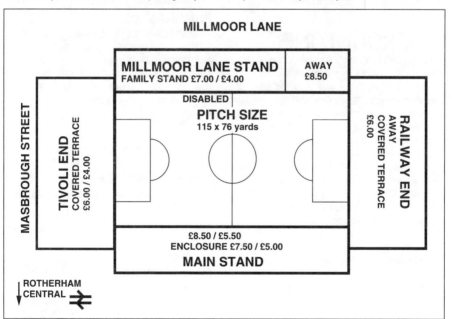

SCARBOROUGH

ADDRESS: The McCain Stadium
Seamer Road
Scarborough
North Yorkshire
YO12 4HF
TELEPHONE No: 01723 375094
TICKET OFFICE: 01723 375094
FAX: 01723 378733
NICKNAME: Boro
Seadogs is an unofficial nickname which is used more often by the fans — Well a Yo! ho! ho! and a bonjour matelot!

RECORD ATTENDANCE:
11,162 v Luton FA Cup 3rd 8 January 1938 (D 1-1)

CLUB COLOURS:
HOME: Shirts: Red and Black stripes;
Shorts: Black; Socks: Black
AWAY: Shirts: Yellow; Shorts: Black; Socks: Black

KIT SPONSORS: To be announced

MANUFACTURERS: Pendle

GROUND INFO

If you are making your first visit to the McCain Stadium, don't expect a brand-new ground à la Huddersfield, Scunthorpe or Walsall; the McCain Stadium is simply the Athletic Ground at which the club has always played but with a bit of sponsorship.

The capacity at the ground was temporarily reduced during the 1994/5, but the rebuilt Seamer Road end opened early in 1995 and work is progressing on the reconstruction of the West Stand. However, more than one cynical fan has suggested that the reduction in the capacity was a management ploy to frighten the opposition by making them play in a half-full stadium. It is encouraging to see that Scarborough offer the same concessions to away as they do for home fans; in fact it has even been known for the club to let everyone in free of charge for the last match of the season.

The away terrace is OK, and although it does get a bit cold in the winter it never reaches Hartlepool style sub-arctic temperatures. What is more, there is a nice grass bank on which you can lie to combine enjoying the game and getting a suntan at the start/end of a season. Given that the away end is currently uncovered there are some very weird acoustics around the place which mean that you can generate a very good atmosphere very easily. The club has recently started development work on the away terrace.

One result of the rebuilding work at the ground is that the tradition of being able to watch the game from houses on the A64 or by standing on the hill behind the ground no longer applies.

One area where the club seems to suffer is with regards to the pitch which whenever I've visited has not worn too well, and from about October onwards don't expect a ball to run in a straight line on it.

CAPACITY: Stands: 2,043; Terrace: 2,851;
Total: 4,894
This will be increased to more than 6,000 with the completion of the current development.

AWAY FANS: There will be accommodation for 1,336 away supporters once the current building programme is completed.

DISABLED FACILITIES: There are about 20 places for disabled fans by the Main Stand and also 14 spaces in the new Seamer Road Stand. Admission is free to the wheelchair-bound, although any helpers are charged. If you go to a match alone and need help then don't be afraid to ask as the club is ready, willing and able to give assistance. Pre-booking is not necessary for other than the biggest of big matches.

There are no matchday commentaries for the visually impaired, nor are there any parking facilities at the ground.

PROGRAMME: £1
Cheap and relatively cheerful, although watch out for the specials that occasionally appear such as that for an Autoglass which retailed at 25p and consisted of four pages: one page of writing, one page for the team sheet and two pages of advertising. There will be some changes for the new season.

FANZINES: None.

TRAVEL

NEAREST RAILWAY STATION:
Scarborough Central (01482 26033 — Hull Enquiries)

BUS: Scarborough and District (01723 375 463)
A number 843 bus will drop you off at the ground from the town.

BY CAR:
FROM ALL PARTS: Take the A64 main York to Scarborough Road. As you approach the town you will see a number of superstores (B&Q, Halfords, etc) and the ground is directly opposite the Do-It-All. The approach to the town takes you through some really remote areas, ideal for making you think about how far you would have to walk if your car broke down, especially at night. This invariably leads to panics (is the engine misfiring?) and thoughts of such fine cinematic feasts as 'American Werewolf in London.' Should you have the misfortune to break down, or run out of petrol I can only say this, 'Stick to the path, and beware the moon'.

PARKING: As you approach the town you will see a number of superstores...Alternatively drive past the ground and take the next left, by the school. Initially this is coned as no parking, but about half-way up the hill the restriction is lifted and there is plenty of street parking available. The attitude of some of the locals may go some way to explaining why it is unlikely that the club is ever going to be a major force in English football, as the last time I went to the ground I parked up here, and as I was getting out a local asked me what I was doing. I said that I was off to the football, but rather than the expected tirade of 'Well you can't park here' I simply got asked the question 'Where?'. At 2.30pm on a Saturday afternoon, this is not good news for the club.

FUTURE DEVELOPMENTS

The club opened the new Seamer End Stand on 8 March 1995, Tom Finney doing the honours. This is a 1,336-seater with an extra 14 disabled spaces — fairly impressive since the initial idea had been simply to put a roof over the terrace. The club is obviously pleased with the new stand as it has obtained planning permission for a replica of it to go up at the Edgehill Road End. However, work will not commence until the finances are in place including a grant from the Football League Trust. Once the development is under way it is likely that visiting supporters will either be given a section within the McCain Terrace (covered), or, if practical, a portion of the Seamer Road End. Provided adequate segregation can be organised, expect the total number of spaces to stay fairly static. There will be no room in the Edgehill Stand up until Christmas; it is hoped that it will be open at the end of the year.

OTHER INFORMATION

If you fancy a pint then you can try the club's McCain Lounge, otherwise the Railway Tavern is about 0.5 mile away from the ground as you go towards the town. As you get closer to the centre there is a rake of pubs to choose from and there should be something there to suit you whatever your taste.

Inside the ground the Bovril looks weak but isn't and the pies although lukewarm were fairly tasty. The biggest plus point about the catering in the ground though is that you are served quickly by people who smile and actually look happy to see you.

The club was the first to go police-free, and the stewards are a good bunch of people who do the job not only because it gets them into the ground for nothing, but also because they love the club. They are also the source of some fairly amusing tales about the ex-Boro chairman and club secretary who 'transferred' to Bradford City a couple of seasons back. I'm sure that these are all grossly exaggerated (although having once had the latter of these men surround me with-stewards and then step forward to ask me what I was up to asking questions such as 'Are there any good pubs around here?' maybe I'm not so sure). Certainly on the basis of my last couple of visits I'd say the atmosphere at the club does seem to have improved over the last 12 months.

A trip to Scarborough will entail a long drive for a lot of supporters and it is worthwhile making a weekend of it. There's a lot of beautiful, if rugged, country-side around, and it is worth paying a trip to Cayton or Filey Bay if you like invigorating sea-breezes, or possibly Flamingoland if you don't or if you have taken the kids with you. You can still pick up a B&B for under a tenner, and while the first 'B' may not be like your 'B' at home, expect a slap-up second 'B' chock full of enough cholesterol to last you the year.

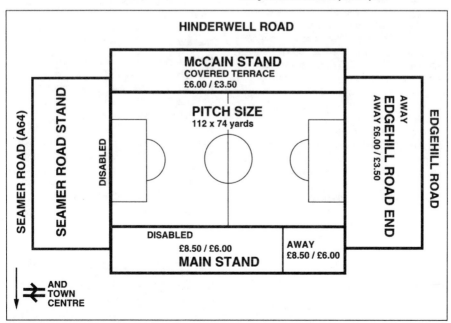

HINDERWELL ROAD

McCAIN STAND
COVERED TERRACE
£6.00 / £3.50

SEAMER ROAD (A64)

SEAMER ROAD STAND

DISABLED

PITCH SIZE
112 x 74 yards

AWAY
EDGEHILL ROAD END
AWAY £6.00 / £3.50

EDGEHILL ROAD

DISABLED
£8.50 / £6.00
MAIN STAND

AWAY
£8.50 / £6.00

AND
TOWN
CENTRE

SCUNTHORPE UNITED

ADDRESS: Glanford Park
Doncaster Road
Scunthorpe
South Humberside
DN15 8TD

TELEPHONE No: 01724 848077
TICKET OFFICE: 01724 848077
FAX: 01724 857986
CLUBCALL: 0891 12 16 52
NICKNAME: The Irons
RECORD ATTENDANCE:

23,935 v Portsmouth FA Cup 4th 15 January 1954 (D 1-1). At Glanford Park: 8,775 v Rotherham Div 4 1 May 1989 (D 0-0)

CLUB COLOURS:

HOME: Shirts: White with Claret & Blue trim; Shorts: Sky Blue; Socks: Sky Blue
AWAY: Shirts: Red with Claret/Blue/Yellow flashes; Shorts: Red; Socks: Red

KIT SPONSORS: Pleasure Island
MANUFACTURERS: Alan Ward Sports

GROUND INFO

The pricing policy at Glanford Park is, it has to be said, excellent and much better than in previous years. For away supporters the £3.70 concession for children's seating in 1994/5, while being a very strange amount, was actually £1.80 cheaper than the cheapest child seat for home supporters. This is even more praiseworthy when you consider that it was only last year the club 'saw the light' and started offering concessionary rates to visitors. Home fans do have the benefit of still being able to go on terracing and the combined cost for one adult and child for this would be £9, which is reasonable by anybody's standard.

The ground itself is functional and offers a good view of the pitch, though it must be said that there is a lack of soul about the place, which together with the bitter wind that is around even at the start of a season, and the grey/sky blue painted metal work that abounds makes for a slightly depressing stadium.

One thing I was less than impressed with were the toilets which were cavernous, resembling something out of the Industrial Zone on the 'Crystal Maze', and the rusty 'stainless' steel of the gents troughs is a novel was not altogether aesthetic addition.

CAPACITY: Stands: 6,410; Terrace: 2,773; Total: 9,183

AWAY FANS: South Stand: 1,678; Total: 1,678
DISABLED FACILITIES: There are 16 spaces for wheelchairs at the ground, and six headsets for the blind. Disabled supporters are admitted free, with helpers paying £7.50. There are both decent toilet and parking facilities for supporters at the ground. Pre-booking is required. The club does seem fairly receptive and geared up towards supporters' needs, which means a trip to Scunthorpe will be one of your easier away days during the season.

PROGRAMME: £1.30
Pretty good, although the printing is not always very pleasing to the eye. The obsession with a Lord Snooty type character is bizarre; this apparently comes from the 1930s when Scunthorpe were known as the Knuts and — I quote — 'The motif is of a well-dressed Knut in top hat and tails'. Words fail me. The programme is available from either the club shop, or inside the ground, but there appears to be few 'wandering' sellers around.

FANZINES: None.

TRAVEL

NEAREST RAILWAY STATION:
Scunthorpe (two miles) (01302 340222 — Doncaster Enquiries)

BUS:
Scunthorpe bus station (two miles) (01724 842233) There are no buses direct from the station to the ground. Instead, go to the town centre bus station (about 10min walk) and get either a 341 or a 335 to the stadium. These leave the bus station every quarter of an hour.

BY CAR:
NORTH/SOUTH/WEST: M180 to J3, then M181. At the end of the M181 turn right on to the A18 Doncaster Road. After 200yd, turn right into the approach to the ground and car park.
EAST: M180 to J4. Take the A18 (signposted Town Centre), continue to the roundabout with the A159 Ashby Road and take the second exit into Kingsway. At the next roundabout (again with the A159) take the second exit into Doncaster Road, and the approach to the ground is 300yd on the left.

PARKING: There is parking for over 600 vehicles by the ground.

FUTURE DEVELOPMENTS
None planned until the club reaches such a position that it would be a league requirement.

OTHER INFORMATION

The ground is a long way out of town, and other than a nearby garden centre which serves tea you are dependent on the club for food and drink. If you decide to go into the town there is a large Safeways on the left as you enter, which is a good place to fill up with petrol and park and is also the site of Scunthorpe's previous home. This is commemorated by a plaque which states not only that you are standing at the site of the Old Showground, but also that Emma loves Leigh (true!).

If you are looking for a watering hole in the town, The Mint or the Royal Hotel are OK, and the Hungry Fisherman is a good chip shop with plenty of tables at which to sit atlf you fancy sticking something up your nose... the newsagent's by the Hungry Fisherman boasts a large selection of snuff.

On my visit, the ground was virtually empty until kick-off time, with seemingly everyone opting for the warmth of their cars and the radio previews until the Scunthorpe entrance music of 'Fanfare To The Common Man' rallies them to the stadium. Inside, the pies were a bit crumbly (with no forks to eat them with) and the tea was of the teabag-on-a-stick variety.

The stewards at the club are both chatty and helpful, and dole out useful advice about getting into town, etc, but will also talk about the forthcoming game — although they tend to find it hard not to express their surprise that anyone should want to travel any distance to see what many refer to as 'this shower'.

Inside the ground, keep an eye open for the ball boy with the pathological hatred of Scunthorpe United who is often observed celebrating with away fans if the Irons let in a goal. Kids today, no sense of etiquette!

Two horror stories for you to end on (and I will leave you to decide which is the most horrible) — on a recent trip to the ground, I got into a discussion with one of the food vendors. When I explained what I was doing, he said 'Oh you'll want to put this in then' and proceeded to belch the team's name for me — lovely! The second is about an old guidebook that talks of strange happenings in the town, and then tells the story of Wesley's Confrontation (which actually occurred in Epworth some eight miles away) when as a child John Wesley, later the founder of the Methodist Church, heard mysterious footsteps on the stairs of his house. His father decided that it must be a ghost and said words to the effect of 'go away ghost', and then — and this is the weird bit — the ghost went, and they never heard from it again (gosh that is frightening, I'll never be able to get to sleep now!).

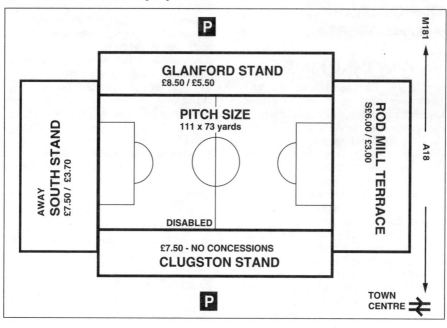

SHEFFIELD UNITED

ADDRESS: Bramall Lane
Sheffield
S2 4SU
TELEPHONE No: 0114 273 8955
TICKET OFFICE: 0114 276 6771
FAX: 0114 272 3030
CLUBCALL: 0891 888 650
NICKNAME: The Blades
RECORD ATTENDANCE: 68,287 v
Leeds Utd FA Cup 5th 15 February 1936 (W 3-1)

CLUB COLOURS:
HOME: Shirts: Broad Red/Thin White Stripes with large White Diamond overlay; Shorts: Black with Red/White Trim; Socks: Black wth Red/White Trim
AWAY: Shirts: Yellow/Purple halves with matching trim; Shorts: Yellow with Purple Trim; Socks: Yellow with Purple trim

KIT SPONSORS: Ward's
MANUFACTURERS: AVEC

GROUND INFO

The John Street Stand was pulled down before the 1994/5 season and the resulting gap detracted dreadfully from the atmosphere at the ground, although it did mean you had a very nice view of Sheffield. The upper tier of the Bramall Lane Stand offers a good if not totally unobstructed view. The Blades' pricing policy does leave a lot to be desired, with away fans paying £5 per adult and £1 per child more than their counterparts in either the lower tier or the impressive Kop Stand (which thankfully no longer seems to be referred to as the tongue-twisting En Tout Cas Stand).

Another peculiarity is the Family Enclosure which starts the season as strictly members only but in which the rule is relaxed as the season draws on, and where membership prices have in the past been reduced from £15 for one adult and child towards the end of a campaign. I was once advised that prices are likely to be reduced 'once our championship challenge has evaporated', which means either that someone dawdled between realising that this was the case in mid-August and changing the prices around March time, or they printed the league tables upside down in 'The Green 'Un'.

If you decide to go into the South Stand (which is OK for not overly vocal away visitors and which I thought offered a much better view than the Stones Stand) then when you go to the ticket office you will be asked for your name. The club states that this is not intended as a hooligan deterrant but more as a reference to help supporters, but it would be a lot more impressive if the club actually bothered asking for some ID. As it doesn't, why not indulge in a spot of personal fantasy and call yourself after your all-time hero. I called myself Edson Arantes Do Nascimento and didn't get pulled up (and if you're wondering who that is, shame on you!).

Two quick hurrahs for home supporters are the club's schemes for Junior Fans and Unemployed Fans which offer considerable reductions.

CAPACITY: Stands: 23,459; Terrace: Nil; Total: 23,459

AWAY FANS: Bramall Lane Stand Upper Tier: 2,200; Total: 2,200
The away allocation can be increased to the whole of the Bramall Lane Stand (total 4,860) if demand is sufficient (note: this is provided that the John Street Stand has been rebuilt and opened).

DISABLED FACILITIES: During the construction of the John Street Stand disabled supporters were temporarily sited at the bottom of the family enclosure. There were 25 spaces for wheelchair-bound supporters and 30 spaces for ambulant disabled fans. There are also 12 Main Stand spaces which offer commentary facilities. There is no charge for either disabled fans or their helpers although you are advised to pre-book, at which time you should also let the club know if you want a parking space. (There are 25 car park passes available for the ground.) Contact the club to pre-book at least seven days before the match. When the John Street Stand reopens, disabled fans will find themselves transferred to this area, although the precise availability of spaces is as yet unknown. Assuming the club maintains its current policy, then expect them to offer a good view and facilities.

PROGRAMME: £1.50
Well above average with a good visitors' section and a fair few general interest articles. One thing that might set your teeth on edge is 'Rusty Blade' which read like an attempt to write a controversial/amusing fanzine-type article which fails on both counts.

FANZINES:
The Flashing Blade	50p
The Greasy Chip Buttie	£1

The Flashing Blade is one of the funniest fanzines around (although Wednesdayites and Leeds Fans may beg to differ). Consistently way above average, a trip to Bramall Lane isn't complete without a copy.

The Greasy Chip Buttie gets its name from the fans' version of 'Annie's Song': 'You fill up my senses, like a night out in Sheffield, like a greasy chip buttie, like a good pinch of snuff' and they say that Yorkshiremen can't express their emotions! A fair publication but suffers in comparison to the *FB*, though is still worth checking out.

TRAVEL

NEAREST RAILWAY STATION:
Sheffield Midland (0114 270 0237)

NEAREST BUS STATION: Pond Street
bus station (opposite BR Station) (0114 276 8688)

BY CAR:
NORTH: M1 to J34. On leaving the motorway take the A6109 Meadow Hall Road (signposted Sheffield). Continue for three miles until this road merges with the A6135, then bear right into the seductive sounding Blonk Street. Take the fourth exit at the roundabout on to the A61. Go past Sheffield station and then take the first exit at the next roundabout, keeping in the left-hand lane for Suffolk Road. Once on Suffolk Road take the fifth exit at the next roundabout into St Mary's Road (signposted Bakewell), and left at the next roundabout into Bramall Lane. The ground is 200yd on the left.

SOUTH/EAST: M1 to either J31 or J33. From J31 take the A57 and from J33 take the A630, until the two roads merge. Continue along the A57 into Sheffield; take the third exit at the roundabout on to the A61, then as north.

WEST: A57 into Sheffield. Just after the University there is a roundabout. Take the fourth exit into Upper Hanover Street. Turn right at the second roundabout into Bramall Lane and the ground is 200yd on the right.

PARKING: Plenty of street parking. Alternatively for those coming from the north/south/east there is a car park by Sheffield station, and for those coming from the west there is a car park by the roundabout at the bottom of Upper Hanover Street. The car park at the ground is for permit holders only.

For those coming by private transport the hassle of driving to United and finding somewhere to park is considerably, and I do mean considerably, less stressful than a trip to their close neighbours and bosom buddies Wednesday.

FUTURE DEVELOPMENTS
The new all-singing, all-dancing 6,500-seater John Street Stand should be fully unveiled to the paying public around September 1995 (give or take a week or so). The club's next step may be the building of corner stands to link the whole ground although precisely when/if this will be implemented is unclear.

OTHER INFORMATION
The local pubs seemed a lot friendlier in 1994/5 than in previous seasons. The Railway Tavern is basic but right by the stadium and welcomes away fans; a 10min walk into the city centre offers a more diverse range if you so desire.

Forget about eating inside the ground; the food is OK, but not a patch on the hot pork batches (rolls for the uninitiated) at Munchies or the cold beef batches at Bri and Irenes (both on Shoreham Street) which are worth the trip up alone! Also on Shoreham Street, though slightly less appealing, is a second-hand book shop which amongst its wares offers would-be buyers a choice of slightly used 'adult' magazines. I don't know if I'm being over sensitive, but the more I thought about this concept the worse I felt!

Finally if you think your club plays dodgy football at times, spare a thought for the Blades. Things are apparently so bad that if you go into the South Stand, by the entrances to the various sections not only are there the seat numbers, but also the legend 'Facing The Pitch'; presumably this counts as the ultimate caveat emptor!

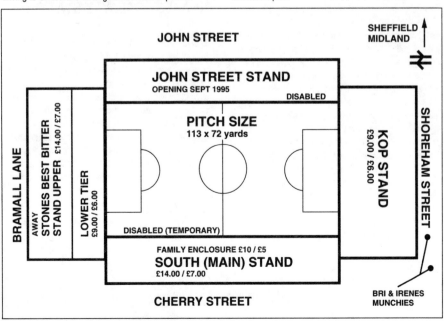

JOHN STREET

SHEFFIELD MIDLAND

JOHN STREET STAND
OPENING SEPT 1995

DISABLED

PITCH SIZE
113 x 72 yards

BRAMALL LANE

AWAY STONES BEST BITTER STAND UPPER £14.00 / £7.00

LOWER TIER £9.00 / £6.00

KOP STAND £9.00 / £6.00

SHOREHAM STREET

DISABLED (TEMPORARY)

FAMILY ENCLOSURE £10 / £5
SOUTH (MAIN) STAND
£14.00 / £7.00

CHERRY STREET

BRI & IRENES
MUNCHIES

SHEFFIELD WEDNESDAY

ADDRESS: Hillsborough
Sheffield
S6 1SW

TELEPHONE No: 0114 234 3122
TICKET OFFICE: 0114 233 7233
FAX: 0114 233 7145
CLUBCALL: 0891 12 11 86
NICKNAME: The Owls
RECORD ATTENDANCE: 72,841 v Man City FA Cup 5th 17 February 1934 (L 2-4)

CLUB COLOURS:
HOME: Shirts: Blue and White Stripes; Shorts: Blue; Socks: White
AWAY: Shirts: Black with Gold trim; Shorts: Black; Socks: Gold
Good news for parents! Wednesday only charge £1 per letter and £4 per number for additions to replica shirts — bad news is your sprog's favourite is Worthington. (Mind you, those replica tops are such good value you can hardly complain at a slight premium to have them customised; after all your kids will get weeks of wear out of them before they're pestering you for a new model.)

KIT SPONSORS: Sanderson Electronics
MANUFACTURERS: Puma

GROUND INFO

It's a bit of a shame that Wednesday seem to have given up on their idea of a mixed family enclosure with excellent concessions for both sets of fans. Perhaps the club didn't like the fact that too many kids were turning up and their high-pitched chanting was upsetting people — although if this is the case then maybe they should also look to saying a fond farewell to the PA announcer who is possibly the most over-excitable man in the world. (Funnily enough he did nearly get into trouble at the end of the 1993/4 season for excessive gloating when Sheffield United went down!)
The away seats offer a good view of the pitch and there is also excellent wooden seating in this section of the ground which is just right for banging out percussion rhythms to accompany your chants! Being in the upper tier means that visitors don't have to worry about where that next cup of tea is coming from when they score, but on the minus side, it is a fair climb to the seats.

CAPACITY: Stands: 36,020; Terrace: Nil; Total: 36,020

AWAY FANS: West (Presto) Stand Upper: 4, 193; Total: 4,193

DISABLED FACILITIES: There are 56 spaces in front of the North Stand. One helper can accompany a disabled supporter, with no admission charge being made for either. The majority of the places are allocated as season tickets to home fans, with any remaining places being up for grabs on a first come, first served basis (pre-book from four weeks in advance). Match commentaries are also available, as is car parking at the ground; pre-book both these facilities.

PROGRAMME: £1.50
Generally not bad although the 25% hike in its price in the 1994/5 season did take the edge off it a bit in value for money terms.

FANZINES:
Cheat!	50p
Boddle — Taking The Wednesday Into Insanity	80p
War Of The Monster Trucks	50p
A View From The East Bank	£1
The Blue and White Wizard	£1

Five fanzines, and the last visit I made to Hillsborough during the 1994/5 season I didn't see one of them on sale (admittedly I was in a rush to get into the ground, and I didn't loiter in the streets looking for vendors). Talking to some Wednesdayites they were raving about *War*, and about two weeks later it got a belting review in *442*. Last time I saw it, it was funny, but nothing brilliant, but it sounds like it's worth another bash.

TRAVEL

NEAREST RAILWAY STATION:
Sheffield Midland (0114 270 0237)

BUS: Pond Street bus station (0114 276 8688)
Pond Street is opposite the railway station, and as the ground is about four miles away is probably worth a visit. After the match away fans tend to be herded straight on to buses, the drivers of which seem to take vicarious pleasure in transforming their vehicles into one of the slowest moving objects known to man. Given the general congestion, it can take ages to get back to the station (and as I found, expect to hear these comments frequently: 'No you can't get out and walk', 'Because I said you can't'). If you have a tight connection to make be afraid, be very afraid.

BY CAR:
NORTH: M1 to J34. Take the A6109 Meadow Hall Road towards Sheffield. After 1.5 miles there is a roundabout; take the third exit on to the A6102 Upwell Street and just over three miles later take a left into Herries Road South (B6395). This brings you on to the A61 and the ground is directly in front of you.
SOUTH/EAST: M1 to J31 or J33. From J31 take the A57 and from J33 take the A630, until these two

roads merge. Continue along the A57 to the next major roundabout at which you should turn right on to the A6102 Prince of Wales Road. Carry on until the road is intersected by the A6178 Attercliffe Road, at which point turn left. After about 100yd turn right into Janson Street, this becomes Upwell Street (A6102), then as north.

WEST: A57 towards Sheffield. As you approach Sheffield the road splits in two; take the left fork on to the A6101 Rivelin Valley Road (if you miss the fork take the next left into Rails Road and about 0.25 mile later turn right on to the A6101). Continue for 3.75 miles until you come to a T-junction with the A61 Penistone Road (and don't think the locals haven't heard all the jokes you can think of about the name, because they have!). Turn left on to the A61 and the ground is 0.5 mile on the left.

Whichever way you go, be prepared for hold-ups. The roads in Sheffield seem to be in a permanent state of rebuilding or repair and the traffic jams can be quite horrendous

PARKING: There is some street parking around Hillsborough. Alternatively, those coming from the north/south/east can continue down Penistone Road (those coming from the west turn right on to Penistone Road) and there is a car park just past Bamforth Street, albeit that this is a good 1.5 miles from the ground. If you do opt for street parking make sure your handbrake is in good working order and that your clutch control is up to scratch as the odds are that you will be on a steep incline, and you don't want to embarrass yourself, now do you!

FUTURE DEVELOPMENTS

The South Stand is being redeveloped; this should be finished in May 1996 for the start of the European Championships, thus increasing the ground's capacity to 40,000.

OTHER INFORMATION

The nearest pub to the ground is the Travellers, but as with quite a few pubs in the vicinity there is not a very welcoming atmosphere for away fans and there seem to be ever more membership/voucher schemes in operation. Stick to the city centre, but remember to allow yourself plenty of time to get to the stadium. Every club has its own celebrity fan who is wheeled out whenever they are doing well for a quick interview on football focus on how they never miss a game and the current side might even be as good as the great team of the 1940s/50s/60s. In Wednesday's case the renowned Roy Hattersley seems to have cornered the market (as well as being — if we are to believe certain satirists — the only geezer who can gob at the ground without running the risk of being hoyed out!).

At one time Hillsborough was associated with Cup semi-finals, huge crowds and surges of excitement on the home and away terraces. The tragedy at the Liverpool-Forest semi put a very different perspective on all that. The seating and renaming of the Leppings Lane End has done nothing to diminish the horror of what happened at the ground. Maybe the renaming of the entire stadium would help lift the pall that still seems to hang around the place, but then again perhaps it's better that the memories aren't fading.

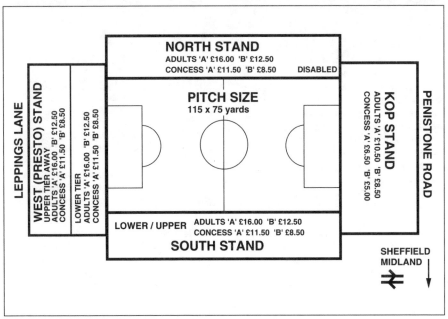

NORTH STAND
ADULTS 'A' £16.00 'B' £12.50
CONCESS 'A' £11.50 'B' £8.50   DISABLED

PITCH SIZE
115 x 75 yards

LEPPINGS LANE

WEST (PRESTO) STAND
UPPER TIER AWAY
ADULTS 'A' £16.00 'B' £12.50
CONCESS 'A' £11.50 'B' £8.50

LOWER TIER
ADULTS 'A' £16.00 'B' £12.50
CONCESS 'A' £11.50 'B' £8.50

KOP STAND
ADULTS 'A' £10.50 'B' £8.50
CONCESS 'A' £6.50 'B' £5.00

PENISTONE ROAD

LOWER / UPPER   ADULTS 'A' £16.00 'B' £12.50
CONCESS 'A' £11.50 'B' £8.50
SOUTH STAND

SHEFFIELD
MIDLAND

147

SHREWSBURY TOWN

ADDRESS: Gay Meadow
Shrewsbury
Shropshire SY2 6AB

TELEPHONE No: 01743 360111

TICKET OFFICE: 01743 360111

FAX: 01743 236384

TOWN TALK: 0891 888 611

NICKNAME: The Town

RECORD ATTENDANCE:

18,917 v Walsall Div 3 26 April 1961 (L 1-2)
Shrewsbury holds the unique distinction of having news of its record attendance share the same newspaper page as the news of Sierra Leone gaining independence. Naturally, the Third Division match which meant promotion for the visitors was the lead story.

CLUB COLOURS:

HOME: Shirts: Blue with White trim;
Shorts: Blue; Socks: Blue with White trim

AWAY: Shirts: Red; Shorts: Red; Socks: Red

KIT SPONSORS: Greenhous

MANUFACTURERS: MG Sportswear

A Kidderminster-based firm. Let's hope the facilities at its factory meet Football League requirements (apparently you need machinery for 6,000 even if you only have 2,000 workers!).

sight of the said 1884 turnstiles, reputedly among the oldest, etc, etc.

CAPACITY: Stands: 3,500; Terrace: 4,500;
Total: 8,000

AWAY FANS: Station End Terrace: 1,500;
Main (Station) Stand: 500;
Total: 2,000

DISABLED FACILITIES: Spaces are available for home fans in the Main Stand Wakeman Wing, and for away fans in front of the Station Wing. Each section holds about 10, with helpers in adjacent seats. There is no charge for disabled supporters, and helpers pay concessionary prices (and from what I can gather even away helpers get this concession!); places should be pre-booked.

The disabled facilities are a bit open to the elements, and there is room for improvement. Even if updating the facilities meant introducing an admission charge, the majority of people who have used them (especially on a rainy day) would agree that it would be money well spent.

PROGRAMME: £1.30

FANZINES:

A Large Scotch 50p

I'm not sure about this one; last time I went to the ground I couldn't find anyone selling it and I was told that it had ceased publication. However, it continues to appear in fanzine listings, so perhaps it is still trundling along after all.

GROUND INFO

1994/5 saw a change in the club's policy towards visitors' concessions. Sadly, as many football clubs were realising they should give them, Shrewsbury went the other way; reciprocal arrangements are, however, retained with other clubs. To make matters worse, if an away fan wanted to sit down, the price for this was hoicked up from £7 to £10. (Thus if one visiting adult and child went into the seats at Gay Meadow in 1994/5 it would have cost them £20 — an increase of 81% on the previous year!) What is even more galling is that the club gives superb concessions to its own fans in possession of a membership card. The Family Stand is members only (as are the Centre Strand and the Wakeman Stand); admission to this is £8 for one adult and one child and £2 for additional children.

The first thing you'll notice on entering the visitors' terrace are the turnstiles, which are reputedly among the oldest in the world, dating back to 1884. The away supporters' terrace is only covered at the rear and naturally it rained on my visit and everyone pushed to the back of the terrace, blocking the entrance to the ground; this meant that if you were outside you were in for a long wait, and were probably heartily sick of the

TRAVEL

NEAREST RAILWAY STATION:

Shrewsbury (01743 64041)

BUS:

Riverside Shopping Centre bus station (0345 056785). Buses 1, 11, 8 and 81 run from the bus station to the ground. Look out for the local penchant for 'naming' the bus stops! Wyle Cup is the nearest to the ground, but beware of Dog Pole, which appears to have been taken a little too literally by some of our canine friends.

BY CAR:

NORTH: A49 into Shrewsbury. When you actually hit Shrewsbury this road is first called Battlefield Road and then Whitchurch Road. In Whitchurch Road there is a major roundabout, take the second exit into Telford Way (A49). Cross the River Severn, then at the second roundabout, take the third exit (in effect turning right) into Monkmoor Road. Follow the road to its end, at which you should turn right into Abbey Foregate, and the ground is 0.5 mile on the right.

SOUTH: A49 into Shrewsbury. As you approach the centre of town the road is called Coleham Head. At the

T-junction at the end of Coleham Head turn right into Abbey Foregate and the ground is immediately on the left.

WEST: A458, the A5 (Roman Road). As you travel down the A5 you will see a playing field on your left, and about 0.5 mile further on there is a roundabout. Take the first exit into Longden Road. When the road comes to a T-junction turn left into Coleham Head, then as south.

EAST: A458 (or A5) into Shrewsbury. Go straight over the roundabout by Lord Hill's Column (who?) into Abbey Foregate. Continue for 1.5 miles and the ground is on the right.

NB: The town is full of narrow one-way streets, so if you miss your turning and hit the town centre be prepared for a lengthy detour.

PARKING: Loads! There is a car park next to the ground, and if you continue along Abbey Foregate across the river, there is a car park on your right; and finally, just before the stadium there is a small left turn off Abbey Foregate which leads to another car park.

FUTURE DEVELOPMENTS

These are currently under negotiation, with the club still considering a possible relocation. If this does not happen (and hopefully it won't as the ground is one of the most picturesque in the league, sited as it is on the banks of the tree-lined Severn), it may be that the existing ground will be shifted slightly towards the away end and turned into an all-seater with work possibly starting on the Station End, followed by the Wakeman and Riverside terraces. However, much has yet to be decided before work commences.

OTHER INFORMATION

If you arrive early, it's well worth a look around the town centre. However, if a cup of tea is not your cup of tea, check out the Crown Inn near to the ground, followed by fish and chips and a jam fritter(?) on your way to the match. Even inside the ground you are unable to escape from the Tudor architecture which is prevalent around Shrewsbury. However, don't rush into the first Olde Worlde building you'll see snapping wildly with your camera and hoping for a picture of the birthplace of Charles Darwin or Clive of India (the town's most famous sons) as you are likely to get arrested; the building is in fact a toilet.

The 1994/5 season saw one very sad event at Gay Meadow with the death of the chap who for years had sat in his coracle on the River Severn and retrieved the balls that were booted out of the ground over the Riverside Terrace. A bit of an unsung hero, this chap loved the club, but never got the chance to see them play at home. However, having rescued literally thousands of balls over the years (his record was I believe 12 in one game) he must have saved the Shrews a good few quid, and it would be nice if the club could do something to remember him by.

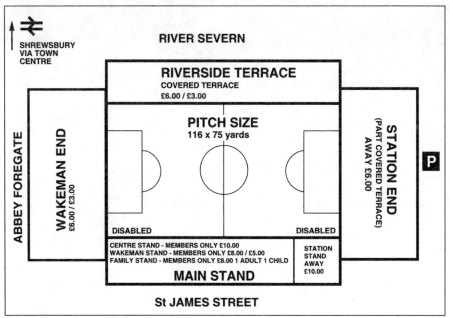

SOUTHAMPTON

ADDRESS: The Dell
Milton Road
Southampton SO15 2XH

TELEPHONE No: 01703 220505

TICKET OFFICE: 01703 228575

FAX: 01703 330360

CLUBCALL: 0891 12 11 78

NICKNAME: The Saints

RECORD ATTENDANCE: 31,044 v
Manchester United Div 1 8 October 1969 (L 0-3)

CLUB COLOURS:
HOME: Shirts: Red and White stripes;
Shorts: Black; Socks: Red/White
AWAY: Shirts: Blue with Yellow stripes;
Shorts: Blue; Socks: Blue/Yellow

KIT SPONSORS: Sanderson

MANUFACTURERS: Pony

GROUND INFO

During 1994/5 away fans were moved from their place in the Archers Road and West Stand, to the East Stand. This is a strange position and gives you a feeling of being slightly cramped; also, because you are stuck in a corner, you have to spend any time that the ball is not in the Archers Road Stand twisted to a peculiar angle in order to watch the game. The old Milton Road double-deck terrace was replaced for last season by a £1.5 million stand which pleasingly has retained a flavour of the architectural peculiarity of the old end, which at places was one person deep, and which expanded like a skewed triangle till at the West Side of the ground it became 'normal' sized.

One thing that hasn't changed during any developments is the goal netting, which must be one of the tautest in the league, and is capable of bouncing even the most timid of shots outside the penalty area. (When Le Tissier lets one of his specials go, he ends up almost respotting the ball on the centre spot ready for the opposition to kick-off.) In fact, if you ever suspect someone of claiming to have 'followed the lads' to the Dell, when in truth they have stayed home, doing the gardening, ask them if after the first goal they saw the ball 'nestling' in the back of the net. If they say yes, your doubts are confirmed.

CAPACITY: Stands: 15,000; Terrace: Nil;
15,000

AWAY FANS: Upper East Stand — Archers
Road End: 770; Lower East
Stand — Blocks J to L: 730;
Total: 1,500

DISABLED FACILITIES: There are places for 12 wheelchair-bound supporters plus eight helpers 'Under West Stand'. Disabled fans are admitted free, with helpers paying £10. Pre-booking is required, at which time you can also organise a parking place. However, due to the limited number of spaces, away fans should consider themselves fortunate if they can secure themselves a spot.

Matchday commentaries for the blind are available; these are provided just behind the manager's dug-out which means that what is initially thought to be feedback on the headphones may well turn out to be The Manager shouting instructions at the team.

PROGRAMME: £1.50
If there is a God of football, then he has got a very strange sense of humour. Given the accusations levelled against one of the club's players last year, the last thing you might expect to find in a programme is any mention of gambling, but there on the back page of the Saints' programme, next to the team sheet, is a list of the odds for the first goal scorer! The programme itself is quite thick, but although the first half is excellent, the second part of it fizzles away disappointingly (and you can place whatever footballing analogy you like on this comment!).

FANZINES:
The Ugly Inside	£1
Red Stripe	£1

The notorious 'Hope You Die' comment over a photo of Ian Branfoot seems to have done for On The March, which was certainly not being sold in abundance the last time I went to the ground. This is a shame really, as while it went way over the top with that particular comment (unlike everyone of the readers of this piece who I am sure will have never said anything they later regretted at a football match) it used to be a fairly good read.

TRAVEL

NEAREST RAILWAY STATION:
Southampton Central (01703 229393)

BUS: Southampton Citybus (01703 553011)
Take a number 5 from the city centre to the Dell.

BY CAR:
NORTH: M3, then A33 towards the city centre. Continue into The Avenue, and take the first right after the Cowherds pub into Northlands Road (if you miss this turning, continue down The Avenue which becomes in effect a massive oval roundabout, drive round 360° and try again). Turn right at the bottom of Northlands Road into Archers Road, and the ground is 50yd on the right.

EAST: M27 to J7. Take the A334 (signposted Southampton, A3024, then follow signs for 'The West'.

This will bring you on to Commercial Road. Once on Commercial Road you will see a car park; turn right here into Hill Lane, then take the second right into Archers Road, and the ground is 100yd on the left. WEST: M27, M271. At the end of the M271 take the A3024 (signposted Southampton). After 1.75 miles you will see Millbrook station on your right; turn left immediately after this into Paynes Road and continue across Shirley Road (A3057) after which the road becomes Howard Road. Go straight across at the next crossroads (over Hill Lane) into Archers Road and the ground is 100yd further on.

PARKING:
There is some street parking available, and one of the best places to try is on Northlands Road. Alternatively for those coming from the north there is a park by the Cowherds where you can leave your car (take the first right after you turn into Northlands Road). There are plenty of car parks within a mile or so of the ground, but watch out for the short stay ones with a maximum waiting time of two hours.

FUTURE DEVELOPMENTS

The Dell is fully developed, but there are still thoughts/hopes that at some point in time the club may move to a purpose-built stadium at the edge of town by the M27, Eastleigh, although the previous assistance afforded to both Southampton and Portsmouth by the powers that be suggests that the term 'full steam ahead' may not be needed.

OTHER INFORMATION

If you're looking for a pub, the Cowherds is fairly good but closer to the ground are the Winston and the Gateway (OK for away fans, but use the side entrance). Keep a special eye out though for the Corner Post; it stands out anyway with its mosaic

patterned outside walls and massive net curtains, but check out the sign outside; now is it me, or is the person taking the corner the ex-bubble head and now greying KK?

The pubs in the city centre aren't bad and it's worth popping into the city for some food as there isn't much around the Dell, although the cheese burgers and coffee from the burger bar behind Milton Road are A1.

If you remember the Tele- as opposed to the Videprinter on Grandstand (oh my God, I'm not about to turn into Dennis Norden here, am I?) then the odds are you shorten the clubs name to Soton without even thinking about it. It took me ages as a kid to realise that Southampton and Soton were in fact the same team. (The teleprinter is sadly missed — it was a better actor than its successor, and every week it seemed to know exactly the right place to stop and cluck provocatively before it gave the away team's score or announced that the home team had scored 3.)

Throughout the land football chants come into being and are subsequently changed to meet different teams' needs. However, some sort of award for the most tenuous derivative must surely go to Saints fans for the following effort to the 'Andy Cole' (or 'Gary Shaw' for those of us with slightly better memories) tune:

Le Tiss, Le Tiss, Matt Le, Matt Le Tiss
He gets the ball
He takes the ----
Matt Le, Matt Le Tiss.

The football team utilises the motto 'Saints, the spirit of Southampton', presumably this means that on recent from the city is well dodgy for the majority of the year, until when faced with the prospect of being downgraded to a village, one person comes up with enough development schemes and projects for it to retain its status for another year.

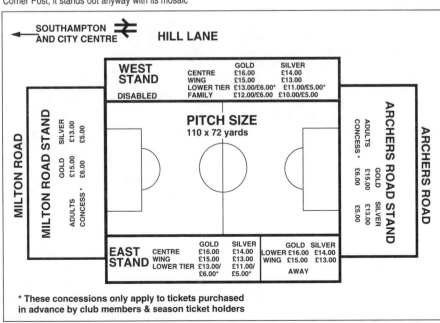

SOUTHAMPTON AND CITY CENTRE		HILL LANE		

WEST STAND		GOLD	SILVER
	CENTRE	£16.00	£14.00
	WING	£15.00	£13.00
	LOWER TIER	£13.00/£6.00*	£11.00/£5.00*
DISABLED	FAMILY	£12.00/£6.00	£10.00/£5.00

PITCH SIZE
110 x 72 yards

MILTON ROAD

MILTON ROAD STAND		GOLD	SILVER
	ADULTS	£15.00	£13.00
	CONCESS *	£6.00	£5.00

ARCHERS ROAD STAND		GOLD	SILVER
	ADULTS	£15.00	£13.00
	CONCESS *	£6.00	£5.00

ARCHERS ROAD

EAST STAND		GOLD	SILVER		GOLD	SILVER
	CENTRE	£16.00	£14.00	LOWER	£16.00	£14.00
	WING	£15.00	£13.00	WING	£15.00	£13.00
	LOWER TIER	£13.00/£6.00*	£11.00/£5.00*	AWAY		

* These concessions only apply to tickets purchased in advance by club members & season ticket holders

SOUTHEND UNITED

ADDRESS: Roots Hall
Victoria Avenue
Southend-on-Sea
Essex SS2 6NQ
TELEPHONE No: 01702 340707
TICKET OFFICE: 01702 435602
FAX: 01702 330164
SOCCERLINE: 0839 66 44 44
NICKNAME: The Shrimpers
RECORD ATTENDANCE: 31,033 v
Liverpool FA Cup 3rd 10 January 1979 (D 0-0)

CLUB COLOURS:
HOME: Shirts: Blue; Shorts: Blue; Socks: Blue
AWAY: Shirts: Red; Shorts: Red; Socks: Red

KIT SPONSORS: Crevette Clothing Co
MANUFACTURERS: Beaver International

GROUND INFO

If you like to arrive at a ground early then expect to spend some time picking your way through the market that is held on the club car park every Saturday. This actually finishes trading around 1pm but by the time everything is taken down and cleared away it is nearer to 2pm. It must be said that the volume of stallholder/customer traffic does little to make your journey easier; be patient!

If you've ever wondered what happened to those old World War 2 air raid shelters, a trip to Roots Hall will provide the answer, as they appear to have been used to provide the roofing at the ground. Not the most attractive of covering at the best of times, they also have the problem of really magnifying the sound of any rainfall until it sounds like you've got a steel band suspended above you.

For away fans the ground is pricey and the North Stand is simply the old terracing with seats bolted on to it. This means that tickets are not sold for the first couple of rows as once you are seated you are practically at sub-pitch level (a situation which is exacerbated by the fact that the club has not taken down the perimeter fencing). Anyway, the club operates a strict policy of sitting where your ticket identifies. Secondly, as there are nine pillars holding up the roof then you have to get very lucky not to have some part of the pitch blocked from your view. Roots Hall is one of the grounds where for away supporters the introduction of the all-seater regulations has resulted in a significant deterioration in facilities offered.

For those that remember the state of the toilets in the North Stand, the good news is that these have been replaced. Further improvements for visiting fans

will also come with the construction of a new stand on the northwest side of the ground.

CAPACITY: Stands: 10,350; Terrace: Nil;
Total: 10,350

AWAY FANS: North (Universal) Stand: 2,158;
Total: 2,158

DISABLED FACILITIES: There are 20 spaces at the front of the West Stand for wheelchair-bound supporters, with adjacent seating for helpers. Disabled fans are charged £4.50, with helpers paying £9. The capacity is often reached, therefore although pre-booking isn't required by the club it is recommended. There is also parking available at the ground which you can sort out with the same phone call. Match commentaries for the blind are available in the Main Stand. A new high-level stand exclusively for the use of disabled supporters is under construction and should be completed by October 1995.

PROGRAMME: £1.50

Once you get past the front cover, which is meant to look like a Victorian photo album but which is just a bit unpleasant, it is not too bad a read, although it does not skimp on the adverts which means that there is a lot less to it than its 40 pages might at first suggest. Talking of adverts, some of these are of questionable taste, especially given that football is once again under the hooligan spotlight. An example of this is the Essex Radio ad which showed a caricature of Chris Tarrant getting a boxing glove in the face, complete with three teeth flying out of his head! (Perhaps most worrying of all was the fact that at the top of the page was the legend 'Southend United Welcome', blimey I'd hate to see what they would do if they had the hump with you!)

FANZINES:
Roots Hall Roar   50p

TRAVEL

NEAREST RAILWAY STATION:
Prittlewell (01702 611811)
Southend Victoria is about 10-15min walk away (heading towards the town), with Southend Central a further five minutes.

BUS: London Road (01702 434444)
Numerous buses run from the town centre to the ground, ie 7, 7a, 8, 8a 12, 12a and 29.

BY CAR:
NORTH/WEST: A127 London-Southend arterial road into Southend. When you get to a large roundabout, take the third exit into Victoria Avenue (A127). Take the third right into Fairfax Drive and the ground is on the left.
SOUTH: A13 into Southend. When you get to Southend there are thousands upon thousands of turn-

ings, especially to the left. Ignore these — this is a lot harder to do than it sounds as you inevitably start to think 'I should turn left here' after about half a mile — until you see a large turning to the left which almost appears to 'fork' the road. Take this and you will turn into West Road. After about half a mile turn left into Shakespeare Drive and the ground is on your left.

PARKING:
Car parking at the ground is for season ticket holders only, and controls have been recently been tightened up. There is loads of on-street parking although with there being so many roads by the ground it is well worth making a note of the one you leave your car in unless you fancy spending a couple of hours after the match looking for your wheels. If you want to park on the main road by the ground you'll need to get there early and watch out for very small parking restriction signs.

FUTURE DEVELOPMENTS
Numerous stories abound about the 'Hall'; a plan to relocate fell foul of the — apparently less than supportive — council. However, that is not to say that one failure precludes another attempt in the future. If the club stays at Roots Hall then further development must be the name of the game. The New Frank Walton Stand — where the old South (grass) Bank used to be — possibly shows the way ahead; it is not massive, but its two-tier structure offers a decent view, fair facilities, and importantly meets the clubs needs. The same type of work may be undertaken at the North End, and to be honest it can't come a minute too soon.

OTHER INFORMATION
Local hostelries include the Golden Lion and the Spread Eagle, both of which serve a decent pint although they do get very busy from about 2pm

onwards, and if you prefer a bit of space then it is as well to wander towards the town centre. The club at the ground which was allocated for away supporters appears to have disappeared during the redevelopment of the ground (which is no great loss, even if it was convenient). The club reports that away supporters will now find a fast-food sit-in cafe/restaurant available at the northeast end of the ground.

The Fish House on East Street serves a truly excellent portion of chips tastewise, but they are not overgenerous with their portions so buy a large bag. Inside the ground everything is fairly expensive but hot and tasty. One peculiarity is why they will give supporters plastic 500ml bottles of Pepsi, but won't give them the caps to go with them, meaning that if you like your fizzy drink fizzy, you have to wolf it down rather than sipping it throughout the match. (Apparently this restriction is made at the insistence of Essex County Council's Safety Committee in order to prevent the bottles being refilled and then used as missiles.)

The question of the plastic cup lids is only one of several mysteries which you will come across. Others include why if, as the club states, the club shop is refurbished does it still have a massive poster of Stan 'The Man' Collymore in the window? (Apparently he still remains popular and the poster still sells.) Policing arrangements are determined according to criteria agreed between the police and the club and this can mean, on occasions, an apparent lack of police. In addition, the club uses a security firm whose employees look like something you'd see either at the door of a night-club or in some film about the marines. Don't let the appearance put you off though, because beneath those eighth of an inch bristle haircuts, beat the hearts of people who are actually prepared to help if they can — and point you in the right direction if they can't.

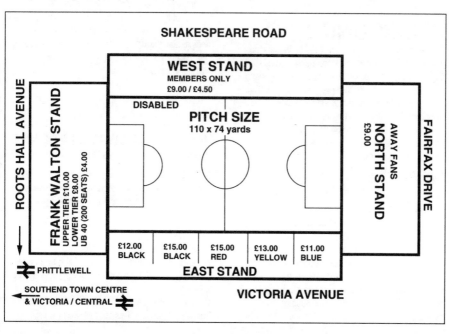

SHAKESPEARE ROAD

WEST STAND
MEMBERS ONLY
£9.00 / £4.50

DISABLED

PITCH SIZE
110 x 74 yards

ROOTS HALL AVENUE

FRANK WALTON STAND
UPPER TIER £10.00
LOWER TIER £8.00
UB 40 (200 SEATS) £4.00

NORTH STAND
£9.00

AWAY FANS

FAIRFAX DRIVE

PRITTLEWELL

SOUTHEND TOWN CENTRE
& VICTORIA / CENTRAL

£12.00 BLACK	£15.00 BLACK	£15.00 RED	£13.00 YELLOW	£11.00 BLUE

EAST STAND

VICTORIA AVENUE

STOCKPORT COUNTY

ADDRESS: Edgeley Park
Hardcastle Road
Edgeley
Stockport SK3 9DD
TELEPHONE No: 0161 480 8888
TICKET OFFICE: 0161 480 8888
CLUB SHOP: 0161 480 8117
FAX: 0161 480 0230
CLUBCALL: 0891 12 16 38
NICKNAME: The Hatters
RECORD ATTENDANCE: 27,833 v

Liverpool FA Cup 5th 11 February 1950 (L 1-2)
Compare and contrast with the 13 people who attended their match versus Leicester in 1921. What many people don't realise about this old footballing chestnut is that the match took place at Old Trafford straight after a Manchester United game, and the 13 refers to the extra people who paid to get in and watch only the Stockport match (presumably Leicester's travelling army).

CLUB COLOURS:

HOME: Shirts: White with Royal Blue pinstripes;
Shorts: White with Royal Blue pinstripes; Socks: White
AWAY: Shirts: Red and Black Stripes;
Shorts: Black; Socks: Black

KIT SPONSORS: Frederic Robinson Limited

MANUFACTURERS: Beaver International

GROUND INFO

The Main Stand was opened in 1967 by those soccer visionaries Matt Busby, Joe Mercer and... David Coleman. Er, quite remarkable! If you are at a boring game then you can wile away your time by watching the planes overhead as the ground is smack on the flight path out of Manchester airport. The new Cheadle Road Stand is due to open on 31 July 1995. The opening will be marked by a commemorative match against Manchester City.

CAPACITY: Stands: 9,410; Terrace: 2,750;
Total: 12,160

AWAY FANS: Main Stand Blocks E and F: 650;
Railway Terrace: 2,750;
Total: 3,400

Supporters of those clubs who choose to reciprocate will be offered the relevant concessions. Seat prices will be £9 (adult) and £3 (child/OAP). Terrace prices will be £7 and £3 respectively. Those clubs that do not reciprocate will have to pay the full adult prices for all supporters.

154

DISABLED FACILITIES: There are 12 spaces for wheelchair-bound fans in the Main Stand. Disabled fans are admitted free of charge, with their helpers paying £9.50. Visitors are welcome, but in all instances pre-booking is essential. County is pioneering a new facility for visually impaired supporters which allows the fan to sit anywhere in the ground and listen to a match commentary via headphones, the signal coming from a transmitter in the commentator's pocket. An excellent idea that will hopefully catch on; telephone the club to book your headset.

PROGRAMME: £1.50

The programme is a massive 56 pages. Given this, it is perhaps slightly disappointing that only a couple of pages are given to the visiting team. Worse still, changes at the club mean that fans have had to say a fond farewell to Danny Bergara's 'Directo Technico' column (a lot like manager's notes, only with a far slower build-up) which used to take at least the half-time break to try and work out. Whether the problem came from the fact that he was South American and his command of English was not that good, or that the editor did not pay full attention to his job was unclear. I tended to lean towards the latter especially when you saw words like turnstyle (sic) amongst the other pieces. On the whole though, the programme remains worth investing in simply as the sheer volume of it means there are going to be some bits that take your fancy.

FANZINES:

The Tea Party	£1
I.O County	£1
No More Pie In The Sky	50p

The last of these is a combined Notts County/Stockport fanzine, which is produced out of Nottingham and tends to lean towards the former of these two clubs. *The Tea Party* is an excellent read; witty and informative, it is worth checking out.

TRAVEL

NEAREST RAILWAY STATION:
Stockport Edgeley (0161 228 7811)

BUS: Mersey Square bus station (0161 228 7811) There is a wide selection of buses which pass the ground, amongst which are the 9, 10 and 11. The railway station is a five minute walk away.

BY CAR:
NORTH/SOUTH/WEST: M63 to J12. Turn right into Wood Street, and left at the lights on to Brinksway Road (signposted Stockport, and directly opposite exit to Heaton Norris). After about 150yd go straight over at the junction with the A560. Follow the road (now called Grenville Street) to a T-junction at which you should

turn left into Caroline Street and first right (still called Caroline Street). Continue to the T-junction with Hardcastle Street, and the ground is directly in front of you.

EAST: A6 towards Stockport town centre. As you approach the town centre there is a cemetery on your right-hand side; about 350yd after this turn left into Longshut Lane West. At the end of this road bear right into Shaw Heath, take the first exit at the roundabout into Mercian Way and then the third left into Caroline Street. The ground is at the bottom of Caroline Street.

PARKING: This can be a bit of a nuisance, as quite a few streets around the ground are either festooned with police bollards or double yellow lines. There is a smallish pay and display opposite the ground which at 10p for two hours or 50p all day won't break the bank; otherwise it's hunt the on-street space.

FUTURE DEVELOPMENTS

The Cheadle End is being developed during the close season, and by the start of the 1995/6 season this should be a resplendent 5,000-seat stand. This will serve to tidy the ground up considerably and has to be better than the old terracing which always filled up very quickly, and which, in certain places, used to have a blind spot of about six yards round the goal.

OTHER INFORMATION

If you go into the pay and display car park you have access to many fish and chip shops and a variety of pubs including the Prince Albert and Sir Robert Peel, which are both worth a visit. If you do go to the latter of these make sure you have a bit of loose change with you to stick in the jukebox, because if you don't you'll be subjected to some very bad sub-supermarket standard piped muzak. Just down the road from these pubs is the Windsor Castle pub, near which is the New Chippy where you can get decent chips. Although the last person I went to County with swears the pie did for them, I can only say mine was fine. Inside the ground there used to be a mobile van dispensing burgers and hot dogs (very slowly). Hopefully this is an area in which some improvement will be seen with the construction of the new stand, as whenever I went there in the past they always seemed to run out of such luxuries as tea and Bovril even before kick-off. Another problem I encountered that County will hopefully work on, is the manning of the away turnstiles which seemed to be staffed in inverse proportion to the number of fans who turned up, thus often leading to longish and irritating queues.

County has become a much nicer ground to go to now that the club has moved away from its old Friday night fixtures, when it used to attract a fair share of idiots and going there as a visiting fan was always a bit tense. There still tends to be a higher than average police presence around the ground but these boys in blue seem too busy chatting amongst themselves to bother about the fans. (What can they be talking about? Their overtime perhaps?)

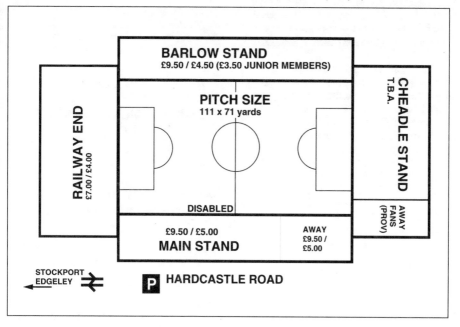

BARLOW STAND
£9.50 / £4.50 (£3.50 JUNIOR MEMBERS)

PITCH SIZE
111 x 71 yards

RAILWAY END
£7.00 / £4.00

CHEADLE STAND
T.B.A.

AWAY FANS (PROV)

DISABLED

£9.50 / £5.00
MAIN STAND

AWAY
£9.50 / £5.00

STOCKPORT
EDGELEY

P **HARDCASTLE ROAD**

STOKE CITY

ADDRESS: The Victoria Ground
Boothen Old Road
Stoke-on-Trent
ST4 4EG

TELEPHONE No: 01782 413511
TICKET OFFICE: 01782 413961
FAX: 01782 745340
CLUBCALL: 0891 12 10 40
NICKNAME: The Potters

RECORD ATTENDANCE:
51,380 v Arsenal Div 1 17 February 1968 (D 1-1)

CLUB COLOURS:
HOME: Shirts: Red and White stripes;
Shorts: White; Socks: Red
AWAY: Shirts: Black and Green stripes;
Shorts: Black; Socks: Black

KIT SPONSORS: Carling

MANUFACTURERS: Asics

GROUND INFO

The away sections of the ground offer a fairly decent view of the ground, and given the reasonable allocation it is unlikely that you will find yourself needing to go anywhere else in the stadium. Should you find yourself in this position, avoid the family enclosure (you need to be a member to get in) and the Butler Street Paddock, where Stoke have a large, noisy (their versions of 'Delilah' and 'I can't help falling in love with you' are sublime) and passionate following (it was on Stoke City that Peter Terson based the play 'Zigger Zagger') as any incursion, especially in a visitors' shirt/scarf can guarantee a hostile reception.

Good news from the Potteries is that the club has begun to introduce concessions for visiting supporters, which hadn't until recently been the case. .

CAPACITY: Stands: 8,494; Terrace: 15,577;
Total: 24,071

AWAY FANS: Stoke End Terrace: 2,615;
Butler Street Stand: 441;
Total: 3,056

The club advises that dependent on the volume of away support this can be increased to a maximum of 6,615 (4,000 seats, 2,615 standing).

DISABLED FACILITIES: There are 45 spaces for disabled supporters (who are admitted free of charge) in the Butler Street Stand. Helpers pay £8 to stand. You should pre-book your place. The club has got some disabled parking facilities at the ground. These are worth examining as the main club car park

is shale and can be an absolute nightmare to manoeuvre a wheelchair over.

Matchday commentaries for the visually impaired are available; again admission is free of charge and should be pre-booked, helpers pay £12 (seat).

PROGRAMME: £1.50

Almost brilliant, but falls down somewhere although it is difficult to put a finger on exactly what the missing ingredient is. Still well worth buying and reading.

FANZINES:
> *The Oatcake*   60p
> *The Victoria Voice*   £1

The Oatcake is an ideal type of fanzine, mixing professionalism in the way that it is put together and edited, whilst retaining the look, feel and spirit of a fans' publication. A new issue is out for virtually every home game (the issue 100 mark was broken many moons ago), and perhaps one criticism of it is that in certain areas it mirrors the official programme.

Wherever the programme is sold, the same person should be able to supply you with an *Oatcake*, which makes you initially query the fanzine's independence. Maybe on some occasions it does lay off the club, but it has never happened in the issues I've seen.

Interesting fact No 2,376: *The Oatcake* gets its name from a local food delicacy which is particular to the Stoke area of North Staffordshire. If you come across one of these it's worth buying and having the next day with a breakfast of egg, beans, bacon, etc, because it's delicious.

The Victoria Voice is a slightly more 'in your face' publication. It is worth a read, but does suffer a bit in comparison.

TRAVEL

NEAREST RAILWAY STATION:
Stoke-on-Trent (01782 411411)

BUS: Hanley bus station (01782 744744)
Staffordshire Bus Line: 01782 223344

BY CAR:
NORTH/SOUTH/WEST: M6 to J15. Take the Queensway (signposted A500 Stoke) and after 0.75 mile you get to a roundabout. Go straight over, but stick to the left-hand lane; 0.25 mile further on there is a branch to the left (signposted A5006), take this road. Almost immediately there is a roundabout, take the second exit into Campbell Road (A5006), then the first right into Boothen Old Road and the ground is 0.3 mile on your right.

NB: Drivers from the north will see 'Stoke A500' signposted at J16 of the M6. You can get to the ground leaving the motorway at this point but it is a lot quicker continuing down to J15.

EAST: A50 towards Stoke city centre. At the bottom

of King Street the road forks into two; take the left fork (A5007). Go straight over both the next roundabout and also Queensway (A500). After you cross Queensway take the second left into Lonsdale Street. Turn left 200yd later into Boothen Old Road and the ground is immediately on your left.

PARKING:
There is a large car park at the ground which is opened two hours before the kick-off. (See directions from North/South/West; at Plough Motel turn right and follow road round — cross over the River Trent.) There is also plenty of street parking. The Michelin Car Park is used for visitors who pass it on the way to the ground from the M6. This is about 0.5 mile from the ground.

FUTURE DEVELOPMENTS

Early in 1995 the club announced that a decision would be made to relocate or redevelop the stadium by March 1995. However, March, April and May passed and no announcement was forthcoming. Enquiries were met by a comment to the effect that the issue was still under review, so it is very much a case of wait and see. The club has got until August 1996 before the ground has to be all-seater, so one way or another expect some serious developments during the 1995/6 season.

Ultimately the dilemma the club is faced with is the same one that many teams have encountered post-Taylor, that being: does it move to a new site, which will be easy to build, or does it remain at a spiritual home which was designed with terracing in mind, and thus which is harder to develop to the required standards (provided you don't do what certain other clubs have done and just stick seats on the old terraces)?

OTHER INFORMATION

Of the two watering holes by the ground the Stoke City Social Club is strictly members only and the Victoria Hotel is either shut or regulars only.

If you come by train there is either the Merry Tippler or the Roebuck Hotel within spitting distance of the station (about 15min brisk walk to the ground), otherwise there are plenty of pubs in the city including Cheers which is just like its namesake in Boston (if you've got a great imagination).

There is a chip shop in Fletcher Road (adjacent to the Victoria Hotel) and also one in Campbell Road (near to Michelin). There are also quite a few mobiles. Of these the Traditional (so called because it wraps the outside of its hygienic containers with a page of local paper The Express and Star) fish and chip caravan does a good 'chips and gravy'.

The facilities inside the ground are fairly standard, although the tea is above average. Just by the tunnel there is a small step up to the pitch and pressed against this is a sign saying 'Welcome to the Victoria Ground'. Whilst this may not have the same ominous ring to it as 'This is Anfield', it certainly provides more potential entertainment as you can wait to see if someone will stumble over it on their way to the pitch.

There tends to be a strong though not too heavy-handed police presence both outside and inside the stadium and away fans may be kept in after the game, escorted to the railway station, etc.

If you're looking to make a weekend of it, you can either go for the culture of the 'China Tour' (plates) or the fun of Alton Towers ('I knew I shouldn't have eaten that oatcake!').

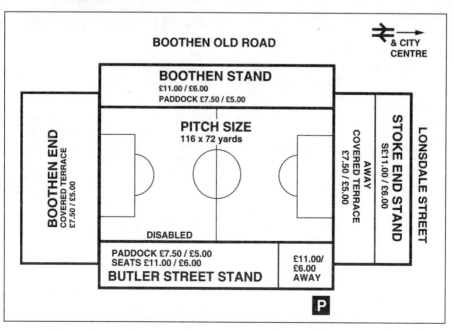

SUNDERLAND

ADDRESS: Roker Park
Grantham Road
Roker
Sunderland SR6 9SW
TELEPHONE No: 0191 514 0332
TICKET OFFICE: 0191 514 0332
FAX: 0191 514 5854
CLUBCALL: 0891 12 11 40
NICKNAME: The Rokerites
RECORD ATTENDANCE: 75,118 v
Derby FA Cup 6th Rep 8 March 1933 (L 0-1 aet)

CLUB COLOURS:
HOME: Shirts: Red and White Stripes;
Shorts: Black; Socks: Red
AWAY: Shirts: Teal;
Shorts: Teal with Red markings; Socks: Teal
Third: Shirts: Yellow and Teal;
Shorts: Yellow and Teal; Socks: Yellow and Teal

KIT SPONSORS: Vaux Samson
MANUFACTURERS: Avec

GROUND INFO

The amount of the Roker End which is allocated to the visitors depends on how many they are expected to bring with them. Initially they get Roker South (323), this will be increased to 1,010, and ultimately they are given the whole end — a total of 3,399.

No matter where you do stand, you can't fail to notice the 'Welcome To Sunderland' illuminated sign at the back of the Fulwell End, which looks like it might have been nicked from an Eastern Bloc airport in about 1953.

The 1994/5 season saw the club designating a couple of matches all-ticket for safety reasons. If you are going to an all-ticket game, make sure.you get yourself sorted before you go up, because this is not the easiest ground in the world to get around the regulation.

It's worth giving the club a call before you travel, because apart from the standard concessions offered, occasionally during the season it will offer free tickets to women, students, OAPs or the unemployed which you will be able to take advantage of if you meet the necessary criteria.

CAPACITY: Stands: 7,753; Terrace: 14,846;
Total: 22,657

AWAY FANS: Roker End: 450 to 6,000;
Total: 323 to 3,399

DISABLED FACILITIES: There are spaces for 23 wheelchair-bound supporters and their helpers at the Roker End of the ground, with free admission. Further there are spaces for 20 blind and 10 visually impaired supporters with their helpers. The club states that it has a fully booked register for the full season. However, it can be as well to give the club a call before your fixture as there may be spaces, or the club may be able to come up with a different scheme or idea that you can use.

PROGRAMME: £1.50
FANZINES:
An Easy One For Norman   50p
Wear All Going To Wembley   60p
A Love Supreme   80p
I always end up buying *ALS* when I see Sunderland, and I almost instantly regret my decision. It is very glossy, has its own sponsors, three or four pages of adverts, and even centre page posters (or portraits as *ALS* calls them), none of which you normally associate with a fanzine. However, when you actually read it you realise that it has plenty of good, well thought out articles, which are sadly often missing from the other club fanzines on offer. It's not a 'must buy' for away supporters, but if you have got 80p spare knocking around in your pockets then it is worth buying, if only for the fact that reading it will make a reasonable dent in the long journey home.

TRAVEL
NEAREST RAILWAY STATION:
Seaburn or Sunderland (0191 232 6262 — for either of the above)

BUS: Central bus station
(0191 232 5325 — PTE Travel Line)

BY CAR:
NORTH: A19 to junction with A184 where you turn left (signposted Boldon). The A184 then joins the A1018 at a roundabout; follow the signs for the City Centre. After 0.25 mile turn left into Mill Bank, go straight on at the roundabout on to Station Road then take the third right into Fulwell Road. Half a mile later turn left into Roker Baths Road and the ground is 400yd on the left.
SOUTH: A1(M) to Carrville then take the A690 (signposted Houghton-le-Spring). Continue on this road following the signs for Sunderland until you see signs for the Tyne Tunnel and Gateshead where you should turn left (on to the A19). After you have crossed the Wear, turn right on to the A1231 (signposted Sunderland North). Follow the signs for City Centre and after two miles you get some traffic lights. Go straight ahead at these (signposted A1289 Roker), and after one mile pick up and follow signs for Roker (A183). Two hun-

dred yards later follow signs for Whitburn and Sea Front (A183). Turn left after 0.5 mile and the ground is in front of you.

WEST: A6, A1 to A1(M), then as south.

PARKING: There is a car park by the ground which fills up very quickly and is no fun to get away from. There is also limited on-street parking. However, a third and possibly the best, option is to park on the sea front which is only a 10-20min walk from the ground (though to call this a 'bracing' walk is a massive understatement), and which also has the advantage of putting you straight on to the A183 for when you are getting away.

FUTURE DEVELOPMENTS

The club should have been looking forward to moving into a 48,000 all-seater stadium this year. However, problems with various sources — not least of them Nissan, mean that Sunderland are no nearer to leaving Roker than they were 12 months ago, and the fans can only watch with mounting frustration as Newcastle and Middlesbrough move further ahead of the club. Expect another extension to be requested from the FLA to keep the terraces open, but one imagines that the powers that be are going to want to see the club cutting through the red tape that surrounds the new stadium relatively quickly. The club is currently awaiting planning permission for a site at Monkwearmouth.

OTHER INFORMATION

The New Derby which is right by the car park is normally fairly safe to drink in as is the Cambridgeshire at the top of Roker Baths Road. However, for a bigger choice try the city centre. The majority of pubs in the area are Vaux's and if you've not been in one before, I can recommend a pint of Samsons.

The Roker Pie shop near the ground is a bit squeaky on filling (what there is is excellent, if rather tepid) so try the chippie on Bede Street which has got an excellent choice of food. (From here you can admire the aquatic shop which advertises that it sells those well-known fishy items 'Guns, Ammo, Knives, Airguns'. Hmmmm, well that's set my mind at ease...)

Roker Park used to be one of the grounds that gave away fans a frisson about visiting: they knew that the Mackems (whatever you do, DON'T call them Geordies!) had a team that could turn over anybody on their day and there was also the Roker Roar to contend with.

Nowadays it's only for the occasional big match that the fans turn up the volume, otherwise it is more of a Wearside whimper than anything else. On their travels though, the club still gets thousands turning up with vocal chords honed to perfection and they often out-sing the home fans just to let them know they can still do it.

There has also been much talk about the training that the stewards have received at the club; you may find this ironic as of all the people I came across associated with Sunderland AFC they seemed to be the least helpful. Still, at least if you are forced to turn to them you can go away safe in the knowledge that you have not been helped in a professional manner.

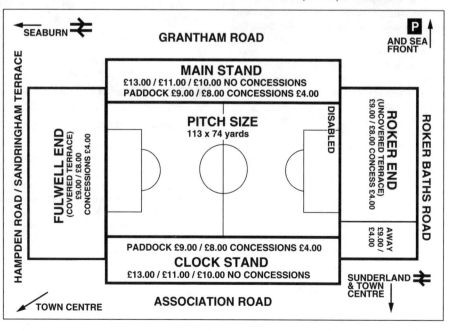

SWANSEA CITY

ADDRESS: Vetch Field
Swansea
West Glamorgan
SA1 3SU
TELEPHONE No: 01792 474114
TICKET OFFICE: 01792 474114
FAX: 01792 464120
CLUBCALL: 0891 12 16 39
NICKNAME: The Swans
RECORD ATTENDANCE:
32,796 v Arsenal FA Cup 4th 17 February 1968 (L 0-1)

CLUB COLOURS:
HOME: Shirts: White with Red/Black/White sleeves;
Shorts: White; Socks: White
AWAY: Shirts: Orange with White/Blue/Orange
sleeves; Shorts: Blue; Socks: Blue

KIT SPONSORS: Gulf
MANUFACTURERS: Matchwinner

GROUND INFO

The club adopts a non-segregation policy in the seated sections of the ground. My own advice would be to go into the East Stand (being careful to avoid the 150 or so restricted view seats), which, although newer and cheaper than the Centre Stand, tends to be used more by families and thus a bit calmer. The away terrace is covered with a bizarre upturned-boat-shaped roof and is fairly basic. There is still a large fence at the front of it, as there is along the North Bank, which means you need to go back a bit to get a decent view (although not too far back or you will find you have a pillar in your line of vision).

If you fancy a trip to Swansea it is recommended that you observe a strict nil by mouth regime for about two days prior to your visit to ensure you don't have to suffer the dark, dingy and pungent abomination that I encountered, that they call the toilets. If you do have to pay a visit, you may wonder how all the leaves got on to the floor as there are no trees around. However, you may find you can't pursue this enigma as your mind is strangely preoccupied with thoughts of cholera and typhoid. Even more worryingly the sign for the refreshments and the gents point to exactly the same place, and this may account for the watery Bovril (and the fact that it wasn't very hot).

The police attitude towards away fans seems to be one of get them in and get them out again as quickly as possible. The street by the West Terrace is sealed off and if you arrive by coach don't expect to be allowed to wander round the town. Equally if you arrive under your own steam, you will have to convince the

person on the gate that you are an away supporter. I know a lot of people who have had trouble at the ground, and heard tales of people with away shirts on getting grief, or even worse, the old 'Have you got the time on you mate?' routine. To be honest I've never had any hassle there myself, and although the ground can be fairly intimidating, I've always found the club and stewards to be fairly helpful. However, it does happen often enough for it to be something to be aware of. Ah well 'Croeso I'r Vetch'.

CAPACITY: Stands: 3,352; Terrace: 13,003;
Total: 16,355

AWAY FANS: West Terrace: 3,500; Total: 3,500

DISABLED FACILITIES: There are 15 disabled spaces in front of the Wing Stand and visiting fans are welcome although it is suggested that you book in advance. Disabled supporters are admitted free, with helpers paying £5 each. There are no match-day commentaries for the blind, nor are there any parking facilities at the ground.

PROGRAMME: £1.20
Quite a bit of interest for away supporters, although the brevity of some of the articles (the Captain's corner is only 150 words, and this isn't the shortest by a long way) means that often items are over before they've said anything.

FANZINES:
A Lot 2 Answer 4   50p
I don't know whether the *Jack* is still going; this used to be an interesting read to say the least.

TRAVEL

NEAREST RAILWAY STATION:
High Street (01792 467777)

BUS: Quadrant (01792 580580)

BY CAR:
NORTH/EAST: M4 to J42, then A48 Peniel Green Road. At second roundabout take first exit on to A4067 Neath Road. Go straight over at next two roundabouts and follow A4067 towards the city centre and turn right on to Alexandria Road (A4118). This becomes Mansel Street, then Walter Road. Turn left into Page Street (if you miss this turn, either of the next three lefts — Nicholl Street, George Street and Henrietta Street — will bring you on to the same road). At the bottom of Page Street turn right into St Helens Road, then second left into Richardson Street. The ground is at the bottom of Richardson Street.

NB: If you go down Henrietta Street cross straight over St Helens Road for Richardson Street.
WEST: M4 to J45, take the A4067 towards the city centre, then as north.

Whichever way you are going, watch out for some very dodgy sidewinds on the M4 especially around Port Talbot.

PARKING: The car park at the ground is for permit holders only, and the one behind the East Stand belongs to the prison. You can either park on-street, or a better bet is to park at the Quadrant or by the Marina. When driving to the ground, the signs for the latter of these are opposite the road you turn into for the pub, and it's a brisk five minute walk at most.

FUTURE DEVELOPMENTS

The Vetch is looking more and more tired with every passing season, and the East Stand, with its excellent bent arm style floodlights, which was built at the time when the Swans were in the then First Division and everything looked rosy for the club, serves only as a reminder of how fortunes can change. Given the option of renovation or relocation it appears that the club may well choose to move, with the possibility that 'within 5 years' they will use the Morfa Stadium which is owned by Swansea City Council.

OTHER INFORMATION

There are plenty of pubs around the ground, with the nearest being a Welsh Brewers' house The Tafarn Clarence (Clarence Arms) in which visiting fans are welcome. The Singleton Arms on the corner of West Way and Western Avenue isn't too bad, but rather than use the chip shop next door, try the Argyle on the corner of Argyle Street and Richardson Way. Inside the ground there aren't any pies on sale, but the pasties are fairly decent. If you want to enjoy them more it is probably as well not to look inside them as the colour of the meat I saw had me worrying about the quantity of 'E' numbers I was likely to be consuming.

Let's face it, it's likely you will face a long trip to Swansea, and if you fancy making a weekend of it it's worth paying a visit to the picturesque Gower coast with its charmingly-named Mumbles! There are loads of B&Bs around and you should certainly walk away with change out of £15.

Of course, you may not be allowed to enjoy this if you are a Cardiff fan, as last season they were banned from attending the Vetch. The reason for this was given as the increased police costs that the match would attract. Given that Swansea was the site of demonstrations against the export of veal last year (which the police controlled at no cost to the exporters) it does bring into question whether football in the area is being used as a convenient way to try and get money into the coffers of the boys in blue.

This final piece of information is not for those with a delicate disposition: on one trip to Swansea I queued patiently for a burger at a mobile van and as I got to the front the person serving sneezed — but instead of turning his head away, he opened up the bun and sneezed into it. Unabashed, he put the burger in and tried to sell it to the (now retching) person who had ordered it.

When he pointed out that he perhaps didn't want that particular one now, the chap serving took great umbrage, and after questioning the person's parentage, turned to me and expressed his disbelief at how fussy people were, and didn't they realise that in the war people would have died for this.

I could only agree with him as I ordered my can of Coke and left.

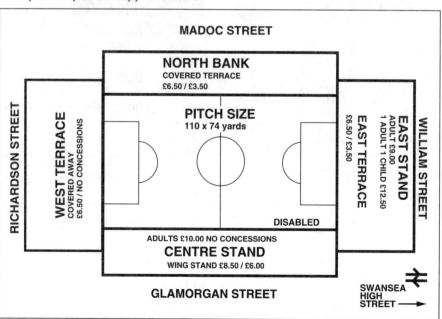

MADOC STREET

NORTH BANK
COVERED TERRACE
£6.50 / £3.50

PITCH SIZE
110 x 74 yards

RICHARDSON STREET

WEST TERRACE
COVERED AWAY
£6.50 / NO CONCESSIONS

EAST TERRACE
£6.50 / £3.50

EAST STAND
ADULT £9.00
1 ADULT 1 CHILD £12.50

WILLIAM STREET

DISABLED

ADULTS £10.00 NO CONCESSIONS
CENTRE STAND
WING STAND £8.50 / £6.00

GLAMORGAN STREET

SWANSEA
HIGH
STREET →

SWINDON TOWN

ADDRESS: The County Ground
County Road
Swindon SN1 2ED
TELEPHONE No: 01793 430430
TICKET OFFICE: 01793 529000
FAX: 01793 536170
CLUBCALL: 0891 12 16 40
NICKNAME: The Robins

The Town are very proud of their nickname and often prior to a match will have a group of cheerleaders strutting their thing to 'Rocking Robin' by the Jackson 5. They are accompanied by someone in a robin costume that looks exactly like Steve McMahon's old Anfield team mate Jan Molby.

An alternative nickname for not just the club, but the good people of Swindon is 'The Moonrakers', based on the legend that a young Swindon lad once saw the moon reflected in a lake, thought it was a cheese (sadly the story doesn't say what he thought a cheese would be doing in a lake) and tried to bring it into the bank with his rake. During his struggle he was joined by half the town, hence 'Moonrakers'.

RECORD ATTENDANCE:
32,000 v Arsenal FA Cup 3rd 15 January 1972 (L 0-2)

CLUB COLOURS:
HOME: Shirts: Red; Shorts: Red; Socks: Red
AWAY: Shirts: Blue/Black; Shorts: Blue; Socks: Blue

KIT SPONSORS: Burmah
I wouldn't mind having a couple of quid on the fact that this might change if they ever got promoted again.

MANUFACTURERS: Mizuno

GROUND INFO

The 1994/5 season saw the opening of the Intel Stand which is very impressive, but not for the use of visiting supporters, who instead were treated to the delight of temporary backless seating being plonked on the old Stratton Bank terrace which had no roof; lovely!

Away fans also were given a section of the North Stand, which is old, but reasonable enough, albeit the fire doors that separate the seats from the facilities under the stand are big and heavy enough that you can't help wondering whether some seven-stone weakling has ever spent an entire 90min trying unsuccessfully to wrestle one of them open. For 1995/6 allocations see future developments.

CAPACITY: Stands: 15,341; Terrace: Nil;
Total: 15,341

AWAY FANS: Stratton Bank: 1,741;
North Stand: 800; Total: 2,541

DISABLED FACILITIES: There are
places for 49 disabled fans in the Town End, and Intel Stand (Town End side), and it is expected that when the Stratton Bank Stand opens there will be a separate away fans' area here (as was previously the case). Matchday commentaries are available, as are parking facilities. Disabled fans should pre-book. Helpers have got their own window by the Town End ticket office at which they can obtain tickets for £5.

Swindon have really got themselves sorted out with regards to disabled supporters. There are large entrances and exits, and a lounge where you can enjoy a pre-match pint (you can almost imagine secretaries up and down the country scratching their heads and saying 'Goodness, I never realised that people in wheelchairs drank lager just like 'normal' people'). The stewards are brilliant, and it is one of the few grounds that I believe disabled fans can go to on their own with complete peace of mind.

PROGRAMME: £1.50
Not a bad read, with enough on the visiting team, and general interest articles to make it worth buying.

FANZINES:
The 69'er	50p
The Randy Robin	50p

The title of the first of these, I am assured, refers to the year Don Rogers et al did for Arsenal in the League Cup final. Not the easiest of fanzines to get hold of, as they are not always on sale on matchdays, but if you do see a seller you could do worse than get a copy.

TRAVEL

NEAREST RAILWAY STATION:
Swindon (0.75 mile) (0117 929 4255 — Bristol Enquiries)

NEAREST BUS STATION: Fleming
Way (01793 523700 — Thamesdown buses)
The 1, 2, 13, 14, 66 and 67 all stop at the stadium end of Fleming Road.

BY CAR:
NORTH: A420 into Swindon until you get to a roundabout with the A345 Queens Drive. Take the second exit (in effect turning right) and the ground is 0.25 mile down the road.
EAST: M4 to J15. Turn right on to the A419, continuing for one mile till you reach a roundabout at which you should turn left on to the A4259. Go straight over at the first roundabout, then left at the second on to the A345 (Queens Drive). The ground is 0.25 mile on the right.
WEST: M4 to J16. A420 (signposted Swindon), go straight over at the first roundabout, and right at the second into Wootton Bassett Road. After 0.75 mile turn left into Westcott Place. Go straight over the next roundabout into Farringdon Road, then after 0.5 mile

turn right into Fleming Way. The ground is at the bottom of Fleming Way on your right.

SOUTH: A361 into Swindon for the A345 and the ground.

Whichever way you go into Swindon the ground is well signposted. However, whichever way you go into the town you will also have to deal with the MAGIC ROUNDABOUT! which is right outside the ground. This abomination is one big roundabout with five mini-roundabouts and various little islands dotted around it. Strangely enough when the road is busy it isn't too bad as sheer volume of numbers tends to sort everything out, but when it is not so packed you get to witness the full splendour of what appears to be traffic going round islands the wrong way and people getting motion sickness as they go into a frenzied dervish-like dance trying to manoeuvre themselves 50yd up the road. This is seriously frightening stuff, and before you set out, it is worth checking that your car insurance is valid, that you've taken plenty of valium, and of course told any members of the family that you love them, where your will is, etc, etc.

PARKING: There is limited parking at the ground. Alternatively, in Shrivenham Road (just keep going round the roundabouts until you see an escape route which is marked as a no through road; this is the one you want) is Hulford Motors where you can park for a quid (though they do like to lock up early after a game). Some street parking is available amidst the residents' zones, and there are two large car parks on the town side of Fleming Way.

FUTURE DEVELOPMENTS

The club intends to develop the Stratton Bank into a 2,700-seat stand. Estimates on when this work will begin range from 'the summer' to '18 months time'. While construction is under way expect away fans to receive a slightly larger allocation within the North Stand. Following its completion the club intends to canvas the views of home supporters as to which areas of the ground they would prefer, and it will be on the basis of the results from this that the away allocation will be decided upon, although wherever it ends up expect it to be about 1,500-2,000 spaces.

Approximate ground capacities:

Pre-Stratton Construction	15,341
During Construction	13,600
Post-Construction	16,300

OTHER INFORMATION

If you like a pre-match pint, the County Hotel by the ground is a bit dingy, but serves its purpose. Alternatively, wander into town (which although it has got a real 1960s precinct feel to it, somehow seems to be able to carry it off) and try out one of the many pubs there; the Mail Coach on Fleet Street is probably one of the better ones. The Red Lion opposite the ground does nice turkey sticks, and banana fritter in syrup, although the chips I had from there were disgusting. Once inside you can indulge yourself in Peter's Pies and Pasties, which taste very nice but, for me at least, kept returning throughout the match and journey home (I don't know what is sadder, the fact that I had indigestion, or the fact that I think you might be interested in it!).

Two unanswered questions: just what is the point of having what appears to be a sign comprising a cucumber in a stetson on the North Stand, and why did my match ticket have printed in large letters across it 'Unauthorised possession is theft!'? (Some would say so is charging £14 to watch a football match.) Are Town perhaps trying to halt the perceived decline in the social environment? As Shaw Taylor would say... 'Keep 'em peeled!'

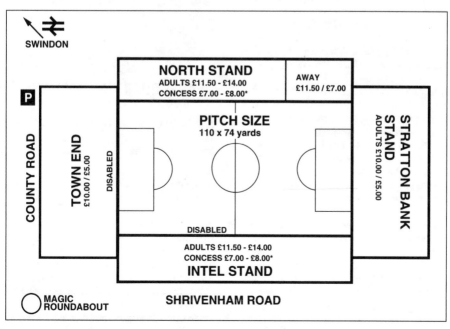

SWINDON

P

NORTH STAND
ADULTS £11.50 - £14.00
CONCESS £7.00 - £8.00*

AWAY
£11.50 / £7.00

PITCH SIZE
110 x 74 yards

COUNTY ROAD

TOWN END
£10.00 / £5.00

DISABLED

STRATTON BANK STAND
ADULTS £10.00 / £5.00

DISABLED

ADULTS £11.50 - £14.00
CONCESS £7.00 - £8.00*
INTEL STAND

MAGIC ROUNDABOUT

SHRIVENHAM ROAD

TORQUAY UNITED

ADDRESS: Plainmoor
Torquay
Devon TQ1 3PS
TELEPHONE No: 01803 328666
TICKET OFFICE: 01803 328666
FAX: 01803 323976
CLUBCALL: 0891 66 45 65
NICKNAME: The Gulls
RECORD ATTENDANCE: 21,908 v
Huddersfield FA Cup 4th 29 January 1955 (L 0-1)

CLUB COLOURS:
HOME: Shirts: Yellow and Navy stripes;
Shorts: Navy; Socks: Yellow
AWAY: Shirts: Blue and White;
Shorts: White; Socks: Blue

KIT SPONSORS: Mod-Dec Windows
MANUFACTURERS: Matchwinner

GROUND INFO

A brilliant pricing system which means that whether you want to sit or stand the cost is the same. Further, it doesn't matter where you want to sit, the price remains static at £6 for adults and £3 for concessions (which from 1994/5 became available for away as well as home supporters!). These prices are for category 'B' matches; respective prices for category 'A' are £8 and £5 and for category 'C' £4 and £1; the club, however, expects most games to be classified as 'B'.

In 1994/5 away fans had 800 uncovered terrace places at the Babbacombe End, together with 200 places in the Main Stand. With the development of the Babbacombe End (see Future Developments), it is believed that away fans will stay in this part of the ground (although the capacity of 1,800 may be reduced if both the visiting team have insufficient support and adequate segregation can be introduced) though this is subject to confirmation.

The development of the Babbacombe End means that there will no longer be the fear for visiting fans if on rainy days they left their seat to go to get a half-time cuppa that it would be claimed by another person (fans were free to transfer from terrace to stands as they wished) thus consigning them to 45min on the exposed open terrace. This is a bit of a shame really as watching someone trying to choose between satisfying a need and the more primal desire to stay dry and warm was always an amusing spectacle at half-time, especially if the person in the stand wanted to go to the toilet, and provided the person in question wasn't you.

The Family Stand (at the Warbro Road End) was the first area of the stadium to be developed and is not only a good place to watch the match from, but also allows for a quick getaway at the end of the match. (Not that five minutes is going to make that much difference on what is likely to be a very long journey home, but every little counts.) This stand also houses the Directors Box making the Board at Torquay possibly the only one in England who enjoy a behind the goals view of the action (Blimey, they'll be leading the chanting next!).

CAPACITY: Stands: 2,375; Terrace: 3,625; Total: 6,000

AWAY FANS: Babbacombe End: 1,200; Total: 1,200

DISABLED FACILITIES: There are 15 spaces for wheelchair-bound supporters at the Ellacombe End of the ground, with both disabled fans and helpers being admitted free of charge. There is no need to pre-book.

There are no general disabled parking facilities at Plainmoor, but if you phone before your visit then you might find that the club can work something out. Match commentaries for the visually impaired are available and once again they do not need to be pre-booked.

PROGRAMME: £1.30
FANZINES:

Bamber's Right Foot	50p
The Gullible Goalpost	50p
You Wot!	50p

The first two are established, well written with a nice mix of humour/criticism and generally seem to have got themselves sorted out so that they come out for different matches, and I'd recommend you try whichever one you found to be 'fresh' that day.

TRAVEL

NEAREST RAILWAY STATION:
Torre (01752 221300 — Plymouth Enquiries).

BUS: Torquay bus station (01803 613226)
Take a number 34 from Torquay town centre to the ground unless you fancy a very long walk.

BY CAR:
NORTH/EAST: M5 to J31 (final junction), then take the A38. Turn left on to the A380. When you get to Kingskerswell there is a roundabout, at which you should take the first exit, and about a mile later turn left (signposted Babbacombe A3022). After 0.75 mile turn left into Westhill Road. This becomes Warbro Road after 0.25 mile, and 200yd further on the right you will find the ground.
WEST: Follow the A380 into Torquay town centre. On Union Street turn right into Lymington Road (signposted Coach Station). Just past the coach station turn

right into Upton Hill, and 500yd further on turn left into St Marychurch Road. After 0.5 mile turn at the crossroads into Warbro Road and the ground is 200yd on the right.

PARKING: Either street parking, or alternatively at the crossroads of Westhill Road, Warbro Road, St Marychurch Road and Manor Road, take Manor Road 0.25 mile down which you will find a car park.

If you are making a weekend of it, it is worth leaving your car in one of the many town car parks and walking to the ground. Depending on how invigorating you find the sea air, it should take 20-30min from Union Street (see route from west).

FUTURE DEVELOPMENTS

The club is redeveloping the away (Babbacombe) end over the summer and replacing it with an 1,800-seat stand. The completion date for this was due to be September 1995 (but has been delayed for about four months). It will represent the third stage in the redevelopment of Plainmoor and means that the ground is light years away from the dilapidated uncovered terraces (considered by many as being unfit for human habitation) of not so many years ago. The chairman and directors deserve a great deal of praise for having quietly brought about a mini-renaissance at the club, and a trip here gets better with each visit.

OTHER INFORMATION

Torquay once provided their fans with the greatest ever pre-match entertainment in the history of the beautiful game. This consisted of the wonderfully named Dave Beer, a local night-club bouncer, standing at one end of the pitch catching cannonballs which were fired at him from the other end of the ground. A millisecond after the moment of impact, Dave was lifted off his feet and deposited about 20yd further back. (Hell of a guy though, he never let go of the cannonball!) This world class act used to be used in the starting titles of 'Match Of The Day', when the BBC knew what football fans really wanted ('It's An FA Cup Final Knockout' etc), as opposed to nowadays when all we get is that silly yellow flag (and less than 15hr coverage on Cup Final day).

There are quite a few pubs in Torquay and Babbacombe, but in all honesty they are not a patch on Boots & Laces, which is the Torquay FC pub. Visitors are more than welcome and it is a great place to go to enjoy a pint, chat about the game, watch 'Football Focus' and get your programme and fanzine. A lot of the locals reckon it is the only reason that they come to matches, and apparently it makes more money than the football club itself. Boots & Laces enjoys a great atmosphere and gives the lie to the idea that we are all animals who cannot enjoy each other's company while having a pint (not that you needed telling that anyway) — for my money, this is the best club-pub in the country.

Inside Plainmoor, when I visited, the food was less acceptable, and you are better off sampling the delicacies of one of the fish and chip shops near the ground, which surprisingly for 'Down South' serve chips and gravy as well.

One thing to be aware of is that there don't appear to be any national bookies in the area, so it can be as well to put your fixed odds on before you leave home (so about Tuesday, if you are travelling down from Hartlepool) or nipping into Torquay town centre or Babbacombe, because if you put it on with a local non-national bookmaker, Sod's law decrees that that will be the week when you win about £50, which should just about cover your petrol when you have to make a special trip to come down and collect it.

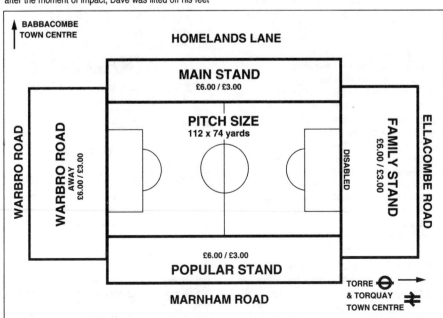

TOTTENHAM HOTSPUR

ADDRESS: White Hart Lane
748 High Road
Tottenham
London N17 0AP
TELEPHONE No: 0181 365 5000
TICKET OFFICE: 0181 365 5050
FAX: 0181 365 5005
SPURS LINE: 0891 100 500
NICKNAME: Spurs
RECORD ATTENDANCE:
73,038 v Sunderland FA Cup 6th 5 March 1938 (L 0-1)
CLUB COLOURS:
HOME: Shirts: White;
Shorts: Navy Blue; Socks: White
AWAY: Shirts: Navy and Purple;
Shorts: Navy/Purple; Socks: Navy/Purple
KIT SPONSORS: Hewlett Packard
MANUFACTURERS: Pony

GROUND INFO

Spurs are one of the most expensive clubs in the Premiership to watch; concessions are only available to club members. The cost of membership is not really worthwhile considering for adults unless they are thinking of going to a fair few matches, but as junior Spurs can get into the Lane for half price in various areas, at the prices Tottenham charge it is worth considering even for one game. If you are not a member, for much of last season the cheapest an adult and child could get into the ground for was £30 (East Lower Cat B), although this did drop to £26 for lower-tier tickets in the reopened South Stand. However, these prices do still seem to send out a message loud and clear to any potential casual supporter. Actually to be fair to the club, on my last visit they had one of several family days they hold throughout the season, when if you bought one East Stand upper-tier ticket, you could get a second one for half price. The standard price of an East Stand Upper Ticket Category B Match is £20, so therefore two tickets cost...er £30 — bargain eh!

As can be gleaned from the above, Spurs also run an — ever popular — categorisation scheme. Hmm, does the expression 'till the pips squeak' ring any bells?

CAPACITY: Stands: 32,960; Terrace: Nil;
Total: 32,960

AWAY FANS: South Stand: 4,000; Total: 4,000
This is the upper and lower tier of the South Stand but is on the opposite side of the ground to that where visiting fans were before the development (ie fans are now next to the East Stand). The capacity can be tailored (upwards or downwards) as required.

DISABLED FACILITIES: There are facilities for disabled fans in both the South Stand (to the right of the Park Lane goal) and the North Stand, and although the club was not prepared to give either total availability or price, it is thought that these number 60ish. In the past disabled fans have been admitted free, with helpers paying the price of a North Lower ticket. One thing that is worth noting is that in the past disabled supporters have HAD to be accompanied by a helper (so don't be getting too big for your wheelchairs by trying to point out that you are quite capable of going to a footie match on your own thank you very much). Apply for spaces one calendar month in advance, and let the club know if you require a parking space at the ground.

Once again the club was not prepared to say whether it offered match commentaries for the blind, but this is thought not to be the case.

PROGRAMME: £1.50
A good read for home supporters, but visitors may find it somewhat lacking.

FANZINES:
> Spur Of The Moment £1
> Cock A Doodle Doo £1.50

Spur Of The Moment has started to appear more regularly than in previous seasons, with Cock A Doodle Doo being a newcomer to the scene. The 1994/5 season saw the demise of the two long-standing publications, Mine Eyes Have Seen The Glory and, after 50 issues, The Spur.

The latter of these was essentially When Saturday Comes, but dedicated to a single team. It cost £2 and there were many who argued that its professional look represented the next stage for fanzines, pointing to the fact that its editors got their readers' opinions aired by the media during the Sugar/Venables débâcle. Equally, others felt it represented the death of the ideal of the fanzine.

Either way, none of the current publications has been able to fill the void it has left, and Spurs fans are worse off with its departure.

TRAVEL
NEAREST RAILWAY STATION:
White Hart Lane (0171 928 5100 — Liverpool St Enquiries)

NEAREST TUBE STATION:
Seven Sisters (Victoria Line)
The term nearest when used in the same sentence as 'tube' and 'White Hart Lane' is a bit misleading as the distance between the station and the ground is enough to make Ffyona Campbell think twice before setting out to walk it.

If the idea of blistered feet does not appeal, then

you can either get a bus from outside the tube station, or transfer to BR at Seven Sisters and take a train to either White Hart Lane or Bruce Grove. The latter is still a little walk from the ground, but does have the advantage of having some decent pubs round it.

BUS: London Transport (0171 222 1234)
Take either a 149, 259, 279 or 359 to the ground.

BY CAR:

NORTH: A10 through Enfield to the roundabout with the A406 North Circular Road and take the first exit (left) on to Sterling Way. After one mile turn right into Fore Street (A1010) which becomes High Road. 0.75 mile down High Road take a left into Park Lane and the ground is on your left.

SOUTH: Cross the river at London Bridge and continue north via Gracechurch Street and Bishopsgate, following signs for A10 Cambridge. Continue for five miles until the A10 branches left into Bruce Grove; at this branch you should bear right into High Road A1010 and turn right 0.5 mile later into Park Lane.

EAST/WEST: Take the A406 North Circular Road following signs for Edmonton. Turn right (if you're coming from the west) or left (from east) on to the A1010 Fore Street, then as north.

PARKING: Parking is a bit of a problem at White Hart Lane. As with their North London neighbours, there is much residents-only parking near the ground.

For those coming from north, east and west, it's as well to park in Edmonton and then either walk the mile or so to the ground or catch a train to White Hart Lane. Those coming from the south are advised to park in one of the side roads around Bruce Grove, again either walking about a mile or grabbing a train. If it rains and you curse Spurs for not having a car park nearer the ground, think yourself lucky you don't have to walk to the tube!

FUTURE DEVELOPMENTS

The new 8,300-seat South Stand was officially opened at Easter 1995, slightly behind the club's original idea of being ready for the start of the 1994/5 season, but impressive none the less. Nothing major is planned for the immediate future but the club is keeping its options open.

OTHER INFORMATION

The nearest watering hole to the ground is the Corner Pin, which even if you can get in takes an age to get served. A better move is to wander down the High Road where there are plenty of other places. The Ship and the Elbow Room by Bruce Grove station are both worth a visit, and neither has a problem about serving away supporters.

There are plenty of places to buy food in the area, and there is also a fairly decent choice in the ground itself, including 'Chinese Snacks' (amongst which is that traditional oriental dish, the samosa), bagels, doughnuts and burgers. The net effect of all these is that the atmosphere under the stands can get fairly pungent at times, and when you queue it can get eye-wateringly smoky.

Whatever the rights and wrongs of the Venables/Sugar affair the club does seem to have got a lot more insular this year, and I've heard various stories about — as well as having witnessed — unhelpful and officious stewarding towards visiting fans, and what was once a good day out in the capital became on occasions a rather strained affair. Hopefully this situation just arose following a time of relative instability at the club, when it was considered the best thing to do was regroup its forces, and it will revert to a pleasant and relaxed day out in the 1995/6 season.

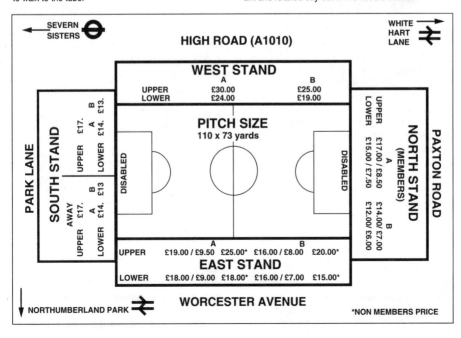

TRANMERE ROVERS

ADDRESS: Prenton Park
Prenton Road West
Birkenhead
Wirral L42 9PN

TELEPHONE No: 0151 608 4194

TICKET OFFICE: 0151 609 0137

FAX: 0151 608 4385

CLUBCALL: 0891 12 16 46

NICKNAME: Rovers

RECORD ATTENDANCE: 24,424 v
Stoke City FA Cup 4th 5 February 1972 (D 2-2)

CLUB COLOURS:
HOME: Shirts: White Green/Blue trim;
Shorts: White Green/Blue trim; Socks: White
AWAY: Shirts: Green;
Shorts: Navy; Socks: Green and Navy
Third: Shirts: Gold and Black;
Shorts: Black; Socks: Black with Gold trim
OK, so no immediate example springs to mind of an occasion when one of Tranmere's first two kits would-n't supply a suitable change to their opponents, but that does not mean the club has acted in an opportune manner in bringing out a third, 'trendy' kit (no, honestly it doesn't!).

KIT SPONSORS: Wirral Borough Council

MANUFACTURERS: Roversports

GROUND INFO
The redeveloped ground was officially opened on 11 March 1995, and considering the club only had 3,646 seats at the end of the 1993/4 season the transformation has been made with impressive speed. (The Borough Road Stand went up in 13 weeks, the Cow Shed Stand in 22 weeks, and the Kop Stand in 37 weeks.) The Kop Stand offers an unrestricted view to away supporters, the first few rows aren't covered by the stand roof, and there is only one food-serving area for visiting fans.

Both sets of supporters share the stand but this doesn't present the sort of problem it might have done 10 years ago, although if your team get a few lucky decisions, you might be aware of a few sets of eyes resting upon you which can be a bit unnerving.

The toilets in the stand are much better than those pre-development when they were open to the eyes of anyone passing by. The new models whilst not massive, are clean, and have designated entrance and exit points which means that the half-time flow is unrestrict-ed (figuratively speaking).

There are no concessions for visiting supporters (although at £8 per seat Tranmere is one of the cheap-est grounds for away supporters), which is quite irritat-ing given that the club has got a scheme whereby home youngsters can get into various parts of the ground (including the Kop Stand) for £3 provided they purchase a book of five vouchers (the books cost £15 and the vouchers get the kids in at no extra cost) which they can use when they like.

CAPACITY: Stands: 16,912; Terrace: Nil;
Total: 16,912

AWAY FANS: Kop: 3,000; Total: 3,000

DISABLED FACILITIES: There are 28 spaces for disabled fans at the front of the family pad-dock. Admission for disabled supporters is free, but helpers pay £8. Away fans are welcome and, although pre-booking isn't essential, it is recommended. Parking facilities are available at the ground, but there are no match commentaries. It is worth noting that the enclo-sure is slightly exposed to the elements so whack on your thermals and fill up the flask!

PROGRAMME: £1.40
One of the all too rare breed of matchday programmes that dares to be different — it's interesting (radical move boys!). There is a decent section on the visiting team, and enough general interest articles to keep you occupied through the half-time break and beyond.

FANZINES:
Give Us An R	£1
White Magic	50p

TRAVEL
NEAREST RAILWAY STATION:
Birkenhead Central or Rock Ferry (from Liverpool Lime Street) (0151 709 9696 — Lime Street)

BUS: Central bus station (0151 236 7676)
Instead of taking the train you may wish to take the ferry across the Mersey — but if you sing the song while you are on board, you are very sad indeed. This will leave you in Woodside from where a number 64 bus will take you to the ground.

BY CAR:
NORTH: Go through the Mersey Tunnel (Kingsway) and once through, follow the signs for the M53. Take the M53 to J3, turning left at the exit roundabout on to the A552 Woodchurch Road. Follow this road for about a mile and on your left you will see a park; shortly after this the A553 is crossed by the B5151 Shoreton Road. Turn right on to this and then second left into Prenton Road West, where the ground is 0.25 mile on your right.

SOUTH/EAST: M6/M56 and M53 to J4. Take the fourth exit at the roundabout on to the B5151 Mount Road. Continue for about 2.5 miles (when Mount Road becomes Shoreton Road you have about 0.75 mile to go), and turn right into Prenton Road West; the ground is 0.25 mile on your right.

On the M56 you will see signs for a picnic area. If you decide to take a break here, don't expect the traditional grassy fields or lake as you will be dining opposite the massive chemical plant at Shotton — lovely!

The police seal off a section of Borough Road on matchdays which only adds to the prevalent congestion.

PARKING:
Parking is a real problem; the car park at the ground is for permit-holders only, so it's either street parking (one of the side streets off Borough Road is probably the best choice), which is a drawn out task among the broken yellow lines and residents-only areas, or drive past the ground and on to Prenton Road East. The third left takes you on to Church Road (B5148) and there is a car park 300yd on your right. If you have any problems parking you may find it really isn't worth asking a policeman for help, as the response I got to the question 'Is there anywhere round here I can park?' was 'Yeah, if you can find a space'.

FUTURE DEVELOPMENTS
The only real changes coming up are that the club is going to build a new ticket office on Prenton Road West at the corner of the main entrance opposite Woodchurch Lane. Secondly, the Main Stand roof is to be re-clad and extended to create a pitched roof, the same as that on the Kop Stand.

OTHER INFORMATION
For a pre-match pint, try either the Mersey Clipper on Prenton Road West or the Prenton Park on Borough Road; both are two minutes from the ground. A little further away is the Sportsman, which is cavernous and might not be to everybody's taste. For food, Chopsticks on Borough Road does a generous portion of chips with gravy, although it insists on putting a sheet of cellophane between the chips and the polystyrene tray, which means that you spend ages chasing the last few chips around trying to get enough of a purchase on them to enable you to lift them to your mouth. Inside the ground, the food is pretty bland, but the hot drinks are hot and come with lids so you don't end up spilling half of them on the way back to your seat.

One of the more interesting sights you might come across is a man called Billy 'The Badge' Wray, who has a massive collection of badges on his jacket from all the clubs he has visited (he reckons the weight of them are what has given him a hunch-back). Recognise the name at all? Well his daughter is (apparently) Emma Wray from, amongst other things, the comedy series 'Watching', which just goes to prove something, although I'm not quite sure what.

Talking of local celebs, ex-Rovers players include Stan Boardman (whose catchphrase 'I 'ate de Germins, dey bombed our chippy' is surely one of the great comedy classics of all time), and Ray Stubbs (who hasn't got a catchphrase, but is adept at looking into the camera like a frightened rabbit). The area is also home to the man with the seemingly immovable hair: Elton (but you can call me Roger) Welsby.

A thing that may concern you on your visit is the sight of the 'Prenton Pups' clubhouse, which is a wooden hut done out like a kennel (and I thought the days of treating fans like animals were over). Children, apparently, love it!

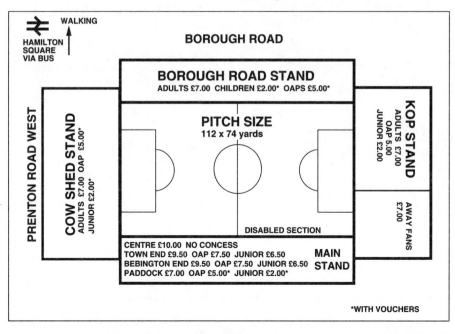

WALSALL

ADDRESS: The Bescot Stadium
Bescot Crescent
Walsall
WS1 4SA
TELEPHONE No: 01922 22791
TICKET OFFICE: 01922 22791
FAX: 01922 613202
SADDLERS HOTLINE:
0891 555 800
NICKNAME: The Saddlers
RECORD ATTENDANCE:
25,343 v Newcastle Div 2 29 August 1961 (W 1-0)
At Bescot: 10,628 England B v Switzerland B 20 May
1991 (2-1)
CLUB COLOURS:
HOME: Shirts: Red; Shorts: Black; Socks: Red
AWAY: Shirts: Claret and Blue Stripes;
Shorts: Blue; Socks: Blue
KIT SPONSORS: Choice Personnel
MANUFACTURERS: Sky

GROUND INFO

There are no general concessions to away fans £10
adults, £6 juniors and OAPsand if the visiting team has
either a junior or family membership scheme and is
prepared to offer a reciprocal arrangement to Walsall,
then the club is happy to let them into the Family
Stand. You will need your membership cards and adult
males will not be admitted alone. (Although if you do
find yourself without your cards, you may discover that
Walsall often will not turn a deaf ear to your plight if
you ask them nicely.)

Wherever you go in the ground you are likely to
have a restricted view, as despite the newness of the
stadium it does not appear to have been built with fans
in mind (well you wouldn't, would you?) as pillars
abound and there isn't much leg room.

If you fancy something a bit different you might try
the Swifts Executive Club. Matchday tickets are £20
and entitle fans to a reserved car parking space, use of
bar facilities, an Executive Stand seat, light refreshments at half-time and a complimentary programme.

Home fans should also note that the club offers a
discounted admission price scheme for those who buy
vouchers for five matches

CAPACITY: Stands: 6,700; Terrace: 2,300;
Total: 9,000

AWAY FANS: William Sharp
Stand: 1,916; Total: 1,916

DISABLED FACILITIES: There are 30
places for wheelchair-bound supporters in the
Highgate Stand; both they and one adult helper are
admitted free of charge. Pre-booking of this facility is
required. The club has introduced specific parking
facilities at the ground for disabled fans and your
requirements should be sorted out when you book your
ticket (if you don't do this, there is enough parking at
the ground for this not to be a problem).

There are no matchday commentaries for the blind.

PROGRAMME: £1.50
This is a programme that keeps winning divisional
awards for programme of the year, and it is easy to
see why. Lots of general interest articles, and one of
the few programmes that when reviewing past encoun-
ters between the teams sometimes includes defeats
for the home team, as opposed to generally when all
you'll get to read about is the one time 73 years ago
when the away team got stuffed 6-1!

There are occasional bizarre articles about 'Aynok
and Ayli' which are written in quite incomprehensible
Black Country dialect.

FANZINES:
Blazing Saddlers 50p
Moving Swiftly On 50p
BS appears regularly, and whilst it is not the thickest
fanzine in the world, what there is of it is good and is
certainly worth 50p of your hard-earned cash. I wish I
could say the same for *MSO* but I can't.

TRAVEL

NEAREST RAILWAY STATION:
Bescot (0121 643 2711 — Birmingham New Street
Enquiries)
There is a fairly regular service from both New Street
and Walsall to Bescot. Allow yourself half an hour from
the former and about two minutes from the latter.

BUS: Central bus station (01922 25515 — West
Midlands Travel Shop)

BY CAR:
FROM ALL PARTS: M6 to J9. When leaving the
motorway take the A461 Bescot Road (signposted
Walsall) and after 0.25 mile turn right into the A4184
Wallows Lane; then turn right at the next set of traffic
lights into Bescot Crescent. Follow this road for 400yd
and the stadium is on the left-hand side.

PARKING: There is car parking at the ground
with a specific area for away fans parking by the
William Sharp Stand which is capable of holding a
massive 80 vehicles! Should by some miracle this not
be sufficient, just use one of the many hundreds of
spaces allocated to home supporters.

There is some street parking available around and

about, but the parking at the ground is cheap enough for most not to bother with anything else. The parking tickets are about 6sq in and are more impressive then the tickets for the match! They include such messages as 'We're glad you're here, enjoy the game' and the ever helpful 'Please lock your car'. (Aww, do I have to?)

One thing you should be aware of is that on my visit the road leading out of the car park got very narrow and became severely congested, which means a choice of either leaving two minutes before the match ends or running the risk of being half-way towards '6-0-6' before you hit the motorway.

FUTURE DEVELOPMENTS

Nothing planned at the moment and it is likely that the ground will remain the same until such time as League requirements dictate otherwise.

OTHER INFORMATION

Whilst the name of Walsall may not conjure up the most seductive of images, the people from the town insist it is the jewel in the crown of the Black Country.

Which reminds me, whilst visitors may not be able to tell the difference between the various linguistic twangs of the people of this area, there are apparently bye-laws which hold a maximum of life imprisonment

should you call someone from Walsall a Brummie. The very mention of the B-word tends to cause psychotic rage, so use it at your peril.

Things to check out include a wine-bottling plant (the exotically titled Chateau Pleck); the Garman Ryan Collection (this is actually considered to be Britain's best-kept art secret and if you are into modern art is a real don't miss); Walsall's Arboretum which is the autumnal site of the indescribable Walsall Illuminations; but most significant to football fans there is the home of Jabez Cliff and Co. Who? Jabez Cliff and Co, manufacturers of all things leather, including the old footballs which used to absorb more water than your average sea sponge and whose weight when wet made any attempt to head them quite foolhardy. The company is still in existence but concentrates nowadays on more lightweight products such as saddles.

The ground is a bit out of the way and apart from the King George V on Wallows Lane (which has a decent chip shop next to it) you are as well to stick to the town for pre-match entertainment. The Saddlers Club is members only, but depending on what the match is and who is on the door you can often get in.

The food inside the ground is way above average, but because the majority of fans end up eating here rather then in the town, expect to queue. When you get to the head of the line you may be surprised to see Walsall FC sticks of rock on the menu, but NO BOVRIL!

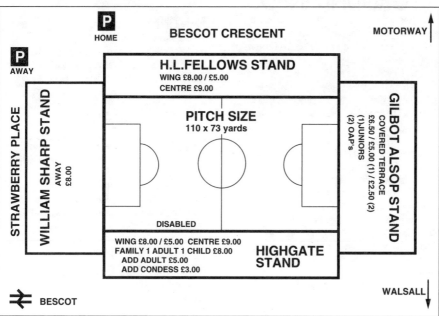

HOME P

AWAY P

BESCOT CRESCENT

MOTORWAY

H.L.FELLOWS STAND
WING £8.00 / £5.00
CENTRE £9.00

PITCH SIZE
110 x 73 yards

STRAWBERRY PLACE

WILLIAM SHARP STAND
AWAY £8.00

GILBOT ALSOP STAND
COVERED TERRACE
£6.50 / £5.00 (1) / £2.50 (2)
(1)JUNIORS
(2) OAP's

DISABLED

WING £8.00 / £5.00 CENTRE £9.00
FAMILY 1 ADULT 1 CHILD £8.00
ADD ADULT £5.00
ADD CONDESS £3.00

HIGHGATE STAND

BESCOT (railway)

WALSALL

WATFORD

ADDRESS: Vicarage Road Stadium
Vicarage Road
Watford WD1 8ER
TELEPHONE No: 01923 496000
(from August 1995)
TICKET OFFICE: 01923 220393
FAX: 01923 239759
CLUBCALL: 0891 12 10 30
NICKNAME: The Hornets
RECORD ATTENDANCE:
34,099 v Man Utd FA Cup 4th 3 February 1969

CLUB COLOURS:
HOME: Shirts: Yellow with Black Shoulders;
Shorts: Black; Socks: Black
AWAY: Shirts: Claret and Teal;
Shorts: Claret and Teal; Socks: Claret and Teal

KIT SPONSORS: Blaupunkt
MANUFACTURERS: Mizuno

GROUND INFO

Away fans are usually sited in the lower tier of the Rous Stand, which offers an excellent along-the-pitch view of the match. In bad weather the first few rows aren't properly covered by the roof of the stand.

The Rous Stand has two distinct features. Firstly there is a quote from Sir Stanley displayed on the structure — 'I don't want to look back instead of forward, but I do hope that football never becomes other than a game' (such sage words are sure to give you a warm feeling... until Watford launch their first attack of the game and you find yourself screaming at your right back to 'do' their centre-forward). The second feature is that it is one of the few stands in the world where light is let in via a series of giant ship portholes.

The big problem with the Rous is that to get to it, away fans have to take a long trek along Vicarage Road, down Occupation Road, round the back of the allotments (now guarded by a massive fence and gate for those who remember the 'potato runs') before heading back up a dirt track to get to the turnstiles which are about 100yd from where you started. If you want to avoid the same 10min journey on departure, find a kind-hearted steward who will let you nip through the top tier of the Rous (the only thing being you will have to leave 5min early); the other alternative is to hang around after the match, until you are allowed out of the North exits, straight on to Vicarage Road (probably bumping into a ragged crocodile of fans who opted for the long walk).

Concessions are available to visiting fans provided that they have been obtained in advance from their own club.

Strangely the atmosphere at Vicarage Road seems to have got worse now that the Rookery End has been constructed, as during its building all the vocal home fans were packed into the North Stand, and this created a definite atmosphere at the ground, but now they have been split up, the volume has been turned down.

CAPACITY: Stands: 22,000; Terrace: Nil;
Total: 22,000

AWAY FANS: Lower Rous: 3,500; Total: 3,500

DISABLED FACILITIES: There are two enclosures for disabled supporters at the ground, one in the North Stand which has 16 spaces, and one in the Rookery End Stand which has 24 spaces. These cost £6 for disabled supporters and £11 for helpers. Pre-booking is not generally required. Parking spaces are not widely available at the ground but if you phone the club it may be able to organise something.

There are also commentary facilities for the visually impaired. Pre-booking is required for this service.

PROGRAMME: £1.50
Looks slightly better than it actually reads. There tend to be a couple of general interest articles per issue which are worth checking out. Not great but not bad either.

FANZINES:
Clap Your Hands And Stamp Your Feet 50p
I've yet to see a copy on a visit to Vicarage Road, so if you do perchance come across one, you're on your own (probably it's worth considering buying if just for its rarity).

TRAVEL

NEAREST RAILWAY STATION:
Watford Halt, Watford High Street, Watford Junction (0171 387 7070)
A veritable plethora of stations are available to the discerning traveller. Watford Halt is behind the ground and is on a direct line from Watford Junction. This operates on matchdays only. Alternatively try the High Street which is walkable, and which offers a few more stopping off points on the way to the stadium.

NEAREST TUBE STATION:
Watford (Metropolitan Line)

BUS: London Transport (0171 222 1234)

BY CAR:
NORTH: Exit M1 at J5 and take the second exit off the roundabout on to the A41 signposted Harrow. Continue for a short distance to the next roundabout and take third exit, Hartspring Lane. Follow this road through a set of traffic lights and continue straight ahead (along what is now Aldenham Road) to another roundabout. Go straight over (second exit) still following Aldenham Road, to next traffic lights. When

through the lights, move into the right-hand lane (marked Watford) and follow one-way system around to Bushey station, then moving into left-hand lane. Turn left under Bushey Arches into Eastbury Road. At traffic lights turn right into Deacons Hill and continue to next traffic lights, turning left into Cardiff Road for visitors' entrance to stadium/coach park.

SOUTH: M1 to J5 and take first exit off roundabout, then as north.

EAST: Exit M25 at J21A and join the M1 at J6. Exit at J5, then as north.

WEST: Exit M25 at J19 and take third exit off the roundabout on to the A411 (Hempstead Road), signposted Watford. Continue for approximately two miles and at the roundabout go straight across (right-hand lane) to the next roundabout, then take third exit into Rickmansworth Road. Take second turning on the left into Cassio Road. Continue through traffic lights, to Merton Road and straight on to Wiggenhall Road. At traffic lights, turn right into Cardiff Road (as north).

PARKING: Matchday car parks are operated by Watford General Hospital (next to Vicarage Road Stadium) and by the Watford Girls' Grammar School (2min walk). Both make a small charge for parking (typically £1 or £2, but prices for 1995/6 have not been confirmed to date).

Alternatively, paying car parks are available in the town centre (5-10min walk). To reach the shopping centre from the Vicarage Road Stadium (on your right), continue to the pedestrian crossing and follow the one-way system around the small shopping precinct (left turn and then bear right around the Hornets). Immediately after the next pedestrian crossing turn left into Vicarage Road and at the end turn left into Exchange Road. This is a one-way system running round the main shopping centre, from which most car parks can be accessed if you keep to the right-hand lane.

There is virtually no on-street parking as many local streets are blocked by the police and side streets are a waste of time for visiting fans.

FUTURE DEVELOPMENTS

The development of the Rookery End now means that Watford have got an impressive stadium on three sides, the odd one out being the East Stand which is a mish-mash of piecemeal stands and, at one place, uncovered seating. This is an obvious area for improvement, although as the ground is now all-seater there is no rush for this to be undertaken.

OTHER INFORMATION

There aren't that many good pubs in the area (although the Red Lion on Vicarage Road isn't bad) and its best is to stick to the town centre. If you come in via Watford Junction, the Pennant just up the road is a popular port of call. It is worth stocking up on grub before you head towards the stadium, as the surrounding streets don't have much to offer. Inside the ground the food is OK but on the pricey side with, in 1994/5, a mushy steak and kidney pie at £1.40 and a Hornet Burger (which much to my surprise is NOT a reference to the amount of meat inside it) a cool £2.20. The tea is OK and is served in a decent 10oz cup. If you do want to eat in the ground get there early, because I found the servers aren't ones to rush. The added bonus of getting there early is that not only do you have a good chance of being served before half-time but also you will get to witness the teams' emergence on to the pitch to the strains of the 'Z-Cars' theme, a piece of music which was introduced in 1963 because the then manager, Ken Furphy, liked it. The toilet facilities are very clean, but also very small, which means more queuing.

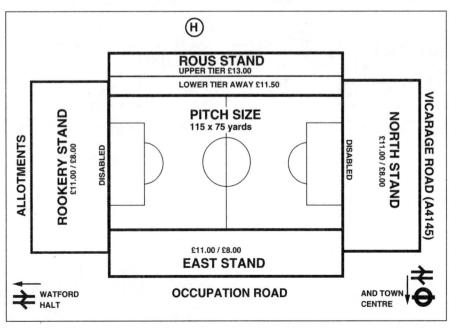

WEST BROMWICH ALBION

ADDRESS: The Hawthorns
Halfords Lane
West Bromwich
B71 4LF
TELEPHONE No: 0121 525 8888
TICKET OFFICE: 0121 553 5472
FAX: 0121 553 6634
CLUBCALL: 0891 12 11 93
NICKNAME: The Baggies,
The Throstles

RECORD ATTENDANCE:
64,815 v Arsenal FA Cup 6 March 1937 (W 3-1)
Interesting Fact Alert: The Hawthorns is the highest
ground above sea-level in England, and it is said that
the next thing a ball would hit on leaving the ground is
the Ural Mountains — sadly for the paying spectators,
Albion have in the past seemed quite intent on proving
this theory!

CLUB COLOURS:
HOME: Shirts: Navy Blue and White stripes;
Shorts: White; Socks: White
AWAY: Shirts: Yellow; Shorts: Blue; Socks: Yellow
Last season Albion moved back to having stripes of
equal thickness on their shirts (with horrible yellow pip-
ing) abandoning those which appeared to incorporate
the bar-code. The club were (allegedly) happy with the
initial design and the fact that it speeded things up at
the club shop, but were persuaded to revert to a traditional look by Baggies who were sick of triggering off
security devices at their local supermarket.

KIT SPONSORS: Guests
MANUFACTURERS: Patrick

GROUND INFO
The ground changed considerably during the 1994/5
season with the redevelopment of the Birmingham
Road and Smethwick Road Ends. For away fans this is
a real blessing as the new Smethwick Road (or to give
it its full title West Midlands Travel Community) Stand
offers a lot more than the old open terrace did, as well
as allowing a much better atmosphere to be generated. Concessions are arranged on a reciprocal basis.

Albion's redeveloped ground is impressive
(although the West Bromwich Building Society Stand
— ex-Rainbow, stands out like a sore thumb now) and
Albion has taken one aspect of it to new levels, namely
'seat writing'! No simple WBA or 'Baggies' in white on
blue seats for them; instead they have gone for 'Albion'
in joined up handwriting in the Smethwick, and a blue
and white scarf at the top of the Midland Road, thus
offering both home and away fans so much more!

Sadly the improvement in the ground seems to
have lessened the atmosphere in the home sections of
the ground and even the legendary 'Boing Boing'
seems to have lost a bit of its sparkle (although naturally this is a far riskier movement on a spring-loaded
seat than it used to be on an open terrace).

The peculiar thing about the home supporters is
that they all seem to have started singing in the style
of the clubs 'celebrity fan' (thankfully more fan than
celebrity) Frank Skinner when he imitates Max
Bygraves on Fantasy Football, which if they are taunt-
ing you can lessen the effect somewhat.

CAPACITY: Stands: 25,100; Terrace: Nil;
Total: 25,100
AWAY FANS: Smethwick Road Stand (P):
2,100; Total: 2,100
This can be extended to 3,100 if required.

DISABLED FACILITIES: Wheelchair-
bound supporters are sited behind the goals at the
Birmingham and Smethwick Road Ends. To be truthful,
what with the advertising boards in front of you, and
the constant flow of traffic from people moving from
various points around the rest of the stand and walking
directly in front of this area, this is not one of the better
grounds to watch football from. Admission is free, with
helpers paying £8. Match commentaries are also available, and these facilities should be pre-booked. No
designated parking at the ground.

PROGRAMME: £1.50
Very thin on readability, and visitors will have probably
got everything of interest out of it within five minutes.
Sadly the reference letters that they print by the other
fixtures taking place that day by are an irrelevance, as
during the reconstruction of the ground the big manual
half-time scoreboard appears to have gone to meet its
maker. All in all, this is one for collectors only.

FANZINES:
The Grorty Dick	60p
Last Train To Rolfe Street	£1

Grorty Dick to my mind is everything a fanzine should
be: absolutely crammed with humour and information
about the Baggies and other topics of interest. Sixty-
four pages long, it has so far eschewed the potential
pitfalls of going glossy in order to keep costs to a minimum. It will certainly take you several hours to read,
and is so good you may even be tempted to subscribe.
LTTRS on the other hand suffers badly in comparison.
£1 for 20 or so below average pages is not what one
would call competition.

TRAVEL
NEAREST RAILWAY STATION:
Rolfe Street, Smethwick (0121 643 2711 —
Birmingham New Street Enquiries). A new station —

The Hawthorns — is due to open in September 1995; this is about 300yd from the ground

Rolfe Street is 6min from New Street, but the frequency of trains is not fantastic. If you're pushed for time check departure times very carefully for connections.

BUS: Birmingham Central (0121 200 2700 — Centro Hotline) Any of the following will do the trick: 74, 77, 78, 79, 450.

BY CAR:

FROM ALL PARTS: M5 to J1. When you leave the motorway, take the A41 Birmingham Road (sign-posted Handsworth, Birmingham). Follow the signs as a new traffic scheme begins in August 1995.

PARKING: Parking at the ground is mainly for season ticket holders only, although there are places available behind the WBBS Stand and off Halfords Lane at £3. Otherwise, continue down Halfords Lane as the road leads to an industrial area with plenty of opportunities for on-street parking. Halfords Lane itself can be a bit of a nightmare to get away from.

FUTURE DEVELOPMENTS

There are provisional plans for a £10 million development of the WBBS Stand although this is very much for the medium to long-term future.

OTHER INFORMATION

The Hawthorns pub on the corner of Halfords Lane and Birmingham Road is members only, but you may be able to get in, especially if you arrive early. The Woodmans on Birmingham Road operates a closed door policy, and for away fans there is no point in trying to discover what is on the other side of it. Either go down Halfords Lane to the Waggon & Horses, or continue along the A41 towards West Bromwich for the Royal Oak. The latter is probably the better bet.

If I tell you that you are best off eating at one of the mobiles outside the ground you will probably have a good idea of the quality of other eateries. The chippies in West Bromwich are very heavy on the grease, and don't seem capable of giving you chips 'open' without the paper unfolding when you are 2min up the road. Inside, the food is fairly bland and inoffensive, although they do serve a very good cuppa.

The ground is policed by the West Midlands Police and seems to be one of the stadia where they are at their most stringent, especially with regards to the treatment away fans can expect to receive, in my experience.

The club appears to pledge allegiance to some strange countries as flying over the Halfords Stand are the Welsh Dragon and the Cross of St Andrew. Mention that you think it is strange that as an English side it doesn't have the English flag flying and (if you talk to the same steward I did) the odds are you will be pointed to the Union Flag which also adorns the stand and be asked 'What do you call that then, stupid?' Oh, my mistake! (The club reports that the flag of St George always flies over the ground; I will check next time I am at the ground.)

Finally, proof (as if any were needed) that West Brom are one of the world's leading club sides can be obtained from the fact that they reached the final of the inaugural 'World Championship Decider'. Mind you this might be slightly more impressive if there had been more than two teams in the competition, or if Albion hadn't gone on to lose 4-1 to those giants of the modern game Renton FC. So sadly for the Baggies it was the Scottish rather than the English Cup Winners who were crowned 'Champions Of The World'.

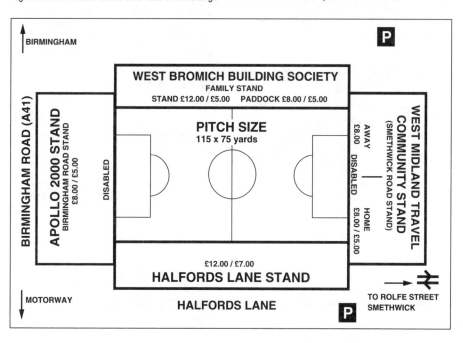

WEST HAM UNITED

ADDRESS: Boleyn Ground
Green Street
Upton Park
London E13 9AZ

TELEPHONE No: 0181 548 2748

TICKET OFFICE: 0181 548 2700

FAX: 0181 548 2758

CLUBCALL: 0891 12 11 65

NICKNAME: The Hammers,
The Irons

RECORD ATTENDANCE:
42,322 v Spurs Div 1 17 October 1970 (D 2-2)

CLUB COLOURS:
HOME: Shirts: Claret with Blue sleeves;
Shorts: White; Socks: White
AWAY: Shirts: Blue with two Claret hoops;
Shorts: Blue; Socks: Blue

KIT SPONSORS: Dagenham Motors

MANUFACTURERS: Pony

When the media describe West Ham they only use three stock phrases: Footballing Academy (although if they are judged on some of last year's performances they run the risk of being downgraded to a Polytechnic); Happy Hammers (when was the last time you saw Julian Dicks smile?); and Chirpy Cockneys. Not hailing from within the sound of Bow Bells myself I could be wrong, but isn't the term 'Pony' rhyming slang (the other part being 'and trap')? If so perhaps we should salute the club for possibly putting out subliminal messages about the whole replica kit issue.

GROUND INFO

The ground has now been fully developed, and whilst it is certainly more grand than it was, it has still retained a lot of its intimacy, and fans are still very much on top of the play. Amazingly the pitch still looks very small, although in terms of square yardage it is bigger than many grounds, including Tottenham and Newcastle.

Having experimented with putting away fans in the Bobby Moore Stand when it initially opened, the club has now decided to site them in the Centenary (ex-North) Stand, which is a bit of a shame as I thought the Bobby Moore Stand was the better of the two. Whilst on the subject of West Ham's, and arguably England's, most famous captain, it is interesting to speak to the home supporters about the naming of the stand, despite many of them feeling it is a fitting tribute to the man, there is a certain undercurrent of belief that they should have done more for him when he was alive, and that the club are playing on their loyalties.

Possibly, the same people might have condemned the club had it named the new stand anything else, but it seems to suggest that there is some unrest at the way the club is being handled. The bottom line, however, is that as a visitor, it is probably true to say the politics of the day-to-day running of the club are unlikely to affect you, and you will be more concerned with how the club respond to your needs; to be fair, whenever I have had dealings with the club I have found it to be prepared to go out of its way to help sort out problems/queries.

The club offers fairly good concessions to home fans via the 'Junior Hammers', and also to students and unemployed fans who can join the 'Irons Clubs' (here, hang on a minute, I know I'm not a Cockney, but isn't Irons...?). But don't expect away kids to get in the North Stand for £6!

CAPACITY: Stands: 26,014; Terrace: Nil;
Total: 26,014

AWAY FANS: Centenary (North) Stand Lower:
Max 3,716.
The entire lower stand will be allocated if there is sufficient demand; otherwise a minimum allocation of 2,290 will be allocated.

DISABLED FACILITIES: There are 87 places for disabled supporters — who are admitted free of charge — at the ground; these are sited in the West Lower, Bobby Moore and Centenary Stands. Helpers pay £10. Places must be pre-booked, and there is no parking available at the ground.

West Ham initially were on for winning top prize in claiming a facility they didn't have when on the initial questionnaire I sent them they replied 'Yes' to having match commentaries, but added the proviso 'only if the blind supporter brings a friend to do the commentary'. However, they have now tempered this claim to a much more modest 'No — not yet' although this may be on the agenda at a later date.

PROGRAMME: £1.50

FANZINES:
On The Terraces	£1
On A Mission From God	£1
Over Land And Sea	£1

Tricky one this. All of the above are worth reading and worth an investment if you support the club; none of them, as yet, are approaching the brilliance of the late and much lamented *Fortune's Always Hiding,* which was not only very funny, but also excellent at campaigning and motivating the 'ordinary' supporter. If you find a back issue even now, it is well worth a read.

TRAVEL

NEAREST RAILWAY STATION:
Barking (0171 928 5100 — Liverpool St Enquiries)

NEAREST TUBE STATION:

Upton Park (District Line)
As with Crystal Palace, avoid the temptation to get out at the stop bearing the club's name.

BUS: London Transport (0171 222 1234)

Any of the following buses will take you to the ground:
5, 15, 15B, 58, 58A, 104, 147, 162, 238.

BY CAR:

NORTH: M11 into London, at the end of which turn right on to the A12 (signposted Wanstead/Leytonstone). After one mile turn left into Blake Hall Road. Just under 0.75 mile later the road forks left towards East Ham Memorial Hospital; at this point continue straight into Centre Road. At the T-junction turn left, then take the fourth right into Green Street, and the ground is one mile on the left.

EAST: A13 into London. Turn right at the crossroads with the A117 and left after one mile into Barking Road (A124). Continue for 0.75 mile, then turn right into Green Street and the ground is immediately on the right.

SOUTH: Pick up the A206 in London, and cross the river via the Blackwall Tunnel. Once through the tunnel, turn right on to the A13 (signposted Canning Town). After 0.5 mile there is a roundabout; take the second exit on to the A124 Barking Road (signposted Plaistow) 1.5 miles later turn left into Green Street and the ground is immediately on the right.

WEST: M40, A40, A40(M). At the end of the A40(M) pick up the A501 and continue on this road past Euston and King's Cross, then follow the signs for Shoreditch and Whitechapel. When in Whitechapel take the A13 (signposted Limehouse and Canning

Town), then at the roundabout in Canning Town take the second exit on to the A124 Barking Road (signposted Plaistow), then as south.

PARKING: Street parking. Alternatively there is a small car park off Green Street in Queens Road, near Upton Park tube station.

FUTURE DEVELOPMENTS

None.

OTHER INFORMATION

If you fancy a drink before the game, be aware that there are some right rough old boozers in the area! And some of the locals may not take too kindly to your replica away shirt. The Queens by Upton Park tube is OK, but for big matches this can be so packed as to make service nearly impossible, and you may find it better to stop off for a drink before making your way to the ground.

Inside the stadium the food is OK. Like many other stadia the 'Snack Attack' bars serve rather stodgy pies but you don't get too many other grounds where the staff are honest enough to advise you against buying the pies if they are cold!

A final conundrum. Why is it virtually every British television actor seems to support West Ham? From London's Burning to Grange Hill, you just know that anyone asked in an interview will state they are an avid Hammers fan. Is this what they are teaching them at RADA these days?? Tsch!

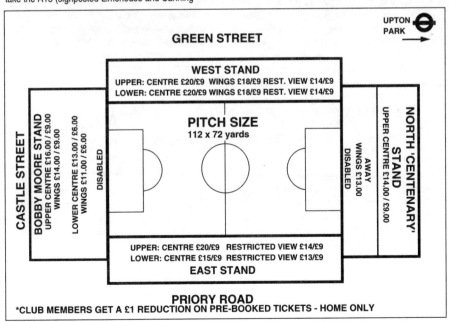

WIGAN ATHLETIC

ADDRESS: Springfield Park
Wigan
Lancashire WN6 7BA
TELEPHONE No: 01942 244433
TICKET OFFICE: 01942 244433
FAX: 01942 494654
CLUBCALL: 0891 12 16 55
NICKNAME: Latics
RECORD ATTENDANCE:
27,500 v Hereford United
FA Cup 2nd 12 December 1951 (D 1-1)
And for the collectors of footballing trivia amongst you,
Wigan were, in 1978, the last team to be elected to the
league rather than be promoted.

CLUB COLOURS:
HOME: Shirts: Blue, White and Green;
Shorts: Blue with Green stripe;
Socks: White with Blue hoops
AWAY: Shirts: Yellow with Blue pin-stripes;
Shorts: Yellow; Socks: Yellow

KIT SPONSORS: JJB Sports
MANUFACTURERS: Puma

GROUND INFO

Springfield Park is one of the more dilapidated stadia
in Britain, and perhaps the only one to have fencing at
the back of the terraces rather than the front (what is
the club trying to do, make sure you don't escape?).
The terraces loop in a semicircle away from the pitch,
and are open to the elements. As the ground is at the
top of a hill, this tends to mean that you have a
Siberian wind whipping around you even in mid-
August. On all other days, however, it is worth considering forking out that little bit extra and claiming one of
the seats in the Phoenix Stand which offers not only a
respite from the weather, but also the opportunity for
any sadists to have a particularly good view of their fellow supporters suffering. In truth the Phoenix Stand is
not rising from the ashes like the mythical bird, but
falling into a state of disrepair, and if you're looking for
luxury, then I can only suggest you take a large magnifying glass with you. Possibly the club thinks otherwise, as in the toilets (which are just as I bet you are
imagining them to be) there is a sign that they are pro-
tected by Pier Security Limited, although quite what
there is in them that warrants such attention is difficult
to ascertain. Concessions are available in all parts of
the ground for under 16s.

CAPACITY: Stands: 1,109; Terrace: 5,565;
Total: 6,674

AWAY FANS: Shevington Road End: 1,500;
Phoenix Stand: 300; Total: 1,800

DISABLED FACILITIES: There is a cabin
at the ground which is used for disabled supporters,
although this only has room enough for four, plus their
helpers. Admission is free. Pre-book your space, and
at the same time organise any parking requirements
that you might have. There are matchday commentaries for the blind, although any supporter wishing to
take advantage of this should bring their own headphones (phone the club in advance to establish
whether a special adaptor will be required). It would
perhaps be easy to take the rise out of the club
because of the b-y-o headphones requirement, but it is
worthwhile flicking through a few other pages of this
book before you do, just so you realise even with this
limitation at least they are offering a service to supporters which some others cannot match.

PROGRAMME: £1.50
Another ex-divisional programme of the year, although
once again it is hard to see why. There really isn't all
that much inside it given the cover price, (the club says
that the programme is likely to be reduced in price for
the 95/96 season.) and it is difficult to see why some of
the articles are included (a classic example being the
profile of Premier League players).

FANZINES:
The Latic Fanatic   £1
One of the many indicators of where the real balance
of power lies within the town is that the most stinging
attacks are not directed at other local football clubs,
but at Wigan Rugby League Club, although several
Wigan fans I spoke to expressed a desire that the publication should be less 'lightweight' in its abuse of
'proper' football teams.

TRAVEL
NEAREST RAILWAY STATION:
Wigan North Western (01942 242231)
Wigan Wallgate station is also situated directly oppo-
site North Western.

BUS: Wigan Central bus station (01942 228 7811)
The ground is a good 15min walk from the town centre, so if you want to avoid this, take a 625 which stops
on Springfield Road by the ground.

BY CAR:
NORTH/WEST: M6 to J27. Take the A5209 to
Wigan (Shevington)and after 0.25 mile turn right on to
the B5206. After a further mile turn left and about 4.5
miles up the road turn left again into Springfield Road
for the ground.
SOUTH: M6 to J25 then take the A49 to Wigan. Turn
left into Robin Park Road and continue into Scot Lane.

Turn right at the third set of traffic lights into Woodhouse Lane, then left at the traffic lights into Springfield Road.

EAST: Take the A557 into the town centre and take a left turn into Robin Park Road, then as south.

If, like myself on my last visit, you find that you have left your directions at home then the best thing to do is ask a policeman. With any luck, you may hit upon the same one that I did who responded 'I could tell you, but it's far too complicated; here let me take you instead'. Whereupon he leapt into his transit, drove round the back streets of the town with me in hot pursuit for about 10min before parking up and telling me that I was in the best street for getting away from, and wishing me an enjoyable afternoon.

PARKING: The parking at the ground is for permit holders only, but there is plenty of on-street parking in the area.

FUTURE DEVELOPMENT

A proposed groundshare with Wigan Rugby League Club at a new stadium in Robin Park has fallen through, apparently due to the rugby club's attitude that ground shares between the two sports do not last. Presumably it hasn't spoken to its counterparts at Huddersfield; there again who in their right minds would rather have a state of the art and architecturally brilliant ground like the Sir Alfred McAlpine Stadium when you've got Central Park — where, I am told, there are places were you can watch the action for nowt from outside the ground.

However, the club states that the project is very much alive with Latics either having sole use of the stadium or perhaps sharing it with Orrell Rugby Union Club. The club are looking to be in their new home for the 1997/8 season.

OTHER INFORMATION

The saying that Northerners are the friendliest people in the world has often been disputed by football supporters, although in Wigan it does stand up to stronger examination than in many other places. On every visit to the place I genuinely find myself overwhelmed by the open, helpful and kind nature of the townsfolk, to whom nothing seems too much trouble, and whose personalities make up for the lack of amenities at the ground and make a trip to Springfield Park far more enjoyable than to certain all-seater stadia with all mod cons.

If you like a pint then either stroll up from the bus station and pop in at the Old Pear Tree, the Colliers Arms, the Guardians Inn, the Brickmakers Arms or the Springfield before you reach the ground, or walk down the path behind the away entrance to the ground for the Prince Of Wales, Traditional or Belle Vue. For food the chip shop by the Guardians shuts at about 1.15pm on matchdays and so a better bet is a hot pie from the corner shop on Meadow Street, which not only tastes excellent and is very cheap (about 55p) but, as usual with the town, is served by a really friendly woman who will tell you amongst other things of an excellent shortcut to Wigan Pier, which is also very useful for avoiding the town centre at the end of a match. Other than that, the meat and potato pie at the ground is worth eating, and the tea is hot and strong. If you fancy a spot of sightseeing then undoubtedly this means a trip to the famous Wigan Pier. This area has been developed quite a lot recently, with the Orwell pub being worth a visit. However, the pier itself is nothing more than a mound of earth behind the canal, and thus it has the dubious distinction of being one of the few sites in the town that is less developed than the football ground!

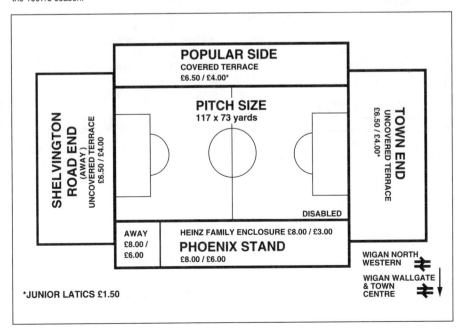

POPULAR SIDE
COVERED TERRACE
£6.50 / £4.00*

PITCH SIZE
117 x 73 yards

SHELVINGTON ROAD END
(AWAY)
UNCOVERED TERRACE
£6.50 / £4.00

TOWN END
UNCOVERED TERRACE
£6.50 / £4.00*

DISABLED

AWAY
£8.00 / £6.00

HEINZ FAMILY ENCLOSURE £8.00 / £3.00
PHOENIX STAND
£8.00 / £6.00

WIGAN NORTH WESTERN

WIGAN WALLGATE & TOWN CENTRE

*JUNIOR LATICS £1.50

WIMBLEDON

ADDRESS: Selhurst Park Stadium
London SE25 6PY

The sharp-eyed among you may have noted that Wimbledon's postcode differs from that of Crystal Palace. This is not a typo (at least not on my part) but the way the addresses appear in the club programmes, as the club offices are sited at sufficiently different parts of the ground to cause the anomaly.

TELEPHONE No: 0181 771 2233
TICKET OFFICE: 0181 771 8841
FAX: 0181 653 4708
CLUBCALL: 0891 12 11 75
NICKNAME: The Dons
RECORD ATTENDANCE: 30,115 v
Manchester United Prem Lge 9 May 1993 (L 1-2)
Prior to the move to Selhurst the club's record attendance was the 18,000 who turned up for the Dons' Amateur Cup Tie against those crowd-pullers from HMS *Victory* on 2 March 1935 (Wimbledon won 3-0).

CLUB COLOURS:
HOME: Shirts: Dark Blue, Gold trim;
Shorts: Dark Blue, Gold trim; Socks: Dark Blue
AWAY: Shirts: Red; Shorts: Red; Socks: Red
THIRD: Shirts: White; Shorts: Black; Socks: White
Wimbledon qualify as possibly the only club with two home kits as when they play at home in the FA Cup and the refs wear their traditional black strip it is considered that the Don's outfit is too similar and might cause confusion (presumably as in 'Hmmm let me see, was that Phillip Don or Vincent Jones who just booted the opposition centre-forward into next week?' 'I don't know; their kits are too alike for me to be able to distinguish them apart!').

KIT SPONSORS: Elonex
MANUFACTURERS: Crazy Gang

GROUND INFO

If nowhere in the ground particularly takes your fancy, why not pick up tickets for the Vice President's Club or Players' Lounge which the club are quite happy to sell you in an attempt to get you through the door. Going in either of these does have the advantage of meaning you're able to get a drink as there is a distinct lack of pubs in the general area. Indeed this probably represents the average football supporter's biggest regret about Wimbledon not playing at Plough Lane any more, where there was always the Sportsman to fill your thirst needs.

CAPACITY: Stands: 26,500; Terrace: Nil;
Total: 26,500
This assumes the Holmesdale Road Stand will be open; otherwise 19,500.

AWAY FANS: A minimum of 2,987 seats are available in Blocks X, Y and Z of the Arthur Wait Stand. Up to 9,844 are available in this stand for visiting fans.

Elsewhere membership restrictions apply for the new Holmesdale Road Stand, the Whitehorse Lane Stand for some matches, the Players' Lounge and the Family Enclosure.

DISABLED FACILITIES: There are 28 places in the Arthur Wait Stand together with a dozen seats for blind and partially-sighted supporters with headphone commentary available. Disabled supporters can gain free admission with escorts paying a nominal £5. A disabled section will also be available in the new Holmesdale Road Stand. It is imperative that seats are pre-booked for high profile matches. Please contact the Box Office manageress, Beryl Whitfield.

PROGRAMME: £1.50
A good programme with plenty of general interest articles which will appeal to both home and away supporters. The amazingly efficient Wimbledon Commercial/Marketing team means that each page is sponsored by a different organisation or fan, but thankfully if anything there are fewer adverts than you'd expect to find in a Premier programme.

FANZINES:

Go Jo Go!!	50p
Yidaho!	50p
Tenants Extra	50p
Sour Grapes	50p
Hoof The Ball Up	£1
Wandering Hans	£1

A cornucopia of reading matter for Dons fans! The top two are the most established and the ones you are most likely to come across. Of the two *Yidaho* (apparently Vinnie's pre-match battle cry) maybe just shades it. It's not brilliant, but anyone who can describe John Jensen as 'Terry from Brookside only with less footballing skill', can't be all bad.

TRAVEL

NEAREST RAILWAY STATION:
Norwood Junction, Thornton Heath, Selhurst (0171 928 5100 — Victoria Enquiries)

The three stations are all about the same distance from the ground. Aim for Norwood Junction, as this seems to have the best service (and the Cherry Trees pub right outside it). See also CRYSTAL PALACE for more details.

BUS: London Transport (0171 222 1234)
BY CAR:
NORTH: M1. Take the A406 North Circular Road (heading west) to Chiswick Roundabout (just before you get there you will see Gunnersbury Park

Underground station on your right). Take the third exit at the roundabout on to Chiswick High Road, then first left on to the A205 (signposted Kew). After two miles you reach a T-junction at which you should turn left (signposted Putney). Continue until the road merges with the A3, then a mile later turn right on to the A214 (signposted Tooting and Streatham). When in Streatham, turn right on to the A23 Streatham High Road. After one mile turn left into Green Lane (B273) which becomes Parchmore Road. At the bottom of the road turn left on to the High Street. Go straight over at the crossroads with the A212 into Whitehorse Lane and the ground is 300yd on the right.

EAST: M25, A20 (signposted London) After approx four miles turn left on to the A224 (signposted St Mary Cray). After three miles turn on to the A232 Spur Road and follow this until you see Shirley Park Golf Club; then right on to the A215 Shirley Road. Turn right again at the top of this road, then first left into Spring Lane (A215). After 1.5 miles turn left on to the B266, and the ground is 0.5 mile on the left.

SOUTH: A23 into London, follow signs for Thornton Heath, turn right on to the A235. (NB: you need to go through a small one-way system; this is no more than an overblown roundabout really.) Once on the A235 turn immediately left on to the B266 Brigstock Road which becomes the High Street, then as north.

WEST: M4 to Chiswick, then as north.

PARKING: There is space for 500 cars at the Sainsbury's car park just off Whitehorse Lane by the ground. There is also plenty of street parking. Alternatively, drive down the A212 towards West Croydon and park in one of the two Whitgift Centre car parks.

FUTURE DEVELOPMENTS

Despite the efforts of the club's owner, Sam Hammam, the club appears to be running against a brick wall in its efforts to move back to Wimbledon, thanks to Merton Council's apparent reticence about having a Premiership Football Club within its confines (despite the fact that this would undoubtedly generate jobs and income for the area). Stories that the club will fold or relocate to Ireland if it doesn't get back to Wimbledon are occasionally wheeled out, but on the whole it appears that these *are* just stories. Expect the current situation to remain in force for at least another year.

OTHER INFORMATION

The club revels in its crazy gang image, and home supporters believe that this togetherness (or insularity, depending on your viewpoint) is a major factor in why the club has enjoyed a level of success only dreamt of by many other teams. As an away supporter though you may have a different opinion; there are occasions when the club is like a breath of fresh air. For example, a charge of 3% (minimum 50p) is levied on all tickets purchased by credit card (together with postage if applicable), but numerous fans tell tales of having phoned up to book tickets only to be told that they should save themselves the money and pay on the door because 'this is Wimbledon, we're hardly going to sell out'. Admittedly it can be hard at times to get information about forthcoming matches, possible postponements, etc, but the club believes that, since its move to Selhurst Park, positive efforts have been made to improve liaisons with both supporters and the media.

The food in the ground is OK but the Chinese on Whitehorse Lane, sells excellent chips — these are reasonably priced and nice and thick, they also have the advantage of coming in those brown paper bags which somehow makes them taste better.

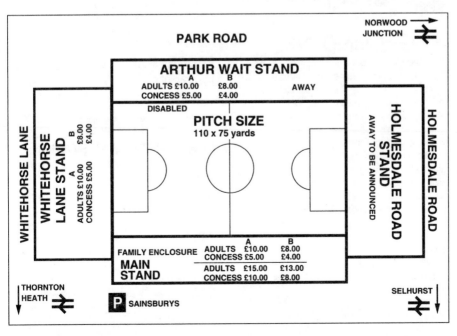

WOLVERHAMPTON WANDERERS

ADDRESS: Molineux Stadium
Waterloo Road
Wolverhampton
WV1 4QR
TELEPHONE No: 01902 655000
TICKET OFFICE: 01902 653653
FAX: 01902 687006
CLUBCALL: 0891 12 11 03
NICKNAME: Wolves
RECORD ATTENDANCE: 61,315 v
Liverpool FA Cup 5th 11 February 1939 (W 4-1)

CLUB COLOURS:
HOME: Shirts: Old Gold;
Shorts: Black; Socks: Old Gold
AWAY: Shirts: White; Shorts: White; Socks: White

KIT SPONSORS: Goodyear

MANUFACTURERS: Nutmeg

The club has stopped using the Picasso-like cubist wolf head as the shirt emblem and returned to the town's coat of arms (the top left item of which appears to be a sink plunger!) with the motto 'Out Of Darkness Cometh Light', although if they had wanted to remind many away fans of past trips to Molineux this might have been more appropriately written as 'Out Of Darkness Cometh A Lump Of Concrete Chucked At The Special'.

GROUND INFO

Away fans get the Jack Harris Stand which can be subdivided into three sections dependent on the quantity of the away following. The John Ireland Stand lower tier has in the past been used as an overspill, which is quite ironic as the fans in the top tier tended to have a problem spilling over their cups of tea on the visitors below (tsch, I don't know!).

The new Molineux may not quite have the atmosphere of the old place but of all the new all-seater super stadia this probably comes as close as any to recreating the noise. Another advantage with the new ground is that at least now all of the stands are in the same postal district as the pitch. If you can't get a ticket for the away end then your best bet is probably the centre of the Billy Wright Stand, but expect a cool reception if this is where you end up. Mind you, getting in the stand is a feat in itself given the number of season tickets the club sells!

The club is rightly proud of its new stadium and unlike many clubs I could mention, if you ask it

questions about the ground it will answer fully. Perhaps it is even more disappointing then that as it does want everyone to enjoy the 'Wolves experience' it does not offer visiting supporters concessions. Talking to various people I was given such excuses as 'No one gives them to us', 'It's not economically viable' and perhaps most strangely 'It's against the rules of the League'! I think not, chaps.

CAPACITY: Stands: 28,500; Terrace: Nil;
Total: 28,500

AWAY FANS: Jack Harris Stand: 5,355;
Total: 5,355

DISABLED FACILITIES: Deep breath, here goes: there is, in total, accommodation for 76 wheelchair-bound supporters in the Jack Harris Stand (for visitors), Stan Cullis and Billy Wright Stands — access being via either the wheelchair lift, or the six specially designed ramps; 300 seats for non-wheelchair-bound disabled supporters; 50 seats for the blind with match commentaries; 50 seats for the deaf with a loop system for PA announcements; 46 disabled parking spaces; and 16 disabled toilets; there is a specially designed lounge area at the ground, and there are 15 stewards who have had specialist training and who will know what to do if you have a problem. Admission for disabled supporters is free, with helpers paying a fiver.

In the words of the Wolves manager 'Can we not knock it?' — No Graham, I don't think we can.

Contact the club to state your requirements and pre-book your seat. Wolves should send a copy of these facilities to every club in the country, and half of them should hang their heads in shame when they read them.

PROGRAMME: £1.50

FANZINES:
A Load Of Bull   £1

TRAVEL

NEAREST RAILWAY STATION:
Wolverhampton (0121 643 2711 — Birmingham New Street Enquiries)

BUS: Wolverhampton bus station (0121 200 2700 — Centro hotline)
The bus station is about 300yd away from the railway station, and although it is only 0.5 mile or so from the ground, it can be worth taking a bus just to avoid having to cross a couple of very busy roads. In addition to the safety aspect, the wait for the bus provided free entertainment on my visit, when some pensioners waiting directed spectacular abuse at the hapless driver of the delayed bus.

If you do opt to go by bus, take either a 503 or 504 (one every 10-15min) from stop R.

BY CAR:

NORTH: M6 to J12. Turn right on to the A5, then left after one mile on to the A449 Stafford Road. Continue until you see the Goodyear factory, go straight over the next two roundabouts until (1.5 miles past the factory) you get to the Five Ways roundabout. Take the third exit into Waterloo Road, and the ground is 0.25 mile on your left.

EAST/SOUTH: M6 to J6. Take the A454 (signposted Wolverhampton) and continue on this road until you pass Wolverhampton railway station. Take the second right into Waterloo Road and the ground is 0.25 mile on the right.

WEST: M54 to J2. Turn right on to the Stafford Road (A449) and continue until you see the Goodyear factory, then as north.

PARKING: There is a 600-space club car park behind the Stan Cullis (the old North Bank) and Jack Harris Stands, and just behind this there is an Asda which has a large car park. Other than this, side-street parking is the order of the day. At a push you can park either at the train station, or in the town centre, neither of which are too much of a trek.

FUTURE DEVELOPMENTS

Nothing major, although the club is continually looking at the service it offers, and if necessary improving it. An example of this, so the story goes, is of the Wolves President and all round cash machine Sir Jack Hayward overhearing two fans complaining about the cramped toilets. He then went down and tried them himself, decided that the fans had a genuine gripe, and hey presto new improved toilets were built.

OTHER INFORMATION

If you fancy a pre-match pint then the Fox or the Feathers are both right by the ground. But, both are real 'home' pubs so it can be as well to stick to the town centre. Inside the ground the food is OK, though in my experience the tea is never more than tepid.

The whole afternoon is musically choreographed; 'Simply the Best' booms out of the tannoy at five to three... and that is just to welcome the ball boys! The team actually appears to 'Fanfare For The Common Man' and warm up to 'Liquidator' (maybe to remind fans of how near the club were to going out of business), but this may be stopped for the 1995/6 season because some rascals in the ground insist on adding a line to the effect that they wish local rival WBA would go away, and the club feels this is against the family atmosphere it is trying to create.

The video walls at two corners of the ground (which apparently plunged half of Wolverhampton into darkness the first time they were used) are real state of the art stuff, and have been sanctioned for use at half-time and full-time provided they don't show anything controversial that might incite the crowd. So if you go to the match hoping for a showing of 'Natural Born Killers' you are likely to be disappointed. Although you will have to be prepared to contain yourself, for the scoreboard not only flashes up 'oohhh' for near misses, but also 'aaahhh' when opposition attacks break down.

Final facts from the club:
- 1986/7 season average gate 12,000; Police 150; Stewards 50;
- 1993/4 season average gate 26,000; Police 35; Stewards 250.

Arrests in the ground down 80%. Yes, football has problems, but these stats hardly suggest a cancer eating the very fabric of a nation.

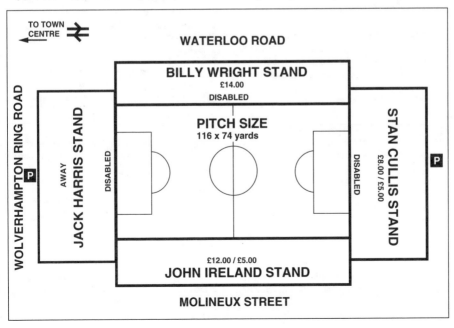

WREXHAM

ADDRESS: The Racecourse Ground
Mold Road
Wrexham
Clwyd LL11 2AN
TELEPHONE No: 01978 262129
TICKET OFFICE: 01978 262129
FAX: 01978 357821
CLUBCALL: 0896 42
NICKNAME: The Robins
RECORD ATTENDANCE:
34,445 v Manchester United FA Cup 4th 26 January 1957 (L 0-5)
Proving that even in the 'good old days' of serious press coverage, journalists were quite happy to throw up a few stereotypes; the headline of one of the 'quality' papers about this match was 'Welshmen too excited to even sing'.

CLUB COLOURS:
HOME: Shirts: Red; Shorts: White; Socks: Red
AWAY: Shirts: Yellow;
Shorts: Black; Socks: Yellow and Black

KIT SPONSORS: Wrexham Lager
MANUFACTURERS: Enkay Sports

GROUND INFO

Although visitors are encouraged to join their fellow supporters in the Marston Stand (hence the concessions), they can also get admission into the Yale Stand Family Section at reduced rates. The Marston Stand has two massive pillars which if you are not careful can lead to a nightmare view. Either position yourself directly behind the goal, or in the first couple of rows as far to the left/right of the main block of seating as you can. The Marston Paddock wasn't used to my knowledge in 1994/5 and as you enter the stand and climb the stairs to your seat you can see loads of wrought metalwork and other assorted rubble which has been dumped underneath the stand. Still closed in 1994/5 was the Mold Stand, which, although the club has tried to hide it by putting boarding around it, is still an eyesore. Its closure wasn't met with too much sorrow as it used to swing in a semicircle away from the ground, meaning that if you were sat at the furthest point from the pitch, the players appeared to be nothing more than specks on a distant horizon. The home Kop is quite impressive and is reminiscent of the Fulwell End at Sunderland. However, the toilets here (as with the Marston Stand) were too horrible for words on my viisit to the ground — if I say to take a surf board with you, you'll get the general picture.

CAPACITY: Stands: 5,024; Terrace: 4,026; Total: 9,050
AWAY FANS: Marston Stand: 2,000; Marston Paddock*: 450; Total: 2,450
* If open

DISABLED FACILITIES: There is a little corrugated hut in the corner of the ground between the Marston Stand and the Mold Road Stand into which about half a dozen wheelchair-bound supporters can fit. If you are not one of the six you can still go, but you will be sat along the touchline and exposed to the elements. Helpers are provided with a chair, but this is little comfort. Still, at least you get a warm welcome, and you can get a parking space right next to the ground, and enjoy a cup of tea and biscuits at the club house. Away fans are requested to pre-book their visit. Admission is free for disabled supporters and £6.50 for helpers.
There are no match commentary facilities for the blind.

RHAGLEN SWYDDOGOL: £1.30
The programme on first sight doesn't appear to be up to much, but rather like Doctor Who's Tardis there is an awful lot more going on inside than you realised. A very good read with plenty of general interest items.

FANZINES:
The Sheeping Giant 50p
This fanzine simply gets better and better; it's very well written and has got a nice 'in your face' style which never crosses the line at being simply offensive (although on occasion some of the jokes are borderline). Lots of information and intelligent well thought out articles. It is available from the club shop, or the Turf pub. One minor complaint is the rhyme used in place of Chester City's last word; this is real old hat and isn't really funny.

TRAVEL
NEAREST RAILWAY STATION:
Wrexham General (0151 709 9696 — Liverpool Lime Street Enquiries)
There are two stations in the town, Wrexham General, which is adjacent to the ground, and Wrexham Central which is about 1.5 miles away.

BUS: King Street bus station (01978 363760) Buses 11, 18a and 21 run from the town centre to the ground, although we are not talking of the longest of walks.

BY CAR:
NORTH/WEST: Take the A483 and Wrexham By-Pass to the junction with the A541. Branch left and at the roundabout follow signs for Mold. At T-junction turn right into Regent Street which leads into Mold Road and the ground.

EAST: Take the A525 or A534 into Wrexham, then follow signs for A541 (Mold), then as north.

SOUTH: M54 to J3, then the A41 to Whitchurch. Take the A525 (signposted Wrexham), then as east. This is a scenic route that takes you through such quaintly named villages as Cock Bank, but it's guaranteed you'll be tearing your hair out when your progress is reduced to 5mph, stuck behind a tractor for miles with little or no chance of overtaking.

PARKING: Parking is available at Wrexham General station, or in the college grounds near the stadium. Some street parking is available in the vicinity of the ground. The car park at the ground is for permit holders only.

FUTURE DEVELOPMENTS

The club have been talking about a redevelopment for quite a while, although the only thing that seems to be happening is that the proposed price of the changes has been steadily increasing (£43 million at the last count). Someone at the club has obviously got a well-honed sense of humour because in reply to the questionnaire I sent them about changes I received a nice typed reply saying that the whole ground would be developed to give a total capacity of 17,000. As to when this would be done they replied 'Not Known', to which someone had added in biro 'Eventually!'

OTHER INFORMATION

When you enter the ground you may wonder what the cricket pavilion is in the corner, and why all the players waiting to come in to bat are wearing woolly hats and scarves. The answer in fact is that this is the Turf pub balcony overlooking the pitch. From here pub regulars can watch the match for free. A word of warning, don't mention how funny/unique this is to anyone at the club as they get very upset about the whole thing.

The Turf itself is very much a home fans' pub and it is probably as well to walk the 5-10min it takes to get into the town centre and go to either the Horse & Jockey (a bit small and poky) or the Talbot (true story — it was inside the former of these two pubs that I was asked to settle a fairly heated argument as to whether Jennifer Rush — 'The Power Of Love' — was Ian Rush's — Liverpool and Wales — wife or sister...Hmmm). If you are a complete wuss, take the road to Chester and continue for about five miles till you get to the Grosvenor, which is just inside the English border.

For food, The Chippies Open which is left through the archway just past the Horse & Jockey serves good food and excellent fat chips. However, as the words fish and chips go together, so do the words slow and service. If you don't fancy the walk, there are burger vans by the ground. Once inside the pies are reasonable, but the tea is bitter and the Bovril grainy.

Away fans are well treated, with police and stewards letting you get on with your own thing. If you come from England then don't worry about the fact that a piano version 'Men Of Harlech' is blasted out over the tannoy as the teams take the pitch as the atmosphere isn't massively anti-English (the town is even called Wrecsam, making it one of the few words in the Welsh language that foreigners can understand). All the same, it is probably as well not to mention that you'll be spending the rest of the weekend in your holiday home whilst enjoying a pre-match pint with the locals.

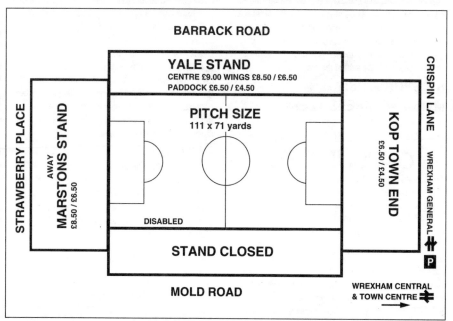

BARRACK ROAD

YALE STAND
CENTRE £9.00 WINGS £8.50 / £6.50
PADDOCK £6.50 / £4.50

PITCH SIZE
111 x 71 yards

STRAWBERRY PLACE

MARSTONS STAND
AWAY
£8.50 / £6.50

DISABLED

STAND CLOSED

KOP TOWN END
£6.50 / £4.50

CRISPIN LANE

WREXHAM GENERAL

MOLD ROAD

WREXHAM CENTRAL & TOWN CENTRE

WYCOMBE WANDERERS

ADDRESS: Adams Park
Hillbottom Road
Sands, High Wycombe
HP12 4HU

TELEPHONE No: 01494 472100
TICKET OFFICE: 01494 44118
FAX: 01494 527633
CLUBCALL: 0891 44 68 55
NICKNAME: The Chairboys
RECORD ATTENDANCE:
15,850 v St Albans City FA Am Cup 4th 25 February 1950 (W 4-1). 9,002 v West Ham FA Cup 3rd 7 January 1995 (L 0-2).

The first of these matches was at the clubs old Loakes Park Ground; the second was at the club's current stadium. In somewhat of a spooky coincidence, the previous best at Adams Park of 7,802 had been against Norwich; this was also an FA Cup 3rd Round tie, and once again Wanderers had gone down 2-0 (fascinating!).

CLUB COLOURS:

HOME: Shirts: Oxford and Cambridge Blue quarters; Shorts: Oxford Blue; Socks: Cambridge Blue
AWAY: Shirts: Yellow; Shorts: Yellow; Socks: Yellow
THIRD: Shirts: Red and Black Stripes; Shorts: Black; Socks: Red

Yes, although they are only relative newcomers to the League, one can only step back and admire the speed with which Wycombe understood the benefits of replica shirts. The introduction of a third kit when it is arguable that only two are required shows they have a financially bright future ahead of them — although the same cannot necessarily be said of their fans.

KIT SPONSORS: Verco
MANUFACTURERS: Vandanel

GROUND INFO

The ground is sited at the very top of an industrial estate, which itself is at the top of a street of very nice 'Terry and June' type houses. My, how the residents must have cheered when Wycombe got themselves promoted into the football league! The ground itself blends in very well with the former of these, having the appearance of a drive-through McDonalds, with the exception of the commercial office which is dominated by two massive round windows similar to those once seen on 'Play School'. The away terrace is covered, and fairly comfortable and offers a reasonable view of the action. The toilets are functional, although as with many things around the ground, a bit on the small size.

CAPACITY: Stands: 1,267;
Covered Terrace: 8,382; Total: 9,649

AWAY FANS: Hillbottom Road End
Covered Terrace: 2,193;
Total: 2,193

This is the maximum allocation available, and this figure can and will be reduced (down to a minimum of 1,424) if there is insufficient demand. The club used to offer 90 places in the Main Stand for visiting supporters, although this appeared to be discontinued as an official policy during 1994/5 — mind you, I've never heard of any away fans wanting to sit down and not being allowed access to the stand, and any problems that have been encountered tend to relate to the small number of seats available.

DISABLED FACILITIES: There are 12 places at Adams Park, which from what I can gather breaks down to six for wheelchair-bound supporters and six for helpers, as opposed to 12 spaces for wheelchair-bound supporters. Away fans are more than welcome but must pre-book (as must home supporters). The cost of admission is £4 for disabled fans and £6.50 for helpers. Match commentaries for the visually impaired are also available and must be pre-booked. There is limited parking at the ground for disabled supporters and it does not appear that this can be pre-booked, so if you want to a space (and believe me with the lack of general parking facilities available this is advisable) then get down to the ground early.

PROGRAMME: £1.30
Fairly good value for money with plenty of space given over to what is going on in the league generally and not just within the confines of Adams Park. Keep an eye open for articles by Wycombe's celebrity fan and Director, Alan Parry, but more especially for Club Secretary John Goldsworthy's bizarre articles. He once dedicated over three-quarters of his allotted space to a rant against Milton Keynes, which whilst perhaps being understandable in some people's eyes, didn't have much do to with the beautiful game (I must say, I didn't really agree with him but I salute his vitriol!).

FANZINES:
The Adams Family   50p
Roo-barb Roo-barb seems to have fallen off the face of the earth and I never seem to be able to grab a copy of *The Adams Family* when I've been to the ground. I checked out the fanzine listing in March 1995's WSC and *Adams Family* does appear to still be going, although it is listed as a non-league fanzine. Good news obviously doesn't travel fast from Buckinghamshire.

TRAVEL
NEAREST RAILWAY STATION:
High Wycombe (01494 441561)

BUS: Central bus station (01494 520941)
A couple of number 300 buses run from the town to the ground. These leave the railway station at 1.55 and 2.25 on matchdays — calling at the bus station 5min later — and prevent a long walk. They are also on hand to whisk fans back to the town after the match, but they do tend to get snarled up in the traffic.

BY CAR:
NORTH/SOUTH/EAST: M1, M25 westbound (signposted Heathrow), then M40 (signposted Oxford) to J4. Take the A404 (signposted High Wycombe) and as you approach the town you get to a major round-about. Take the second exit on to Abbey Way. Continue for 0.75 mile to the next major roundabout at which you should take the second exit on to the A40 Oxford Road. Continue past Desborough Industrial Park and after this take the next exit into Mill End Road. Turn left at the T-junction/roundabout with Chapel Lane. Almost immediately there is another mini-roundabout at which you should turn right into Lane End Road. When this road forks in two, bear right into Hillbottom Road; the ground is at the top of this road.
WEST: A40 towards High Wycombe. Turn right into Chapel Lane, right again at the second mini-round-about into Lane End Road, then as north.

PARKING: There is a small car park at the ground, and also suitable places around the industrial units in Hillbottom Road. If you are reduced to street parking, and you don't arrive early, count on a walk of around one mile. The nearest public car parks are in High Wycombe which is a couple of miles from the ground.

FUTURE DEVELOPMENTS
The club is to be commended for its development pro-gramme which has been made slowly and surely, with-out financially over-stretching the club. The start of the 1995/6 season should see the opening of its most ambitious project, the Davenport Vernon Stand, which runs along the side of the pitch where the old Woodlands terrace was sited. This stand will hold approximately 5,000, and the capacities given above are post-opening. The club is subsequently to review other areas of improvement in line with its league posi-tion and the need to meet requirements. Nothing firm has been decided on as yet, but expect the continu-ance of current strategies.

OTHER INFORMATION
The bars at the ground are for social club members only, so apart from an off-licence at the junction between Hillbottom Road and Lane End Road the nearest place to get alcoholic refreshment is the Hourglass at the bottom of Lane End Road which is just under a mile from the ground. It is a reasonable size, but if it gets packed the management seem happy enough for fans to take their drinks and stand in the car park.

As you approach the ground there is a stall selling that traditional fare of football fans, the doughnut, as well as a couple of burger vans. Inside, both the tea and Bovril are OK, while the food was a bit nondescript and overpriced.

The people involved at the club are friendly, helpful and polite; the stewards even call you Sir! and it remains the only ground where I saw a mum get a steward to let her through several gates so she could check her ball boy son was well wrapped up (he wasn't embarrassed at all!).

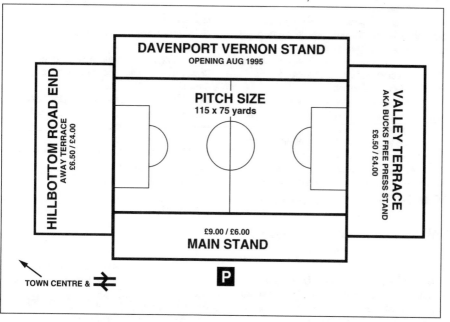

DAVENPORT VERNON STAND
OPENING AUG 1995

PITCH SIZE
115 x 75 yards

HILLBOTTOM ROAD END
AWAY TERRACE
£6.50 / £4.00

VALLEY TERRACE
AKA BUCKS FREE PRESS STAND
£6.50 / £4.00

£9.00 / £6.00
MAIN STAND

TOWN CENTRE &

P

YORK CITY

ADDRESS: Bootham Crescent
York
YO3 7AQ
TELEPHONE No: 01904 624447
TICKET OFFICE: 01904 624447
FAX: 01904 631457
HOTLINE: 0891 66 45 45
NICKNAME: The Minstermen
RECORD ATTENDANCE: 28,123 v
Huddersfield FA Cup 6th 5 March 1938 (D 0-0)

CLUB COLOURS:
HOME: Shirts: Red; Shorts: Blue; Socks: Red
AWAY: Shirts: Blue; Shorts: Blue; Socks: Blue

KIT SPONSORS: Portakabin

MANUFACTURERS: Admiral

GROUND INFO

The first thing that strikes you when you arrive at Bootham Crescent is that it is one of the few grounds where the outside of the Main Stand is done up in a wooden mock-Tudor style (on stilts!). Sadly the inside of the ground does not reflect this grandiose style.

Because much of the seating is designated members only on big match days, if you don't get there early you can be struggling. Don't be fooled into thinking that you can get to the away section of the Popular Stand via a transfer from the home section as the two areas are separated by about half a ton of wrought ironwork. The view from the Popular Side isn't brilliant anyway — although it has got plenty of leg room — but this segregation fencing certainly doesn't help matters. If in any doubt, stick to the terracing (provided the weather is not too inclement).

The club has a family section in the Main Stand, but it also offers the use of a family room before and after the game.

Perhaps the most worrying thing about a visit to York is the fact that the ground is outside the city walls, so if the Vikings decide to have a pop at the place while your team are playing, you've had it!

CAPACITY: Stands: 3,670; Terrace: 5,789; Total: 9,459

AWAY FANS: Grosvenor Road Terrace: 2,603; Popular Stand H: 636; Main Stand: 300; Total: 3,539

DISABLED FACILITIES: There are 18 places for disabled supporters at the front of the Main Stand, and although booking is not essential, due to the restricted capacity I would recommend it.

Admission for disabled fans is free, and for helpers it is £7.50. The club advise that there is no match commentary facility available (although I seem to remember in the past that you could pre-book this service — check it out) nor are there any parking facilities at the ground.

PROGRAMME: £1.30
In places excellent and in others dire. Still, it has a very nice picture of the Minster on the front. It's a programme that you will find difficult not to buy, because as you approach the ground there are hundreds of sellers strung across the road defying anyone to try and breach their luminous orange line without coughing up.

FANZINES:
New Frontiers	50p
Win Lose or Draw	20p

Both are on sale inside the ground at the supporters, club hut. If you want one, then in most circumstances a steward will let you nip down the side of the pitch to get it. *New Frontiers* is OK, but to call *Win Lose or Draw* sparse is something of an understatement.

TRAVEL

NEAREST RAILWAY STATION:
York (01904 642155)

NEAREST BUS STATION:
Rider York (01904 624161)
There are no buses direct from the station to the ground, instead get either a number 8, 8a or 8b from Rougier Street (by the Tourist Information Centre).

BY CAR:
NORTH: A1, then the A59 until you cross a railway bridge. Two miles after this turn left into Water End, and at the next T-junction turn right (signposted City Centre). 0.5 mile further on turn left into Bootham Crescent.
SOUTH: A64, turning right after Buckles Inn on to the Outer Ring Road. Turn right on to the A19 (following City Centre signs), then 1.5 miles further on turn left into Bootham Crescent.
EAST: Get on to the Outer Ring Road, turn left on to the A19, then as south.
WEST: Get on to the Outer Ring Road, turn right on to the A19, then as south.

PARKING: There is parking at Marygate car park about 0.25 mile on the right after the turn-off to the ground. However, this is quite pricey and puts you at the back of the queue when it is time to go home. The best bet is to park on the A19 itself; if you leave the car facing the direction you want to head in (and also on the correct side of the road) you can count on saving yourself around half an hour's queuing at the final whistle.

FUTURE DEVELOPMENTS

None at present.

OTHER INFORMATION

There are lots of excellent pubs in the city; nearest to the ground are the Bootham Tavern, the White Horse and the Exhibition, all of which are on Clifton Road, on the city side of the ground. If you want to venture a little further afield, try the Maltings in Tanner's Moat (about half-way between the station and the ground) which serves a fine pint of Black Sheep.

There is a chip shop tucked behind the ground in Newborough Street but you might as well wait till you get inside the stadium, because not only is there an excellent choice of foods, but also one of the best meat and potato pies you could hope to come across.

York is a brilliant place to spend the weekend, especially if you take the family. There's plenty to see — check out the Jorvik Centre if you've got a spare four days to spend queuing — as well as decent nightlife. There are B&Bs all over the place including about 15 in Bootham Crescent itself, and you should be able to get a room for about £12-£15.

A trip to York gives you a chance to see how mature and intelligent you are. Simply answer the following question as you leave the ground, 'Did the teams emerge on to the pitch to 'The William Tell Overture' or the theme from 'The Lone Ranger'?'. If you say the first then give yourself 10 'grown up' points, if you said the second, good on you, Heigh-Ho Silver Awayyyy!

I was wondering how I would finish off the last league ground in this book, and had pretty much settled on the very sad and anoraky question of 'York City are one of five clubs whose first and last letter are the same, who are the other four?' However, the club came to my rescue. When I undertook this project I sent a questionnaire to all 92 clubs asking for certain information. York were the first to answer (thus displaying the very helpful attitude that away supporters are likely to encounter at the ground) by virtually return of post. I anxiously scanned through the information but was perplexed to see that although they said they had enclosed a list of ground prices, there was no evidence of this. Yes, with a breathtaking absentmindedness they had forgotten to put it in! Cheers chaps, you encapsulated the magnificence and utter frustration of being an away supporter in one beautiful movement! (To be fair the club did subsequently send the form.)

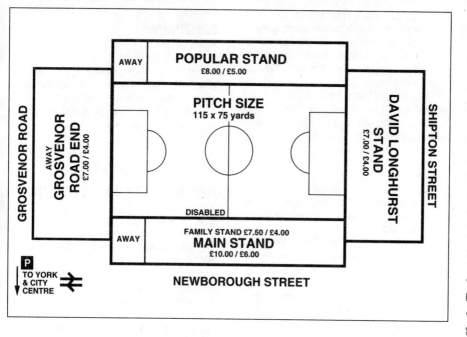

WEMBLEY STADIUM

ADDRESS: Wembley Stadium
Wembley
Middlesex HA9 ODW
TELEPHONE No: 0181 902 8833
TICKET OFFICE: 0181 900 1234
FAX: 0181 900 1055
CLUBCALL: 0891 66 44 33
NICKNAME: Venue of the Legends
or How Much?!?
RECORD ATTENDANCE:
126,047 Bolton v West Ham (2-0) FA Cup Final 28 April 1923. And that's just the ones who paid! It's thought there were well over 150,000 in the ground.

GROUND INFO

Prices for the 1994/5 Cup Final ranged from £17 to £60 with the Olympic Gallery at £90 and £100. Entry to the Olympic Gallery is via turnstiles E and H.

If you are trying to work out whereabouts in the ground you'll be, turnstiles A-F serve the Tunnel End, and G-M the West End, while the Block Numbers are prefixed by a '1' for Lower Tier, '2' for Upper Tier and '3' for Olympic Gallery.

The seats at the front of the Lower Tier are virtually level with the pitch and have an inadequate rise between each row. What is more, here, the leg room is laughable, and your seat will not have a back on it.

As a general rule of thumb, if you're allocated one of the red seats give up any thoughts of sitting down to watch the match. The blue seats on the lower tier give perhaps the best view in the stadium as long as you are along the side of the pitch. However, because the people in the red seats are going to be standing up, then so inevitably will you.

In the Upper Tier, the seats at the front are good, though as you move backwards there are various pillars and obstructions virtually guaranteed to get irritatingly in your way at vital moments.

The Olympic Gallery offers a terrific view of the pitch, but you will need 20/20 vision to be able to make anyone out.

With the introduction of the Criminal Justice Act, touting is illegal, but there are still plenty of touts by the tube station and all the length of Wembley Way. If you must buy a ticket from one of these gentlemen I can only recommend that you leave it as late as possible. At five past three, you'll find you can pick up some real bargains. Never forget to check your ticket for a hologram and watermark, and once you've bought it go straight into the ground so that if it is rejected and you get turned away at least you'll have a chance of catching up with the lovable rogue who flogged it to you.

CAPACITY: Stands: 80,000 Terrace: Nil
Total: 80,000

DISABLED FACILITIES: The stadium management appear strangely reticent about giving details of their disabled facilities. If you are going to watch a club match then you will have to get in touch with your team, who then have to get in touch with Wembley. If you are going to an international, get in touch with the box office who hopefully will be able to sort you out.

PROGRAMME: Costing £5 for major matches, the programme has the feel of a brochure for the Ford Mondeo, and comes in a very unhandy A4 size — hardly the sort of thing you can (or would want to) casually fold up and stick in your back pocket.

Open a Wembley programme and you cannot fail to be impressed by the brilliant pictures, excellent graphics and superb printing styles, but the actual content is disappointing. Apart from being even more out of date than club programmes normally are, it's a bit shallow and you can't help feeling that you've read it all before.

FANZINES:
(National Team)
Flair's Back In Fashion   50p
Not one you normally see sold in large numbers if you go and watch England, and annoyingly when I sent money to the address in WSC I received nothing in reply, although I'm sure this was a one-off and other people would have better luck.

TRAVEL

NEAREST RAILWAY STATION:
Wembley Stadium (0171 262 6767), Wembley Central (01923 245001)

Wembley Stadium station is at the bottom of South Way, and is served by Marylebone-Banbury trains on the Chiltern Line. Very handy, but trains are infrequent and don't run at all on Sundays.

Wembley Central is about 10min walk from the stadium, and is served by Euston-Watford/Milton Keynes/Northampton services.

NEAREST TUBE STATION:
Wembley Park (Jubilee and Metropolitan Lines). The tube station is about 5min from the ground when you arrive for a game, but after a match it is a different story entirely and you should allow 20-30min at least getting from the ground to the station.

Parents with young children should be aware that some of the crushes that can develop going to the station can be frightening and particularly dangerous, especially given that once you're in one, it is very difficult to get out.

BUS: London Transport (0171 222 1234)
Buses 18, 83, 92, 182 and 297 serve the stadium.

BY CAR:
NORTH/EAST: North Circular (A406) to right turn into Neasden Lane. Keep straight on for Forty Lane and Empire Way; turn left into Engineers Way for car parks.

SOUTH/WEST: North Circular (A406) to left turn into Harrow Road. Bear right past Wembley Stadium railway station and take second right for car parks. Alternatively, take the North Circular to left turn into Drury Way, then left at the second (Tesco) roundabout into Great Central Way. Follow the road for car parks. The road to Wembley is well signposted from all parts.

PARKING: There is car parking for about 7,000 by the stadium, but expect to pay between £5 and £10 for the privilege. Also expect to spend an awfully long time trying to get out of the car park (under 30min and you've done well; above an hour and you're unlucky, but certainly not unique).

FUTURE DEVELOPMENTS
So many projects are flying about that it is difficult to know where the truth lies. Perhaps the key issue is how much cash the stadium can get out of the Millennium Fund. A choice will be made in the near future as to which of three major projects (Wembley, Birmingham or Manchester) will get a nice slice of the lottery pot, with which they should redevelop the (or build a new) national stadium. The talk is that if Wembley gets the nod, it would be completely redeveloped, and all that would remain of the original structure would be the Twin Towers. Capacity would be around the 100,000 mark.

While there are naturally advantages about starting

anew, for all Wembley's faults there is something very special about the place, and one of the greatest feelings in the world must be walking down Wembley Way on a sunny day, towards the stadium, knowing you are going to see your team. Enter the stadium, and you can feel the ghosts from years gone by all around you. Almost magical, it is something that I hope every reader of this book gets to experience in their lifetime.

OTHER INFORMATION
For a pre-match drink, the Torch is one of the best places to go. It may be lacking in refinement but does serves a reasonably-priced pint quickly. The staff and management understand that it is a big day out and are happy to let the fans have a good time. Turn left out of the station and it is 200yd on the right. If you do go to the Torch then on the way to the ground there is a chip shop, which is well worth popping in at to refuel.

Wembley is one of the most awesome stadiums you could wish to see. The Twin Towers, Wembley Way, the sweeping oval... how I wish I could put a full stop here and say, 'Well that's the end of the book', but sadly I can't: the prices of refreshments are astronomical. It's well over £2 for a 500ml bottle of lager (which brings it to around the £4 a pint mark!!), and burgers start at over £2 and go through the £3, £4 and £5 barriers without even trying.

The toilet facilities are perfectly adequate, but there's simply nothing they can do about the fact that everyone wants to use them at half- and full-time: first big queues form, then minutes later any available wall space becomes a legitimate target (for men), which in turn almost inevitably leads to one or two people getting lifted by the police (although, to be fair, they are VERY restrained).

One thing you can be sure of; you'll not forget a trip to Wembley!

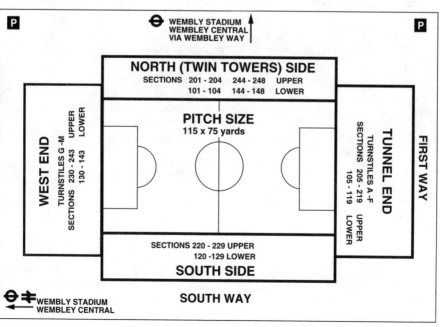

An aeriel view of West Ham United's ground. *Aerofilms.*